The Great Tradition

The Great Tradition

CONSTITUTIONAL HISTORY AND
NATIONAL IDENTITY IN BRITAIN
AND THE UNITED STATES, 1870-1960

Anthony Brundage

Richard A. Cosgrove

STANFORD UNIVERSITY PRESS

Stanford, California 2007

Stanford University Press
Stanford, California
© 2007 by the Board of Trustees of the
Leland Stanford Junior University

Library of Congress Cataloging-in-Publication Data

Brundage, Anthony.
   The great tradition : constitutional history and national identity in Britain and the United States, 1870–1960 / Anthony Brundage and Richard A. Cosgrove.
      p. cm.
   Includes bibliographical references and index.
   ISBN-13: 978-0-8047-5686-0 (cloth : alk. paper)
   1. Constitutional history—United States. 2. Constitutional law—Study and teaching—United States. 3. United States—Politics and government. 4. Great Britain—Politics and government. 5. Constitutional law—Study and teaching—Great Britain. 6. Constitutional history—Great Britain. I. Cosgrove, Richard A. II. Title.
   K3161.B78   2007
   342.02'9—dc22   2006033689

Printed in the United States of America on acid-free, archival-quality paper

Typeset at Stanford University Press in 10/13 Minion

Frontispiece: Professor H. B. Adams's Historical Seminary (seminar) at Johns Hopkins University, 1890. Adams sits at the head of the table, flanked by his graduate students. On the left is C. H. Haskins, America's preeminent medievalist in the first half of the twentieth century. Toyokichi Iyenaga, on the right, would become Japan's leading constitutional historian. A portrait of English historian E. A. Freeman (to the left of the doorway), together with his famous aphorism about history and politics, were meant to inspire the fledgling historians and to underscore the doctrine of the Anglo-Saxon origins of modern government in Britain and the United States. Courtesy of the Ferdinand Hamburger Archives of the Johns Hopkins University.

For MARTHA *and for* LORETTA

Acknowledgments

In an undertaking of such magnitude and duration the authors have incurred many debts. For their assistance with archival research in Britain, we thank Pauline Adams, Somerville College, Oxford; Richard Childs, West Sussex Record Office; Michael Carter, Centre for Kentish Studies; Colin Harris and his efficient staff in Room 132 of the New Bodleian; Alun Ford, University of London Library; Anna Sander, Balliol College, Oxford; Jane Maxwell, Trinity College Library, Dublin; Kate Perry, Girton College, Cambridge; Peter Nockles, The John Rylands University Library; Anne Whiteman, Oxford; Michael Bott, University of Reading Library; and the staffs of the National Archives, Kew and the Cambridge University Library. Archivists and librarians in the United States were equally helpful. Particular thanks go to Jeffrey M. Flannery of the Library of Congress Manuscript Division; Joan Grattan and James Stimpert of the Johns Hopkins University Library; Susan Halpert of the Houghton Library, Harvard University; Christine Weideman of the Yale University Library; Susan Summerfield Hammerman, University of Chicago Library; and Malgorzata Myc of the Bentley Historical Library, University of Michigan.

Thanks for permission to quote from unpublished materials go to the Principal and fellows of Somerville College, Oxford; Llyfrgell Genedlaethol Cymru, The National Library of Wales; the West Sussex Record Office; the University of Chicago Library; and the Mistress and Fellows, Girton College, Cambridge. For permission to use the frontispiece photo, we wish to thank the Ferdinand Hamburger Archives of the Johns Hopkins University.

We are also grateful to our friends Jack Marietta, Hermann Rebel, Richard

Davis, Reba Soffer, Henry Weisser, and Michael Hurst for many helpful suggestions. Finally, our special thanks go to colleagues in the Pacific Coast and Western branches of the North American Conference on British Studies as well as the American Historical Association who listened patiently to papers that eventually formed the bases of this book.

Contents

Preface

———◆◆◆———

This project had its inception in pondering the cycles of academic fashion. Why did constitutional history, once the mainstay of the history curriculum in 1900, suffer such a loss of prestige by 2000? For that matter, how had it risen to such preeminence in the first place? The explanations, we found, were far more complicated than we had originally suspected. Constitutional history's loss of prestige certainly depended upon developments within academe, but it also hinged upon accelerating political, social, economic, and international transformations. Historians were expected to provide national narratives that were at once compelling and reassuring. Armed with a newly won sense of professional expertise and a belief in the scientific nature of their scholarship, historians in Britain and America fastened on a narrative of constitutional evolution within a framework of Anglophone exceptionalism. A belief in the institutional superiority of Anglo-American law and government had crystallized by the early twentieth century into a central tenet of both national identity and historical scholarship.

In this book, we seek to illuminate these processes by analyzing the public and private writings of historians, while placing them within the context of wider societal and cultural change. In addition to the relevant secondary literature and the publications of leading constitutional historians starting with William Stubbs, the book is based on over seventy different manuscript collections (mostly the letters and papers of historians) in the United Kingdom and United States. At one level, we develop the theme of the emergence of constitutional history as the dominant field in the discipline in the half century or so after the onset of professionalization, and its gradual decline as new modes of historical inquiry, chiefly in social history, took hold. At another level, we distinguish the various strands of constitutional history (e.g., racial, institutional) and the ways in which they affected and were affected by broader cultural patterns and national policies in both societies. We show that while constitutional history became the dominant mode of discourse within the profession and influenced wider (especially elite) circles, it was by no means uncontested. Sharp "culture wars" over rival forms of national identity based on history resulted, especially in the interwar United States. We also pay considerable attention to the role of constitutional historians in promoting the growth of empire and the Anglo-American "special relationship." Finally, the small but growing role of women historians within the field is considered in a separate chapter, as is the field of legal history.

The Great Tradition

Introduction

Constitutional history as a discrete (and, for over half a century, dominant) subfield of the discipline emerged in the second half of the nineteenth century. But as a more broadly conceived approach to the past, it is of course much older. Medieval chroniclers did not, on the whole, concern themselves overmuch with the major milestones of constitutional change that later scholars would take up. It was in the highly charged polemical atmosphere of the seventeenth century, with the rising tide of resistance to Stuart "absolutism," that scholars of law and history, many of them in leading positions in the law courts and parliament, began developing a comprehensive historical critique of James I's and Charles I's policies. These were, according to leading critics like Sir Edward Coke, contrary to a long-established constitutional tradition of limited government and respect for the rights of free-born Englishmen. The professional respect for the historic precedent cited in common law courts was as important as the worship of such milestone documents as Magna Carta.

A growing interest in the Anglo-Saxon period, originally stimulated by Tudor-era scholars and antiquaries, was readily grafted onto this constitutional historical consciousness. For some commentators, Anglo-Saxon freemen came to be seen as the essential progenitors of English liberty, crystallizing a racial element within constitutional history. In all the major constitutional conflicts from the late seventeenth century on, the degree to which Anglo-Saxon village councils were invoked as justification of resistance to tyrannical regimes served as a marker of the movement's radical nature. Thus the aristocratic Whig revolution makers of 1688 chose, on the whole, to anchor their cause on Magna Carta and later parliamentary restrictions on royal power, rather than on the more egalitarian, if more ancient, practices of village councils.

The latter half of the eighteenth century saw the radical deployment of Anglo-Saxonist arguments on both sides of the Atlantic in the American Revolution. While much of the radical assault hinged on ahistoricist "rights of man" doctrine, it was accompanied by historical references to ancient rights. Thus Thomas Paine, otherwise firmly grounded in a demotic brand of Enlightenment argument against the absurdity and injustice of hereditary privilege, also invoked the Anglo-Saxons by playing the "Norman Yoke" card—the belief that the Normans in 1066 and after had suppressed but not destroyed ancient English liberties. These were seen by Paine and other radicals to be in vibrant ascendance not only in America, but in the growing opposition to royal and aristocratic misrule in Britain. In the French Revolution, English "Jacobins" and radical Whigs again grounded their movement partly in "free-born Englishmen" rhetoric. Of course, champions of established forms and entrenched privilege could also muster constitutional historical arguments, holding up monarchy, aristocracy, and church as long-enduring and essential components of English national identity. This argument, especially when used by Edmund Burke, served not only to polarize constitutional views between radicals and conservatives, but to split asunder the Whig party itself. Burke's "Appeal from the New Whigs to the Old" sought to anchor Whiggism in the elitist arguments of the leaders of 1688, seeing in their reverence for long-established forms a safe and trustworthy restraint on dangerous change, yet one that allowed some room for reform, albeit in cautious increments.

By the start of the nineteenth century, two substantially different forms of English constitutional history vied for supremacy, a radical Whig view favored by proponents of democracy and a Burkean version with the greatest appeal to those of property and station. At times of intense political excitement, as at the time of the Great Reform Bill of 1832 or during the Chartist era, these arguments became politically charged to an intense degree. In quieter years, a more consensual atmosphere prevailed. The new appreciation of the Middle Ages spawned by Romanticism helped to inculcate further a historically informed constitutionalism into English national identity. Another element of constitutional historical consciousness grew out of the new philological studies, in which German scholars took a leading part. This work traced the antecedents of Anglo-Saxon liberty back to primitive, supposedly freedom-loving Teutonic tribes and beyond them to that ur-people of remote antiquity, the Aryans. While this component may be said to have had a somewhat limited impact on the English public's sense of national identity, it made considerable inroads among intellectuals and racial theorists. In combination with Darwinism, it offered a "scientific" demonstration of English racial superiority.

The second half of the nineteenth century saw the formulation of the classic Whig theories of the origins and development of the English constitution. The three writers who dominated this era, William Stubbs, Edward Augustus Freeman, and John Richard Green, are often considered to have constituted the "Whig" school of historiography. In spite of significant differences, they shared a belief in the long-term development of the English constitution and the placing of that development at the center of the English national story. The country's history was considered to be largely one of incremental progress, punctuated indeed by some dramatic events and even a few setbacks, yet overall moving majestically forward toward greater inclusion and freedom. Throughout their history, the English held fast to a belief in freedom and self-government, the priceless legacy from their Anglo-Saxon forebears. Institutional continuity from the age of Alfred through the Norman Conquest and beyond was a firmly held tenet of the Whig school.

The professionalizing of the discipline in the waning years of the century was not kind to Green and Freeman, whose work was viewed as overly colorful and based too much on chroniclers and other "soft" evidence. In the new, more rigorous practice of academic historians, Stubbs, whose careful collection, publication, and analysis of primary source materials had helped inspire the professionalizing of the discipline, alone survived the transition. His *Constitutional History* and *Select Charters* remained essential reading for students well into the twentieth century. British elites studying history in universities during this period were subjected to a painstakingly analyzed but reassuring national story based on gradual, incremental change, illustrating both the fundamental soundness of the nation's institutions and the natural English gift for governing. This included a presumed genius for ruling other races, a most useful belief for the many graduates taking up posts in the far-flung Empire.

In many respects, the evolution of constitutional history in the United States in the second half of the nineteenth century mirrored that in Britain: the reverence for ancient, especially Anglo-Saxon antecedents, the rapid advance of professionalization, the emphasis on close analyses of primary sources, the reassuring sense of the gradual unfolding of sound governmental and legal structures. Initially, the labors of early academic leaders like Herbert Baxter Adams of Johns Hopkins University served to bolster the Teutonic "germ" theory of Anglo-American institutions. However, the new generation of seminar-trained historians largely repudiated this view as fanciful, focusing instead on the post-conquest period, for which there was an abundance of extant sources. As in Britain, constitutional history came to be concerned largely with post-1066 England, and the Anglo-Saxon era was relegated to the status of a promising but chaotic preamble to the main event.

The changes in academic approaches and methodology in the United States did not merely affect views of English constitutional history. Applied to American history itself, they wrought dramatic changes in the national story and ushered in several decades of intense debate. Most importantly, the new constitutional history challenged the conventional heroic narrative of the American Revolution. Secondarily, it called for a sharp revision in the dominant view of the history of Anglo-American relations. The pre-Revolutionary period, looked at through the dispassionate lens of constitutional studies, dissolved into a series of administrative problems and attendant transatlantic misunderstandings, resulting in an unfortunate rupture of the English-speaking world. This repudiation of a deeply rooted heroic narrative challenged the very essence of American national identity. A related view held by many American historians at the turn of the twentieth century—that the United States and Britain were temporarily estranged cousins who needed to mend relations and cooperate in world affairs—had immediate relevance to pressing issues of empire.

On both sides of the Atlantic, growing world commitments and fresh international dangers called for corresponding changes in historical national identity. The earlier Anglo-Saxon version of English constitutional history stressing individual liberty, localism, and small central government had suited early to mid-nineteenth century conditions. As Britain and the United States moved into a period of overseas expansion, the form of historical identity shifted forward in time to the vigorous, expansionist Normans. Constitutional history's emphasis on the post-1066 period had to do with something more than the availability of a large documentary base. It also provided satisfying antecedents in the form of the Normans, whose wide-ranging military successes throughout Europe were matched by their supposed genius for creating powerful organs of central government. Expanded government was also viewed, by Progressives in the United States and New Liberals in Britain, as necessary for addressing growing social problems. A suitably enlarged administrative state could be seen to have antecedents in Norman and Angevin England, yet the majesty and antiquity of the English constitution and Common Law served as an effective barrier against socialism's threat to the regime of private property and capitalism. In short, a "Normanized" version of constitutional history provided a highly usable past for both nations' elites.

The dominant role of this conservative version of constitutional history also served to facilitate Anglo-American rapprochement. With the American Revolution no longer either a fundamental watershed or an embittering memory, the way was paved for the coming together of the two English-speaking powers as they confronted other imperial contenders like Germany and Japan. A number of the leading scholars in the field were themselves strong advocates of a close alliance, and a few even argued for an enlarged imperial federation that would include the United States. Their efforts assisted in the emergence of a close relationship by the outbreak of the Great War and in bringing America into the conflict at Britain's side. Transatlantic educational opportunities, academic visits and friendships, and new international institutions helped cement this "special relationship" (as it came eventually to be called), secured firmly in shared beliefs about English and American constitutional history. In America after the war, this Anglophilic version of constitutional history not only was entrenched in a number of universities, but had also begun to penetrate high school textbooks. The ensuing "culture war" over what those espousing traditional patriotic views called "treason texts" was a bitter, politically charged conflict.

The cultural struggle in the United States in the interwar period did not occur in Britain for the simple reason that the radical Whig view had never entrenched itself as the dominant national story. This did not mean that that constitutional history went unchallenged. As in America, the period after World War I witnessed the rise of new approaches and methodologies, principally those associated with social history. The new social historians, many of them driven by a progressive or radical (in some cases, Marxist) agenda, saw in constitutional history a powerful intellectual prop of capitalism and the imperial order. The ensuing struggle within history departments was sometimes as bitter, at least in America, as the more public dispute over treason texts. By the 1930s, the citadel had been breached, and constitutional historians found themselves on the defensive, though it would not be till after World War II that the enormous increase in nonelite higher education led to the marginalization of the Great Tradition.

Such, in brief compass, is a chronological overview of what is to follow. Ensuing chapters are organized on a largely topical basis, around themes such as race, professionalization, empire, gender, law, politics, and diplomacy. A central subtopic is the impact of constitutional history on the Anglo-American connection, both diplomatically and culturally. Throughout the book, the focus is on the various contested national identities that emerged in Britain and America during the period 1870–1960, the role played by constitutional historians in fostering them, and the impact on broader cultural patterns.

CHAPTER ONE

"The Paragon of the World"

―――◆◆◆―――

English Constitutional History as National Identity

In the past two decades no issue has engaged scholars of English and British history more than that of national identity. This research and reflection has fostered an outpouring of scholarship that has turned national identity into a growth industry that demands the plural: identities. In the wide variety of approaches to and interpretations of these issues, it is clear that different conclusions have arisen from debates about chronology, authenticity, religion, sources, and cultural modes. To enter into the labyrinth of national identity, English, British, or both, requires a careful appreciation of the many facets that affect this complex problem. Nor is this a scholarly issue alone. In the 1960s and 1970s, the era of agonizing reappraisal, or in the forthright Thatcherite appeal to Victorian values in the 1980s, or in the years of New Labour at the end of the twentieth century, the composition of the United Kingdom and its identities have assumed political importance.[1] Scholarship aimed at those outside the academy has made this quest a popular topic as well.[2]

What is central to these debates is the consensual verdict that history plays the ultimate arbiter. Whether that history is nostalgic, romantic, antiquarian, scientific, elitist, or popular, the past, often imagined or invented, has defined the boundaries for understanding national identity issues. Prior to 1870, historians tended to emphasize writing about famous political events without much regard for the discovery of new knowledge. Arguments about identity touch diverse areas of inquiry and epochs, but this book focuses on the period 1870–1960, when constitutional history took a primary role in narrating the English story. As Stefan Collini has written, jurist A. V. Dicey (1835–1922), in his *Introduction to the Study of the Law of the Constitution* (1885), "managed to make the ordinary operations of the common law central to the characterization of the distinctive identity of the English nation."[3] English constitutional achievement epitomized theories of English exceptionalism, especially the famous (or infamous) Whig interpretation of history. In order to gain perspective on the claims of constitutional history with respect to the national identity issue, a review of alternative explanations will help fix its place.

Even the premises of identity discourse are not specific, for a definition of national identity acceptable to all scholars simply has never existed, nor is there agreement about what constitutes the nation and nationalism. The reassessment of the latter two phenomena began with Benedict Anderson's famous definition of the nation: "It is an imagined political community—and imagined as both inherently limited and sovereign."[4] Another formulation placed emphasis on the nation as a "cultural entity with principles of coherence," where "to talk of national identity requires us to analyse processes of inclusion and exclusion."[5] Yet another scholar has written that "nationalism may be described as the myth of the historical renovation that rediscovers in the depths of the communal past a pristine state of true collective individuality."[6] This rediscovery occurs in the assortment of myths, memories, values, and symbols that constitute national identity.[7] Nation and identity may be political or cultural, both or neither; given this situation, no wonder the issues have taken on such disparate dimensions.

Discussions of national identity sometimes turn into concern for national character, a phrase that historians have usually regarded with suspicion. National character has implied attachment by an overwhelming majority to a unique value system that set the nation apart from other countries. Or, conversely, alleged idiosyncrasies have served as the symbols of national identity. Historians have found it difficult to identify such a code in the light of racial, class, and gender differences within a specific society. Proponents of English exceptionalism have rarely succeeded by an appeal to a unique national character. In one area, however, this situation did prevail: "the relationship between national character—a preoccupation of the Victorians—and the constitution was central to both academic and political perceptions of the nation, and especially to Conservative patriotism."[8] Theodore Marburg (1862–1914), American ambassador to Belgium in 1914, wrote that "the English are eminently a people of political genius."[9] In 1908 foreign secretary Sir Edward Grey (1862–1933) recorded the following opinion. Baron Wilhelm von Stumm, upon completion of his tour as German ambassador in London, told Grey in a farewell interview that "he had realized that in some ways we were different from other people."[10] Granted that these represent a few instances only, but was the German diplomat onto something? Many in England would have agreed.

In the end, scholars confront a series of dichotomies, some mutually exclusive: popular versus elite visions of identity, the chronological fluctuation of identity from era to era, and the changing images of historical figures. No single identity has prevailed, because alternative versions always compete for acceptance.[11] The plural is appropriate because identities have always taken a variety of expressions and have changed over decades and even centuries. At any specific time, whose identity is meant depends on a variety of social factors. The formulation of national identity may be both positive and negative, internal and external. Does this failure to reach consensus mean that the issue should not matter? On the contrary, historical inquiry into the contingent elements of its multiple forms has made the study of national identities even more crucial, because few other categories offer such a record of change and continuity. Krishan Kumar's impressive review of the complexities associated with national identity has provided an extensive framework for consideration of its puzzles.[12]

Inevitably historians turn to chronology when confronted by vexing questions. When, if ever, did a specific English identity become evident? Patrick Wormald has addressed this issue through an examination of Anglo-Saxon society. He disputed the claim that the nation is essentially an invented community; this latter argument denied its essential historicity, a point that Wormald considered specifically.[13] As he argued, one need not embrace Whig history to recognize that some forms of institutional continuity persisted from Anglo-Saxon times into the modern period, because "this system's endurance rested on the unusual size of a political nation whose depth and coherence was in turn sustained by the access of its members to the king's law."[14] This may strike some readers as unduly Stubbsian, but more than a century after the *Constitutional History*, Wormald's continuing research into Anglo-Saxon history has perhaps provided the evidence for similar conclusions that Stubbs himself lacked. At the very least the resurrection of Anglo-Saxon studies has reconfigured the national identity question, for continuity, after decades of denigration, might after all really have a place in the national narrative.

Emphasis on 1066 and the period thereafter has continued to provoke interpretive differences, however, much as the Norman Conquest did in the heyday of William Stubbs (1825–1901) and Frederic Maitland (1850–1906). For the proponents of the Normans as the crucial ingredient in identity formation, the conclusion resulted from the long synthesis of Anglo-Saxon and Norman. Those who resisted the teleology and (by implication) continuity of the Whig interpretation, such as John Horace Round (1854–1928) and Maitland, focused on the postconquest era in order to argue for the Norman rather than Anglo-Saxon basis for English history. In retrospect, this emphasis depended upon a view of identity that stressed biological descent perhaps more than institutional inheritance.[15] It took the work of Frank Stenton (1880–1967) to advance beyond the "quirky genius" of Round; in *The First Century of English Feudalism, 1066–1166* (1932), Stenton built upon Round's obsession with archival records "to use them as a basis for the reconstruction of a society."[16] Stenton provided a nuanced account of the synthesis between Anglo-Saxon and Norman after 1066, and the controversy has continued. When now the venerable term *feudalism* appears on its last legs, the postmodernist search for identity in symbols and contexts has displaced the traditional representation of postconquest England as a polity held together by feudal bonds. In the era to 1307, therefore, issues of identity formation have remained problematical.

The period from the death of Edward I in 1307 to 1485 has often seemed dreary in contrast to the heroic age of the Conqueror, Henry II, and Edward I himself. For many historians, the period has reeked of decay and decline, domestically and beyond England's borders. Among the more obvious examples of this transition were the political instability symbolized by the deposition and murder of monarchs, the social unrest typified by the Peasants Revolt in 1381, population loss accelerated by the Black Death, the rise of religious controversy, and the ultimate loss of practically all the Angevin Empire. Feudalism and manorialism, the institutional bulwarks of the post-1066 era, disappeared without obvious replacements. For the constitutional historian, however, no such gloom pervaded this epoch, for whatever else the origins of parliament and the existence of a Lancastrian constitution provided ample opportunities for research. Parliament in particular, that potent symbol of the English gift for representative government, "meant the creation of that national and political unity which, until quite modern days, was the highest achievement of European statesmanship; it meant the appearance on the world's horizon of that new star, which was to light the nations on their march to freedom."[17] Add to this the debut of equity as a complement to the common law, the formal retention of recorded case law, and the development of parliamentary precedents that would have later importance, and the constitutional historian never lacked topics for investigation. Once parliament became a badge of identity, its remote origins took on greater significance in order to illustrate how England had so fortuitously evolved such a prestigious institution.

With the accession of the Tudor dynasty in 1485, the claims of different eras to formulate national identity became clearer. The Protestant Reformation ushered in decades of profound change that occupied most of the sixteenth century; indeed, from the perspective of the medieval church, "the Reformation was the greatest revolution in English history."[18] A new identity as a Protestant nation, forged in the dramas associated with Bloody Mary, John Foxe, and the Spanish Armada, resulted from the covenant that God had made with His elect nation, the New Jerusalem of England. In recent years the pace of this change and the process by which the country adopted a Protestant culture has led to arresting work on the entire Tudor age. Whether this transformation in religion created a new nation historians still debate.[19] In the end the "combination of patriotism with intolerant Protestantism is a factor in 'Englishness.'"[20] In the seventeenth century the Civil War and the Glorious Revolution helped resolve the settlement of religion in national life, although the extent to which religion had become *the* pillar of national identity has remained problematic.[21]

By the eighteenth century the religious dimension to the national history had taken a central place: "The absolute centrality of Protestantism to the British experience in the 1700s and long after is so obvious that it has often been passed over."[22] A triumphant Anglican church, secure in law and status, occupied a substantial part of the national narrative. Foxe had taken a role second only to scripture in forging an alliance between religion and national memory. By the middle of the nineteenth century, when James Anthony Froude (1818–94) narrated the history of the sixteenth century, he articulated a cosmic vision that endured for many decades. A righteous people suffering from clerical corruption and papal tyranny responded spontaneously to the liberation presented by the Reformation and the battles to defend religious liberty against Queen Mary and Spain. The subtext to this struggle implied the defense of English liberty against Spanish oppression; the superiority of the common law prevailed against the arbitrary strictures of the civil law: "Popery was deadly for constitutional reasons; it encouraged despotism and was incompatible with free political institutions."[23] God's chosen nation enjoyed the providential blessings of constitutional liberty as well.

Protestant triumphalism was not uniform. On one level Roman Catholicism played the role of religious Other to a significant degree. On another level the great cultural divide that separated the Anglican establishment from Dissent added an additional ingredient to the national story. Dissent represented to the established church those traits of zeal and enthusiasm so foreign to the true English virtues of moderation and toleration. Stubbs, great historian and ultimately bishop of Oxford, wrote that he doubted whether a Dissenter could write the history of England.[24] The centrality of religious experience to English history, Anglican or otherwise, often denigrated in the twentieth century, has placed the relationship of religion to national identity in a revised light.[25]

Whether or not one accepts J. C. D. Clark's model of England as a confessional state in the long eighteenth century has not affected the recognition that religion helped define English identity as the nineteenth century believed and the late twentieth century has rediscovered.[26] Even in the middle of the nineteenth century, "there were still many people who saw Britain as an elect nation, a second Israel, with a divine mission to uphold and propagate pure Christianity."[27] The inroads of secularism and unbelief eventually corrupted this perception, but as with so much of Victorian history, it is the endurance of traditional attitudes rather than the rapidity of change that surprises. At the end of the nineteenth century the links between religion and constitutional liberty still endured: "The function of the Church of England was to be the church of free men."[28] Ultimately, from the time of the Protestant Reformation forward, religion has staked its claim as a fundamental component in the complex appraisal of national identity.

To this religious sense of national self-realization the tumultuous events of the seventeenth century added further nuances. In this period it was Parliament, not Protestantism, that symbolized the permanent characteristics of English history. The struggle for the ancient constitution embodied in the prelude to civil war accentuated the role of Parliament as guardian of historic English liberties. The definition of a common-law mind in political and legal culture placed law at the center of political debate and permitted widely varying interpretations of its legacy.[29] Even the resort to military action proved beneficial to the emphasis on institutional continuity by its singular place in all English history; it was the exception that proved the rule whereby consensus had governed national development. The truth of these arguments became less important than the manner in which they came to claim belief: "The radical tradition and the sinews of the state had combined to create an imagined national identity already in the seventeenth century."[30] At the end of the nineteenth century Samuel Rawson Gardiner (1829–1902), in his eighteen volumes on the years 1603–56, resolved Stubbs's doubts by demonstrating that Anglican exclusivity no longer served the national narrative: "He offered the Victorians a comprehensive interpretation of the seventeenth century that was broad enough to contain the nation's Puritan as well as its Anglican past."[31] The Glorious Revolution sealed the place of the seventeenth century in national consciousness by virtue of its relative freedom from violence. The resolution of constitutional issues in 1688 had secured the primacy of constitutional achievement in the unfolding of English history. When, however, the Act of Union with Scotland in 1707 created the United Kingdom of Great Britain, the identity issue became more complex.

The parallel existence of English and British identities complicated matters greatly; the task of untangling the intricacies has proved just as difficult. Was identity determined by internal factors, contrasted to some external Other, or a mixture of these categories? For much of the twentieth century, historians treated nationalism as a political and cultural construct that affected continental countries, from which Great Britain, as with bureaucracy, was blessedly free. In Britain imperialism had served as the greater patriotism, the role played by nationalism in other countries. Without attempting to account for every contribution to the vexing question, two theories of the English versus British distinctiveness have emerged. Linda Colley in *Britons* famously traced the shaping of British identity from 1707 to 1837 by stressing Protestantism, war and especially the rivalry with France, empire, profits, royal culture, and a patrician renaissance.[32] Colley provided a succinct version of this interpretation: "If we look at Great Britain in this way, as an invented nation that was not founded on the suppression of older loyalties so much as superimposed on them, and that was heavily dependent for its raison d'etre on a broadly Protestant culture, on the threat and tonic of recurrent wars, especially war with France, and on the triumphs, profits and Otherness represented by a massive overseas empire, a great deal becomes clear."[33] Thus British identity depended primarily on negative perceptions of others rather than a celebration of its own virtues.

The other major contribution to this debate on the eighteenth century came from Gerald Newman's *Rise of English Nationalism,* with its emphasis on English identity and tracing its definition to a somewhat different chronological period: 1740 to 1830. Newman and Colley certainly shared many positions, such as the crucial importance of external influences, and their accounts coincided on many points. In the end, however, Newman found national identity located much more in traits of national character: innocence, honesty, originality, frankness, and moral independence.[34] The conclusions of Colley and Newman were not mutually exclusive, because in many, but not all, ways they depended on a similar roster of historical materials. Was it accurate to interchange English and British? Was Scotland, for example, merely North Britain? Changing contexts of historical inquiry have provided new avenues for investigation into the identity issue.

These innovative changes, pioneered by J. G. A. Pocock, stressed a departure from the conventional history of nation-states toward a broader geographical perspective. Emphasis on the British Isles as the preferred unit for narration, especially the relationships among the three kingdoms of England, Ireland, and Scotland, replaced specific focus on just one nation. As Norman Davies phrased it: "How Anglocentricity distorts our islands' changing story."[35] Davies rejected the English story as the cornerstone of British historical narrative that privileged English history at the expense of Irish, Scottish, and Welsh history and interpreted the latter national histories as appendages to the dominance of England. This change in historical fashion helped recast the English/British dichotomy and offered new opportunities to examine the identity question from a fresh perspective.

While the study of eighteenth-century English history has broken away from its post-Namierite malaise, the exact nature of its place in the national identity has remained a matter of contention. On the one hand the eighteenth century has received this assessment: "In this process [identity formation], the eighteenth century was crucial; it is the historic battleground of the formation of Great Britain, and subsequent historians have viewed it as such."[36] Great Britain, as with other nations, was invented to express new constitutional arrangements. On the other hand the historian of the long eighteenth century has written: "Britain was not invented; it developed. It was not devised by a small number of cultural entrepreneurs, acting like advertising executives to package and market a new product; it grew, the often unintended result of actions by men and women in many walks of life often, too, the result of conflicts and cross-purposes."[37] Such divisions of opinion have made clear that the eighteenth century had important significance for the British/English identity issue. Answers as to why this should be so, or what forms the answers should take, have not generated any kind of scholarly consensus.

The place of the constitution in the expression of national identity in the eighteenth century rarely has received attention. The additions of the prime minister and cabinet occurred without fanfare, even much notice, so unlike the dramatic events that had characterized the century before 1688. The Glorious Revolution had defined the constitution, so mundane developments thereafter did not have the same cachet. The most influential of the century's constitutional authorities, Sir William Blackstone (1723–80), transformed common-law history into the comfortable scheme so prized by the political elite: "Not only did his system imply that there remained no major resumptions of past liberty to be worked for but he venerated the wisdom of the ages that had brought forth the law and approached even cosmetic change with caution."[38] Blackstone established that one of England's glories was its unique and unrivaled constitutional splendor. More specifically one scholar has argued that the legal system itself contributed to identity formation because "we can see the extent to which 'England' and 'Englishness' were themselves invented through rules of ownership and through the state's use of rules of ownership to project and to enforce certain ideas of desirable Englishness."[39] When the French Revolution challenged fundamental assumptions of English society, the English constitution symbolized the divide between the rivals. During the turmoil generated by the events in France, Richard Sheridan in the Irish House of Commons quoted an observer that "in England there were two parties; they were rivals, they hated each other but loved the same mistress—the constitution."[40] This attachment to the constitution reflected a sentimental vision of the past entertained by the politically active and increasingly placed before a wider audience to offset the appeal of revolutionary ideology.

Under the broad influence of romanticism in the first half of the nineteenth century, national identity took yet another turn as history itself became a fertile ground for self-definition. The surge in historical interest at a popular level resulted in an antiquarianism at odds with later academic professionalism.[41] By later standards, romantic history erred in focusing on the particular at the expense of the general and by its fascination with the arcane. As long as the university study of history emphasized the world of classical antiquity, domestic history as a subject of academic study still lagged.[42] The antiquarian interest explored the byways of the English past and provided a satisfactory outlet for the popular imagination to examine the deeds (and sometimes misdeeds) that composed English history. Elite history in the Whig vein joined with romanticism's appeal to the public to establish a usable past for all society: "The Victorian cult of English history reflected and revivified national consciousness, pride, and identity."[43] The romantic encouragement of an uncritical nostalgia accelerated the search for national identity by rummaging through centuries of history.

When school reform in 1870 produced a mass reading public, the educational system became the front line in inculcating ideas about national identity within each succeeding generation.[44] After 1870 the topics that might reflect national identity multiplied significantly. At present any subject, with appropriate justification, might illuminate the British/English identity issue or any permutation thereof. Identity research has now become a favored research area, perhaps in part from the post-1945 loss of such verities as empire that had seemed to anchor national life. Devolution and the potential dissolution of Great Britain itself have accentuated the political relevance of these issues. In this fashion appraisal of national identity will continue to provide an important context for both contemporary academic culture and political debate.

As long as university culture stressed familiarity with classical antiquity, English national identity defined itself in part both on its own internal history and by comparison to past societies and the way that English history had replicated values found in earlier periods. In the eighteenth and nineteenth centuries, classical Rome provided a model of civic virtue that legitimated the post-1688 constitution by an idealized analogy to Republican Rome.[45] In the Victorian era, ancient Greece also served as a surrogate for English identity, when "the Athenians became transformed into the ancient equivalent of modern Englishmen who had mastered the art of self-government and who had achieved a civilization wherein artistic excellence, positivistic thought, and individual liberty had largely, if not always perfectly, flourished."[46] When the empire grew dramatically in the nineteenth century, imperial Rome superseded the earlier republic as a source of historical comparison. Some Victorians even found in the Vikings a source of institutional life that reflected the accomplishments of English society.[47] The Vikings served as both a positive and negative influence as the English sought to define themselves: "Confronted by Vikings, the English, ancient and modern, have oscillated between repulsion and association. English identity has been constructed against a Viking Other, as a narrative of shared victimhood and resistance, personified by King Alfred the Great."[48] This penchant for seeing themselves reflected in other societies added a remarkable ingredient to the Victorian taste for self-fashioning.

If external models did not work, then examination of domestic personalities and periods presented a wide variety of identity sources. For example, Alfred the Great and the Anglo-Saxons served well as racial discourse became more prominent in the 1870s. Emphasis on the Germanic sources of English identity asserted the primacy of Anglo-Saxon roots for English society.[49] In other cases an individual alone offered a model for national emulation; the depiction of Edward I, for example, as the English Justinian stressed his role as shaper of the common law: "In his person, his character, his position, and his policy, are summed up the essential elements of that great English nation which came into existence during his lifetime."[50] Despite the reservations of academic historians on the ground of Tudor despotism, popular historians looked to the Tudor age as "Merry England," a treasure trove of social history and other traditional elements of the English past.[51] For other Victorian historians, the constitutional triumphs of the Stuart era made that period suitable for exploration as a standard for the national past.[52] This brief review makes plain that national identity might be found in every direction, for traveling through the past offered ample opportunity literally to choose any topic and make it a reflection of some sense of national identity. Rather than resolving the issue, the search for identity in the nineteenth century revealed how complex unraveling its strands had become.

If the Victorians struggled with making sense out of these materials, the political structure of Great Britain added a complicating dimension as well. Emphasis on the contrasts between English and Celtic societies assisted in the quest for identity within the United Kingdom. On the one hand, anti-Celtic, particularly but not exclusively Irish Catholic, prejudice put Celtic societies in opposition to English superiority.[53] The Irish suffered from stereotypes of violence, fondness for alcohol, and economic backwardness that stood in stark contrast to the "English" values of political consensus, sobriety, and economic innovation that made the achievements of English society so laudable. On the other hand, the Irish helped generate Celtophiliac attitudes through admiration for the simplicity of peasant life in contrast to the urban ills that affected industrial England. Add to this the rich variety of Irish literature and many in England found much to praise about Irish life and history: "It would be truer to say that Englishmen had drawn from their long experience of the Irish a national stereotype which had both its good points and its bad: as good and bad points were defined by the Irish themselves."[54] If the ambiguities of the Anglo-Celtic relationship haunted the search for English identity, it did the same for Irish, Scottish, and Welsh efforts as well. Recent scholarship on Irish history has prompted numerous attempts to define the Irish national narrative.[55] Within the constituent elements of the United Kingdom, therefore, the Victorians discovered no magic formula to resolve questions of national identity, and if anything, found them more difficult.

In yet another direction, national identity became located in a strand of nostalgia that stressed the essentially rural nature of Englishness. From the time of John Constable's *The Hay Wain* and William Cobbett's *Rural Rides* in the 1820s, country landscape, whether verbal or visual, exercised an increasingly strong hold on the English imagination. "Representations of English morality" have focused attention on the rural values embedded in this particular expression of identity.[56] These virtues included "insularity, artifice, stability and order."[57] Other aesthetic endeavors spawned different forms of an essential English vision. For example, one strand accentuated the golden days of rural life, as in Flora Thompson's *Lark Rise to Candleford*, a reminiscence of Oxfordshire village life that made the small agricultural community a microcosm of stability and permanence for all England to envy: "memories of childhood when the sun shone all summer, and there was always snow at Christmas."[58] Deep England, depicted by the village, the country inn and church, and the farm, became a powerful expression of Englishness.[59]

A similar motif animated the English garden city movement, a "vision of the future from a mythic past, constructing a green and pleasant heaven to replace an ugly and unhealthy urban hell."[60] Dreams of medieval or early modern England, invented or realistic, emphasizing hierarchy and continuity, have made their mark on national consciousness. So appealing that their truth rarely matters, these idealized pasts compelled attention and allegiance. Even competing models of the English garden reflected broader political and cultural conflicts in the period after 1870. The Crystal Palace exhibition of 1851 had powerfully evoked the English image as workshop of the world, yet the trope of rural tranquility continued to battle the urban, industrial realities.[61] Each of these aspects of identity contributed to the Victorian mosaic of national self-image.

A sense of place permeated yet another contribution to the identity discussion. In this interpretation a particular region might play the part of progenitor to a view of Englishness. One scholar has noted, for example, how the Cotswolds became singled out to reflect what were presumed to be the unvarying virtues of country life: "It is predicated in part on the notion that landscape is a powerful idiom for representing national identity, but stresses the construction of *regional* identities and their connections with national identities in England."[62] Or in the case where absence made the heart grow fonder, travel abroad reinforced Englishness through contrast to foreign destinations. Going overseas often increased patriotic feelings, religious identification, and the blessings of English liberty in equal measure.[63] In light of this Victorian legacy, by 1914 matters of identity had become more complicated than ever.

In the twentieth century, total war, loss of empire, and changing cultural norms combined to challenge many perceptions that, rightly or wrongly, have been called Victorian. After World War I, for example, the inauguration of commemoration rites started new means of defining identity and preserving it within the context of military virtues.[64] Even the role of intellectuals and their relative lack of influence within British society have illuminated the identity issue.[65] As historians multiplied investigatory schemes, the uncovering of Englishness in more and more categories occurred. The political debates surrounding the transition from subject to citizen helped to polarize discussions of inclusion and exclusion with respect to who qualified as British.[66] National identity had entered the political arena, where whether to be British or English or an imperial resident stoked the fires of immigration debates.

The debut of the cinema as a potent force for representation opened up additional areas whereby different perceptions of identity might find expression. Film fans will not soon forget *Mrs. Miniver,* Mel Gibson as William Wallace in *Braveheart,* Liam Neeson as Michael Collins, or the Welsh mining community in *How Green Was My Valley,* all powerful projections of values or perhaps stereotypes associated with the four parts of the United Kingdom. As one historian has concluded: "The ideological function of British cinema as a national cinema is thus to pull together diverse and contradictory discourses, to articulate a contradictory unity, to play a part in the hegemonic process of achieving consensus and containing difference and contradiction."[67] One might easily substitute descriptions of the Whig interpretation of history and arrive at the same conclusion.

The extensive recent work on empire has produced a historiography all its own that finds identity inextricably linked to the acquisition and ultimate loss of a vast imperial enterprise. Whereas earlier generations of historians had explained the impact of the metropolis on the periphery as the primary importance of the imperial experience, reassessment of this relationship has reversed the equation led by the word *Orientalism,* originally explored by Edward Said (1935–2003). This scholarly path has made the national identity issue more difficult because it added the imperial dimension into the discussion. When English, British/English, and imperial evidence come together, it is little wonder that answers have taken such a varied form.

Given the disparity of evidence and conclusions, even in this brief survey, it seems clear that national identity is an issue on which scholars will never fully agree. Kathleen Wilson's argument that "identity is tentative, multiple, and contingent, and its modalities change over time" was right on target.[68] Signs and symbols of national identity were and are omnipresent, but the one constant that pervades the issue is the primacy of historical inquiry. With due respect for the variety of interpretations that have attempted to answer national identity questions, shared history, whether continuity from the age of Athelstan to the collective memory of the world wars, dominates the issue: "National memory is shared by people who have never seen or heard of one another, yet who regard themselves as having a common history."[69] Perceptions of the past ran throughout each interpretation of national identity formation. As national identities have changed, the necessity to place these shifts in historical context became even more crucial. History provided the matrix upon which the national story is recorded and resolved, if that task can ever be completed. Consciousness of the past as national identity is but one of many explanations; yet it is surprising how little this sense of the past has figured, or how it has been simply dismissed as Burkean or Whig rhetoric, in analyses of the national identity disputes. History itself is a, not the, significant contributor to national identity after 1870; but it alone has created the national narrative that made other interpretations plausible.[70]

When constitutional history began to dominate discussions of the English past around 1870 and national identity, the quarrels that resulted resembled modern culture wars. The multiple identities that already existed in the Victorian era made plain that no single sense of the nation had triumphed. The challenges of empire made this task even more difficult. From the time that Gerald Newman observed in 1987 that "it is strange to think how greatly nationalism has eluded our scholarly attention," state and nation have claimed increasing importance in the identity issue.[71] Control of the past implied command of the national present and future. And, if "a nation is a named community of history and culture," then history dictated who was included in and excluded from the national narrative.[72] Such debates were inevitably political; historical controversies appeared in the national media, not the narrow confines of the academy. History engaged public intellectuals in an English Kulturkampf for the definition of nation and society.

The concept of culture wars as a heuristic device was reinforced, in Dwight Culler's phrase, by the Victorian mirror of history: "the habit . . . of drawing analogies between their own age and various historical periods in the past."[73] Prior to 1870, history had served many masters in random fashion, particularly romanticism and antiquarianism; only after that date did the new standards of science and professionalism impose rigorous criteria upon the study of history. Whether study of the distant past or part of an elite celebration of "evolving political institutions over at most the past two centuries,"[74] history provided the sources for rummaging in the past in order to support appropriate comparisons to demonstrate the path by which England had arrived at its privileged position. A usable past helped forge a hegemonic sense of exceptionalism, but precisely what made England so unique remained a source of controversy.

Whatever evidence a particular historical perspective demanded, one fact remained: English history stretched over many centuries. In the nineteenth century the construction of national identity demanded emphasis upon historical continuity.[75] A seamless continuum represented only one of several underlying traits in competing historical explanations, but it did provide one significant ingredient. By the time Stubbs published the *Select Charters* in 1870, earlier historians such as Henry Hallam (1777–1859) and Thomas Babington Macaulay (1800–1859) had already made the case for continuity, but even Hallam had started only at the accession of the Tudors. The pageantry of English history required an even grander backdrop, for "the sense of historic continuity is essential to the greatness of the nation as well as to the mental elevation of the individual."[76] To fill this need, Stubbs introduced his emphasis on the importance of medieval constitutional history. His *Constitutional History* in three volumes (1874–78) transformed English history into a panorama in which he featured "an orderly, unifying principle of study in the systematic and organic narrative of constitutional history."[77] For Stubbs and many others in his scholarly train, constitutional history, the superiority of a governing race, recounted the saga of English exceptionalism.

Attachment to the constitution, of course, had a long history well before

1870. The Norman Yoke, or the existence of a free Anglo-Saxon constitution before 1066, had long fueled radical political movements, especially in the battle in the seventeenth century to secure the recognition of historic rights. After the Glorious Revolution of 1688, praise for the "settled" constitution became a regular part of political discussion. Opposition to the political principles associated with the French Revolution resulted in even stronger devotion to traditional constitutional arrangements, in particular a renewed reverence for the monarchy. Simultaneously reformers of the era "turned more often to a radicalized constitutionalism than to the ideas of the French Revolution in order to draw legitimacy for their own political actions."[78] Admirers of the constitution who stressed the virtues of continuity and consensus, such as the Earl of Chatham, invoked the genius of the constitution. In 1849 Joshua Toulmin Smith wrote: "Born to Free Institutions as his Birthright, the Englishman rejoices to see . . . the cause of constitutional freedom."[79] In *The British Bee Hive* (1867), George Cruikshank placed the constitution second only to the monarchy and cited law and equity, trial by jury, and religious freedom as its principal glories.[80] Even as late as the 1950s, Winston Churchill (1874–1965) described the work of Henry II and the advent of the common law in a manner that accented constitutional exceptionalism.[81] Only after 1870, however, did the focus of historical inquiry switch to previously remote eras in the Middle Ages in order to emphasize the long record of constitutional achievement. In 1912 American historian George Burton Adams (1851–1925) wrote: "The importance of the English Constitution in the political history of mankind is so great that the question of its origin is of unusual interest. The unanimous judgment of the world at the beginning of the twentieth century is that this is the best system of government yet devised."[82] Americans recognized the links between constitutional achievement and national pride and appropriated that legacy for themselves.

The increasing connection of constitutional glories to national identity issues in the 1870s provided ample ammunition for self-congratulation as well as a basis for critiques of other countries that did not enjoy the blessings of English liberty. The constitution reflected political virtues that had turned Great Britain into an imperial power whose jurisdiction spanned the globe. The unwritten constitution symbolized the attainments of a free people who also dominated the world's commerce. James Bryce (1838–1922), politician and scholar, described this constitution as "The Paragon of the World," a beacon of hope to other nations still struggling to find constitutional success.[83] The arbitrary nature of French constitutionalism, with its enhancement of the state at the expense of the individual, or the impotent parliamentary system of Wilhelmine Germany proved the superiority of the English structure. The supposed authoritarianism of continental countries made English constitutional superiority all the more gratifying. For example, Eyre Crowe (1864–1925) of the Foreign Office, just two weeks after he had distributed his famous memorandum on Anglo-German relations of 1 January 1907, wrote of the Germans: "Of any genuine determination to bring on constitutional or parliamentary government, I cannot see any signs anywhere."[84] The constitution as icon in popular and academic culture came into its own in the 1870s and succeeding decades.

The allusion to the constitution conferred stability upon a country that faced serious challenges in the years after 1870. In a period when the previous sense of domestic and international security changed to jittery anticipation of the future, adherence to and praise of the unwritten constitution gave an element of permanence in an uncertain world. Increased economic competition, imperial disputes, and the ebbing sense of global ascendancy made the international scene increasingly fraught with danger. At home disrespect for the law in the home rule movement in Ireland, bitter clashes between capital and labor and an assertive trade union movement, and the erosion of political consensus made the constitution appear more fragile. These events after 1870 caused the constitution to represent the nation in forthright fashion, presenting an opportunity for constitutional history to encompass the contradictions of the political system.[85]

The foremost expression of constitutional history as the national narrative appeared in the famous Whig interpretation of history, the subject of Herbert Butterfield's (1900–1979) treatise in 1931.[86] This book acquired a fame of its own despite the fact that the author never attempted a philosophical analysis of historical causation and mentioned few Whigs. Most of the work actually dealt more with problems of continental history than with issues from the English past. Butterfield's conclusions were not even particularly novel; H. A. L. Fisher (1865–1940) had just published an article in 1928 in which he had examined trenchantly constitutional history and historians since 1870.[87] Butterfield's critique of his version of Whig history became trivialized into the aphorism that God had sided with Protestants and Parliament in English history. The terms *Whig history* and *Whig historian* had acquired many diverse meanings, including the privileging of constitutional history, historical teleology, and the primacy of historical continuity; but the Whig interpretation had embraced the triumph of Protestantism as well as English constitutional exceptionalism in general. In the end, therefore, the evaluation of Whig history suffered from the failure to analyze sufficiently its contradictory historiographical assumptions.[88] Despite the many muddles and false paths created by Whiggish assessments of English constitutional development, even Fisher conceded that the study of constitutional history made its singular achievements "a pearl of great price."[89]

Historians were not solely responsible for pushing constitutional history to the forefront of historical inquiry. Walter Bagehot (1826–77) in *The English Constitution* (1867) and Dicey in *Introduction to the Study of the Law of the Constitution* (1885) played a part in making the constitution the centerpiece of English history: "The political constitution described by the former, and the legal constitution described by the latter, have long held a complementary sway over the corridors of Westminster and Whitehall, as well as countless law school lecture halls."[90] Bagehot rescued the constitution from contempt by demonstrating that it could still function efficiently even after the monarch had withdrawn from public life in a protracted period of mourning. Dicey achieved his first great success when he reduced the complexities of constitutional law to the triad of the rule of law, parliamentary sovereignty, and the conventions of the constitution. In this enterprise he "achieved the improbable fusion of the Whig interpretation of history, the Austinian analysis of law, and the Individualist conception of the state, the whole amalgam presented as the dispassionate conclusion of academic legal science."[91] Promoted by both historians and jurists, constitutional history became fixated on the need to trace the origins of this English success story in order to explain how the constitution had evolved so successfully into its Victorian manifestation.

The initial suspects in the promulgation of Whig history included Stubbs, Edward Freeman (1823–92), and John Richard Green (1837–83). Often lumped together indiscriminately as partners in the crime of Whig history, their differences now seem to outweigh their similarities. They did agree, however, on the claim that the English constitution originated in Teutonic institutions, so its history needed research into its most remote antecedents. Stubbs in particular, despite the many improbable scholarly temptations to which he succumbed, still deserves respect because he inaugurated a new standard for historical research by his thorough utilization of original documents. His *Constitutional History*, as John Burrow rightly concluded, was "one of the great books, in fact, of the nineteenth century."[92] Whig history was public history, so it invariably conformed to high literary standards. Whig history became synonymous with stylistic craftsmanship, so an individual such as George Macaulay Trevelyan (1876–1962), not famous for his contributions to constitutional history, would later epitomize other aspects of the Whig interpretation. In the 1870s and for the next several decades, the conclusions of constitutional history became "so irresistible that the constitution had come to be regarded as the sole explanation for the development of English history as such. It became the ideal angle from which to illustrate the growth of the British nation, and its development was the axis of the history of England, *tout court,* the factor explaining especially the uniqueness of British political development."[93] Political progress fused with moral instruction to provide a singular tone to the story of constitutional accomplishment in which Victorians celebrated "the way in which England's native genius for liberty and representative government had brought it a far more fortunate history than had been the lot of less happy peoples."[94] Constitutional history fused with national identity to create the Great Tradition.

The Great Tradition may be defined as the process by which English constitutional history both as a research field and as a teaching field acquired a status that placed it at the apex of historical scrutiny. It rested on many assumptions shared with the Whig interpretation but also transcended the latter's limitations in important ways. The Great Tradition accepted the centrality of constitutional history but insisted on the highest scholarly standards in its study. This approach to English history privileged constitutional history above other avenues of inquiry because "constitutional history is concerned with the *working* of government; that is, with the interplay of *forces.* It is bound therefore to take notice of the social and economic factors, which determine forces, as well as with legal conventions which regulate the relation of the different parts of the constitution. Thus the constitutional historian has to keep his eye on all the other types of history."[95] The Great Tradition regarded public law, the relationship between the individual and the state in any period, as the foundation of national history, and therefore national identity.

This quest for the foundations of identity might lead the historian into any century since the Anglo-Saxon triumph in the seventh century. Henry W. C. Davis (1874–1928), for example, wrote of the medieval manor as a constitutional issue because it was "the type, the symbol, of an economic system which reacted powerfully upon the welfare and general habits of life of two important classes—lords and cultivators."[96] Constitutional history, therefore, encompassed all forms of human endeavor. The historian who coined the phrase, Michael Powicke, did so because the Great Tradition remained "both a rewarding and liberating ideal."[97] Its allure as a research field soon diminished, yet its eminence as a teaching field remained for decades, extending into the 1960s. The rise and decline of the Great Tradition possessed a symbiotic relationship, because for a few decades it represented to a remarkable degree the collective memory upon which that history existed. T. S. Eliot perhaps caught the links between history and identity best in the *Four Quartets:*

> A people without history is not redeemed from time,
> For history is a pattern of timeless moments.
> So, while the light fails
> On a winter's afternoon, in a secluded chapel
> History is now and England

The Great Tradition, with its focus on constitutional history set so carefully, marked an era when it defined England more specifically and more appreciatively than any other competing interpretation. A country hallowed by its history as much as or more than any other, England found in constitutional history a brilliant medium of expression:

Whether or not the English constitution is "written" in one document matters little because it is written into the political consciousness of the English nation. Indeed it describes the mythology that describes England. The whole idea of England, a chosen nation with a particular crusading destiny, is dependent upon the myths presented by the likes of Spenser and Shakespeare, Milton and Wordsworth. It gives England an identity, a sense of purpose, a reason for existence, its only reason.[98]

The lessons of English constitutional history extended into the ongoing relationships between imperial possessions and the mother country in which to varying degrees the experience of England was replicated. In addition, after the American Civil War, English common law served as one element of a broader Anglo-American rapprochement. The medieval origins of English constitutional history received illumination and came to symbolize a shared constitutional inheritance as well as closer cultural and political bonds.[99] The study of English history, especially constitutional history, flourished in the United States, where the publication of *The Common Law* (1881) by Oliver Wendell Holmes (1841–1935) opened new directions in American historical endeavors.[100] Concentration on the common constitutional underpinnings of the two countries fostered a greater sense of community; at the time of the Spanish-American War in 1898, Dicey wrote: "The immediate result to my mind of this is to make an *entente cordiale* if not an actual alliance between England and the U.S. imperative. This may save Anglo-Saxon principles of law & liberty & nothing else will."[101] Later, when famous New York attorney Joseph Hodges Choate (1832–1917) served as ambassador to the United Kingdom, at a Bench and Bar dinner in London, in his speech he noted that the event gave "a signal proof that neither time, nor distance, nor oceans, nor continents can weaken the ties of sympathy and fraternity between the members of our noble profession wherever the English law has reached or the English tongue is spoken. . . . There is no difference between American law and liberty and English law and liberty."[102] This view was endorsed by English scholars such as Sir William Holdsworth (1871–1944), who wrote, "one of the chief intellectual ties between us—our common legal heritage."[103] English constitutional history stood as a visible embodiment of national identity, not only to its own citizens, but also to its imperial subjects and to other countries. Nowhere did that heritage have greater influence than in the United States.

CHAPTER TWO

"A Three-Step Waltz, Germany, England, and New England Eternally Round and Round"

Constitutional History as Racial Hierarchy

On first consideration the connection of racial solidarity to constitutional achievement has never seemed a promising path of inquiry. Race is now such a thoroughly discredited concept, and tarnished by the odious use of the word in the twentieth century, that its utilization for sober discussion of English constitutional history remains slightly jarring. In 1870, however, race in its many cultural manifestations enjoyed a place in political and social discourse on both the past and the present without the disapproval that posterity has conferred. The idea, and indeed ideal, of an Anglo-Saxon population that shared racial characteristics in order to account for British global leadership, had offered a neat explanation of complex phenomena. The greatest challenge to an analysis of race in 1870 came in the way that Victorians defined the word to mean so many different things, an amalgam of biology, ethnicity, culture, tradition, and language.[1] The most frequent engagement with issues of racial classification occurred in the long struggle against slavery and the slave trade that had peaked in the first decades of the nineteenth century. Although this crusade enlisted the moral capital of many, hatred of slavery as an institution rather than anticipation of social equality motivated most participants.[2] Prior to 1870 interest in race, especially Africans, had taken a backseat to debate about the plight of those enmeshed in the slavery gulag: "As a result of the anti-slavery movement, nineteenth-century Englishmen had a well-defined stereotype of blacks and at least a tradition of concern and interest in their welfare."[3] After 1870 the varied meanings of race led to more pernicious conclusions.

In the first instance, the biological definition of race derived from the Victorian argument about monogenesis versus polygenesis. Monogenesis, seemingly supported by the powerful evidence supplied by Charles Darwin (1809–82) after 1859, postulated a common origin of all human beings; polygenesis argued that races were "species with separate origins and distinct, biologically fixed, unequal characteristics."[4] Monogenesis assumed that unequal historical evolution accounted for racial differences, so that both theories took for granted the fact of racial inequality and a hierarchy that placed European civilization at the apex.[5] In 1850, Robert Knox (1791–1862) had published his polygenetic treatise, *Races of Man,* whose message emphasized racial dissimilarity. Pseudoscientific discussions of race provided the context for the expression of popular racial constructions. The Indian Mutiny of 1857 and the Jamaican uprising of 1865, both with a legacy of repression against the nonwhite inhabitants, helped put a racial edge to public policy decisions. The Governor Eyre controversy lent support to polygenesis enthusiasts, who regarded racial subordination as the only solution to the problem of race relations.[6] Biological classification fostered belief in the inherent inequality of the races, for empirical evidence appeared to demonstrate the truth of this proposition.

By 1870 race also served as a synonym for cultural difference. While skin color certainly acted as a primary indicator of race, anti-Irish prejudice on the basis of their Celtic origins showed that color alone did not furnish a basis for racial analysis.[7] Utilization of the comparative method, so popular in many emerging disciplines, provided a tool that emphasized distinctions among cultures. The comparative temptation confused race and culture, blurring the boundaries of both concepts.[8] Cultural difference was regarded by many as part of the lineal inheritance carried in the blood, and it reflected the bewilderment that race caused when thought of as both biology and culture. The equation of cultural and physical characteristics supported by such indices as cranial measurement or shades of skin color only added to the problematic use of the word *race.*[9] Victorian anthropology, led by Edward Tylor (1832–1917), offered seemingly substantial evidence for racial inequality: "Many anthropologists were irresistibly drawn to the conclusion that the gradual evolution which Darwin described in the Descent applied to intellectual and moral qualities and this was the best explanation of the cultural differences recorded in Tylor's theory of 'primitive' religion."[10] The result was the near automatic use of racial superiority and inferiority to explain the disparities in development so obvious to the Victorians.

Another complication that made race such an amorphous term after 1870 stemmed from its use as a surrogate for national character, a way to classify individuals and groups so that race became a convenient shorthand for behavioral differentiation.[11] In the process of drawing generalizations, the dominant group attributed putative character defects to inferior bands and claimed opposing virtues for itself; for example, Africans were lazy and succumbed to an uninhibited sensuality, whereas the English possessed a strict work ethic and controlled sexual appetites. Closer to home, the Irish penchant for drink and violence stood in contrast to the sobriety and personal restraint of the English. Such transparent stereotypes often acquired the authority of scripture with little regard for reality. The tendency to equate race with national character had certainly existed well before 1870 and would continue long after, evidence of the links that bound them so strongly.[12]

Finally, race possessed sociopolitical implications that offered criteria for the inclusion or exclusion of different individuals or groups. In this manner race defined self as well as identified others. When race projected political and social overtones, miscegenation and other forms of racial mixing required boundaries beyond which the races could not trespass. Racial separation marginalized those racial inferiors whom society constructed according to its prejudices. In tandem, Knox and Darwin popularized the belief that racial categories provided an important tool for historical research: "To a large extent, the history of social science is a history of a series of accommodations of the sciences to the demands of deeply held convictions about the 'naturalness' of the inequalities between human races."[13] These interpretations of racial contrast in Victorian England found expression most forcefully in the creed of a superior Anglo-Saxon race.

Fascination with the Anglo-Saxons did not originate in the nineteenth century. To the established radical tradition of the "Norman Yoke" theory of history, with its vision of self-governing Saxons tyrannized by despotic Normans and their aristocratic successors, were added the inquiries of generations of scholars that began in the sixteenth century. Antiquarians, ethnographers, historians, jurists, philologists, and poets found much to intrigue them in early English government and society. Sharon Turner's (1768–1861) *History of England from the Earliest Times to the Norman Conquest* (1799), often considered the foundational text for the modern study of the Anglo-Saxon period, was followed over the next half century by the work of scholars such as Sir Francis Palgrave (1788–1861) and John Kemble (1807–57). The latter, in *The Saxons in England* (1849), displayed in full measure the Teutonic philology he had studied under Jacob Grimm in Göttingen. Kemble provided the first fully articulated theory of the Teutonic origins of free government, singling out the primitive Germanic mark, for him not merely a plot of cultivated land but a self-governing community and the progenitor of all subsequent free institutions.[14] In 1850 Knox argued that the racial future belonged to the descendants of the Anglo-Saxons, so over the next two decades the adaptation of this genetic ideology to constitutional history came as no surprise.

The appeal of the Anglo-Saxon era for historians rested in part on the assumption that the term *Anglo-Saxon* described a coherent, identifiable set of Germanic tribes who had conquered England by 600 after serial invasions that began in 449 with Hengist and Horsa. These Germanic forebears had shared a common culture, institutions, and ethnic identity that gave to England a racial unity that ultimately led to political centralization. In the process, the previous Romano-Celtic population had disappeared through conquest, disease, and assimilation. The articulation of Anglo-Saxon ideology conflated race and national character as an explanation for the triumphs of English history and its contemporary global dominance.[15] The Anglo-Saxon legacy was evident not just in physical appearance but in the character that the English displayed: "love of liberty, courage, patience and reserve, honesty and plain dealing."[16] This attractive view of national identity played a major role in the construction of a national origin myth; a distinct race favored by God who had survived the Norman Conquest to keep alive their libertarian traditions, the Anglo-Saxons, once the favorite of political radicalism, now confirmed the stability and continuity of English history.[17] All that remained was to uncover the historical proof upon which this interpretation of English history rested.

The cult of Anglo-Saxon constitutional exceptionalism after 1870 depended on claims of racial purity and historical descent that now seem preposterous. Although widely embraced by historians, the construction of the Anglo-Saxon legend hinged in the first instance upon the premise of a singular degree of uniformity among the Germanic tribes who succeeded the Roman era of the English past. This Anglo-Saxon race had a special partiality for individual liberty, and thus this trait had become the hallmark of Teutonic societies. Blessed with racial uniformity, the Anglo-Saxon progeny possessed a unique civilizing mission, especially in the area of constitutional liberty. In particular, the English people held a monopoly on the love of freedom and ordered self-governance, those virtues that distinguished the race.[18] By 1870, in the minds of many Victorians, "the idea of a superior Anglo-Saxon race regenerating a world of lesser races was firmly ingrained."[19] The affinity between race and constitutional history appeared secure.

To understand the fate of this dimension of constitutional history, it must be emphasized at the outset that this alleged racial unity never existed. *Anglo-Saxon* was not a name, for example, that the various Germanic tribes called themselves, and any fusion that may have occurred came much later: "When a single kingdom was formed in the tenth century within boundaries that more or less approximate those of what we think of as England, it was called the kingdom of the English—not of the Anglo-Saxons, nor yet of the Anglo-Danes."[20] After all, from the time of the Beaker people to 1870, a series of invasions had brought successive waves of Iberians, Celts, Romans, a variety of Germanic tribes, Danes, and Normans to English shores. Some of these immigrants had stayed longer than others, but to argue for some sort of specific historical legacy was difficult at best. That the Teutonic origins of English constitutionalism could be claimed at all testified to the strength of racial thought that held sway in late Victorian England. Given this faith in the purity of racial Anglo-Saxonism, it is all the more ironic that modern DNA research has postulated that the permanence of the original Celtic peoples dominated the demographic history of England at the expense of the Anglo-Saxon invaders.[21] One can only wonder about the reaction of the Anglo-Saxon enthusiasts if they had known the true population record of England.

The ranks of Anglo-Saxon true believers who subscribed to the Anglo-Saxon vision of history included a disparate assembly of historians, politicians, and public intellectuals. While the language might have varied in individual instances, the commitment to an Anglo-Saxon world order remained the same. Goldwin Smith (1823–1910), for example, the Regius professor of modern history at Oxford from 1858 to 1866, embraced the United States in what he termed "Anglo-Saxonry": "a vision of the rapprochement of the English-speaking peoples of the world."[22] The empire of English law, language, liberty, and literature created ties so strong, in Smith's opinion, that political and diplomatic disagreement over issues such as the American Civil War or the later Venezuelan boundary dispute in 1895 should not lead the Anglo-Saxon powers into a fratricidal war. The American Revolution had created a schism in the Anglo-Saxon race, and this rupture required permanent mending.[23] Smith's interpretation of history stressed the primacy of race: "Race seems, of all physical influences, the strongest."[24] Such a quarrel would undermine the community of Anglo-Saxonry that he supported so strenuously.

In a similar vein, future member of parliament Charles Dilke (1843–1911), who journeyed throughout the United States in 1866–67, also concluded that the Anglo-Saxon achievement in Great Britain was replicated in the new world: "Through America, England is speaking to the world."[25] More remembered now for a political career that brought him near to the Liberal party leadership and then foundered on the shoals of scandal, Dilke conceived Greater Britain as an Anglo-Saxon commonwealth, and his book helped inaugurate the revision of British attitudes toward the United States in a more positive way.[26] Dilke thought of the extended Anglo-Saxon community in specifically imperial terms, anticipating a political alliance, formal or informal, that would spread the blessings of British civilization.

Another noteworthy Victorian, Charles Kingsley (1819–75), publicized the cult of the Anglo-Saxon in fiction and what he thought of as fact. In 1864 Kingsley published a set of lectures whose purpose was to inform his audience "of the causes which urged our Teutonic race to attack and destroy Rome."[27] Idiosyncratic in its evidence and argument, the book focused on the contrast between the late Roman Empire and the Germanic invaders. Kingsley accentuated the deep respect for rank and blood that characterized the Teutonic peoples; and he presented the simple morality of the barbarians against the decadence that had overtaken the Romans. Two years later, Kingsley published *Hereward the Wake* (1866), in which he gave a fictional account of the last Anglo-Saxon warrior to battle against William of Normandy and his minions after 1066. Uncritical admiration of the Anglo-Saxon race and its uncomplicated relationship with the Victorian world deprived Kingsley of scholarly distinction, yet his ideas symbolized the widespread permeation into contemporary culture that Anglo-Saxondom enjoyed.

Historian James Anthony Froude has remained a significant figure in Victorian historiography, with his epic narrative of the sixteenth century the greatest contribution. In his attitudes toward contemporary public affairs, Froude also demonstrated a firm commitment to the Anglo-Saxon illusion of race, nation, empire, and the superiority of the Anglo-Saxons. One biographer wrote that Froude presented "the most powerful expression of the Anglo-Saxon myth"; this resulted in the advocacy of the Anglo-Saxon mission: "to civilize the uncivilized, to impose order, and, in the process, to settle the uninhabited regions of the earth with men and women of its own kind."[28] Similar sentiments motivated Cecil Rhodes (1853–1902), whose scholarships aimed to secure "the unity of the Anglo-Saxon race and the propagation of Anglo-Saxon ideas of democracy, justice, and individual liberty."[29] These racial views were not merely intellectual constructs, for they had political consequences as well.

Examples of how Anglo-Saxon expression entered mainstream politics, and how standard such racial language had become, may be seen in the careers of Joseph Chamberlain (1836–1914) and Lord Salisbury (1830–1903). The most obvious assertion of Chamberlain's views came in 1898 and after, when, as colonial secretary, he attempted to establish an alliance of Germany, Great Britain, and the United States. His plan rested on one aspect of Anglo-Saxon ideology, that race bound the three countries together as the past, the present, and the future hope of the human race. Racial unity provided the fundamental basis for this political dream.[30] Salisbury shared these sentiments, most dramatically in an imperial context where he evinced contempt for the class of educated Indians who resisted racial discrimination. Imperial power allied to the Anglo-Saxon vision inevitably produced a sense of racial superiority among the governing class.[31] The appeal of the Anglo-Saxon argument transcended conventional political boundaries to form a small but significant part of Victorian culture.

Before the mid-nineteenth century, Anglo-Saxon studies had a limited impact on American attitudes toward England, although race had already become a fundamental issue in American history. One of the earliest enthusiasts, Thomas Jefferson, was fascinated enough by early England to study the language and even suggest that one side of the Great Seal of the United States depict those fifth-century founding heroes, Hengist and Horsa.[32] Francophilia and a profound mistrust of Britain, however, remained central to his worldview. For other Americans, early nineteenth-century Anglo-Saxonism provided a justification for slavery and for Manifest Destiny but seems to have done very little to overcome deep-seated American suspicions of the British Empire.[33] This changed markedly after the Civil War, in spite of the temporary worsening of Anglo-American relations during and immediately after that conflict. Key figures drawn from the Boston Brahmin class, hitherto a bastion of anti-British patriotism, paved the way.

John Lothrop Motley's (1814–77) *Rise of the Dutch Republic,* though originally published before the war, became immensely popular in both Britain and the United States in the 1860s and 1870s. Motley, who had studied in Germany, set forth an Anglo-Saxonist line with transatlantic appeal in his introduction: "To all who speak the English language, the history of the great agony through which the Republic of Holland was ushered into life must have peculiar interest, for it is a portion of the records of the Anglo-Saxon race—essentially the same, whether in Friesland, England, or Massachusetts."[34] Motley, whose three daughters all married prominent Englishmen, was an ardent Anglophile who served as minister to the Court of St. James after the Civil War. He spent his final years in Dorset and after his death in 1877 was memorialized at Westminster Abbey by A. P. Stanley. Moved by the eulogy, John Richard Green observed that Motley had "knit together not only America and England, but that Older England which we left on Frisian shores, and which grew into the United Netherlands. A child of America, the historian of Holland, he made England his adopted country, and in England his body rests."[35]

In the United States, especially in New England (a notable noncartographic designation), Anglo-Saxonism drew sustenance from contemporary racial beliefs as well as the identification of New World institutions in a continuum with those of the Old World. Edward Freeman, for example, on an American tour in 1881–82, proclaimed: "Men of New England, I claim you as Englishmen. Sprung as you are of English blood, speakers as you are of the English tongue, sharers as you are in the great inheritance of English law, neither my feelings nor my

reason will allow me to call you by any other name."[36] Anglo-Saxon racial overtones affected political attitudes when, in the minds of some, the United States
appeared on the verge of succumbing to a rising tide of Irish and other ethnic
immigration: "A belief in the innate superiority of the 'Anglo-Saxon race' was
part of the prevailing orthodoxy in both Great Britain and the United States in
the late nineteenth and early twentieth centuries."[37] Josiah Strong's *Our Country* (1885), for instance, indicted immigration as the principal threat to American Anglo-Saxonism. Racial and cultural unity tied the two countries together
in bonds that grew ever stronger in the last decades of the nineteenth century,
even as political rapprochement increased as well.[38] Reconciliation between the
two countries constructed a framework for a growing sense of historical continuity that would eventually center on constitutional history.

A scion of an eminent Massachusetts family introduced Anglo-Saxon ideas
concerning history into the nation's oldest university. As the first professor of
medieval history at Harvard, Henry Adams (1838–1918) directed his doctoral
students to the study of early English law, resulting in the publication of *Essays
in Anglo-Saxon Law* (1876).[39] Two of America's newest universities, however,
constituted the real driving force in fostering close relations between American
and English historians: Cornell and Johns Hopkins. Andrew Dickson White
(1832–1918), Cornell's founding president as well as the first president of the
American Historical Association, attracted leading English historians to his
campus. The most prestigious recruit was Goldwin Smith, whom White lured
to Ithaca in 1868. Smith, who had just resigned his Regius professorship at Oxford in 1866, inspired Cornell students to regard England as the mother country in the Anglo-Saxon relationship. To underscore the connection, Smith even
arranged to have some ivy shipped from Oxford to Cornell to grace the new
university buildings.[40] On the memorial tablet in Goldwin Smith Hall on the
Cornell campus, there is inscribed a declaration of his "attachment as an Englishman to the union of the two branches of our race on this continent with
each other and with their common mother." Smith's place in the transatlantic
historical community was recognized by his presidency of the American Historical Association in 1904. Yet by that time, he was widely viewed within the
profession as having nothing of value to add to the rapidly evolving discourse
on constitutional history. Moreover, his racial views had become repugnant to
some leaders of the profession. As James Bryce remarked after Smith's death in
1910: "He was more prone to racial antagonism than a historian ought permit
himself to be, was markedly anti-Semitic, and had the old fashioned English
suspicion of the Gallic race."[41]

An even more important conduit for early English history as crucial to

American history was Herbert Baxter Adams (1850–1901) of Johns Hopkins. With a newly minted doctorate in history from the University of Heidelberg, he secured a position as instructor at Johns Hopkins upon its foundation in 1876. An ardent Teutonist, Adams established the rigorous seminar method he had learned in Germany. Of old Massachusetts Congregationalist stock, Adams was fascinated by the task of tracing New England civic and legal institutions to their European antecedents. The continuity of the Germanic village community in the United States had been suggested by an 1870 article in the *Nation* by W. F. Allen of the University of Wisconsin. Allen, describing a review in *Historische Zeitschrift* by the eminent Prussian historian Heinrich von Sybel of a book comparing village communities in Germany and England, wondered whether an extension of such studies to include New England might not bear fruit: "It would be worth while to examine how far the early settlers in this country were influenced by the traditions and surviving remnants of this system and how far, on the other hand, similar causes led to similar results."[42] Clearly, Allen was suggesting an open investigation. When taken up by Teutonist enthusiasts like Herbert Baxter Adams, however, to pose the question was to answer it.

Students in Adams's seminar (or "seminary," as he called it) worked intensively in primary sources in order to reveal the organic links to old England. To President Daniel Coit Gilman (1831–1908) of Johns Hopkins, he explained in detail the ambitious projects he set for his students:

We have in the Johns Hopkins University this semester a class of graduate students who are pursuing the subject of institutional history, with special reference to the continuity of the English system of local self government in the United States. We are greatly interested in such topics as popular assemblies, the historical village community, the English parish and township, the manor, the hundred, the shire. Sheriffs, constables, tithingmen, borough-elders, and the like; also in local representation and local taxation. As you doubtless are aware, many institutions of an anarchic character have been perpetuated in the towns of New England and in the parishes of the South, and we are anxious to discover their full significance on the light of the most advanced knowledge upon the institutional history of the mother country.[43]

To their credit, many of Adams's graduate students were skeptical about Adams's grand interpretive scheme. Charles McLean Andrews (1863–1943), subsequently a leading historian and president of the American Historical Association, wrote incredulously to his mother about Adams's History of Politics course starting "way back at the Arian [*sic*] migrations and coming down to American times."[44] Another future American Historical Association president, John Franklin Jameson (1859–1937), described to his father a "tiresome" meet-

ing of the seminar in 1882, "where a fellow read a paper on the origin of the
military system of England, which he traced back *nearly* to when our ancestors chattered in the tree-tops. He couldn't *quite,* because, as I suggested to
him, standing armies were impossible among those who held on to branches
by their tails."[45] And Woodrow Wilson (1856–1924), a few years older than his
fellow Hopkins graduate students, complained that Adams compelled his students to adopt as a research framework the institutional continuity of European and early American settlements.[46] As far as Wilson himself is concerned,
this was an unfair charge, for Adams allowed him to write his dissertation on
contemporary politics, later published as *Congressional Government.* As we will
see in the next chapter, Andrews framed his research strategies in a way that
produced conclusions diametrically opposed to Adams's views.

The early publications in the *Johns Hopkins Studies in Historical and Political
Science,* begun in 1883, exemplified the type of local studies carried on under
Adams's direction; in the first of these he asserted: "The science of Biology no
longer favors the theory of spontaneous generation. Wherever organic life occurs there must have been some seed for that life. . . . The town and village life
of New England is as truly the reproduction of old English types as those again
are reproductions of the village community system of the ancient Germans."[47]
The germ theory explained the historical process by which Teutonic institutions originated in ancient Germanic forests, then passed to England with the
Anglo-Saxons, and then arrived in North America with the English colonists.
The political values that underlay this theory are evident in Adams's claim that
such studies would have a "wholesome conservative power . . . in these days
of growing centralization."[48] And when Bryce suggested an Anglo-American
scholarly partnership in founding a history journal, Adams responded enthusiastically: "To my mind there is a peculiar propriety in united English effort in
the direction of historical science; for the history of the countries is one. The
whole tenor of our researches at J.H.U. is to show the continuity of English institutions in America."[49] Other proponents of Teutonic triumphalism included
such luminaries as Albert Bushnell Hart (1854–1943), Moses Coit Tyler (1835–
1900), John Fiske (1842–1901), and James K. Hosmer (1834–1927), all of whom
subscribed in one fashion or another to the interpretation that America's past
depended specifically on its English heritage.[50]

That race should have played such a major role in the thinking of many of
America's leading historians during this era is hardly surprising. In addition to
the pervasive belief in black inferiority in the north as well as the south, and
the exaltation of racial "science" fostered by Darwinian biology, there was also
the deeply unsettling influence of mass immigration. In the view of long-es-

tablished Americans of northern European, and especially British, antecedents, the onslaught of alien peoples threatened the very fabric of their civilization. Such feelings were pronounced in New England, still in the throes of meeting the challenge of a massive influx of Catholic Irish. John Fiske, one of the most popular historians of the day, lectured and wrote about the growing menace. Subscribing to the "germ theory" of American freedom, he agreed with Francis Parkman (1823–93), George Bancroft (1800–1891), and other intellectual leaders that the future belonged to the Anglo-Saxon peoples. Moreover, in 1894 Fiske became honorary president of the Immigration Restriction League, a pressure group whose tireless harangues began to bear fruit by the end of the First World War.[51] Like many American "Teutonists," Fiske believed that it was England and America, rather than Germany, which were the real transmitters of free institutions in the modern world. In 1900, he declared that in any future war between England and Germany, the United States would inevitably be drawn to England's side.[52]

Most American "Teutonists," including Fiske and Herbert Baxter Adams, increasingly downplayed the Germanic and Aryan element in their scholarship, focusing instead on America's English constitutional roots. John W. Burgess (1844–1931), who taught at Columbia for many years, was an exception. His reverence for Germany, which he had acquired during the 1870s as a graduate student at Göttingen, Leipzig, and Berlin, never faltered. Studying under such luminaries as Johann Gustav Droysen (1808–84), Theodor Mommsen (1817–1903), and Rudolf von Gneist (1816–95), the foremost authority on comparative constitutional law, left an indelible mark. A key figure in the professionalization of both history and political science, Burgess embraced Droysen's assertion of the Teutonic race's innate genius for government and superiority to all other races. Burgess was a tireless champion of a German-American alliance and was one of the few leading academics to argue for assisting Germany rather than Britain in the Great War. An avowed opponent of socialism and other "alien" ideologies, he shared Fiske's fear of the new immigrant masses from southern and central Europe. He told an audience at Cologne in 1907 that, while the earlier immigrant stock in the United States had been chiefly Teutonic, "now we are getting people of a very different sort—Slavs, Czechs, Hungarians. . . . They are, in everything that goes to make up folk character, the exact opposite of genuine Americans."[53]

There was a significant regional variant to the overall pattern of American views of English constitutional history. The South, led by its planter elite, had traditionally entertained a favorable view of the Anglo-Norman aristocracy. Even though Jefferson was the leading proponent of Anglo-Saxon studies, his fellow Southerners were less enthusiastic, finding in postconquest feudalism a suitably noble antecedent for their own hierarchically structured society. The Civil War altered Southerners' historical sense dramatically. With the Confederacy prostrate at the hands of a conquering army, Southerners began to compare themselves with post-1066 Anglo-Saxons, a reassuring identity considering the dominant Whig interpretation of the era, in which the Normans were themselves eventually absorbed by those they had conquered.[54] A certain sleight of hand was required to cast Northerners in the role of Normans, as it continued to be an article of Southern faith that the Northern states were without culture or gentility. Ironically, by the turn of the century, Northern scholars were ascribing a dominant constitutional role to the Normans. For the South to accept this shifting paradigm, a major change in views about the cause of the Civil War was required, one that transformed it from a moral issue (slavery) to a constitutional one (states' rights). As we will see in Chapters 6 and 7, such revisionism was well under way by the early twentieth century.

The ascendancy of the American germ theory did not last long. Although prevalent in the 1880s, by the 1890s the frontier thesis proposed by Frederick Jackson Turner (1861–1932) superseded it as an alternative explanation for American institutions.[55] More sophisticated research on Anglo-Saxon history revealed that the idyllic portrait of a democratic village life had little basis in reality. A contrite Henry Adams symbolized this academic change of heart: "For some six or seven centuries they [Anglo-Saxons] muddled their brains with beer and cut each other's throat for amusement, and did not even leave an institution worth preserving, for a rottener society never existed than that which the Normans so easily extinguished."[56] Although Anglo-American amity, despite the Venezuelan crisis of 1895, flourished in the 1890s as a result of a shared imperial ideology, Anglo-Saxon history fell by the wayside. Race no longer supplied the paramount historical interpretation for the continuity of English and American history as it had done just years earlier.

If the western shores of the Atlantic proved fertile ground for the influence of the Anglo-Saxons, in England some Victorian historians looked to the east and those primeval German forests, not just for the sources of Teutonic liberty, but for the rigorous techniques of scholarship necessary for the advancement of history as a discipline. John Burrow has observed: "The idiom of English historiography was German."[57] The work of Gneist on the English constitution at midcentury had not only fixed attention on this specific topic but also legitimized the nation as a proper subject of study against earlier cosmopolitan histories.[58] As late as 1914, despite worsening political relations between the two countries, German historians represented a major influence on historical writing in England as opposed to other continental scholarship.[59] The acceptance of racial kinship brought a special admiration for the undoubted accomplishments of German historians that spilled over into the manner in which English liberties were expressed; for example, Bryce had faith in the existence of "Teutonic freedom"—a notion shared by many of his academic contemporaries."[60] Few English historians of the period, especially those who undertook *Verfassunggeschichte*, had not read and esteemed authors such as Georg Waitz (1813–66), Otto von Gierke (1841–1921), and Felix Liebermann (1851–1925). Dedication to discovery of new knowledge through careful archival research had a profound impact on the development of constitutional history after 1870.

The most enigmatic symbol for the attachment to German scholarship was Lord Acton (1834–1902), a Catholic, liberal, and German-trained historian who took the Regius chair of modern history at Cambridge in 1895. Although in the past his reputation seemed in inverse proportion to what he had actually published, Hugh Tulloch has shown that the lingering sense of promise unfulfilled no longer has merit.[61] That Acton had acquired immense learning few doubted. In a disquisition on Irish home rule in 1888, for example, Acton roamed through the history of Poland, Belgium, Norway, Hungary, Holstein, and Iceland in a quest to identify appropriate historical comparisons.[62] The sense that Acton did not share the concerns of English historiography rested on his belief that "ideas were the mainspring of history, not institutions, constitutions, borders, battles, dates of reigns; and fresh, innovative ideas by definition transcended and crossed borders."[63] More specifically, Acton rejected the evolution of English freedom from Anglo-Saxon roots, for he was "ironical at the expense of the Whig enthusiasm for the barbarian liberty inherited from the German woods."[64] Acton's place in the pantheon of Whig historians did not note this latter nuance. While Acton's philosophy of history opposed the emphasis on a nation's institutional evolution, his commitment to the highest standards of scholarship sustained within England the achievements of German historians. The racial inheritance of Anglo-Saxonism, intellectual links east and west to Germany and the United States, and dedication to emerging standards of scholarly endeavor joined to focus attention upon the research into and within English constitutional history.

The germ theory of modern representative government, or the liberal descent of Burrow's title, depended upon a substantial degree of racial thought. Darwinian language typified constitutional history as well as individual, group, or national struggles for survival. After 1870 Teutonism grafted to constitutional history in a fashion that proved persuasive to two decades of scholarship: "This was a constitution seen to grow from Germanic, or at least Anglo-Saxon, roots in a natural and inexorable way. It was organic, not just cumulative, and it was morphological, not haphazard or without a planned structure. No one can read these constitutional historians without noting how gripped they were by teleological and biological concepts (evolution, maturation, struggle)."[65] At a welcoming ceremony for Prince Henry of Prussia in 1902, Harvard president Charles William Eliot (1834–1926) made sure that this point was understood by his guest: "Our students of history know the Teutonic sources, in the dim past, of many institutions and public customs which have been transmitted through England to this New England."[66] Even as historians rejected the germ theory, it persisted in broader public circles.

This Darwinist veneer made it easy for constitutional historians to slide into the nether world of racial language and thought. When racial ideas increasingly prevailed, English constitutional history utilized their emotive power at all social levels: "As the nineteenth century progressed, racism became ever more widely diffused and achieved an acceptance, almost a consensus, in educated society as well as at deeper levels of popular culture."[67] In this respect the synthesis of race with constitutional history provided a unique interpretive framework through which to understand the English experience: "The history, or perhaps the embryology, of the constitution was to be the putative story of a continuous process of cellular multiplication, amalgamation and expansion, whose code was contained in its nuclear primal cell, 'the original basis on which all Teutonic society rests,' the mark-community, vicus or self-regulating township."[68] The net result of such a combination became A. F. Pollard's (1869–1948) conclusion that "the failure of parliamentary institutions in semitic or Negroid communities is proof, not of the defects of parliaments but of the political incapacity of those who cannot work them."[69] Race and constitutional history attracted many adherents, but no individual symbolized this marriage better than Edward Freeman.

Freeman has remained an important figure in Victorian historiography despite his now diminished reputation and the eccentricity of his views. Freeman enjoyed in his lifetime an audience and respect that his present lack of appreciation does not reflect. On his American tour in 1881–82, for example, Freeman reported to close friend John Richard Green: "You will be glad to hear that we are all, you, I, Bryce, Stubbs, much honoured on this side of the river Ocean."[70] To Freeman was granted the honor of writing the first essay in the *Johns Hopkins Studies in Historical and Political Science:* "An Introduction to American Institutional History." In order to ensure that Freeman's influence would remain paramount, Herbert Baxter Adams had a large portrait of him placed in the history seminar room at Johns Hopkins, along with Freeman's famous dictum: "History is past politics, and politics present history." In 1884, upon the resignation of Stubbs, Freeman sought and gained the Regius professorship of modern history at Oxford, a position he held until his death in 1892. Freeman represented the best example whereby history and race combined to offer a grand interpretive scheme, because he addressed racial issues in direct language as well as himself embodying many of the unpleasant racial stereotypes of his day. What now seem like the vulgar racial animosities of Victorian convention were in fact "part of a process of seeking an identity, a unifying theme linking past and present."[71] Belief in the primacy of constitutional history enabled Freeman to identify national character that best reflected a racial inheritance.[72] Freeman's theories, as with most racial ideologies, possessed both positive and negative elements incorporated within a single viewpoint; race defined who did and did not constitute the national community.

If Freeman's belief in race furnished one foundation for his historical conclusions, his approach to history added the other element of his mature work. From Thomas Arnold's work, Freeman internalized the emphasis on the moral unity of history; this gave to Freeman his faith in the "intelligible design and purpose of history."[73] From this starting point, Freeman moved to the conclusion, adding race to the mix, "that the Aryan nations in Europe should be studied as one great continuous whole."[74] Freeman constructed a research design to seek the fundamental explanation of history in racial unity. His intellectual path returned to the Anglo-Saxons, as he spelled out to anthropologist Edward Tylor: "What I want to do is to carry out the same line of thought which you and others have applied to the language, the mythology, and the customs of different nations to their political institutions, and to show that the forms of government of the Aryan nations . . . all spring from a common source, an Urbrunnen, to use the language of Langenschwalbach."[75] The unity of English history hinged on the racial affinities and institutional similarities that tied the ninth century to the nineteenth. The passion to find the present in the past gave rise to curious opinions and conclusions; for example, on a visit to Bayeux, Freeman wrote of the "extreme folly" of the local population in speaking French when they should have retained their natural Danish, if not their earlier Anglo-Saxon.[76] The unity of history meant for Freeman that the supremacy of the Anglo-Saxon extended to cultural and political matters as well as racial solidarity. Freeman also stressed philology in accounting for racial origins in order that he might incorporate national character in terms of common inheritance and traditions.[77]

For Freeman, as for Green and William Stubbs, English history originated in the remote forests of ancient Germany, where free villagers formed self-gov-

erning communities and became the predecessors of subsequent free institutions. This led Freeman to articulate the full panoply of Anglo-Saxon influence:
Parliament descended directly from the witan, political democracy originated
in the gatherings of early German villagers, the Norman Conquest represented
a minor break in the continuity of English history, and the positive aspects
of Victorian national character derived from Anglo-Saxon forebears.[78] Anglo-
Saxon society elected kings and created self-government, Freeman asserted, so
critics argued with justification that Freeman regarded the Germanic village
community as the cradle of Gladstonian liberalism.[79] The historical process
had begun in 449, when Hengist and Horsa had landed in Kent and initiated
the transformation by which Teutonic institutions had flourished on English
soil. In the centuries that followed, the English had improved on the "original
genius of their Germanic forefathers."[80] Green expressed this vision best: "It is
with the landing of Hengist and his war-band at Ebbsfleet on the shores of the
Isle of Thanet that English history begins. No spot in Britain can be so sacred
to Englishmen as that which first felt the tread of English feet."[81] Only an epic
national narrative based on racial affinity could do full justice to the pageantry
of the island story.

Freeman's racial ideas, in the sense of affirming a positive national identity based on the Anglo-Saxon heritage, seemed innocuous enough. When he
turned to groups outside the Anglo-Saxon community, however, the pernicious
consequences of race took center stage. In the first instance, Freeman shared
the conventional prejudices of Victorians against blacks, although in private his
language possessed a virulence that did not appear in public. His negative views
received strong expression after Freeman toured the United States in 1881–82, a
series of lectures that one American friend termed "quite a failure" because the
theme of Anglo-American community was "now rather trite."[82] Freeman wrote
after this visit that the best remedy for social problems in the United States
"would be if every Irishman should kill a negro and be hanged for it."[83] The
only drawback to this scheme Americans reported, Freeman added, was the
depletion of the available servant pool. The more vitriolic versions of his attitude toward race relations included references to niggers as big monkeys or as
great black apes.[84] Blacks, whether resident in America, Britain, or the empire,
had no redeeming racial virtues and certainly did not belong to the greater
Aryan community.

In a similar vein Freeman harbored an unrelenting bias against Jews. This
animus was based in part on his theory of the unity of Western Christendom,
to which Jews posed the major exception. His prejudice extended even into the
scholarly world, where Freeman, an admirer of German historians and research

methods, paid a compliment to his friend Stubbs in this fashion: "Waitz the Stubbs of Germany; Stubbs the Waitz of England"; yet he referred to the equally illustrious Felix Liebermann contemptuously as "Stubbs's Jew."[85] Freeman's commitment to Liberal politics would have led him to oppose Conservative policies and politicians in any event; still he referred repeatedly to Benjamin Disraeli as the Jew, or even the "Dirty Jew."[86] About Jews in general, Freeman wrote while on his American tour:

If the Chinese controlled the press of half the world, as the Jews do, there would be a cry everywhere of "Frightful Religious persecution in America," because of the bill which has just passed Congress. The only difference is that the Russians have punched some Hebrew heads irregularly, and the heathen Chinee has before now suffered from California mobs; but there is no religious persecution in either case, only the natural instinct of any decent nation to get rid of filthy strangers.[87]

This remarkable passage cited an important anti-Semitic stereotype, press influence, as well as a remarkable indifference to the murderous pogroms of Tsarist Russia. More notable perhaps was that Freeman's biographer felt no compulsion to edit these sentiments, an indication of how prevailing these racial attitudes were in Victorian Britain and how little controversy they would have aroused.

Both politics and scholarship dictated the hatred that Freeman exhibited toward the French. With respect to politics, France remained the hereditary enemy of England, and Napoleon III represented the antithesis of liberal democracy; the Franco-Prussian War served the French right, and the unification of Germany guarded against French pretensions. For example, during the Franco-Prussian War, Freeman wrote: "I need not tell you, that my sympathies go wholly and unreservedly with the North Dutchmen [Germans]."[88] Freeman found it loathsome that anyone in England could possibly favor the French cause. On another occasion Freeman insulted doubly when he referred to John Morley (1838–1923), "who, after all, is little better than a Frenchman."[89] Freeman spread his racial venom across a wide spectrum; the political eclipse of France by Germany after 1870 he regarded as the natural outcome of his racial ideas on superiority and inferiority. Ultimately Freeman's bias against the French stemmed primarily from the Teutonic basis for his historical writing. As the principal rival to the dominance of Germanic institutions in European history and the carrier of the Romanist case for centrality in the construction of Western civilization, France stood in direct opposition to Freeman's beloved Teutonism. In Freeman's lifetime the question of historical primacy in influence took on considerable scholarly significance because it went to the heart of the debate about who had and who should dominate European history.[90] Freeman took the German part without reservation, although his anti-French feelings never prevented him from making frequent trips to France, nor did they diminish his interest in medieval French architecture. The chilling nature of Freeman's racial views, to add another perspective, came because of "his unfairness to men and writers of whom he thought ill" and his "absolute blindness to certain aspects of things which were of no interest to himself."[91] Racial passion in the end determined the scope and nature of his historical inquiries, and the French were invariably on the losing side.

Liberal politics also explained Freeman's antipathy toward the Turks, whose presence in the Balkans undermined European unity, and he denounced them accordingly. The Gladstonian campaign on behalf of Christian minorities within the Ottoman Empire focused Freeman's attention on the dangers of Islam to his ideal of Europe: "Now Austria is by her geographical position the only European state fitted to introduce European civilization into the Balkan peninsula."[92] This civilizing mission he denied to the Serbs and Hungarians, as he sorted out those who belonged within the European family from those who did not. The Turks remained a menace to the European civilization he treasured, for as his friend Sir Frederick Pollock (1845–1937) wrote to him: "Turks with Krupp guns and paper money are a monstrosity."[93] Although Freeman's racial language was extreme even by contemporary standards, his ambiguous use of the word *race* illustrated the difficulties associated with its emotive content. Freeman acknowledged that race as blood descent bowed to culture, language, and religion as additional sources of racial unity: "For Freeman, then, 'physical purity of race' was neither an established fact nor even a desirable possibility."[94] Despite the private fulminations against various racial groups, Freeman never went that far in public, acting more on stereotypes of his favored peoples.[95] Given the various ways in which Freeman invoked racial principles, that his conclusions possessed neither consistency nor coherence came as no surprise.

The confluence of race, unity of historical development, and the supremacy of institutional history led Freeman in 1872 to publish *The Growth of the English Constitution*. Two years prior to Stubbs's great work on the same topic, Freeman's work appeared while he was in the middle of his five-volume account of the Norman Conquest. In the *English Constitution,* the virtues and vices of Freeman's scholarship were on display: the preoccupation with Teutonic antecedents, the desire to make history a contemporary political conflict, and a literary style that engaged a large public audience. Based on exhaustive reading, but not archival research, Freeman presented the first of the modern constitutional histories, although the work did not command the field for long.

His work soon suffered eclipse by that of Stubbs, but it set the standard for the incorporation of racial thought as the primary agent of constitutional history. Consistent with his belief that English institutional history originated in early Germanic life, Freeman started his account with a long disquisition on the contemporary political traditions of the Swiss cantons Uri and Appenzell. In these customs Freeman located the ultimate sources of the English constitution: "We may see the institutions of our own forefathers, the institutions which were once common to the whole Teutonic race, institutions whose outward form has necessarily passed away from greater states, but which contain the germs out of which every free constitution in the world has grown."[96] The English story began in the Germany described by Tacitus, where Teutonic institutions supplied the core of life before one branch of the Germanic race sought new homes between the Humber and the Thames. Freeman was so concerned to argue the essential unity of the Aryan race that he also asserted that the basis of the English constitution derived in part from the civilization of classical antiquity: "In the Homeric poems we see a constitution essentially the same as that which is set before us in the Germany of Tacitus."[97] Determined to construct a constitutional metanarrative at the expense of specific details, Freeman assumed "that what is Teutonic in us is not merely one element among others, but that it is the very life and essence of our national being."[98] For Freeman the comparative method "provided the means of ordering the new knowledge about the antiquity of man into a coherent pattern of development, while retaining belief in cultural and racial hierarchy."[99] With these racial foundations firmly established, Freeman moved to the specifically English phase of the work.

The second characteristic of English constitutional history that Freeman stressed was the unbroken, although sometimes strained, continuity that persisted through the centuries. One famous example of this resolve came in his description of the Anglo-Saxon witenagemot, where he insisted that Parliament, and the House of Lords in particular, descended directly from its Anglo-Saxon forerunner and that the witan enjoyed powers before 1066 similar to those of the Victorian Parliament: "Be it Witenagemot, Great Council, or Parliament, there has always been some body of men claiming, with more or less of right, to speak in the name of the nation."[100] Continuity also fit well into the biological metaphor, so that a verb like *grow* served to reinforce his general interpretation. English common law did not possess a *grundnorm,* or founding constitutional document, so history itself offered the record of gradual evolution, and the English Parliament was therefore "immemorial."[101] In retrospect, this argument, now so discredited, should have exercised little influence, because it rested on such shaky intellectual foundations.

Yet it was clear that Freeman's volume did, in fact, provide an important legacy, because he conflated two different strands of historical thought about the constitution. On the one hand, Freeman symbolized the new constitutional history: "at once populist and Whig: populist in the assumed primitive democracy of the folk-moot, Whig and Burkean in its insistence on continuity, on the creation of the constitution without design."[102] On the other hand, however, "Freeman's writing was an extraordinary inversion of Whig history. It conceived of progress, but of progress through retrogression, and considered the postmedieval world as a declension from purity and unity to racial mix and diversity."[103] These two assessments of Freeman in the context of Whig history showed clearly how multifaceted the Whig interpretation of history has become and the various ways in which Freeman straddled its contents. The resolution of this paradox, one presumably with which he would have agreed, came in the desire for a popular audience. The English constitution must demonstrate progress, because if it merely relied on the past alone, constitutional history would only provide ammunition for conservative principles. Writing of constitutional history, therefore, required a widespread reception, for the results would not only strengthen national identity but also simultaneously make the case for the Liberal principle of political democracy. Freeman's ideas about history, progress, and continuity were intended to illuminate issues of contemporary Victorian politics.

In conformity to his aphorism that history was past politics, Freeman rarely missed an opportunity to vindicate Liberal politics at the expense of Conservative politics and personalities. Constitutional history in Freeman's hands owed some of its popularity to its culture wars dimensions, transforming a potentially labored topic into one that might engage the educated reader. In this vein, Freeman proclaimed: "As the continuity of our national life is to many so hard a lesson to master, so the continuity of our political life, and the way in which we have so often fallen back on the very earliest principles of our race, is a lesson which many find specially hard."[104] He asserted further that "our ancient history is the possession of the Liberal, who, as being ever ready to reform, is the true Conservative, not of the self-styled Conservative who, by refusing to reform, does all he can to bring on destruction."[105] This pugnacity had the desired result in that Freeman's work did secure a large audience (although never as many as he wished), and it also invited thorough scrutiny; Freeman was happy to succeed in both areas.

The vehicle by which Freeman gained his greatest fame was the five volumes of the *History of the Norman Conquest* (1867–79), ostensibly a political narrative but in many places a commentary on the constitutional history themes that he prized. This work is certainly more referenced at present than read in its entirety; its organization, judgments, and style strike the modern reader as well over the top: uncritical and injudicious, remorselessly detailed, and a prose that adored long, languid sentences. Despite its many flaws, Freeman's narrative did possess a dramatic rhythm that unfortunately led to an endless flow of information, not all of it relevant. Too many sections of the work came colored in bright purple hues, a habit that too often hid his insights in endless pages of obsessive detail. Volume 1, for example, did not even reach 1066 before its close. Finally, in opposition to the presumed objectivity of modern scholarship, Freeman made the work a political polemic that indulged the racial ideas he had embraced.

From the extended argument that Freeman offered came motifs similar to those advanced in the *Constitutional History*. These included, but were not limited to, the assertion that the English people before 1066 constituted the same nation as after 1066, with respect to race, laws, language, and national character. The Normans presented a challenge to this Anglo-Saxon nation, "but in a few generations we led captive our conquerors; England was England once again, and the descendents of the Norman invaders were found to be among the truest of Englishmen."[106] This represented the continuity thesis with a vengeance, for from 600 to 1066, England had become so predominantly "Low-Dutch" in blood and language that it could absorb any foreign element: "Long before the Norman Conquest the various Low-Dutch tribes in Britain had been fused into one English nation."[107] In addition to an enduring Anglo-Saxon national identity, a settled constitution reinforced the definition of a racial self.

The third chapter of volume 1 Freeman devoted to a consideration of the Anglo-Saxon constitution as it had existed in the tenth and eleventh centuries. He conceded that this period's constitutional arrangements were not exactly the same as in Victorian Britain, but he did insist that the historian could discover "the germs alike of the monarchic, the aristocratic, and the democratic branches of our constitution."[108] The alleged democratic elements of this pre-1066 constitution existed primarily in the relationship between the witan and the king, where the witan elected the monarch and he could do little without its express consent. This highly romanticized view of a protodemocratic Anglo-Saxon constitution gave great self-satisfaction to his readers as well as made the political points that Freeman wished. Finally, his articulation of the connection between past and present fit neatly into his overall vision of historical unity. A summary of Freeman's five volumes would require much space and effort for little return, but perhaps the most important hypothesis he put forward involved the racial nature of the Norman conquerors. William of Normandy brought his Romanized Scandinavian followers to rule over Germanic England:

A chief of Danes and Saxons who had fallen from their first love, who had cast away the laws and the speech of their forefathers, but who now came to the Teutonic island to be won back into the Teutonic fold, to be washed clean from the traces of their sojourn in Roman lands, and to win for themselves, among the brethren whom they were to meet as momentary enemies, a right to an equal share in the name, the laws, and the glories of Teutonic England.[109]

This quotation neatly encapsulated Freeman's assumptions and prejudices, for in his interpretation, the conquest eventually united the English nation even more strongly than before, and ultimately, the continuity of Anglo-Saxon life had incorporated the Normans and completed the circle of racial unity. By the inception of the reign of Henry I in 1100, the Normans had started down this path to Englishness, and the reign of Edward I (1272–1307) had completed the process. The *Norman Conquest* brought fame and notoriety in equal measure, for other scholars soon commenced an evaluation of the work that proved fatal to its racial ideas.

Freeman's reputation suffered a rapid diminution because he gave ample ammunition to his critics through a series of scholarly eccentricities that detracted from the serious goals that he had set for himself. The first of these idiosyncrasies appeared in his mania for Old English diphthongs, certain that authentic spelling of Anglo-Saxon was crucial to an understanding of postconquest history. Freeman carried this quirk to an extreme, and when the *Dictionary of National Biography* refused to accommodate this pedantic preference, Freeman boycotted the great enterprise in a huff after volume 1 appeared.[110] In addition, Freeman insisted to no avail, then or now, on calling the decisive victory of 1066 Senlac instead of Hastings, even though only Orderic Vitalis among contemporary and subsequent chroniclers had done so.[111] Freeman believed that a proper Germanic word alone could do full justice to the great battle, instead of the unpatriotic Hastings with its French connections.[112] More serious, because it contradicted the research ideal of the fledgling academic history, was Freeman's aversion to work on manuscript materials in archives or even to visit research libraries: "I tremble at the notion of going to the Vatican library, I, who never in my life had any dealings with any library at all, save very slight once with our Bodleian."[113] He found it more congenial to work in the study of his Somerset home surrounded by his own books, for this also excused him from acquiring the paleographic skills to work with manuscripts.[114] Add to this mix the substitution of *High Dutch* where others used the word *German* and his insistence upon other points of pedantic nomenclature, and the result made Freeman an easy target to satirize. Finally, his advocacy of antivivisectionism, certainly not an ignoble cause, nevertheless in the Victorian context contributed to a suspicion of his probity. These attitudes might have been dismissed as petty foibles except that Freeman would not excuse this propensity in others, especially Froude.

For an individual with such fervid opinions, Freeman's extended personal and scholarly (it is difficult to distinguish them) quarrel with Froude still retains an air of inevitability. If Freeman had not feuded with Froude, surely another scholar would have provoked Freeman's wrath. Their long and bitter rivalry was all the more remarkable because, although not identical, the racial ideas of the two men possessed a striking similarity. They both believed in the "racial" superiority of the English people, and both harbored doubts about the future of the elect nation. The details of the long-standing controversy with Froude were never as important as the way the bitterness reflected Freeman's personality and historical methodology. In 1864 Freeman, anonymously, launched a series of critical attacks in the *Saturday Review* that cast doubt on Froude's epic twelve volumes *History of England from the Fall of Wolsey to the Defeat of the Spanish Armada* (1858–70). In this enterprise, Freeman inaugurated a controversy that highlighted aspects of Victorian historiography and the future path of constitutional history.

From a modern perspective Freeman, first of all, was on the wrong side of the archival research issue, for Froude had used Spanish archives as a basis for his work. Next, Freeman had the unhappy habit of focusing not on Froude's overall interpretation of the English story in the sixteenth century, but rather on minor errors that Freeman blew all out of proportion in order to cast doubt on Froude's credibility. When Bryce made this point to him, Freeman replied: "So you think I was hard on Froude. Most men say I let him off too easily."[115] Freeman's penchant for nitpicking became so obvious that Freeman felt compelled to deny the practice: "But I don't think that *in my writings published with my name* I am open to the charge of constantly challenging on small points etc."[116] Anonymity apparently condoned such tactics and legitimized Freeman's no-holds-barred critiques. Finally, Freeman envied Froude's success in attracting an audience, complaining that "one thing which puzzles me is the seeming belief that Froude can tell a story & that I can't. I believe that I can tell a story much better. Could he have done my battle stories in Vol. III [of the *Norman Conquest*]? Besides that he would have fought Senlac on a plain in Northumberland on a Monday in April, & set the English on horseback & armed the Normans with axes."[117] This latter sarcasm soon came back to haunt Freeman when other scholars turned Freeman's methods on his own work.

This dispute would have little value for posterity except for its revelation of Freeman's character.[118] In the context of constitutional history, Freeman, fairly or unfairly, was judged by contemporaries to have vanquished Froude; this was significant because it established Freeman's reputation to the point where he pursued successfully the Regius professorship at Oxford when Stubbs resigned the position in 1884.[119] This prestigious appointment made Freeman an inviting target for critics of his *Norman Conquest* in particular. When experts analyzed his work in much the same fashion as Freeman had done to Froude, Freeman could not handle the reversal of his scholarly fortunes. Once John Horace Round began his onslaught against Freeman's reputation as a historian, Freeman complained about Round's criticism because it dwelt "on the smallest point."[120] Freeman, the "brutal controversialist," simultaneously was "unduly sensitive to criticism."[121] Paybacks in this case returned to haunt Freeman, who had lived by the scholarly sword and then died by it. Freeman's reputation never recovered, and when he died in 1892, in a final irony, Froude succeeded him as Regius professor.

John Kenyon, after a litany of Freeman's deficiencies as a scholar and as a human being, wrote that "the respect in which he was generally held in his lifetime is difficult now to understand."[122] There are, we think, two significant reasons why Freeman's treatment of English constitutional history deserves remembrance. In the first instance, the epic history of the Norman Conquest thrust interpretation of that event to the heart of English medieval history, a place that it has never relinquished. Freeman's interpretation of the conquest as a milestone during which a stout Anglo-Saxon constitution resisted the inroads of the Norman invaders has lost its conviction; but the discussion of change versus continuity in 1066 and afterward has remained central. No matter whether the historian sides with Anglo-Saxon continuity or Norman innovation, or some safe scholarly haven in between, the conquest has remained since Freeman's day at the core of scholarly discussion, and it has truly remained an argument without end.[123] Historians ever since have wrestled with this issue in a continuing line that leads directly back to Freeman. For all its faults, Freeman's history of the conquest has, in the opinion of one medievalist, "never been superseded, and it is those best versed in the history of eleventh-century England who are most conscious of its value."[124] In the phrase of Clare Simmons, Freeman played a principal role in "reversing the Conquest."[125] The exaltation of the Anglo-Saxons and their survival after 1066 made a majestic story for his readers, one that Freeman continued in two further volumes on the reign of William Rufus (1087–1100) in 1882. The combination of race with "anachronistic nationalism" made the *Norman Conquest* a "notorious high-water mark in studies of 1066."[126] The causes and consequences of the conquest have continued to intrigue successive generations of historians as much as they did Freeman.

More importantly, Freeman, by his emphasis on linking racial solidarity to constitutional development, placed constitutional history at the center of national identity issues. Freeman's success in uniting race as national identity with constitutional destiny reassured his readers that the fate of England was secure in spite of the many challenges of the 1870s and 1880s: "To the pragmatic English, unschooled in German idealism, a physical, largely inalienable and genetically-determined basis for their national growth and character was to have immense appeal, particularly when linked to the dominant constitutional form of historiography by writers like Freeman. This was the importance of the Victorians' sense of belonging to an Anglo-Saxon race."[127] By giving to the English of the late Victorian period an identity rooted in fifth-century liberty and institutions, Freeman fixed national identity firmly in constitutional history. The importance of Teutonic antecedents, particularly their survival after 1066, was crucial to who the English people were.[128] For Freeman it was also important to American national identity. Addressing an audience of over a thousand people at the Peabody Institute in Baltimore in 1882, he hammered away relentlessly at the theme, to the extent that even a devotee like Herbert Baxter Adams had to admit that the lecture was "a three-step waltz, Germany, England, and New England, eternally round and round."[129] In a sense, therefore, it no longer matters how strained Freeman's conclusions were, because constitutional history itself had in part become prominent through his efforts. His victory was not total and in some ways short-lived, but his role in placing constitutional history at the forefront of English historiography regains some respect for his industry.

In retrospect Freeman's definition of constitutional history as primarily public law that encompassed only the political sphere carried within it the seeds of its decline. Although he often invoked the legal accomplishments of his Anglo-Saxon heroes, Freeman had little but contempt for lawyers, a group whose infamy began with their genesis by the Norman Conquest. For the history of law, an integral part of constitutional history, Freeman expressed only indifference. In a commentary of his friend's achievements, A. V. Dicey wrote about the narrow perspective that Freeman brought to his work: "He was quite capable, for example, of understanding law; but he never seemed to me to see that the law of a country, & especially of a country like England, was part of its history."[130] Constitutional history based on race in Freeman's expression did not have sufficient breadth, and his synthesis of the two did not survive him.

Having helped place constitutional history at the intersection of public discussion, national identity, and academic inquiry, Freeman's version barely lasted two decades.

The decline of the racial factor in the primacy of constitutional history was complicated because race remained an underlying theme of public discourse even as its importance to historical study eroded. Green, for example, so often lumped together with his friend and putative mentor Freeman, nevertheless held views in some respects at variance with those of Freeman. In his most acclaimed work, *A Short History of the English People* (1874), Green certainly subscribed to the Teutonic origins of English society, but simultaneously he refrained from some of the prejudices that distorted Freeman's conclusions. On the issue of Anglo-Saxon village democracy, for instance, Green argued for its reality, although this interpretation soon vanished.[131] Yet against Freeman, Green had no illusions about the considerable political and social inequality of Anglo-Saxon society, the growing incidence of slavery, and the violence associated with predatory kings; Green was no uncritical admirer of Germanic liberties, nor did he imbibe Freeman's anti-French bigotry.[132] Green, to the chagrin of Freeman, sold more copies and received greater praise because he wrote with a more accessible narrative style and his conclusions were more judicious. Freeman bred no true successor to his vision of constitutional history, not even his protégé Green.

By the 1890s the reaction against the genetic inheritance argument within English constitutional history had begun on the part of both historians and jurists. Andrews, in the introduction to his *The Old English Manor*, asserted that a racial explanation of institutional history simply no longer persuaded.[133] Pollock suggested that specific statements about the organization of the manor and the land system "must be to a great extent hypothetical, and to some extent conjectural."[134] Freeman's ideal of an Anglo-Saxon democracy populated by individualist-minded free men vanished before the conclusions of research that utilized documentary research. The history of the English constitution might reveal a strong attachment to the pursuit of liberty, but this record did not depend upon some imaginary racial traits.

Other contentions of Freeman also fell before the advent of archival investigation; Luke Pike (1835–1915) concluded that "the ideas which William the Conqueror brought with him were, therefore, the ideas of Frenchmen."[135] At the end of the 1890s, Pollock wrote about the legal principles and institutions of the common law, that "we have acquired or preserved them, peculiar as they are, not by some spontaneous genius of the Anglo-Saxon race, but through the course of a long and complex national history."[136] To this, the American

Charles McIlwain added: "The Anglo-Saxon freeman, proud of his liberty and consciously preserving for future nations those institutions which England was later to hand on to the civilized world, is harder to see than he was twenty-five years ago."[137] Finally, James Baldwin wrote an epitaph for the tomb of Freeman's scholarly reputation: "As a general rule for the study of the English constitution, the nationalist theory of its origin no longer stands."[138] Freeman's attempt to link racial classification to the development of the constitution had failed; in the end it represented, in the phrase of Geoffrey Elton (1921–94), "nineteenth-century fantasies."[139] Yet the commingling of racial thought and constitutional history had not quite run its course.

In the broader Victorian intellectual context, other reasons helped explain why simplistic Anglo-Saxonism disappeared after its brief tenure at the core of constitutional explanation. The idea of race was transformed by recognition of the complex meanings attached to the word.[140] In addition, other forms of historical inquiry surfaced for the study of constitutional history as academic fashion changed. Historians acknowledged significant influences other than the Germanic forests of the distant past. This trend emphasized the Norman contribution to English history after 1066: "The Norman Conquest, despite the vehement protests of Anglo-Saxon historians, did in a real sense mark the beginning of English history."[141] The retreat from Anglo-Saxon history also occurred in the United States, symbolized by Charles Homer Haskins's (1870–1937) *Norman Institutions* (1918): "Hence one effect of Haskins's concentration on the Normans was to maintain the traditional orientation of American scholars toward British history but at the same time subtly to redefine what was best in Britain as 'French' (Anglo-Norman)."[142] Even as the Anglo-Saxon argument waned, Anglo-American ties were strengthened by the experience of wartime comradeship and organizations such as the English-Speaking Union (1918). The decline of the Anglo-Saxon factor as a category of historical causation did not weaken Anglo-American affinities to any noteworthy degree.

In addition, a generation gap developed when older scholars retained race as a crucial dimension of constitutional history, whereas younger colleagues adopted subdisciplines such as economic or administrative history to offer new insights into the field. Historian, jurist, and member of Parliament James Bryce personified this evolution best, for his later writings expressed an ambiguity of belief that indicated an element of doubt had modified his earlier conclusions about race. On one hand, his historical lectures continued to stress the transplantation of English institutions to the New World; yet he also wrote of "the extraordinary vainglorious spirit in which the achievements and the claims of 'Anglo-Saxondom' as it is called are being vaunted."[143] To this end, he proposed in 1920 a center in London where American students might locate, "bringing them into touch with our institutions, such as Record Office & libraries, with British historical teachers and students. A well furnished house with library, reading rooms, lecture rooms & other facilities would be essential."[144] In this sense, the Anglo-American dream never died.

On the other hand, Bryce continued to synthesize sincere speculation with conventional racial stereotypes on formal occasions, such as the Romanes lecture (1902) and the Creighton lecture (1915).[145] In these and other late writings, racial hierarchies dominated his approach to the historical dimensions of racial issues.[146] His distinction between permissible economic rights and impermissible social relationships for inferior racial populations persisted in his conclusions about race and history. The first generation of Anglo-Saxon enthusiasts could never fully escape the racial boundaries that they had embraced; younger scholars rejected the racial blandishments upon which Freeman had insisted.

In the 1870s Freeman, Stubbs, and Green had published their most influential books with respect to constitutional history, and the racial foundations of their work did not vanish immediately. The racial argument, however, could not sustain its academic influence for long.[147] Even those scholars who had once given allegiance to racial categorization sometimes had second thoughts. Dicey, for example, conventional in most racial expressions, also referred to "the insolence of race" when the possibility of constitutional government on the English model for indigenous peoples was discussed.[148] A more genteel, restrained form of constitutional assumption that would not use such crass, discredited notions as Anglo-Saxon heritage or genetic descent of institutions nevertheless still took for granted the superiority of English constitutional culture, whether past or present. Race became an understated fashion rather than an avenue for vociferous exposition. The former adopted its own codes for the expression of racial triumphalism; for example, jurist Carleton K. Allen (1887–1966) wrote in the 1930s of a Rhodes scholar from South Africa: "He strikes me as distinctly the better type of Jew that one finds in South Africa."[149] Race and English constitutional history continued their relationship in the muted tones of English exceptionalism.

Between 1870 and the 1890s, however briefly, the racial interpretation of the English past had pushed constitutional history to the forefront of historical concern. In 1889, for example, Theodore Roosevelt (1858–1919), future president of the United States, called the American westward movement "a mighty epoch in the career of the mighty English race."[150] Although the racial explanation was soon eclipsed in terms of scholarly fashion, the heritage of Anglo-Saxonism persisted. As late as 1918, Bryce had written to American historian William Dunning (1857–1922) of the common law as the "one ancient root" from which Great Britain and the United States had sprung; and he finished with the admonition that "[constitutional] history, no less than philosophy, is the guide of life, national as well as private."[151] The legacy of the racial explanation foundered in part because it could not meet one criterion, pioneered by Stubbs, of academic history: the necessity of archival research to discover new knowledge. Constitutional history moved past its racial assumptions in order to fulfill this new demand, and its prestige prospered even more as a result.

CHAPTER THREE

"I Do Not Believe in the Philosophy of History and I Do Not Believe in Buckle"

Constitutional History as an Academic Profession

William Stubbs, Regius professor of modern history from 1866 to 1884 at Oxford, and then successively bishop of Chester and Oxford, has remained a major figure in the story of constitutional history because of the influence exercised by his three-volume *Constitutional History* (1874–78). As with so many other classic histories, especially the multivolume ones, Stubbs's work is more frequently sampled in small portions than read in its entirety. For nearly a century Stubbs's broad conclusions survived with piecemeal (and usually apologetic) revisions; not until H. G. Richardson and G. O. Sayles launched a frontal assault on the *Constitutional History* in 1963 did the Stubbsian enterprise fall from grace. Even when subjecting Stubbs to a withering scrutiny, however, the authors paid tribute to the legacy: "For Stubbs's misconceptions will be found repeated, it may well be unawares not only in textbooks . . . but in books that purport to be the fruit of original research"; this influence was malign, for the "*Constitutional History* is an inadequate and misleading book."[1] The shortcomings of the three volumes are easily acknowledged, for no scholar now accepts their conclusions without significant reservations. In a real sense this matters little. The work, whatever its faults, placed constitutional history at the center of historical inquiry based on archival research and firmly associated it with history's transition to an academic discipline founded in part on the rigorous standards set by German scholarship. The *Constitutional History* not only established Stubbs's reputation but also led to the field's hegemony as a research area. Edward Freeman, his great friend and admirer, wrote of Stubbs as "the greatest of living scholars" upon the completion of the *Constitutional History* in 1878.[2] Even Stubbs's student John Horace Round, who usually had a bad word for everyone, wrote respectfully of Stubbs as "our greatest historian" even while making revisions to his mentor's work.[3] Stubbs's legacy bequeathed by the *Constitutional History* placed the field at the center of academic prestige.

Equally important to the fate of constitutional history was the publication in 1870 of Stubbs's *Select Charters,* which became the essential foundation of the field's eminence as a taught tradition.[4] The emphasis on documents fit neatly with the new research ideal, while the fifty-six-page introduction anticipated the later arguments of the *Constitutional History.* The extensive influence of the *Select Charters* derived from its role as the basic teaching device for constitutional history in a teaching curriculum begun at Oxford, then spread to Cambridge, and ultimately around the world. Whereas English constitutional history as a research field enjoyed its day in the sun and then succumbed to other forms of historical inquiry in terms of academic status, the subject endured at the center of a teaching tradition that lasted much longer, one that privileged knowledge of constitutional history above other topics. The success of this taught tradition at home and abroad rested upon the *Select Charters* because the documents collection introduced the student directly to original sources. In this respect, therefore, the *Select Charters* served equally with the *Constitutional History* as a basis for Stubbs's legacy to the field as both a research and a teaching tradition.

Despite the conservative aspects to his politics and theology, with respect to historical scholarship based on archival materials, Stubbs proved a revolutionary; indeed, as Charles Firth (1857–1936) noted, he was "probably the first Regius Professor who ever penetrated the recesses of the [Public] Record Office."[5] Originally a student of mathematics and philosophy as an undergraduate at Oxford, Stubbs was self-trained as an editor and a historian. He had learned German as a youngster, and he combined language proficiency and admiration for German scholarship with "the greatest confidence of all in the Teutonic origins of English institutions."[6] Stubbs took holy orders in 1850 and became the vicar of Navestock in Essex until his appointment as Regius professor at Oxford in 1866. In the pre-Oxford period, Stubbs established his reputation by editing a number of medieval chronicles that set a new standard for scholarly excellence: "It is generally agreed that no one has ever edited medieval texts more beautifully or gracefully."[7] His rising fame as a historian and his impeccable church credentials made Stubbs, somewhat fortuitously after the controversial tenure of Goldwin Smith, the choice of the Derby government for the Regius professorship in the summer of 1866.[8] While his selection may reflect political as much as academic considerations, Stubbs used his new dignity to transform the study of English medieval history.

Unlike most of his contemporaries, who wrote history for the educated public, Stubbs never enjoyed the luxury of a private income; he needed every shilling of the compensation that his positions provided. His perseverance and ambition coincided neatly in the furtherance of his career. The Rolls Series, begun in 1857 to publish medieval records, became in 1863 a primary outlet for Stubbs's work and he eventually produced nineteen editions for the project. Taking his model from the strengths of German erudition, Stubbs possessed the languages, paleography skills, balanced judgment, and boundless enthusiasm that made his edited works superb examples of the genre. These accomplishments had provided the foundation for his selection as Regius professor, although in 1866 his "professorial qualifications would have been regarded as adequate in Germany."[9] Stubbs made significant contributions in several areas of the historian's craft, in the process winning this accolade from William Gladstone (1809–98) in 1883 as "the first historical authority of the day."[10] Yet in the end, even with the reputation that he earned, his life ended on another career path.

Stubbs's religious vocation superseded his commitment to historical research; in 1884 he resigned the Regius professorship in order to become the bishop of Chester. God's work removed the greatest English historian of his generation at the peak of his skills and fame. The scholarship that had awed his contemporaries virtually ceased; as A. V. Dicey predicted correctly: "Chester I dare say will gain but I fear we shall never have any further installments of constitutional history from him."[11] Stubbs chose his spiritual obligation in preference to his secular career without hesitation: "His letters reveal him as a generous, kind, and extremely intelligent and perceptive man, a fervent Christian, and a strong nationalist who firmly believed in the innate superiority of English parliamentary, common law, and ecclesiastical institutions."[12] In retrospect Stubbs has remained an unlikely candidate to push historical scholarship in new directions.

For all of Stubbs's achievements in editing and ecclesiastical service, in the context of constitutional history he made the consultation of original documents an absolute requirement for the aspiring professional historian. Any reader of this book who has earned the doctorate in history will understand this criterion because it has long been enshrined in the standards set for a dissertation: a contribution to knowledge based on the utilization of original sources. It should be noted, however, as James Campbell has done, that Stubbs "paid no attention to unprinted sources in the Public Record Office, and had not grasped their scale."[13] This caveat notwithstanding, Stubbs emphasized the methodology of the German academy as he sought to distance himself from the "popularizers" or "amateurs" or even serious scholars who had not made a pilgrimage to archives, for the previous generation of English historians had failed "to adopt the standards set by German scholarship when it came to the use of primary sources."[14] The advance of historical knowledge must proceed through evidence obtained from original documents subjected to critical analysis. In this fashion only could more general conclusions about a topic gain validation. Constitutional history encompassed the public domain, and as the treasures of eight centuries of records became apparent, the subject seemed perfectly suited to embody Stubbsian ideals about research and teaching: "The publication in 1870 of his *Select Charters* was at once a tribute to German methods and a vindication of English scholarship. Henceforth any medieval study not founded upon original sources was an anachronism."[15] In the long run, Stubbs helped to focus the parameters on a conversation among academic historians that continues to the present.

In general the study of history within the academy has stressed methodology at the expense of theory. Since the nineteenth century, scholars have usually assumed that historical inquiry into original sources based on scientific principles should result in empirically verifiable conclusions. Debates among historians often have revolved around matters of interpretation, not the philosophical assumptions upon which historical knowledge is founded. The primacy of radical empiricism in the quest for new sources has continued to dominate. When postmodernism questioned the long tradition of fidelity to the sources by casting doubt on their representational authority, it caused resentment and excitement in equal measure throughout the profession. Arthur Marwick reasserted what might be termed the Stubbsian citadel: "History is the study of the human past, through the systematic analysis of the primary sources, and the bodies of knowledge arising from that study, and, therefore, *is the human past as it is known from the work of historians.*"[16] In response, Hayden White wrote that postmodernism at its best questioned this paradigm and attempted to stimulate historians to reflect more seriously on the nature of their work: "History is rather a craftlike discipline, which means that it tends to be governed by convention and custom rather than by methodology and theory and to utilize ordinary or natural languages for the description of its objects of study and representation of the historian's thought about those objects, based on 'research' of the 'primary sources' and efforts to co-ordinate those with 'secondary sources.'"[17] To this exchange, with its focus on the role of original documents, Stubbs contributed at far remove by his original emphasis on the importance of archival research.

Stubbs denied that he had formulated a philosophy of history, for he had adopted German methods, not German theory. As early as 1857, upon the publication of H. T. Buckle's (1821–62) *History of Civilization,* Stubbs wrote: "I do not believe in the Philosophy of History and I do not believe in Buckle. I fear you will make me out a heretic indeed after such a confession."[18] Stubbs, of course, possessed a sophisticated philosophy of history carefully disguised by the posture of objectivity. He took the emphasis on sources seriously because this guaranteed objective findings and it inculcated a mental discipline, primary aims of historical study:

Truly we may say the study of Geschichtsquellen is not to be approached without clean hands and an open mind. And after the initial investigation comes the criticism; first we have to identify, then we have to value our historical inventory. Both these processes are involved in the study of original sources; it means not merely the reading, or the restriction of reading to, the primary authorities, but the weighing and critical analysis of the primary authorities themselves.[19]

Work on sources demanded technical skills such as paleography and languages, plus the development and exercise of judgment on complex matters of historical explanation.[20]

For the apprentice scholar, such training and experience led to dispassionate objectivity. Goldwin Smith, Stubbs's predecessor as Regius professor, had engaged in numerous contemporary political discussions; Stubbs wished to avoid this behavior at all costs.

Stubbs valued the English Middle Ages far more than the pagan world of classical antiquity, so he differed from his friend Freeman on the unity of all human history. Christianity imparted historical unity, no more so than in English history: "I hold a religious unity, he [John Richard Green] a philosophical & you I suppose an actual continuity."[21] From the synthesis of original documents and religious faith, Stubbs constructed a providential interpretation of English history: "The most precious Histories are those in which we read the successive stages of God's dispensations with man, the growth of the highest natures, under the most favourable circumstances, in the most fully developed institutions, in the successive contributions which those natures, regions and institutions have furnished to the general welfare of the whole."[22] Divine providence ordered human affairs, no better illustrated than in the unfolding of English history: "Not only are God's will and purpose invoked, but also the idea of a relationship between the divine plan and the human apprehension of it."[23] Add to this interpretation Stubbs's advocacy of Germanic constitutional origins, and the rationale for the *Constitutional History* became obvious: "He wanted to make English history a teleological history because of the association he made between liberty and Christianity."[24] To this mix Stubbs then attached that "it is to Ancient Germany that we must look for the earliest traces of our forefathers, for the best part of almost all of us is originally German."[25] These contexts permit Stubbs's reader to understand the premises of the majestic *Constitutional History*, which contained no Calvinist determinism and featured individuals who retained freedom of action in varied circumstances.

Stubbs harbored no doubts about his enterprise because he subscribed to the scientific underpinnings of the quest that "must be rigidly factual and empirical, shunning hypothesis; the scientific venture was scrupulously neutral on larger questions of end and meaning; and, if systematically pursued, it might ultimately produce a comprehensive, 'definitive' history."[26] That Stubbs never attained this utopian goal did not diminish his scholarship or his influence. The *Constitutional History* presented a framework for the writing of English history that propelled the general subject to the forefront of academic consciousness. Religious conviction provided the foundation for its teleological narrative: "He saw English history as manifest destiny."[27] Stubbs believed that constitutional history embodied ethical lessons for the student to discover: "History was a theodicy in which moral forces always triumphed over the immoral."[28] His work stood at the epicenter of constitutional history's rise because it affected agendas for the field's influence both as a research field and as a taught tradition. The former did not last as long as the latter, but Stubbs's dicta on the crucial importance of original documents lay at the heart of both. His conclusions no longer possess the same authority as when first published, but it is still remarkable for how long his legacy exemplified constitutional history itself: "He displayed a learning and an intellectual command which enabled him, so it seemed conclusively, to establish how the English were to understand the nature of their early Germanic and medieval past, and of the determinative debt which they and the world owed to it."[29] In the process, Stubbs alleviated the concerns of those in the 1880s who fretted about constitutional decay through the portrayal of a mythic past.

When Stubbs published volume 1 of the *Constitutional History* in 1874, he produced the first comprehensive treatment of the topic from its remote origins by an English scholar. The work of Henry Hallam (1827) had begun only with the advent of the Tudors, so the medieval story had not received a full scholarly treatment.[30] Freeman's 1872 effort had consisted of topical lectures with no goal of a systematic account. To venture backward into the medieval period connected to the terra incognita of constitutional history; by the 1870s, the belief that the events of the Glorious Revolution had "settled" the constitution in its modern guise had prevailed. Gladstone, upon receipt of the first volume, alluded to this convention when he wrote: "The history of our Constitution, one of the most instructive subjects in the entire field of national experience, has been too often regarded, like the history of the Church, as having died a natural death, or passed into Nirvana with the Revolution of 1688."[31] To trace the specifics of this "settled" constitution by reference to the seemingly endless medieval records in numerous archives offered a monumental challenge, one to which Stubbs responded brilliantly. In so doing, he made it clear that, his own work notwithstanding, medieval documents existed in such profusion that the field could support the endeavors of many other historians. Constitutional history met the criteria for a documents-based history to an extraordinary degree.

The *Constitutional History* rendered an epic version of the national past in part because it located the origins of the nation and its history earlier than previous historians had done.[32] As noted previously, Stubbs began his narrative with the assumption that the English people and institutions had germinated in early Teutonic society. Volume 1 began in somewhat mundane fashion as Stubbs lingered lovingly over the local institutions that he thought at the core of Anglo-Saxon society. For the period before 1066, Stubbs apparently relied too heavily on the work of Rudolf von Gneist, whose two volumes on the English constitution and administration had appeared in 1857 and 1860. Stubbs's conclusions on Anglo-Saxon liberties were wrong, but only because he had misinterpreted the tradition upon which these beliefs were founded.[33] Gneist in turn had learned from the eminent Friedrich von Savigny (1779–1861) that similarities in early social organization had furnished the fundamentals of legal development in both England and Germany.[34] Unfortunately Stubbs did not get past his admiration for Gneist, and the racial rationale for Anglo-Saxon history meant that his conclusions introduced little new, or they were erroneous and quickly superseded.[35] This section did not make an auspicious start to the project.

Stubbs's real contribution began with his interpretation of the Norman Conquest. Whereas Freeman had regarded this event as a barely mitigated disaster for the Germanic nature of English society, Stubbs declared that the Normans had played a providential role in the evolution of English constitutional history. Stubbs argued that the Normans brought an indispensable "national" element to England that imposed the growth of a broad popular consciousness that went beyond the spirit of local institutions so quintessentially Anglo-Saxon. Norman centralization complemented Anglo-Saxon local self-government. The Anglo-Saxons, on the verge of political disintegration, were saved by the Normans.[36] The Norman monarchs created a centralizing energy crucial to the creation of the modern (post-1066) English nation.[37] Although the Normans governed in despotic manner, they could not crush the habits of Anglo-

Saxon independence;[38] the Normans played a pivotal role in the formation of a new national community that grafted the traditions of local communities onto a centralized state. Anglo-Saxon and Norman institutions gradually harmonized into a political community typified by self-government, albeit under the auspices of a strong monarchy. Henry II best illustrated the process of synthesis because he codified what was best from the past and introduced new elements in order to safeguard royal power. As a result, by 1215, the English nation had acquired a specific expectation of government that harmonized effective kingship with local self-government.

Volume 2 of the *Constitutional History* is now regarded with good reason as the most successful segment of the work, for it covered the period when a national party emerged that spoke for the nation and parliament originated as the voice for the political group. From the diverse conglomeration of local communities came a national polity in a series of dramatic confrontations that exemplified the country's destiny. As a result of his debt to German historiography, Stubbs envisioned England's history as one where "the growth of national consciousness gives the state a life which is real and characteristic."[39] Stubbs thereby inaugurated the custom that defined constitutional history as almost exclusively public law, the relationships between individuals and the state. Private law, the rules governing relationships between individuals, had little place in Stubbs's intellectual universe. When noted jurist and legal historian Sir Henry Maine (1822–88) left Oxford for Cambridge in 1878, Freeman reported that Maine would lecture on bailments, a topic well beyond himself and Stubbs.[40] The history of public institutions took center stage as the primary vehicle for explanation of the nation's history.

In the second volume Stubbs also indulged most dramatically his penchant for moral judgments. If the Whig interpretation of English history, simply put, divided historical actors into good guys and bad guys, then Stubbs more than merited the label in this category. He believed that the moral lessons of historical study required that appropriate assessments of individual actions form an important part of the historian's duty. King John, for example, because he attempted to thwart the national consensus during the crisis that led to Magna Carta in 1215, was "the very worst of all our kings: a man whom no oaths could bind, no pressure of conscience, no consideration of policy, restrain from evil; a faithless son, a treacherous brother, an ungrateful master; to his people a hated tyrant."[41] About Edward I, however, the verdict was quite different. The reformer of constitutional practice a century after Henry II, Edward earned great praise for his part as midwife to Parliament. About this hero, Stubbs wrote: "He had inherited to the full the Plantagenet love of power, and he possessed in the highest degree the great qualities and manifold accomplishments of his race."[42] We emphasize that revision by subsequent historians has not tarnished the overall intellectual achievement; as Norman Cantor wrote: "On no one point can it be said that Stubbs's judgment was completely without merit or that the thesis he propounded did not have a plausible basis in the contemporary documentation."[43] The narrative and interpretations of volume 2 have left an indelible mark on later constitutional historiography.

The final volume of the *Constitutional History* reflected Stubbs's inundation by records and a consequent loss of the deftness displayed in the previous installment. The proliferation of medieval records meant the impossibility to master them in their entirety in the way that his editing made impeccable his work with chronicles. An increasing abundance of court and government records, the sinews of public law, overwhelmed Stubbs as they would have any other historian. The finale to the medieval constitution was located in the synthesis of Anglo-Saxon and Norman institutions, of which Parliament was the great culmination. Development of private law doctrines enshrined in the common law interested Stubbs far less. The balance among royal government, local self-government, and representative institutions, the core of the English constitution, had come into existence.[44] Continuity represented the key to this institutional evolution, but the path had been neither smooth nor preordained; as Stubbs emphasized: "[L. O.] Pike you know shirks the great point, the continuity of Teutonic as opposed to Roman or Celtic institutions in law & judicature."[45] Constitutional progress reflected in many instances the realization of unintended consequences, although even T. F. Tout (1855–1929), a sophisticated critic of Stubbs, wrote: "We are still rightly proud of the English constitution, of the continuity between our modern democratic institutions and our parliamentary institutions of the middle ages, and of the way in which in modern times the English parliamentary system has suggested the form of free institutions to nearly every civilized nation."[46] Policies and initiatives designed to secure one result had often led to a different outcome. Freeman and Stubbs both wrestled with the impact of Darwinism, but ultimately "they interpreted evolutionary biology in terms of order and purpose, rather than in terms of chance and natural selection."[47] From the long record of purpose and chaos, however, a national consensus had embraced individual liberty and public order.

Stubbs's influence on the growth of constitutional history as a research field was so great that it was soon taken for granted. As J. Goronwy Edwards (1891–1976) wrote of the Stubbsian legacy, the confluence of constitutional history with academic scholarship inaugurated a new genre of investigation, the more impressive because Stubbs had no English models to imitate.[48] Even when the field itself declined in academic prestige, Stubbs continued to set the research agenda. Only when his student Tout changed the emphasis from institutions to administration did the parameters of research begin to change: "After the death of King John, Stubbs was content to relegate administrative details to the antiquarian. . . . There is no reason to regret that Stubbs thus narrowed his field. It was only through such limitation that he was able to give us what still remains the classic presentation of the whole history of our mediaeval parliamentary institutions."[49] As late as 1938, K. B. McFarlane (1903–66) thought it necessary to outline new boundaries for constitutional history in order to move the subject into non-Stubbsian areas by focus on new topics, "namely local surveys to investigate the power of the great noble families and collective biographies of the gentlemen who sat in parliament."[50] Stubbs's students such as Round and Tout went their separate ways, but the work of their mentor never faded. Even Frederic Maitland recalled that he had discovered Stubbs at a London club and read it because he found it interesting. This experience did not transform Maitland's life, but the incident demonstrated how Stubbs's influence worked at many levels.

For academic historians especially, ever after, a primary criterion for the assessment of published research rested on the diligence in exploring relevant archives. This unleashed for some in constitutional history a mania to discover cartularies, charters, and manuscripts that knew few limits. The cult of the archive frightened some, but it became central to the academic pursuit of reputation based upon publication.[51] The *Constitutional History* "taught that history should be rooted in original sources, balanced and temperate in judgements, highly detailed and analytical, and severe and austere in tone."[52] Contrary to the argument of Piet Blaas that emphasis on documents contributed to the decline of constitutional history,[53] we believe that Stubbs helped establish an archival standard that placed constitutional history at the forefront of the new academic discipline. Research in original documents, in the form of the adage that theoretical argument means simply a paucity of evidence, became central to the ethos of the academic historian. Constitutional history in its guise as surrogate for public law provided ample opportunities to the intrepid researcher from the dooms of Ine through the pipe rolls that dated as far back as 1130 to the formation of the common-law courts.

The Stubbsian legacy promoted careful imitation in the 1880s and 1890s. Readers may recall the five-hundred-page monuments to this tradition in which two hundred pages represented analytical text and the remaining three hundred pages reproduced in full the sources for other scholars to share. The foundation of the Pipe Roll Society in 1884 and the Selden Society in 1887 stressed the publication of documents germane to the study of legal and constitutional history. In 1886 the anniversary of Domesday Book "produced some solid results, & in particular a movement to found a *Selden Society* for the historical study of English law—which all or nearly all the right people have promised to support."[54] Constitutional history had turned into a growth industry for the nascent academic profession.

The cult of the archive meant a two-way street, for careful identification and organization of documents as well as prompt production of them were essential to scholarly enterprises. When Maxwell Lyte (1848–1940) became deputy keeper of the Public Record Office in 1886, inaugurating his four-decade tenure in the position, "he was able to execute his wide-ranging reforms precisely because by that date he headed a professional and competent staff well-versed in archive management."[55] Lyte, and his longtime assistant Hubert Hall (1857–1944), who served in the Public Record Office for forty-two years, worked diligently to provide information to scholars; both traded letters with historians on the potential significance of some new manuscript discovery. Lyte made publication of research aids a priority once he was in charge.[56] Hall, long retired, died in 1944 as a result of enemy action, and a letter in support of his widow's application for a pension from the Royal Literary Fund summarized his achievements:

He was a guide, philosopher and friend to several generations of Assistant Keepers of the Public Records and to numerous students, especially from America, many of whom have written appreciative notes since his death. As Secretary of the Royal Commission on the Public Records [1912–21] he collected a great mass of useful evidence on the keeping of archives of all sorts and their availability to historians. The Officers both of the Royal Historical Society and the Selden Society have expressed to me their great appreciation of his services to their Societies over a long period and their hope that this application will succeed.[57]

Hall published, for example, the valuable *Studies in English Official Historical Documents,* which reflected his commitment to research, his own and the work of others.[58] The cult of the archive by the 1880s thus depended on the synergy between the new class of professional archivists and the historians keen to explore the treasures of the Public Record Office.

More importantly, Stubbs had created constitutional history as the national narrative. Constitutional history, as Richard Southern (1912–2001) wrote, "was a wonderful instrument for the purposes with which the History School was coming to be identified. Intellectually it was highly respectable. It was systematic; it gave an organic unity to a large assortment of otherwise disconnected events. It was difficult."[59] Stubbs had transformed the study of medieval documents into a panorama that transcended its archival parts: "a bold account of the development of the English Constitution which, though in certain respects High Church or quasi-Tractarian, could more generally have been written by any patriotic Liberal (like Freeman) who believed that mediaeval constitutional history was about progress, liberty and national cohesion."[60] Stubbs wrote constitutional history with a purpose, to prove the working of divine providence in granting to England a set of principles that restrained government power in favor of individual liberty.[61] This theme resonated with every segment of the population and reinforced pride in representative government through parliamentary institutions.[62] Its organization and style made the *Constitutional History* eminently readable despite the documentary evidence that supported the narrative: "It is not surprising that continuity, as epitomized by the slow, orderly development of the English constitution, should have been thought of as a distinctive national virtue."[63] Not only did the work stress the Anglo-Saxon period for serious study; it pioneered the professional interest in medieval history. For Stubbs, "the role of constitutional history did not stop at national cohesion, however; it gave history itself cohesion."[64] In this fashion the field attracted the admiration of citizen and scholar alike.

In a long but never discursive work, Stubbs had successfully made constitutional history *the* fashionable subject for historical research. So great did Stubbs's reputation grow that Tout complained about the "excessive cult of his great book."[65] Oxford don H. A. L. Fisher once complained that "this is a very dull letter, but the French Revolution, the Lombards and Stubbs with his everlasting Constitutional History are making a hole inside me."[66] Stubbs achieved a pinnacle of fame granted to few historians, and academic imitation became the sincerest form of flattery. Even after the field as a research tradition faded from academic glory, as late as the 1930s, the book was still "the point of departure for all constitutional research after 1066; and those who neglect it do so at their peril."[67] In the 1980s John Kenyon still referred to the *Constitutional History* as "the Ur-text on medieval English history."[68] All good things must come to an end, and eventually the subject lost much of its academic luster. Indeed excellent work in the field never declined; what did change was the perception that constitutional history represented the cutting edge of research. Such were the vagaries of academic history.

In the first instance, constitutional history as a research field fell victim to the aforementioned cyclical nature of academic status. The subject spun off administrative history, but scholars looked to ostensibly broader areas such as economic or social history for new inspiration. With his ecclesiastical appointment in 1884, Stubbs virtually abandoned scholarship, even book reviews, so that by the time of his death in 1901 historians had already begun to place him in the unfashionable category when compared to scholars in other subfields. The pace of discovery, stimulated in part by Stubbs himself, made his work increasingly removed from the discipline's goals. Perhaps this was predestined, for Stubbs had provided the means to critique his work in the code of documents-based history. Unearthing of new records and a more sophisticated reading of their importance, as in the case of Magna Carta, revised his reputation. His grand narrative soon suffered from the work of successors who pointed out that there was more to the Stubbsian forest than the trees he had used. Excellent research continued in the field, usually with a salute to Stubbs as a pioneer, but other historians no longer accorded constitutional history the same approval. Academic culture became in the process a cruel taskmaster, because published work in many cases enjoyed a brief recognition and the profession then moved on to different topics.

Stubbs's emphasis on Germanic origins suffered the same fate as the broader category of racial ideas in general. More detailed and certainly more nuanced monographs on constitutional history, but without his epic majesty, cast doubt on this portion of his scholarship and soon resembled variations on a familiar theme. Once race had run its course as historical explanation, the Stubbsian canon survived, but not in a manner that retained an exalted state for its subject. This transition diminished his reputation in the broader world of academic history, but not within his specialized field. Reference to Stubbs as a pioneer in research became something of a cliché, and the *Constitutional History* remained an obligatory footnote. Stubbs, however, had more to give.

Stubbs's other great book, the *Select Charters*, inaugurated the longer tenure of constitutional history as a taught tradition. Long after the relative eclipse of the field as a research tradition within the academy, the *Select Charters* served as the essential basis for the teaching of English constitutional history; the first two selections came from Julius Caesar and Tacitus respectively, an indication of how far into the past Stubbs went to convey the importance of Germanic institutions. So successful was the work that it reached an eighth edition by 1895, and a ninth edition, substantially revised by Henry W. C. Davis, appeared in 1913, and it was reprinted as late as 1957. Although Stubbs wrote a long introductory essay to the volume, the collection of documents was intended primarily as a "treasury of reference" and secondarily as "a manual for teachers and scholars."[69] "The study of Constitutional History," Stubbs wrote, "is essentially a tracing of causes and consequences; the examination of a distinct growth from a well-defined germ to full maturity: a growth, the particular direction and shaping of which are due to a diversity of causes, but whose life and developing power lies deep in the very nature of the people." Stubbs placed "the greatest importance" on constitutional history as a critical element in a "regular English education." Stubbs included these basics in his expectation of a taught tradition: a sense of organic development, institutions springing from the character of a select racial group, and the strong sense of why knowledge of constitutional history was essential to contemporary society. He commended "this little book to the good offices of teachers, and to the tender mercies of pupils." Few books of its kind have succeeded as well as the *Select Charters,* perhaps surprising even Stubbs himself. Even after World War II, Bertie Wilkinson (1898–1981), in his own extensive work on constitutional history, wrote "Stubbs's *Select Charters* was a masterpiece of selection and condensation."[70] Wilkinson, in further testament to the Stubbsian legacy, also included documents he had selected for the reader to ponder.

The eighth edition, published in 1895, well after Stubbs had turned to his episcopal duties, came from the demand by the target audience, students and teachers. Criticism of the *Constitutional History* had already challenged several of his major research conclusions, so Stubbs attempted to sustain his belief that continuity of institutional development was essential to the understanding of constitutional history. The scientific basis for this inference he now attributed to astronomy instead of biology, for the "accepted theory of continuous History" rested on arguments as valid "as those on which Copernicus and Kepler worked out their astronomical conclusions." Constitutional history grounded in archival research and systematic evaluation of source materials gave special training to the student, who had to replicate the historian's task when study of Stubbs's selections was required.

Although Stubbs always projected himself as an opponent of abstract historical theories, he in fact helped inaugurate a technical study of history and its relation to undergraduate education that still persists. Stubbs stipulated three reasons for the importance of history: (1) the subject was a worthy field for its own sake; (2) history provided a fundamental mental discipline; and (3) history imparted the contexts of a cultivated life.[71] The modern teacher might argue that the study of history offers skill acquisition along with information accumulation. Practically all departments emphasize writing and analysis, including preparation of an extensive research paper, for the undergraduate. In this process many courses use a documents reader of one sort or the other, varying between readings from original documents or secondary authorities. The other variable is whether selections are a few pages from multiple authors or extensive choices from a smaller number of the available options. Stubbs cannot be given sole credit for this pedagogical innovation, but the assumption that student involvement in small discussion groups creates a learning environment better than large lecture sections still remains a contentious issue. His own professorial career at Oxford did not include teaching success, for his lectures were not well attended.[72] The presumption that immersion in original documents provided the best introduction to history started a continuing argument within Oxford and other universities about whether undergraduate history education should focus on professional training, a general introduction to specific areas of study, or character formation. For Stubbs the issue remained moot because constitutional history could meet all three demands.

The justification for a professional training at the center of the undergraduate experience at Oxford soon showed a limited appeal. Not every student had the ability or the desire to make the study of history a lifetime vocation. In the latter part of the nineteenth century increasing numbers of students studied history, and the controversy between tutorial instruction and professorial teaching never was fully resolved. Proponents of the professional ideal generally fought a losing battle. Preparing students for examinations took precedence over encouragement of a scholarly temperament. A. L. Smith (1850–1924), advocate for tutorial education and eventually Master of Balliol, was remembered in this way: "Modern history was considered a subject especially suited to students of high social rank but only moderate intellectual abilities and 'A. L.' proved to be outstandingly successful with undergraduates of this type."[73] It is one measure of Stubbs's influence that his ideas could be used on both sides of the question. Although his teaching career ranked well behind his outstanding research record, Stubbs believed that the undergraduate study of history did not necessarily have only a professional pursuit as its goal: "The thing that vexed him when he came back to Oxford was that it was undervalued in its true character of mental training."[74] Stubbs's admonitions about historical argument also triumphed. The cult of objectivity permeated the tutorial ranks; as George Otto Trevelyan (1838–1928) wrote in 1912 of an unnamed tutor at Balliol: "[he was] extraordinarily disgusted at there being any attempt at moral or political judgements in history. Happily other Oxford students can get other teaching from Firth."[75] Aspects of the teaching controversies were never mutually exclusive, for the relationship between teaching and research still generates discussion, and Stubbs's work provides ammunition for both sides.

Firth represented the professorial ideal in the post-Stubbsian decades. His concern that undergraduate education go beyond simple reading of documents never abated; with respect to clerkships at the Public Record Office, for example, he complained of the low standards required in language training and examination results.[76] Hubert Hall at the Public Record Office also expressed doubt about teaching only to examinations and failure to stress true engagement with archival materials. Candidates for employment did best "*above all who are intimately acquainted with the actual texts of constitutional documents*"; and in a special Stubbsian fashion, Hall also grumbled that other graduates were "inevitably forgetting all about the 'continuity of English history' within six months of the Examination."[77] James Bryce had written in 1882: "The sense of historic continuity is essential to the greatness of the nation as well as to the mental elevation of the individual."[78] The long reign of constitutional history as a taught tradition in part resulted from the tutors who taught to examination material. In the end, Oxford tutors "saw their curricula as meant especially to empower a generous conception of intelligent citizenship rather than to further a professional discipline."[79] Despite some professorial victories, the war went to the tutors: "Unlike Smith, Firth never understood that external fame, based on scholarship, had little to do with the reputation of history tutors, which was confirmed rather by the national careers of their former students."[80] Edward Jenks (1861–1939), a legal historian who taught at the universities of Melbourne, Liverpool, and London in addition to Oxford, reflected on the ethic of the tutor: "The great rewards of the teacher are the consciousness that he is, all his life, deliberately spending his time and strength in helping to make smooth the rough places for others, and to lay for them a sure foundation for future success, and the rich satisfaction which an honest and hard-working teacher may count on receiving, in the knowledge that his efforts are remembered with gratitude and affection, by those for whom he had laboured."[81] For these tutorial goals, nothing served so well as initiation into the Stubbsian vision of constitutional history.

English constitutional history as a taught tradition concentrated on giving to the student the historical evidence to inspire good citizenship and public service. Among its many lessons was the exceptionalism of this constitution, from its "unwritten" form to the long history that had resulted in the individual liberty and parliamentary government that served as a beacon to the rest of the world. As a taught tradition, constitutional history embodied specifically Stubbs's contention that its study instilled character.[82] In this sense Stubbs thought that constitutional history went far beyond the confines of public law to the point that it encompassed just about every aspect of national life. This broader conception "contributed largely to its double intellectual significance in Victorian and earlier twentieth-century England."[83] It defined academic professionalism and yet also reflected broader standards of public life. The conjunction of moral lessons and historical evidence made constitutional history a curricular centerpiece that aimed at reinforcing values as much as imparting information: "One explanation for the flourishing state of English political and constitutional history at Oxford and Cambridge is that it appealed to a wide spectrum of both liberal and conservative historians as a conclusive demonstration of the values that they all thought most important."[84] In the final analysis Stubbs "gave the (History) School an ordering, unifying principle by basing the study of history upon the systematic and organic narrative of constitutional history. That narrative was consistent, optimistic, without troubling ironies or ambiguities, and, above all, satisfying as a majestic panorama."[85] The ideology of constitutional history stressed that it, better than any other topic, gave to the student a set of values that emerged from the national history, "to train the good citizen, not the professional researcher."[86] In the end Firth acknowledged the success that Stubbs had enjoyed: "His influence was most marked in the direction he gave to the study of English history, to a certain extent in Oxford, to a much greater extent outside it, by the publication of his Constitutional History."[87]

Foremost in the pantheon of constitutional virtues was political consensus, an antidote to the revolutionary traditions that beset most other countries, which Stubbs attributed to debate about the constitution, now buttressed by documentary evidence. National character had formed in the crucible of this long evolution where "independence of character" came from "rootedness and continuity."[88] John Clive has left an elegant summary of the emphasis on constitutional continuity:

The high point of that [Whig] interpretation in its original form included an ancient, free, Teutonic constitution under the Anglo-Saxons; the immemorial antiquity of common law and the House of Commons; the continuity of Saxon freedom which could not be destroyed either by William the Conqueror or by the feudal system brought to England by the Norman Conquest, but which, indeed, were confirmed and endorsed by Magna Carta, the revitalization after a period of absolutism of the power of the Commons as well as the flowering of constitutional government under the Tudors; and the inevitable as well as providential defeat by the forces of freedom, as they manifested themselves in the English revolutions of the seventeenth century, of the wicked attempt by tyrannical Stuart kings to turn the clock back to despotic, personal rule.[89]

The *Select Charters* introduced the student to the early sources of this tradition and provided within limits the experience of working with original texts. Hall advised that the *Select Charters* should serve as a surrogate for Stubbs himself: "The boys examine their books for themselves as though they were inquiring of a living master!"[90] The result was that "tutors taught students receptive to a reading of national history that made harmonious institutions depend upon individual capacity and responsibility because it confirmed and justified their elite place within society."[91] Consensus, not conflict, had characterized the growth of the constitution, with the implicit message that radicalism in any guise simply would not do. Stubbs's version "demonstrated a historical ability to accommodate social groups, political conflict, and institutional change."[92] Engagement with the fundamental documents in the making of the constitution inculcated these lessons in a way that reinforced the Stubbsian legacy.

At Oxford in particular college tutors made character formation a life's work rather than the research agenda for the discovery of new knowledge. In lamenting the relative lack of students studying law, Dicey wrote: "It must be remembered that in other schools, such as that of History, the colleges are far more capable of supporting good teachers than in the Law School."[93] The *Select Charters* attained scriptural status and became the cornerstone of the Oxford history curriculum to such an extent that A. L. Smith lectured on "Steps to Stubbs," an attempt to focus student attention on the key passages and documents in the book.[94] Stubbs's "optimistic and gratifying narrative of organic constitutional growth" created teaching lessons and research opportunities in equal measure.[95] His version of English constitutional history spread throughout history departments in the United Kingdom, the United States, and the Empire because it recounted a model of ordered liberty that these other polities admired.

Fortunately we have an excellent example of how Stubbs's legacy worked in J. Goronwy Edwards, who entered Jesus College, Oxford, in 1909, took the master of arts at the University of Manchester in 1915 under the direction of T. F. Tout, and then joined the military. In 1919 he became a tutor at Jesus, became the editor of the *English Historical Review* from 1939 to 1958, and still served as director of the Institute of Historical Research at the University of London from 1948 to 1960. Although too late to study with Stubbs in person, Edwards was a scholarly grandchild. His undergraduate notes and essays addressed such issues as these: discuss fully the statement that Edward I reaped where Henry II had sown; sketch the form, privileges, and weaknesses of Parliament in the fourteenth century; and what were the causes of the collapse of the Lancastrian constitutional experiment?[96] The readings designated to answer these questions included Freeman, Round, Maitland, and Sir Paul Vinogradoff (1854–1925) among others, but these authorities paled in comparison to the stature of Stubbs. Edwards's notes reflected constant attention to subsequent scholarship where others had corrected Stubbs as well as those instances of later research that had vindicated his conclusions. By the time Edwards himself had entered the history profession at Oxford after World War I, Tout wrote with pride to his student: "You combine the great gifts of the ideal pupil, loyalty and productivity."[97] These attributes Edwards retained until his death in 1976, enjoying a full, distinguished career.

In his own work as tutor Edwards sustained the Stubbsian legacy. In Hilary Term 1930, for example, he prepared a seventy-six-page syllabus on sources of English constitutional history to 1307, the date at which the *Select Charters* ended.[98] In discussing the nature of historical evidence, Edwards informed his pupils that "it involves the study of facts," but the historian must also play the detective "by studying the traces which the facts have left behind them."[99] In another exercise for his students, Edwards devised a pro and con lesson called The Constitutional Experiment in which the undergraduates had to read selected quotations from volume 3 of the *Constitutional History* and then decide whether Stubbs's conclusions still were valid.[100] How enduring this bequest was may also be seen in notes that Edwards prepared for a proposed revised edition of the *Select Charters*:

English constitutional history has, in general, been characterized by two outstanding features. Firstly, the development of the English constitution has, on the whole, been singularly free from violent revolution and abrupt change. This fact has given an unusual degree of continuity to its institutions. . . . Secondly, the English constitution has developed as the constitution of a small, well conquered, much governed kingdom. . . . English constitutional history cannot therefore be intelligibly studied without a good deal of attentive regard to judicial institutions & judicial procedures.[101]

Nearly eighty years after the *Select Charters* Edwards still preached the gospel according to Stubbs that he had first learned at Oxford as a young man before World War I. Edwards's essay on Stubbs, published in 1952, in which he tried to protect the reputation of the master completed the scholarly circle.

For how Stubbs's ideals influenced an individual not known as a constitutional historian, there was the example of R. G. Collingwood (1889–1943). A remarkable philosopher of history in a country where that achievement has never merited great recognition, Robin Collingwood exhibited some elements of the Stubbsian legacy as well. After a period of relative indifference after his death in 1943, in recent decades scholars have begun a thorough reassessment of Collingwood's work. A typical appreciation called Collingwood "one of the key figures, alongside Hegel and Croce, in the history of the history of philosophy."[102] We wish only to make the point that Collingwood, famed for his construction of an idealist philosophy of history against what he thought were the failings of positivism, also held views of a decidedly Stubbsian nature. Christopher Parker detailed Collingwood's hesitations about English historiography: "too much concern with detail and 'unprecedented weakness in dealing with large-scale problems'; a refusal to judge; an inability to get under the skin of people in the past; a concentration upon political history."[103] These criticisms certainly applied to Stubbs and created a divide between the two historians. On several other issues, however, Collingwood held a position more like Stubbs's than Hegel's. On one hand, Collingwood asserted that academic historians caused "intellectual myopia"; on the other hand, he wrote that "the specialisation of modern historical research is a necessary and a fine thing."[104] The argument here is that Collingwood showed a strong preference for Stubbs's ideals when it came to the practical labor of the historian: "The historian is bound by his evidence. His business is to interpret it. . . . The real business of history begins when . . . authorities vanish and we are left with sources instead."[105] Idealism worked for Collingwood when it came to theoretical analysis, but when the historian went to work, he sounded far more like Stubbs in focusing on original materials.

On the issue of impartiality, Stubbs had enjoined historians to avoid putting their own values and prejudices into their writing, even though his own work reflected an opposite result: "Stubbs wanted to be judicious, fair-minded, and objective. But dedication to truth and justice was often mediated by his unexamined theological, psychological, ethical, and political commitments."[106] Complete objectivity had some adherents, and at the end of the nineteenth century it remained, in the phrase that Theodore Clarke Smith coined in 1935, a noble dream.[107] When Collingwood delivered a paper to Oxford's Stubbs Historical Society, he argued: "Our own eponymous, the great Stubbs, said that no historical work could be done without an element of spite in it. In short: we may take it as an axiom that the unprejudiced historian does not exist."[108] Stubbs, despite his official pronouncements, recognized that in practice the objective historian could not happen. Collingwood added that "people who deny this are either too stupid to recognize their own prejudices or else ashamed to avow them; what we cannot do is to continue playing with historical research & yet shirk the responsibility of judging the actors we narrate."[109] The historian must act as a judge, not an advocate. In spite of his pretensions to objectivity, Stubbs had certainly engaged in moral judgments that betrayed his clerical, conservative perspectives. The obvious differences notwithstanding, such as Collingwood's belief that "political ideas are not innate ideas, biologically annexed to the pedigree of something called the Anglo-Saxon race,"[110] what Stubbs had achieved through constitutional history continued to provide a variety of lessons from which his successors might choose.

With English constitutional history in the vanguard, "by 1900 modern history had become a subject of commanding importance in British universities." In the first decade of the twentieth century, history was the most popular subject among undergraduates, taken by 23.4 percent, and as late as 1948 the proportion had risen to 26.6 percent.[111] In the 1930s, Marjorie Chibnall recalled: "The pattern stamped on the History School in the nineteenth century by William Stubbs still persisted; the mainstay of the syllabus had been English constitutional history with particular emphasis on parliamentary institutions."[112] In his 1968 survey, Brian Harrison reported that constitutional history was compulsory at seven and optional at nine of the pre-1945 universities, but was neither at any of the redbrick institutions.[113] Kenyon added that as late as 1980, the shade of Stubbs still fell across the School of Modern History at Oxford.[114] Constitutional history had proved that it could deliver on the three goals of the taught tradition: (1) to provide students with the opportunity to cut their teeth on primary documents, (2) to inculcate sophisticated skills of analysis and synthesis that would last a lifetime, and (3) to foster good citizenship and the importance of public service. In addition, as Peter Slee has written, constitutional history gave "a strength and dignity to the [Oxford History] School which it might otherwise lack."[115] The subject exercised an imperial influence all its own, for it spread throughout English-speaking environs. In Canada, for example, the teaching of English history, especially constitutional history, dominated even against Canadian history.[116] As a taught tradition, therefore, English constitutional history retained its influence well past the relative decline of its status as a research field.

The long ascendancy of constitutional history also resulted in part from the canonical role that Stubbs possessed for so long. Maude Violet Clarke (1892–1935), when teaching constitutional history at Oxford in the 1930s, introduced her pupils to the two greatest constitutional historians that England had produced, Stubbs and Maitland. Clarke conceded that Stubbs had made significant mistakes, for his conclusions about the Anglo-Saxon period especially had become less persuasive with the advent of additional sources and new interpretations of those materials. Stubbs had also erred in his reluctance to revise the *Constitutional History* and the *Select Charters* in any important way. As a result "others destroyed the myth of the Anglo-Saxons as a constitutionally minded people with a national army, local gov. & a central Parliament."[117] Stubbs still kept his standing in the field after decades had passed. Clarke wrote of this continuing stature: "The 3 vols. of his great work were regarded as the sacred books of the Vedas. It was said by students that to read the 1st was necessary to salvation. To read the 2nd was to acquire grace while to penetrate to the unnatural austerities of the 3rd was reserved for the elect ascetic."[118] Sixty years after its initial publication, the *Constitutional History* still remained at the center of the taught tradition.

After World War II, however, the centrality of constitutional history started to wane. We acknowledge that precise measurement of this phenomenon is impossible. If we use medieval history in general as a proxy for constitutional history, Campbell's examination of the history syllabi at British universities documents this decline: "The twenty-five universities founded before 1949 all required the study of English medieval history: none of the twelve founded in and after 1949 required it: only three made provision for it."[119] Although Richardson and Sayles justified their severe critique of Stubbs in 1963 in part on the ground that "the cult of Stubbs has persisted wherever Oxford historians abide, but even at Cambridge," that day had passed.[120] The two critics surely overstated the case, for as early as 1952 Edwards had noted: "The upshot is that the *Constitutional History* is not now regarded by anybody as containing in itself all that is generally necessary to salvation. There is no longer any 'cult' of it, either in Stubbs's university or in others. Least of all is there a 'cult' of it among the undergraduates."[121] So the taught tradition slowly ebbed away, but other aspects of constitutional history's influence still flourished. In particular, its primacy led to increasing scholarly specialization, one result of which was the foundation of the *English Historical Review* in 1886.

The impulse to start a professional history journal on the German model and free from antiquarian articles first appeared in the late 1860s. John Richard Green wrote to Freeman about discussions for a "purely Historical Review" that would have Stubbs as the first editor.[122] When Freeman wrote to Bryce about the possibility of such a venture, he stressed that the journal must be substantially different from the general periodicals that were the staples of Victorian culture.[123] While the initiative did not succeed at that time, the discussion gave a context to the foundation of the Royal Historical Society in 1868. One leader of this process was the ubiquitous Oscar Browning (1837–1923), who became a lecturer at King's College, Cambridge, after his controversial dismissal from Eton in 1875. A scholar who reaped much benefit from the sole episode of Louis XVI's flight to Varennes, Browning used the Royal Historical Society originally as a platform for his ideas about the reform of history teaching at secondary levels. Browning was far more interested in the teaching of history than in the discovery of new knowledge; and he was defensive about his unwillingness to adapt to the new research ideal. For example, on the death of Maitland, Browning had this criticism for the much-admired scholar: "He had, perhaps, too strong a contempt for knowledge which is not based on research."[124] The project for a professional periodical thus failed in the 1860s.

The *Transactions of the Royal Historical Society*, as John Burrow has written, now a mainstay of historical scholarship, originally published work of little distinction.[125] In the short run, the *Transactions* failed to meet the demand for an outlet for historical investigations based on original research. Charles Oman (1860–1946) wrote to Browning in 1890, after the *English Historical Review* had made its debut, that the *Transactions* had been "full of uninteresting second hand matter," but the addition of "Bishop Stubbs, Canon Creighton and Prof. Seeley" gave the society a new respectability.[126] The tensions produced by the teaching-versus-research ideals reflected in part the Stubbsian emphasis on archival work. Jenks, a legal historian of some distinction, wrote to Browning: "I agree with you in your general policy of making the Historical Tripos rest on a basis of more or less exact and inductive science, rather than on masses of more or less connected records"; and he added that Stubbs used the facts of history as achievement instead of illustration, "& for history specialists it may be the right one."[127] The default of the *Transactions* to provide an opportunity to publish original research meant the opportunity still existed for those who had subscribed to the research ideal.

In the mid-1870s, Freeman, Green, Stubbs, Bryce, and others once again attempted to push the historical journal goal forward. At this point, Freeman appeared to offer the greatest enthusiasm, but the impetus evaporated because of publishers' hesitancies about the financial viability of the endeavor. In the period from 1867 to 1886, the tension between the nascent ideal of scientific history and the need to consider audience and monetary issues plagued endeavors to initiate a new journal.[128] In 1883 the desire for a professional journal on German lines surfaced once again. Bryce wrote to Freeman that "the idea of a Historical Review is again coming on the carpet & is to be proposed to the Cambridge University Press in October."[129] Additional time was still needed, and in the end Longmans gambled on the finances and undertook the task. Simultaneously jurists pursued the same quest, a professional periodical dedicated to the scientific study of law. In 1884 Pollock wrote to Freeman about the *Law Quarterly Review,* which first appeared in 1885: "Our new Review will be a Law, not a History, Review. But we hope to give a good proportion of our space to the historical treatment of law, the more so because there is not in England any periodical devoted to historical science—and we hope also that we shall derive special advantage in this respect from our headquarters being practically at Oxford."[130] The foundation of the *Law Quarterly Review* in 1885 and the *English Historical Review* in 1886 marked an influential conjunction of the desire for a professional approach to the respective disciplines.

In 1883 Bryce laid out the proposal that eventually came to fruition in 1886, although certainly not in all particulars.[131] Bryce hoped for a volunteer (unpaid) editor, an editorial committee of three or four scholars, and market payment for authors. He wished, not surprisingly, that a share of the review, from one quarter to one third, would be devoted to American history. Bryce also stipulated, wisely, that the publisher must not expect profits for the first three years at least. The outreach to Browning tried to include those for whom research and publication were not a high priority in the expectation that teachers at all levels might support the enterprise. The organizers received exactly what they had envisioned, a journal with little appeal to the public that published the fruits of original research. Bryce had anticipated real problems because profits were scarce and readers in short supply, and even as late as the 1920s the subscription list still had not risen much over a thousand.[132] Despite all these travails, the *English Historical Review* finally appeared with Mandell Creighton (1843–1901) as the first editor.[133]

In the prefatory note to the first number of the *English Historical Review,* Bryce announced what the founders hoped to achieve. In the first instance, the review would offer a venue to demonstrate the accomplishments of historical research, and it would in time become the organ through which adherents to the research ideal would triumph. Bryce specifically repudiated Freeman's definition of history as past politics in a bid to open the journal to an ecumenical vision of scholarship, a belief he harbored in private as well: "I could never agree with his [J. R. Seeley's (1834–95)], or Freeman's, view of history as politics."[134] The *English Historical Review* from the outset conformed to the Stubbsian emphasis on documents and original research. How this played out was soon shown by the stress on the "Notes and Documents" section, which subsequent editor Reginald Lane Poole (1857–1939) thought the journal's strongest asset: "I hope you realize that the articles are normally the least important things in the *Review*. They are mostly, or largely, derelicts abandoned by other periodicals. The really good feature is the section on *Notes and Documents,* and it is this feature I am endeavouring to extend."[135] As the hitherto undiscovered document became an important cog in the advance of historical scholarship, Stubbs's focus on this dimension of research and teaching won more and more academic converts. Given the long history of public law in England, constitutional history benefited most from the triumph of the two ideals.

The popularity of constitutional history was both cause and consequence of the adoption of rigorous standards in the process of professionalization within the academic community. Oxford and Cambridge led the way in recognizing that teaching and research went hand in hand in the brave new world of higher education. Faculty accomplishment depended on the "cognitive superiority of historical writing based on critical use of source materials, archival research, and a historicist view of human societies . . . [where] professors combined research activity and teaching functions . . . [with] specialists responsible for the continued progress of their discipline through both their own scholarly work and the training of neophytes."[136] The ancient universities blended professorial research with college teaching "for the sons of the landed and professional classes preparing for careers in the public service, including politics, the home and Indian Civil Service, colonial government, and the liberal professions."[137] When other universities joined this bandwagon, the same logic and language prevailed; in putting forward a call for recognition of the University of London and its research agenda, A. F. Pollard wrote: "The advancement of knowledge and understanding is the true function of universities."[138] English constitutional history in the form of Stubbs's two great works met the demands of research and teaching admirably.

The subject offered simultaneously the chance to establish one's scholarly reputation for original research, yet it also offered a body of knowledge whose mastery became a focal point of the taught tradition. In all of this, Stubbs had a major part to play. The *Constitutional History* especially was a milestone in the transformation of academic research and teaching: "It bears the image and communicates the spirit of a great scholar."[139] In 1948, Helen Cam (1885–1968) offered this testimonial to Stubbs: "I would say at once, with all the force at my disposal, that there is no nineteenth-century historian towards whom it is less possible to be condescending without condemning oneself as unfit to study history."[140] More recently Stubbs received this assessment from Richard Southern, another distinguished Oxford medievalist: "Stubbs is a name always to be mentioned with veneration in the Oxford History School. He is without doubt the greatest of Oxford historians, as Maitland is equally preeminent among Cambridge men. They have no peers."[141] Stubbs's role in founding the Great Tradition remains worth considering in the light of these latter sentiments.

In the United States, while the professionalization of historical writing followed a somewhat different trajectory, the results were similar. Stubbs had a less direct influence than in England during the early stages of the process, though ultimately both his *Constitutional History* and *Select Charters* found their way to the top of the constitutional history canon. Moreover, the rise of the specialized, document-centered mode of historical scholarship was hatched, for the most part, at the nation's newest universities. Finally, the impact of the modern German research ideal was more pronounced than in England. Among America's oldest and most prestigious universities, only Harvard took an early part in the process, with the appointment of Henry Adams to teach medieval history in 1870. He made a promising start, especially in Anglo-Saxon legal history, but with his wide-ranging interests and role as a social critic, he was restive with his circumscribed role and resigned after a few years. At any rate, he lacked an advanced degree and had relatively little experience in archival research. The early locales for promoting the professionalization of history were the University of Michigan and Johns Hopkins University. On both campuses the lead was taken by men also named Adams (no relation to Henry or indeed to each other): Charles Kendall Adams at Ann Arbor and Herbert Baxter Adams at Baltimore.

While Herbert Baxter Adams is rightly credited with initiating the process at Johns Hopkins in the late 1870s, Charles Kendall Adams (1835–1902) claimed to have started in the professional direction at Michigan in 1869, though he admitted that the work was "rather elementary for a number of years." He acknowledged his predecessor at Michigan, Andrew Dickson White, following White's appointment as professor of history in 1857, for having "brought an enthusiasm to his new chair that sent a sort of historical glow through all the veins and arteries of the university.[142] White's importance extended nationwide and is difficult to exaggerate. He ranks as one of the foremost reformers of higher education in the nineteenth century and later served as ambassador to various countries, including Germany and Russia. A thoroughgoing freethinker and secularist, he was unable to secure a position at Yale (his alma mater) because of his radical views. However, the founding of new state and private universities, free of sectarian affiliations and the attendant mission of training clergy, provided him with the institutional matrix with which to begin the transformation of American higher education. As professor of history at the University of Michigan from 1857 to 1865, White helped establish the foundations on which Charles Kendall Adams was to build.

While White's long presidency of Cornell University, starting in 1865, was even more important in providing a powerful model of the modern university, it was far less successful in fostering the appropriate environment for the study of constitutional history. This was because of his unfortunate selection of Goldwin Smith. What had seemed, in the 1870s, a stunning coup of academic entrepreneurship in luring the Regius professor of history from Oxford to Ithaca had a relatively small impact on the professionalization of history. Smith was not a research scholar and made no attempt to fashion a rigorous program at Cornell based on the study of primary sources. While the *Dictionary of National Biography* might have been overly harsh in identifying Smith as a "controversialist" rather than a historian,[143] many of his publications were shallow and propagandistic. It was during White's earlier, shorter tenure at Michigan that the enduring groundwork was laid for the professionalization of historical research and teaching.

Charles Kendall Adams had enrolled in White's initial class of students and distinguished himself to his professor and to the reforming president of the University of Michigan, Henry Philip Tappan (1805–81), an advocate of the German method of higher education. On White's departure for Cornell, Adams was named assistant professor of history. A full professorship was conferred on him in 1867, along with a year and a half leave of absence to study in France and Germany. On his return he put into effect the seminar method of instruction for advanced students that he had experienced in Germany. His career continued to be mentored, indeed guided, by his ongoing close friendship with White. When the latter left the Cornell presidency in 1885, Adams succeeded him, and it was under Adams's direction that Cornell, thanks to his insistence on hiring talented new faculty members, became a vital institution, especially in the fields of history and political science. From 1892 he performed a similar function at the University of Wisconsin. Even after his transition from teaching to administration, C. K. Adams continued to be involved in instructional matters and in 1882 published an important bibliographic guide (updated in 1888) to works in all fields of historical study.[144] Although his primary field was the history of France, English history received by far the most fulsome treatment in his 660-page manual, with approximately a hundred pages, roughly the same space as that accorded to the United States and a great deal more than was allotted to any other country's history.

Herbert Baxter Adams's role in spearheading English constitutional studies at Johns Hopkins has been described in Chapter 2. There the emphasis was on his racially charged view of constitutional history in his teaching, an approach that was largely discredited in the profession by the 1890s. However, H. B. Adams's place in the transformation of history in general and constitutional history in particular was important and enduring. Whatever the deficiencies of Adams's conceptual framework, there was considerable scholarly rigor in his seminar, with a strong emphasis on primary source research. His students developed important critical skills in analyzing and discussing primary sources and deploying them in their written work. Adams inculcated a healthy dose of skepticism and did not insist that his students reach conclusions similar to his own. The Hopkins historical seminar was also surprisingly international in its composition. In 1886 Charles Andrews (1863–1943) wrote to his mother: "Our Seminary is about the most cosmopolitan affair I ever was connected with. Besides a great variety of Americans composing it with Japanese and Jews and Germans, we have been addressed in the last two meetings by a Russian, an Englishman, and an Italian, who were exceedingly interesting."[145] Toyokichi Iyenaga (1862–1936), a Japanese scholar whom Andrews described as "one of the brightest and cleverest of the students here," went on to a celebrated career as a professor and constitutional historian of Japan.[146] Although a number of

Adams's students turned against the germ theory of institutional development, they all seemed to have accepted the primacy of constitutional history. Whatever their views of Edward Freeman, whose portrait Adams had placed prominently in the seminar room (sometimes called "the laboratory"), few of them dissented from Freeman's famous dictum, inscribed in large letters on the wall: "History is past Politics and Politics present History."

Many of the students trained under Adams's guidance at Hopkins fanned out to other leading universities, establishing similarly rigorous programs. John Franklin Jameson, the first member of the history seminar to receive the doctorate (1882), was appointed full professor of history at Brown University in 1888. He quickly shaped the history program at Brown into one resembling that at Johns Hopkins. Several years later, he sent his mentor Adams a printed description of graduate study in history at Brown, which was arranged in a three-year cycle:

Thus in the European field, two terms of each year being given to English history and one to that of the Continent, the first year's work will consist of a critical study of the earliest period of English history and that of the reign of Charlemagne. The second year's work will relate to the constitutional history of England from the Conquest to Magna Carta, and to one of the Crusades. The third year will be England's constitutional history under Elizabeth and James I, or in the time of the Commonwealth, and certain aspects of the Thirty Years War.[147]

Thus was English constitutional history given pride of place and the seminar method institutionalized in departments colonized by Hopkins graduates. Luminaries among American historians such as Andrews, Charles Beard (1874–1948), and James Harvey Robinson (1863–1936) started with research or study on topics in English history.[148] It would be simplistic, however, to apply an academic "germ theory" to this process. While a fair amount of propaganda on behalf of the new course of studies emanated from Baltimore, there were many independent developments, so that by the 1890s, most of the leading private and state universities had acquired similar programs and methods. At Harvard, for example, in the 1880s the history department was overhauled in the professional mold by, among others, Charles Gross (1857–1909), a Göttingen PhD soon to emerge as a leading constitutional historian of England. Accompanying this was the rise of the *Harvard Historical Studies* to a position rivaling if not surpassing the *Johns Hopkins Studies in Historical and Political Science*. Yet even while Harvard was an example of autonomous progress within the profession, it also showed how compelling a model was the system established at Hopkins.

Herbert Baxter Adams's place in professionalization was enhanced by the founding of his monograph series at Johns Hopkins. He had responded enthusiastically to Bryce's suggestion for Anglo-American partnership in setting up a scholarly journal,[149] though that particular transatlantic publishing project did not succeed. Instead, the *English Historical Review* began publication in 1886 as a purely British scholarly enterprise, while the *American Historical Review* did not debut until 1895. Adams did not welcome a new scholarly journal that would compete with his monograph series. A year before the start of the *English Historical Review,* he told Jameson: "The Englishmen wish me to cooperate with their new review. I think I shall, but the Studies will beat the Britishers in American circulation."[150] Gilman promoted the new publications to eminent constitutional historians in England and reported to Adams in 1883: "I have seen Prof. Stubbs today and told him of your work in which he seems to be much interested. I have promised him some of your *tracts. Will you send them*; also the diagram of your historical laboratory. Sir H[enry] Maine was also very appreciative."[151] These monographs provided a vehicle primarily for Adams and his doctoral students. In the first two years of the *Johns Hopkins Studies,* there appeared Adams's own *The Germanic Origins of New England Towns* (1882), *Saxon Tithing-Men in America* (1883), *Norman Constables in America* (1883), and *Village Communities of Cape Anne and Salem* (1883). While these works were informed by the Teutonic germ theory of institutional transmission, other works in the series, mostly by his students, were not. *The Constitutional Development of Japan 1863–1881* (1891) by Toyokichi Iyenaga was an excellent example of the editorial latitude allowed by Adams. So also was the work of Charles Andrews.

Andrews, who taught at Bryn Mawr before moving on to Johns Hopkins in 1907 and finally to Yale in 1910, emerged as the major figure in challenging Whig doctrine on both the Norman Conquest and the American Revolution. Herbert Baxter Adams had encouraged him to study the origins of early towns in Connecticut (Andrews's home state), with the purpose of demonstrating their descent from Anglo-Saxon communities of freemen, and this became his dissertation topic. Once launched on the project, however, Andrews discovered disparities between Adams's grand theory and the documentary evidence, which, of course, he had been taught to revere in Adams's seminar. In his dissertation, published in the *Johns Hopkins Series* as *The River Towns of Connecticut* (1889),[152] Andrews made clear that the new towns of the seventeenth century were creations of the colony rather than its building blocks. This rejection of the Teutonic "germ theory" of institutional origins had profound consequences. By emphasizing the importance of central government policy as opposed to local community initiatives, Andrews called into question a key tenet of Whig orthodoxy: the postconquest mark community of self-governing freemen in England. Furthermore, Andrews reasoned that if local environs had not formed the building blocks of the American colonies, then perhaps the same was true for England with respect to German antecedents. This became Andrews's next project.

By the 1890s several other notable scholars contested the theory of the mark community. Frederic Seebohm (1833–1912), Vinogradoff, and others in England had already demonstrated how slender was the evidential base and how tortured the chain of reasoning used by a proponent such as Freeman to bolster the case for the free mark community. Andrews, encouraged by Gross of Harvard,[153] joined the revisionist ranks when his book on manorial organization in late Anglo-Saxon England appeared in 1892. *The Old English Manor* received praise from scholars in the field, though Andrews was chided by Vinogradoff, William J. Ashley (1860–1927), and Sir Frederick Pollock for not presenting his views more forcefully, which Ashley attributed to Andrews's reluctance to offend his mentor.[154] In spite of this soft-pedaling, however, the conclusion was clear: the Anglo-Saxon manor bore little resemblance to the supposed ancient Teutonic *tun* and was characterized by servility and lack of self-government. Andrews argued that little liberty existed in England before 1066, and therefore William and his "armed banditti" no longer played a sinister role, because the conquest itself had lost a key aspect of its former significance. The common man of early England, far from being an ardent rustic democrat, had been politically inert. Andrews declared in his conclusion: "With few wants, without the consciousness of others . . . the Saxon ceorl and the Norman villain seem to have been contented with their position. This simple and self-dependent life, though destined to change with the industrial growth of the kingdom, and to expand under the influence of a greater economic inter-dependence, lasted with little variation for four centuries."[155]

With the Anglo-Saxons consigned to constitutional limbo, historians could concentrate on the post-1066 period, for which there was a relative abundance of documentary evidence. Reverence for the close study of primary sources had of course become an essential virtue of the historian by the 1890s. Stubbs, the one historian whose scholarship was still held in high regard throughout this period of major historiographical change, had exhibited those qualities all along. His *Select Charters* continued as the essential documentary compilation for scholars and students alike well into the twentieth century in the United States. In the work of Maitland and Round in England and Andrews in America, English constitutional history focused on the gradual evolution of later medieval institutions. Their sober, painstaking analyses of the documentary evidence served to strip away any supposedly innate impulse toward freedom and to denigrate revolutionary agency, particularly that of the common people. Thus, while the barons of 1215 retained and even enhanced their significance, the peasant rebels of 1381 were reduced to utter inconsequence.[156] The result was a "Normanization" of English constitutional history on both sides of the Atlantic, a profound paradigm shift that was accompanied by a similarly sharp interpretive revision regarding the American Revolution. These linked revisionist processes, which were paramount in the two decades leading up to World War I, will be discussed in detail later.

Two remaining elements of professionalization in the United States require consideration: (1) the establishment of the American Historical Association in 1884, and (2) the first appearance of the *American Historical Review* in 1895. The scholarly journal might have preceded the organization had Herbert Baxter Adams not already established his monograph series at Johns Hopkins in 1882. There still existed a need for a serial publication to handle articles and book reviews, something the *English Historical Review* began doing in 1886, and that the *Historische Zeitschrift* and *Revue Historique* had done since 1859 and 1876 respectively. Prior to 1895, articles on history appeared in either general periodicals, such as the *North American Review,* or in the one publication devoted to history, the *Magazine of American History.* Even in the latter, the great majority of pieces were by amateur historians.

The American Historical Association (AHA) was established largely as the result of the tireless efforts of Herbert Baxter Adams, at Saratoga, New York, in 1884. At that time there were only about twenty professors of history in the entire country, most of them unknown to the wider community; the bulk of the scholars who assembled for the birth of the AHA were not academic specialists.[157] The formation of the new organization took place at the annual meeting of the American Social Science Association, from which the historians were, in effect, seceding, beginning that process of the hiving off of academic specialties that was continued by political scientists, economists, and sociologists. The approximately forty historians who established the AHA at Saratoga chose Andrew Dickson White as their first president, with Herbert Baxter Adams as secretary, and resolved to open membership to all with a serious interest in history. From the outset, the AHA followed an inclusive strategy, and the mixture of "amateurs" and "professionals" can be seen in the fair number of nonprofessorial scholars occupying the presidency in the first decades. Such figures were often well known to the general public, such as George Bancroft, a widely revered historian of the United States who held the presidency in 1885–86 (at the age of eighty-five). Inevitably tension arose within the new organization, much of it generational. Some leaders of the expanding professoriat in the AHA resented what they believed to be the excessive deference paid to the older, and in their view, amateur historians. The ever-diplomatic Herbert Baxter Adams tried with considerable success to preserve the peace. When Albert Bushnell Hart of Harvard complained of the undue influence of the older members, Adams wrote to Jameson, also a "professionalizer": "In my recent letter to Dr. Hart, I had no notion of suppressing young men, but of properly representing the 'old boys' at the next annual meeting. . . . I believe in young blood, but we must preserve a proper balance between the boys and the patriarchs."[158]

From the initial meeting, scholarly papers were presented, and some of them were published from 1885 to 1891 in the annual *Papers of the American Historical Association*. When Congress granted a federal charter in 1889, it stipulated that the Smithsonian Institution should publish the AHA's annual reports, the first of which appeared in 1890. With no publication or postage costs to the AHA, the annual report quickly expanded beyond executive council meetings and financial reports to become a vehicle for scholarly articles, documentary collections, and similar materials. While this free ride diminished in the late 1910s and was finally eliminated in 1945, it provided important opportunities for new scholarship.[159] Still, for the United States to lack a professional journal of history, while other advanced nations boasted theirs, was galling, especially to the younger academic members of the AHA. In April 1895 a group of professors, headed by George Burton Adams of Yale and Albert Bushnell Hart of Harvard, founded the *American Historical Review* as an independent publication, appointing Jameson as managing editor. Three years later the AHA began subsidizing the journal and acquired control over its editorial board.[160]

The lead article of the *American Historical Review*'s first number, by William M. Sloane (1850–1928) of the six-man editorial board, offered readers a sense of the new journal's nature and direction. Sloane castigated the narrow Anglo-Saxonist approach to American history, a stricture consistent with the move away from a racial sense of constitutional history to one that was based on institutional analysis. Sloane further urged teachers to ensure that their students were well grounded in general history before introducing them to American history, a radical challenge to the conventional pedagogic strategy of building a nation of patriots through an early introduction to the national narrative. He declared that the *American Historical Review* would "display the largest catholicity possible," but that "mediaeval, modern, and Contemporaneous history" would be preferred over "ancient history, oriental or classical."[161]

Noteworthy among the other pieces in the first number of the *American Historical Review* was Moses Coit Tyler's article on the loyalists in the American

Revolution. Tyler, a historian of American literature who had been a classmate of Andrew Dickson White at Yale, was, thanks to White, appointed professor of American history at Cornell in 1881, the first such post in the United States. Tyler was also among the founding cadre of the AHA. An ardent Anglophile, he sought in his 1895 article to rescue the loyalists from the obloquy to which they had been consigned by generations of patriotic historians. Pointing out the loyalists' many failed attempts to reform the Anglo-American relationship while avoiding a permanent breach with the mother country, Tyler concluded that their success "would have given us political reform and political safety, but without civil war and without an angry disruption of the English-speaking race."[162] To dispute so central a tenet of patriotic history was, in effect, to support the recent friendly overtures made to Britain by key figures in American political, social, and economic life. The maturation of the historical profession in the United States at the end of the nineteenth century, accompanied by an institutionally based constitutional history, helped shape a new Anglo-American relationship. The history and identity of the United States, spurred by the traditions of constitutional history, now took a consensus path; in the process, the revolutionary origins of the nation faded into the background.

CHAPTER FOUR

"A Too Acrimonious Spirit"

---◼◗◆◖◼---

Constitutional History as Culture Wars

The emphasis on record history and its ultimate triumph within the academy had a number of unintended consequences. The adoption of new "professional" standards affected the role of narrative in constitutional history, the growing chasm between academic and public history, and the position of the national narrative, the Whig interpretation of history. John Horace Round, who died in 1928, is now remembered primarily as an individual who took no prisoners when engaged in scholarly disputes that occurred throughout his lifetime; Noel Annan, for example, wrote of "the horrible Horace Round, who in controversy had the manners of a ferret."[1] Not until 2001 did a comprehensive biography appear, almost as if the subject's infamous reputation for pugnacity kept posthumous assessments at bay.[2] Books such as *Feudal England* and *Geoffrey de Mandeville* are now rarely read, certainly not in their entirety, and languish in reputation.[3] As our interest in Round increased, we hoped to revise the prevailing view that he had been a footnote ogre who had destroyed the weak and flattered the strong. No individual, we hoped, could have been so unpleasant as to deserve such opprobrium from posterity. How wrong we were! Round used his undoubted abilities in essentially unfair ways on numerous occasions, and when he had once identified a victim, he never ceased to repeat his charges of slipshod scholarship.[4] Throughout his four decades of active scholarship, Round remained a terrier who never relaxed his grip on enemies, real or imagined.

Round never joined the ranks of academic historians who matured within the universities during the 1880s. A student of Stubbs at Balliol in the 1870s, along with such future academic luminaries as Charles Firth, Reginald Lane Poole, and T. F. Tout, Round never pursued an academic appointment. He enjoyed a private income that freed him from the obligation of employment. After a period of residence in London that began in 1887 upon the death of his father, Round returned to live the remainder of his life in the house where he had been born, 15 Brunswick Terrace in Brighton, in July 1903. This seaside citadel provided the haven from which he made his scholarly forays. In addition, Round suffered from chronic ill health throughout most of his adult life. His correspondence literally teems with references to prolonged periods of illness, most of which derived from bronchial attacks in youth and then disabling migraine headaches in later life. During periods of recuperation, when confined to bed rest for months at a time, Round trained his nurses to fetch materials from his library. Even when the academy beckoned, fate intervened, as in the case when sickness forced Round to decline to give the Ford lectures at Oxford in 1910–11.

Round's physical tribulations played a role in determining the nature of his scholarship and his reluctance to engage in sustained narrative writing. His work came primarily in short, incisive articles that he could complete when enjoying intermittent spells of good health. Prolonged periods of intense pain no doubt contributed to the "acerbity which too often colours Round's style."[5] The challenges his condition presented appeared in Round's reflection that "work is a great effort to one in delicate health, and I have made many sacrifices for it. If it were not for the *occasional* appreciation of competent scholars I should give it all up."[6] Yet Round soldiered on, leaving one to wonder how much more prodigious his productivity would have been if he had escaped his frequent bouts of illness. Never married and with little else in his life other than politics and an obsession with the discovery of medieval documents, Round possessed a penchant for scholarly combat that knew few limits.

To his opponents, Round's demands for high standards of scholarship appeared craven because he adopted an obsequious attitude toward his mentor, William Stubbs. About Stubbs, he wrote of the "vastness of his learning, the soundness of his judgment or the supreme merit of the work he did for English history."[7] One historian has suggested that Round's initial excursions into constitutional history were written "to illustrate or carry forward Stubbs's work."[8] Certainly Round often paid homage to his tutor's appreciation of the importance of genealogy in medieval history, a topic that fascinated Round throughout his life. In fact, however, much of Round's work subjected Stubbs to careful criticism, but it was veiled in a rhetoric of adulation. Before a thorough critique of Stubbs on Magna Carta, for example, Round wrote: "No one I think, will suspect me of imperfect appreciation where our great historian is concerned."[9] His professed sentiments notwithstanding, Round became increasingly aggressive about Stubbs's mistakes after the great man died in 1901; this circumstance gave additional ammunition to those who denounced Round's want of scholarly courage. Indeed, Round brought Stubbs's *Constitutional History* into question on several substantive issues, but he never launched a search-and-destroy attack on his teacher as he did with scholars of lesser reputation.[10] In similar fashion, Round refrained from any disputes with Frederic Maitland, especially after the latter had reproved Round in the *Athenaeum* in 1899 for his scholarly bad manners.[11] This episode involved Round's abuse of Kate Norgate (1853–1935) and came at the end of a string of disputes in which Round's ferocity was on display; but Round never attempted to confront Maitland directly. Round was a scholarly bully, pure and simple.

In addition, Round held racial views that, although they were shared by many contemporaries, added to the unpleasant side of his personality. Round, for example, frequently expressed an especially repugnant anti-Semitism. In 1910 he wrote: "I noted lately a fearful result of miscegenation observing in an illustrated paper a young Jew with strongly marked Hebraic features addressing the house, I looked to see if it were a Simon or a Samuel. . . . It had the same effect on me as the Mongol-European half caste in Burma."[12] About the Marconi scandal in 1912, Round observed to his Liberal friend Oswald Barron: "Our friends the Jews seem to be on 'Queer Street' at last. I wonder what you, ever quickest to scent scandal, would have said of this Isaacs Marconi business, now being investigated or of this Samuel 'Montagu' India Office deal—if they had been Conservatives."[13] Nor did Round keep his hatred private, for it intruded into his published work as well. In an introduction to a pipe roll of Henry II, Round observed: "Another Jew Moses 'with the nose' (cum naso) must have possessed in no ordinary manner the distinctive feature of the race of Shem."[14] Even by the standards of his day, Round conflated racial and political prejudices to a remarkable degree.

Anti-Semitism did not exhaust Round's fund of intolerance. On one occasion, after a period of good health that permitted him to work industriously, Round described himself as "toiling like a nigger."[15] Irish Catholics were also on Round's list, as when he wrote in 1912 in a period of home rule excitement: "We owe this humiliation (for us English) to the sordid vote of Irish members at the crack of the Roman whip. Which fact, I hope, will shake your pathetic belief that Home Rule does not mean Rome rule."[16] Round became an equal opportunity bigot by also denouncing socialists, trade unions, and Americans with equal fervor. Even the Welsh earned his enmity upon the establishment of the National Library in Aberystwyth in 1909 on the grounds that: (1) it presaged a call for home rule and thus portended the dissolution of the United

Kingdom; (2) it might also result in the transfer of medieval documents pertaining to Welsh history away from London.[17] In this reprehensible catalog of hatreds, we have found only one sentiment that illustrated a softer side to his personality. In 1908 Round wrote: "I adore cats, and it is a standing grief to me that my servants will not let me keep one, a nice *fluffy* Persian. . . . But a lonely man craves for them."[18] Despite this solitary example, Round still remained a most unattractive person whose traits and isolation affected his approach to scholarly research and writing. Round suspected conspiracies against his work at every turn, and no attempt at reassurance could placate him.[19]

One instance in particular illustrated Round's tactics in scholarly disputes that earned him such a ferocious reputation. In 1890 Hubert Hall, then junior clerk at the Public Record Office, had persuaded Round, on the basis of a long friendship based on a shared interest in medieval manuscripts,[20] to become coeditor of an edition of the *Red Book of the Exchequer* for the Rolls Series. Round and Hall had major disagreements about the project, and eventually Round withdrew from the collaboration. Still on friendly terms, Round twice offered to read the proofs for the finished project, and Hall had these sent to him.[21] Round apparently made some minor suggestions, but he did not inform Hall of major reservations he had on some issues. When the edition was published in 1897, Round then reviewed it in hostile fashion on problems he might have earlier called to Hall's attention. Hall's editing was problematic, and even Maitland, who liked Hall, tried to convince Round that Hall was not worth the effort.[22] Round would not rest in attacking Hall and the *Red Book* until "its heresies should be exposed."[23] Ultimately Round published a ninety-one-page diatribe against Hall in August 1898, to which Hall responded the following November. Hall regarded Round's conduct as unethical and a special betrayal because the two had been friends prior to the controversy. Hall wrote: "Mr. Round has striven with all the perverted learning at his command to darken and blight my official and literary life—to denounce me as an imposter, a fraud."[24] Round's style of scholarship came at a cost; historian William Stevenson (1861–1924) wrote to Frederic Maitland: "I cannot get him [G. J. Turner] to admit that J. H. R. has an ounce either of integrity or merit as a researcher: this is a prejudice founded upon the somewhat brutal treatment of Hubert Hall."[25] At the turn of the twentieth century, Round's intimidating manner made him the most feared book reviewer in Britain.

In view of this loathsome combination of personal and professional behavior, why does Round now deserve our attention? In the first instance, Round played a significant role in undermining English constitutional history in its research dimension as the national narrative by his emphasis on short, analytical articles. The work of Edward Freeman, Stubbs, and others had established constitutional history as the primary vehicle for the ostensible Whig interpretation of history that privileged the subject in the nascent field of academic history. The reputation of Freeman and Stubbs, as well as their friend John Richard Green, had rested in considerable degree on their narrative flair. Narrative in this case is defined as "the organization of material in a chronologically sequential order and the focusing of the content into a single coherent story, albeit with sub-plots."[26] Other Victorian historians such as Froude on the Tudor century, Samuel Rawson Gardiner on the Stuarts, and W. E. H. Lecky (1838–1903) on the eighteenth century had all constructed multivolume meta-narratives on their periods. As a result, all attracted a public audience as well as academic colleagues. Round helped to discredit that form of historical explanation by offering an alternative vision of what scholarship meant.

Round took the task of discovering new documents and then subjecting them to minute analysis almost to the point of obsession; for example, he once wrote to Maxwell Lyte: "I am happy to say that I am on the track of a fine series of nearly 30 charters of a French abbey relating to England, and wholly unknown it would seem."[27] In addition to information on the state of his health, Round filled his letters with arcane discussions of this charter or that manuscript.[28] Without teaching obligations in which the necessity to generalize predominated, Round focused on single documents as his preferred genre of research. Round himself called this the "modern ardour for discovery,"[29] a spirit of archival adventure that dominated his work.

The best evidence for this attitude came in his efforts on behalf of the Pipe Roll Society. Round devoted much of his energy to editing the pipe rolls in the belief that this work, publishing original records for the benefit of other scholars, was his foremost mission. In 1909, for example, he noted that "I am writing the preface to the forthcoming Pipe Roll volume, an annual labour of love with me."[30] When the outbreak of World War I threatened the existence of the society, Round tried to obtain a grant from the Carnegie Trust to sustain its publication agenda.[31] Like many other historians of his era and after, Round found that the lure of editing original documents superseded the satisfaction of turning the records into an original account.[32] After the war, when historian Doris Stenton (1894–1971) became secretary of the Pipe Roll Society and rescued it from impending demise, Round showered her with his gratitude: "I fear that I may never have congratulated you on the production of the Pipe Roll volumes. It is a real triumph to have made so good a start."[33] Perhaps the most indicative symbol of Round's commitment to archival research came when he refused election to the British Academy on the ground that Oxford historian

Charles Oman, not famous for such industry and a frequent target of Round's criticisms, was already a member.[34] The widely shared ideal of documentary research took special form in Round's work.

In the felicitous phrase of John Kenyon, Round was a "destructive miniaturist."[35] In his many articles and reviews, Round usually concentrated on a single point from another author's work and subjected it to withering analysis. Round dissected the conclusions of others in a manner that seized upon a single point (a mistake in a date or an erroneous translation of a single line) and exaggerated its significance to impugn the author and the argument. His lack of perspective led him to take an error on one page of a two-hundred-page book and use that as a weapon to invalidate a thesis for which the other 199 pages provided ample, accurate proof. In his zeal for undiscovered manuscripts, Round made himself a parody of the archival ideal, for the documents became the end, not the means of advancing knowledge. His excursions into narrative exposition were relatively few, and his attitude was well exemplified when Round declined the invitation of Lord Acton to contribute to the *Cambridge Medieval History* on the ground that the projected work "is somewhat alien from that of my minute researches."[36] In the end, however, this concentration steered Round into a parochial view of the expanding nature of historical scholarship.

Round gloried in the style he had perfected; it was what he did best and afforded him the opportunity to pursue his pugnacious career. The loneliness he endured was self-inflicted, for friends and colleagues attempted to deter him from his aggressive path. From the start of his work in 1884, other historians urged him to tone down the nature of his remarks. In 1894 Gardiner warned Round about his "unparliamentary" language in dealing with other scholars.[37] The best example of how Round grafted his undoubted analytic skills onto his refusal to abandon past disputes occurred in 1914 when he submitted a brief article to the *English Historical Review* that ostensibly corrected a statement by Stubbs. Editor Reginald Lane Poole advised Round that the critique of Stubbs was valid, but Round had also used the occasion to launch once again a bitter attack on Hall for the work that had appeared nearly twenty years earlier. Poole explained: "What I expected was an explanation of the manner in which Stubbs was misled into altering a statement for the worse; but I did not expect an elaborate criticism of a forgotten book which Mr. Hall published."[38] Poole informed Round that he would not publish the assault on Hall precisely because no justification existed.

Documents meant everything to Round, and when he detected errors, he pounced like an avenging angel on unsuspecting authors. No one faulted Round for this habit except perhaps on the ground of excessive enthusiasm.

His refusal to forswear scholarly grudges and his habit of using every opportunity to repay real or alleged slights made his work appear all the more quarrelsome. To compensate for his weakness in synthetic writing, Round emphasized his own analytic gifts. On one occasion he wrote to George Burton Adams: "I am very glad that you like the critical study of records in my last book."[39] The consequence was a format of historical inquiry that precluded narratives, for Round's books were short polemics, compilations of previous articles, or an unorganized mass of arguments that defied rational arrangement. With a remarkable absence of irony, Round wrote of William Stevenson: "He suffers from excess of learning 'made in Germany.' So he cannot see the wood for the trees."[40] He found satisfaction only in the short pieces that revised a conventional conclusion, usually at the expense of a previous authority.

Round's belligerent scholarship characterized by attention to detail helped provide an alternative to traditional narrative in the research and writing of English constitutional history. In the first four decades of the *English Historical Review,* from 1886 to July 1923, Round published sixty-five articles or notes and forty-three book reviews, a record unmatched for that period, we believe, by any other scholar. His work helped determine what sort of scholarship the *English Historical Review* published. In 1920 Poole noted that Round's type of research had gained an ascendancy: "It is curious that, while Notes abound, Articles come in very scantily."[41] In a similar vein, George Burton Adams lamented to Round: "If only the merely narrative history did not take so much time."[42] As analysis of particular events and documents replaced narrative in constitutional history, despite Round's personal quirks, his methods attracted many imitators.

The attention to detail so beloved by Round permitted him to indulge his taste for controversy, and yet it also raised the bar for scholarly exactitude. One imagines, for example, that medievalists took extra care with their text and footnotes lest Round pounce upon some careless statement or reference to savage the work and to disparage in unpleasant terms the abilities of the author. As one victim of this venom wrote, Round possessed "a too acrimonious spirit."[43] Early in Round's career, Poole patiently explained to him that "what I complain of is not the pointing out of mistakes, but the magnifying of them."[44] Poole advised in vain, for Round's skills eventually placed second to the reputation for "gotcha" scholarship that he acquired. In the end, sadly enough, his scholarly record "may not have been wholly unconnected with the irritability of an ailing and somewhat lonely scholar, but it was also deliberate and adhered to in the face of many remonstrances."[45] This verdict was all the more regrettable because it obscured what Round had achieved in his lifetime.

Round's enduring renown for scholarly battles has overshadowed his positive contributions to medieval English history. In the first instance, given his obsession with precise analysis, Round introduced a higher standard for historical genealogy. He published close to a hundred articles on the subject in the journals *The Ancestor* and *The Genealogist*. From 1914 to 1922, in recognition of his expertise, he served as adviser to the Crown on peerage cases. His concern for accuracy allowed him to expose embarrassing cases in which historians had confused father and son or brothers. Round pioneered the historical genealogy that resolved puzzling aspects of postconquest patronage and governance.

Next, Round made significant advances in the study of Domesday Book by emphasis on the "principle that the clue to the understanding of Domesday Book lies in the contemporary system of assessment to the Danegeld."[46] His statistical compilations "for the first time brought out clearly the varieties of regional assessment beneath the system of the national taxation which was a principal achievement of the Anglo-Saxon state."[47] As a result, Round "first unlocked the secrets of Domesday Book."[48] Round's articles in the early 1890s paved the way for Maitland's 1897 *Domesday Book and Beyond* by explaining how the great survey was created: "Maitland did not have to answer this question himself because John Horace Round had already explained how Domesday was made."[49] This type of detailed analysis suited Round's intellectual interests best, although as so often happens, subsequent research has cast doubt on many of his conclusions.

Finally, the most important piece of scholarship that Round ever published was the three-part article in 1891–92 on the Norman Conquest and the introduction of knight service.[50] In the aftermath of this innovative work, Round showed an uncharacteristic breadth of vision when he wrote: "I have also been much struck of late by the difficulty comparing the administration of our kings on the two sides of the channel, though such a comparison would bear fruit if the means existed for making it."[51] Round did not acknowledge the irony that this great contribution came in fifty-nine pages, not the five or six pages he preferred. Round argued that the feudal obligation of military service for the Anglo-Norman tenant-in-chief in no way derived from the Anglo-Saxons. This posed a serious challenge to previous continuity arguments about 1066, the survival of Anglo-Saxon institutions, and the impact of the conquest. Round supplied significant evidence to buttress those who argued for a cataclysmic change in medieval society in consequence of the Norman victory.

Round's argument on this controversial topic gained immediate acceptance from his peers and prevailed for several decades. Poole assured Round in advance of publication that "I do not hesitate to say I think you have made out your point."[52] One later historian, however, has noted that Round, the champion of documents history, based his claim on one writ and the words of three chronicles.[53] Nonetheless, Round had a major role in reversing the conquest, putting to rest the racial theories that Freeman had expressed.[54] Even now this piece is still considered "his most striking historical achievement."[55] A. L. Smith at Oxford recorded in his notes for undergraduates: "Hence also N.C. becomes the centre & starting point of E. const. hist."[56] The problem of long-term synthesis remained, however, for as Poole wrote to Maitland: "There is, I believe, no period of English history which so thoroughly needs re-writing as that which lies between William the Conqueror and John. It needs the criticism of Round joined to the constructive gift which he has not."[57] Round worked in an intellectual atmosphere that took the concept of feudalism for granted, and as that construct has come under increasing attack, it is little wonder that Round's work is now so dated. Domesday Book and the Norman Conquest continue to spawn sophisticated scholarship that has made Round as irrelevant as he made his predecessors. His work had an even broader impact, however, on the issue of national history, or, as we would put it, the culture wars of the late Victorian period and the issue of audience for historical writing. National identity and political debate had united in the guise of constitutional history.

That historians have other agendas, implicit or explicit, in the depiction of the past triumphed in the twentieth century against the original ideal of objectivity in which facts would speak for themselves. In 1870 historians such as Buckle, Froude, and Macaulay represented major arbiters of cultural authority, but the development of "professional" history challenged this hegemony over the next several decades.[58] At midcentury the lessons of history had served the purposes of all classes, whether the radicalism of the working class, demands for reform by the middle class, or the emphasis on continuity and the constitution by the upper class.[59] When constitutional history came to the fore as a preferred historical discourse, its emphasis on public law stressed ruling elites and their deeds. History had many uses, however, as the political differences among authors demonstrated. Indeed, the whole point of historical study was to make the putative lessons of the past available to the present.[60] Stubbs, for example, had written with a Conservative slant; Freeman was an unabashed Liberal; and Green's *Short History* was decidedly radical and antiestablishment.[61] A usable past also appeared in museums, statuary, and great houses among other manifestations, and more recently in movies and television.[62] It is now a commonplace that those who control the past dictate the present and the future; debates about the past, therefore, usually reflect differing political viewpoints, as an examination of the controversies surrounding adoption of history standards for a national curriculum in the United Kingdom and the United States has demonstrated.

Round made his contribution to history as a usable past by initiating a frontal assault on Freeman just before the latter's death in 1892, ostensibly on the subject of the Norman Conquest. Freeman's supporters defended him in both popular and scholarly periodicals to the point that the controversy became known as the second battle of Hastings. It soon became obvious that accusations about details of the original battle in 1066 served as proxies for arguments about politics in the 1890s. Lamentations for a past golden age or optimism about prospects for the future found a particular haven in the idiom of constitutional history. An appeal to history provided a standard framework for discussions of the issue of home rule for Ireland.[63] William Gladstone wrote: "The historical argument has the most important judicial bearings on our argument as to the Act of Union."[64] Round's warfare with Freeman and his friends started out as a debate about historical details, quickly turned into a confrontation of political viewpoints, and ended in public apathy. Its significance came from raising the issue of for whom should historians write, a subject still argued within the academy.

Round's campaign against Freeman began in 1884 and continued until after the latter's death in 1892. The episode has become proverbial for the heat, if not the light, that characterized the controversy.[65] It has remained notable for the acrimony among the various participants and how arcane evidence about the Norman Conquest acted as a surrogate for contemporary political dispute, sealing Round's reputation for ferocity. In the context of Freeman's appointment as Regius professor at Oxford in 1884 and his long record of vituperation directed at the historical work of Froude, Freeman made a tempting target for scholarly impeachment. Round declared that he would simply hold Freeman accountable based on the standards that Freeman had applied to Froude. The first stage of the Freeman-Round imbroglio came in 1884–86, when Round called attention to some inaccuracies in Freeman's *Norman Conquest,* but this prelude hardly attracted much attention and Freeman barely deigned to acknowledge his upstart critic. The preview did illustrate important aspects of Round's participation. For example, Round criticized Freeman for mistakes in the first edition, errors Freeman himself had already corrected before Round made his charges public.[66] This struck others as a particularly lame avenue of criticism, to which Round responded that readers should not be required to purchase every new edition that appeared. The other element was advice from others about the unfair nature of his tactics; "what I complain of is not the pointing out of mistakes," wrote Poole, "but the magnifying of them."[67] These considerations brought a brief respite, but Round could not be deterred.

The fireworks in earnest began in 1892 with an anonymous *Quarterly Review* article by Round that questioned in unsparing language Freeman's abilities and conclusions.[68] Through no fault of his own, Round had the bad luck for the article to appear after Freeman's unexpected death. This unfortunate circumstance made the author of the critique appear a master of bad taste, but also cowardly in the bargain because Freeman could no longer defend himself. Round eventually argued that the article was written and accepted well before Freeman's demise; yet Round made things worse by not admitting authorship of the offending article until 1894. By this time, a posse of Freeman's friends had targeted Round for retribution.

After having portrayed Round in such a dismal personal fashion, we feel that an important point must be made on his behalf. Round had a double purpose in the attack on Freeman, because he loathed Freeman's skills as a historian and hated his politics as well—turning the battle of Hastings into a contemporary battle. In the first case, Round's criticisms were valid, although expressed in his usual vindictive style, while in the latter Round engaged in political polemics rather than scholarly debate. As far as issues in the past were concerned, in keeping with his documents mania, Round indicted Freeman for his lifelong refusal to consult archival documents. Round explained that Froude, the foremost victim of Freeman's aggressive criticism, had used such resources in England and in Spain, and thus Freeman could be liable for criticism on this issue.[69] Round discredited Freeman's "account of the battle of 'Senlac,' his league of the western cities, and a whole series of lesser magnitude errors; and traced them with precision to their ultimate origin in the misinterpretation of an original source."[70] Whatever other consequences ensued, Freeman's stature as a historian suffered permanent eclipse. His death precluded any attempt to salvage his reputation: "I think I ought to tell you that the last time or nearly the last time I saw Freeman, he told me of your article on knight service, and said that he meant to read them together that he might see what they proved."[71] A final confrontation between Freeman and Round never materialized, and the latter won the historical arguments decisively.

What transformed Round into such a vicious critic was his hatred of Freeman's politics, "dangerous nonsense incarnate."[72] Round denounced Freeman "a democrat first, an historian afterwards, history was for him unhappily, ever 'past' politics."[73] The unity of history, in Freeman's view, justified the commingling of past and present. Freeman's attempt to portray 1066 was "these fantasies of a brain viewing plain facts through a mist of moots and 'witan,' we have what can only be termed history in masquerade."[74] Freeman made no secret of his anti-French opinions, and it was these that made him so hostile to the Normans: "they disturbed the peace of Europe, they were Catholics, and unlike the

Teutons, they were dishonest."[75] Round then proceeded to turn the conquest into a Conservative lesson by portraying the end of Anglo-Saxon England as a proxy for the lack of strong Tory government. Anglo-Saxon England suffered from an "excess of liberty" and "the want of a strong rule."[76] The protodemocratic susceptibilities of Anglo-Saxon society, "an almost anarchical excess of liberty," had been no match for the realities of Norman power.[77] Yet in the end it was the new liberalism of government growth that Round hated more than the limited authority of the old liberalism: "It always strikes me as odd that the Radical-Socialist gang will not understand that apart from politics and the merits of this or that act, Englishmen have a stubborn hatred of being *dragooned*."[78] Round, of course, rejected any implication that he had embraced Freeman's historical bias in the guise of an opposed political program.

Friends and admirers of Freeman took up the fight by attempting to rebut Round's criticisms on behalf of their fallen hero. The primary participants in this regard were historians Kate Norgate and Thomas Archer. Norgate in particular hammered Round for hiding so long behind a dastardly anonymity and charged that he "had not the courage of his opinions."[79] Such charges drew the full fury of Round's personality, and Norgate remained a special target ever after for his venom. Round responded that he had worked on Freeman's scholarship since 1884 and that Norgate's imputation of cowardice was a personal insult "so reckless, so offensive, and so capable of instant disproof [that it] could only have been made by the advocate of a desperate and routed cause."[80] Where his honor was concerned, Round found that a fifty-page article was no difficulty at all. The bitterness of the public quarrel Round attributed not to his own conduct but to the fact "not merely that I have ventured to assail Mr. Freeman's sacrosanct authority, but that I have been successful."[81] In this determination, Round was surely correct.

Given the demeanor Round displayed and the short scholarly pieces in which he specialized, it was surprising that Round also sought public acclaim as well as academic acceptance. In a letter in 1910, Round made this point specifically: "Our chief differences are (1) that you write avowedly for scholars, while I keep always in view the intelligent 'general public'; and make the broad, effective points that will tell on *them*. (2) that you are apt to make general assertions while I—by instinct, not design—prove my way step by step."[82] In retrospect, Round demonstrated an uncharacteristic capacity for self-deception. With such an emphasis on the detailed analysis of obscure medieval charters and pipe rolls, his appeal to the public stood little chance of success. Round's desire to reach a public audience and his patent inability to do so made an interesting sidebar to the role of constitutional history in public discourse. History of every sort came increasingly to fall within the purview of the academy, where appropriate standards applied and historians wrote monographs mostly for other historians.[83] The role of public intellectual, to which Round aspired, fell by default to "amateur" historians. His work illustrated in several ways the transition of constitutional history as a research field from broad survey to narrow documentary text.

Constitutional history served as a battleground for contemporary political debate with respect to many issues. Several of the most dramatic disputes from the 1880s to 1914 had, ultimately, a constitutional dimension. Home rule for Ireland possessed sinister implications for the traditional doctrine of parliamentary sovereignty as a cornerstone of the constitution; whatever political implications the issue had, many believed that constitutional concerns loomed large in the debate.[84] Goldwin Smith wrote in 1888 that "this sort of lamentation helps make the case for Constitutional history in that the past is a utopia against which the perils of the present may be contrasted. It goes to the political uses that constitutional history supplied."[85] Women's suffrage involved constitutional reform, and opponents used the agitation on its behalf as an argument to refuse the vote:

Never was there a time when a novel experiment in constitution making could be tried at greater risk to the country, and further it was absolutely necessary that both Englishwomen & Englishmen should be taught that a change in the constitution cannot be obtained by methods of illegal violence. The strange thing about many women who deserve the highest respect both morally and intellectually, was their incapacity to perceive that the existence of peace & progress really depends upon the permanent determination of a country to enforce respect for the law.[86]

Specific constitutional events such as the Taff Vale decision and the Osborne judgment caused major political repercussions. Finally, the argument between capitalism and socialism often invoked legal definitions of property and proposed modifications of traditional private property rights. In all these conflicts, knowledge of constitutional history offered one measure by which to evaluate the complexities of these problems.

For those historians who wished to qualify as public intellectuals, a choice between academic legitimacy and a wide audience frequently seemed difficult. Often this decision came down to a belief in historical writing as the discovery of new knowledge or as a mental discipline to promote good citizenship. These categories were never mutually exclusive, but each side often treated the other warily. Stereotypes of the turgid monograph versus the oversimplification of popular history created an uneasy relationship within the historical community. As A. F. Pollard, founder of the Institute of Historical Research at the Uni-

versity of London in 1921, once wrote: "Writing books is slow work if they are
to be done well and not merely works of fiction."[87] The negative implication
about popular history was no doubt unfair, but it illustrated the suspicions that
over time became more transparent. In this respect, mammon played its part as
well, for academic books rarely, if ever, sold close to the numbers sold by colleagues who wrote for the general public. In 1929, for example, in a discussion
of Lewis Namier's (1888–1960) just published *Structure of Politics,* Philip Kerr
(1882–1940), then secretary to the Rhodes trustees who had supported Namier
financially, wrote: "'The Structure of Politics' has had a most resounding success. Few historical works of this nature have received such good press notices
but of course it is not the kind of book which will produce revenue as it is
of interest only to historians and scholars."[88] Or was it a matter of style? Did
the uneasy alliance of accuracy and literary skill come undone in the jargon
of academic history? J. H. Plumb (1911–2001) provided an anecdote about this
potential rivalry in writing how Lucy Sutherland (1903–80) vetoed C. V. Wedgwood's (1910–97) candidacy for the British Academy "on the grounds that she
wrote so well that it brought a kind of superficiality to her work."[89] The issues
that had emerged in the 1870s apparently were no closer to resolution.[90] In this
muddled atmosphere of amateur versus professional, constitutional history
rendered several examples of individuals who attempted to resolve in part the
issues raised by Round.

W. E. H. Lecky, for example, whose studies of English history in the eighteenth century, and Irish history in particular, earned him a formidable reputation, remained more the historian than public figure, although he did sit in
the House of Commons from 1895 to 1902. As early as 1892, Lecky published
his straightforward *The Political Value of History.* Lecky used the language and
emphases of constitutional history to make his argument. English constitutional history as a usable past served well in stressing political exceptionalism:
"There is probably no better test of the political genius of a nation than the
power which it possesses of adopting old institutions to new wants; and it is,
I think in this skill and in this disposition that the political pre-eminence of
the English people has been most conspicuously shown."[91] Institutional continuity provided an essential organic unity that only history could clarify. Such
Stubbsian pronouncements were crucial for Lecky, a prominent Unionist, in his
political arguments against Home Rule. The study of history "greatly expands
our horizon and enlarges our experience."[92] Lecky also served as a resource for
nonhistorians who desired to obtain historical information on the debate over
home rule.[93] On the issue of history as literature, by the end of his career, Lecky
had decided: "But in general the depreciation of the literary element in history

seems to me essentially wrong. . . . It is always the temptation of those who are dealing with manuscript materials to overrate the small personal details which they bring to light, and to give them much more than their due space in their narrative."[94] Lecky's modern biographer has confirmed this attitude: "Lecky regarded manuscript material and documents as of far less significance than the artistic creation in historical composition."[95] On these issues Lecky remained very much the Victorian scholar who operated outside academic boundaries.

For the spousal team of John (1872–1949) and Barbara (1873–1960) Hammond, the outcome to these issues differed dramatically in that they earned greater fame as public intellectuals than the esteem they held within the academy. Their work has survived more for its moral intensity than its interpretive framework because the Hammonds placed themselves outside academic culture: "An historian, Lawrence once remarked to a younger colleague, requires an intellectual and moral base outside the prevalent assumptions of his day and his special sphere of work."[96] Yet the Hammonds were among the first scholars to use Home Office documents in their many works on the working class during the Industrial Revolution. They designed their histories to inspire political reflection and perhaps to influence policy. History was crucial, they believed, because it "was a schooling in citizenship," and it was needed "to encourage a sense of civic responsibility in all intelligent readers."[97] The Hammonds also prized literary flair in the hope of creating a wide readership. Their work drew praise for "literary power" in the presentation of their ideas.[98] The Hammonds functioned as public intellectuals, yet their utilization of moral outrage had a political impact that placed them in the tradition of earlier constitutional historians.

Perhaps the single most symbolic historian for these issues was George Macaulay Trevelyan, who left an academic career for twenty-four years (1903–27) only to return as Regius professor at Cambridge and yet retained his position as a popular historian throughout the first half of the twentieth century. His hiatus from university life gave Trevelyan the opportunity to embark "on a crusade to bring history back fully into the public eye."[99] In order to accomplish this goal, history had to pursue a "didactic public function."[100] History had ceased to be part of national literature, and the influence of history had greatly diminished. In reaction against the search for scientific laws of historical explanation, Trevelyan thought this enterprise utopian. He once wrote to Oxford historian H. A. L. Fisher that he was the "rising hope of the small but stern and unbending school of idealists who think that history is both a science and an art."[101] This discipline staked its claims on the ability to educate the general public and teach the values of good citizenship.[102] Studies of smaller and smaller topics written for the few betrayed what history stood for in the Victorian period.

In addition, Trevelyan in 1913 argued that literary excellence was fundamental to the writing of history and that the principal craft necessary for success was the art of narrative: "Until quite recent times . . . historical writing was not merely the mutual conversation of scholars with one another, but was the means of spreading far and wide throughout all the reading classes a love and knowledge of history, an elevated and critical patriotism and certain qualities of mind and heart."[103] The decline in literary elements boded evil for the scope of history, for "a history book is treated as an historical monograph, and consigned to 'historical students' unless it violently proclaims that it regards itself also as literature and appeals to the general public."[104] Within this general public Trevelyan wished to attract readers from the intelligent laity, among whom the values of English history would best be appreciated. "The literary coherence of the Victorian was an invitation to belief," Rosemary Jann has written, "a pact between the writer, the reader, and the past."[105] This relationship Trevelyan sealed by reference to the English people as being "of history's royal blood . . . with the greatest record of ordered progress in the world," a statement of exceptionalism expressly within the Great Tradition.[106] The concern for literary excellence and the goal of a wide audience always remained with Trevelyan. Even Herbert Butterfield in the twilight of his career reflected on his "misfortune to have neglected at a late-ish stage of my life" the literary side of history.[107] The conjunction of Trevelyan with Butterfield unites two major figures in the most famous expression of a usable past in English history: the Whig interpretation of history.

Few if any phrases in modern English historiography have gained more fame than the Whig interpretation of history. Butterfield, in 1931 a young and relatively unknown scholar, earned a substantial reputation, if not notoriety, by publishing a slim, denunciatory volume of that title. Critics ever since have noted that Butterfield never attempted a philosophical analysis of historical theory, that he mentioned few Whigs, and that his ostensible target, Acton, was a Catholic and a Tory. Most of the book actually dealt more with problems of continental history than with English history. In retrospect, *The Whig Interpretation* struck such a responsive chord because it focused on a well-established tradition of historical writing, and the book functioned as a vehicle to reassess the validity of conclusions that had served both the general public and the history profession so well for so long. The attention generated was remarkable for a book "really perilously thin—truly an essay, lacking in substance, and in particular lacking in history."[108] In the era after World War I, it was perhaps inevitable that what some recognized as eternal historical verities should face new challenges.

Ironically, at the end of the 1930s, Butterfield prepared a series of lectures (published in 1944 as *The Englishman and His History*) so unabashedly patriotic that the book seemed to repeat many of the defects he had attributed to Whig history.[109] In 1931, however, Trevelyan believed that Butterfield had aimed the polemical *Whig Interpretation* at him on the ground that he was the only Whig historian still living. Butterfield maintained for the rest of his life that his intended target had been Acton.[110] For all his later denials, Butterfield may well have targeted both historians:

My youthful devotion to the ideals of *Clio* mattered more to me than Whiggism or Anti-Whiggism, and I remember feeling a shock when T. told P. C. Vellacott that the *Whig Interpretation* must have been directed against him, since he was the only Whig historian left. I believe I wrote that piece because I had jumped to the idea that "historical revisions" of Whig History—so that it was a particular type of general historical error (rather than Whiggism as such) which caused a lot of history to seem loaded on the side of the Whigs. Your paper makes me wonder whether Trevelyan was in my mind somewhat below the level of consciousness—but Acton (whom I mentioned, and to whom I was always particularly devoted) was certainly much more in my conscious mind.[111]

Regardless of Butterfield's real prey, the book immortalized the phrase to the point that it became part of the special lexicon with respect to English history. It became an analytical shorthand used as peremptory dismissal. By the end of the twentieth century, most historians of England (and Great Britain) agreed that Whig history, in the spirit of *1066 and All That*, was and is a Bad Thing. Too often the Whig interpretation was regarded as a single entity,[112] when in fact the phrase gave rise to multiple meanings.

Examination of commentaries on Whig history makes plain that historians have specified different eras, discussed various issues, and clearly had multiple meanings in mind when they attacked the Whig interpretation. Victor Feske made this point well when he alluded to the "confusion" among historians and described some of the variable senses in which critics had defined Whig history.[113] Butterfield had defined what he intended to criticize in clear language: "What is discussed is the tendency in many historians to write on the side of Protestants and Whigs, to praise revolutions provided they have been successful, to emphasize certain principles of progress in the past and to produce a story which is the ratification if not the glorification of the present."[114] Yet, as a recent Butterfield scholar has noted, "the more we read the more we realize that Butterfield is actually attracted to the very people he attacks."[115] Since 1931, a di-

alectic of accusation and rebuttal has served only to show that the Whig interpretation of history has remained a problematic phrase for the understanding
of English (British) history and one that ought ultimately to disappear because
its variable shades of meaning preclude significant agreement. Yet the Whig
interpretation remains worth revisiting precisely because it has continued to
symbolize fundamental questions relating to English constitutional history.

The various uses of Whig history are exemplified by the numerous ways
in which historians have defined the phrase, which will be classified into ten,
sometimes conflicting and sometimes overlapping, categories. In the first instance, a point that Butterfield emphasized, was the Whig predilection for turning the past into a human or even cosmic drama in which moral judgments
prevailed as the final arbiter of evidentiary selection and interpretation. Butterfield wrote: "It is the result of the practice of abstracting things from their
historical context and judging them apart from their context."[116] This argument was the more ironic because few historians in the twentieth century held
as steadfastly as did Butterfield to the existence of providential intervention
as the foundation of history.[117] Morality infused the approbation and censure
bestowed on both individuals and nations in equal measure, for Whig historians employed moral language to trace the lessons of the past (that they clearly
thought existed). History too often became reduced to a linear narrative in
which the good guys contested the bad guys in an unending struggle for right
and justice. Whig historians were too eager to parcel out praise and blame,
"distracted by teleology, anachronism, and present-mindedness."[118] Human affairs proved impervious to such neat moralizing, even if any agreement should
emerge about what value system should serve as criterion.

Second, Whig historians read the present back into the past: "the study of
the past with direct and perpetual reference to the present."[119] In the process,
Whig historians committed that most notorious historical sin: anachronism.
Political teleology occurred most often in chronicling the history of parliament,
where the temptation to describe the House of Commons at any historical moment in terms of later developments proved irresistible. Past events derived
their importance from the extent to which they contributed to the present. In
this view, institutions, especially the constitutional kind, that survived were inherently more significant than those that had disappeared. Historical research
became a scavenger hunt for examples that appeared persuasive in explaining
how the past became the present. Too often the past resembled a rummage sale
from which the Whig historian selected only the evidence that supported pre-
conceived ideas. In fairness, however, Whig historians were not the only ones to
adopt the ideal of a usable past in their approach to history.

The third way that Whig history operated in practice reflected the assumption that the story of constitutional liberty took pride of place among the subdivisions of historical inquiry. By the 1870s, as we have argued, constitutional history had taken over as the national narrative. When the story of individual liberty in England compared favorably to its fate in other countries, tracing this development from start to finish, from medieval to modern, became necessary. The prominence of the unwritten constitution within English history exhibited its role as the carrier of English political genius. The centuries of unbroken history conferred an additional dimension to ordinary patriotism. Constitutional history added a special value to mundane accounts of the national past.

The stress upon constitutional maturity led to the next feature of Whig history: the continuity of English history in general, and its legacy of legal traditions and constitutional precedents in particular. In addition to the description given by John Clive in the previous chapter, Linda Colley has produced another elegant account of this aspect of Whig history:

The Whig interpretation was never as monolithic or as crude as its critics suggested, but its broad characteristics are clear enough. As disseminated by E. A. Freeman, Henry Hallam, W. E. H. Lecky, Thomas Babington Macaulay and his nephew, George Otto Trevelyan (to cite only the better-known exponents), it was both present-minded and intensely nationalistic, concerned to celebrate Victorian constitutionalism by stressing those episodes of England's past in which freedom seemed to triumph over oppression and injustice. This might involve chronicling the supposed extent of Anglo-Saxon democracy before the Norman Conquest or the barons' efforts to wrest Magna Carta from King John. But many Whig historians preferred to start their story in the early modern period, showing how Parliament had resisted the more extortionate demands of Tudor and Stuart sovereigns, how it had brought Charles I to heel and to the scaffold, and how in 1688 James II's schemes to establish papist and arbitrary rule had splintered in the face of the Glorious Revolution. On this Whig victory was founded religious toleration, Cabinet government, the two-party system and constitutional monarchy: in short, all the blessings that distinguished England from absolutist Europe. But every Eden has its serpent, and England's was King George III. When he came to the throne in 1760, he tried to reassert royal authority as the Stuarts had done. The American colonies were driven into rebellion and into secession from the Empire. In England itself, it was not until the Reform Act of 1832—naturally a piece of Whig legislation—that liberty and sound government were once again secure.[120]

In the end, the idea that continuity represented such a dominant feature of constitutional history proved illusory: "The major drawbacks to this view lay in its tendency to fashion precedents where there were only superficial resemblances and to attribute causality where only sequence existed."[121] In light of such sentiments, it is difficult to distinguish whether insular pride fueled the Whig interpretation, or whether the historical record supplied the basis for national chauvinism, or perhaps a little bit of both. Such discrete categories mislead to some extent because each had a reciprocal influence on the others; continuity certainly represented a unique element of constitutional history.

Next among Whig characteristics was the emphasis on consensus that sealed historical continuity. Revolutions were usually anathema to Whig history because they negated the seamless pageant so essential to constitutional history, as in the case of 1641.[122] These convulsions were turned into relatively minor disruptions within the unfolding drama of constitutional liberty versus Stuart despotism. The interregnum from 1649 to 1660, after the execution of Charles I and the abolition of the House of Lords, two-thirds of the historic triumvirate of King, Lords, and Commons, marked the exception that proved the rule of continuity. The rapidity with which the nation returned to traditional institutions reinforced the importance of continuity. In similar fashion the Glorious Revolution of 1688 was the more glorious, and indeed the more English, precisely because it preserved Protestant liberties with such a minimum of disruption and bloodshed; as G. M. Trevelyan wrote in classic manner:

> The conduct of Whigs and Tories between 1678 and 1685 is so mad and bad that it is a psychological puzzle to recognize any of the better elements usually found in the English political character—humanity, decency or common sense. Whigs and Tories act like the nervous and hot-blooded factions of a South European race. They rant, scream, bully, assassinate men by forms of law, study no interest but their own, and betray even their own interest through sheer folly and passion. Yet, a few years later, these same men took part in making and observing the Revolution Settlement, the most English thing that was ever done—if, indeed, it is English to take stand on good sense, compromise and toleration.[123]

Consensus blunted the sharp edge of Marxist analysis as well, for cooperation, not conflict, best depicted the centuries when squires played games with their tenants, unlike the continental countries where class tensions proved so divisive.[124] The absence of sustained social conflict added another aspect of continuity to the island story.

To distinguish English history from that of European countries offered the opportunity to focus on English exceptionalism, the sixth trait of Whig history. Although this description might apply to any era, its impact began with England's deliverance from the Spanish Armada, which in turn gave way to England's destiny as the New Jerusalem, God's elect nation. England might not have become the Puritan New Jerusalem, but it was enough to have become Shakespeare's "Scept'red Isle." Constitutional ontogeny had helped England attain its global eminence, a fitting testament to its unique constitutional arrangements. Whig historians "took English exceptionalism for granted: it existed, it was good, and it was the historian's task to explain it and to applaud it."[125] Whig history celebrated English triumphalism despite the ambivalence that occasionally colored its expression, particularly with respect to placing it in a broader British context.

In the next instance, Whig historians took an unhesitating Protestant perspective, discovering in the Anglican church those virtues of moderation and toleration that embodied English history as a whole. Roman Catholicism, with its international authoritarian structure, played the perfect foil for a national church. Spain (and by implication Catholicism) personified the villain for England in the sixteenth and early seventeenth centuries, while Catholic France eventually superseded the Spanish as national enemy. Even the Puritan revolution could not long deflect the supremacy of the established church. After 1688, the de facto toleration extended to Dissenters demonstrated anew the quintessential virtues of religious liberty. Nonconformists remained suspect because of their dreadful enthusiasms that undercut Anglican national values. In the national narrative, therefore, the chronicle of English liberty meant not only the struggle against the crown for constitutional rights, but also the long battle against papal tyranny that ended only with deliverance in the Reformation. God indeed was a Protestant.

Next came the political agenda(s) within Whig historiography that encompassed several conventions. Whig history justified the past and confirmed the present, but its lessons might apply equally. Individuals of every political persuasion could find solace in its teachings or attempt to hijack its dogmas in support of particular causes. Whig history offered a forum from which a usable past might be constructed; in this sense John Burrow wrote of the Whigs' "political annexation of the past."[126] Selective memory presented a convenient medium through which to interpret the past. Political programs were encoded in phrases like the Norman Yoke for radicalism and the cult of local institutions for the Toryism that opposed government centralization.[127] Whig historians, however, distrusted radical ideologies of either the right or the left because they treasured political consensus.

Reliance on the proven principles of orderly political change ensured progress, the penultimate trait of the Whig interpretation. Progress extended to political, social, and economic endeavors in an optimism that resembled religious faith. Here Whig historians "married belief in continuity with faith in progress . . . change occurring within the confines of tradition, and hence controllable; tradition made malleable by change, and hence progressive."[128] Whig history offered a blueprint for permanent national improvement: "Ideas of progress and the Burkean conception of tradition, however, are the warp and woof of all those nineteenth-century interpretations of English history which, in contrast to the lamentations, whether Tory Radical or simply radical, for a forfeited or corrupted social and constitutional idyll located somewhere in the Saxon or medieval past, may safely or loosely be described as Whig interpretations."[129] The Whig historians succeeded in making their vision of the past triumphant over rival views in order to reflect national confidence.

Finally, the tenth distinct sense in which the Whig interpretation has received definition is in terms of its style, not its content. It emphasized high standards of literary craftsmanship in order to reach the general public. Most Whig historians presented their arguments in brilliant fashion, for history was as much an aesthetic experience as a research mission. Brilliant style sometimes supplanted analysis, because for Whig historians the expository narrative mattered more than the sustained evaluation of evidence. A good story counted most of all: "The 'literary' historians had assumed that history's purpose was to make the world morally and intellectually intelligible to a wide audience."[130] The Whig canon, with several notable exceptions, aimed at the educated public, not professional colleagues. In the first half of the twentieth century, debates about the preferred audience permeated historical conversations; in 1946, for example, "C. V. Wedgwood launched a blistering attack on those historians who turned away from their audience towards their archives, and thus forgot their main purpose, which was to educate and edify the public ... most history, and most historians, had cut themselves off completely from the general national culture which they existed to enhance."[131] No other school of historical interpretation has replicated the cultural hegemony won by the Whig historians in the nineteenth century.

When all these varied elements of the Whig interpretation are taken into consideration, however, two fundamental questions have remained: who, exactly, were the Whig historians, and is it still useful to use the term anymore? Part of the problem in answering these questions lies in the fact that few historians have sought the designation except for someone such as George Macaulay Trevelyan: "The phrase 'Whig history' has long been used as a term of historiographical criticism, in such a way as to imply, firstly, that everyone knows what it means, and secondly, that nobody wants to be 'whiggish.'"[132] One might nominate the Venerable Bede, because of his assertion of purposeful evolution in English history in the seventh and eighth centuries. Should the term begin with John Selden, that noted scholar of parliamentary history, whose research uncovered significant precedents useful to the House of Commons in the seventeenth century? Henry Hallam might qualify, because although his *Constitutional History* in 1827 started only at the end of the medieval period, it began with the following assumption: "The government of England, in all times recorded by history, has been one of those mixed or limited monarchies which the Celtic or Gothic tribes appear universally to have established, in preference to the coarse despotism of eastern nations, to the more artificial tyranny of Rome and Constantinople, or to the various models of republican polity which were tried upon the coasts of the Mediterranean Sea."[133] Hallam neatly sidestepped the task of proving what he had assumed about English constitutional history since 600.

In more recent times, the term *Whig* described the extended Macaulay family; Thomas Babington Macaulay, who was born in 1800; George Otto Trevelyan; and George Macaulay Trevelyan, who died in 1962. The problem here is that Joseph Hamburger has argued that Macaulay attacked the "attitude which assumed that what was established in the past should be a model for the present."[134] This conclusion suggested that not even Macaulay fit neatly into the Whig paradigm. George Otto Trevelyan's scholarship dealt with imperial history rather domestic matters, which, according to the particular intellectual perspective chosen, made him either an innovator in Whiggish imperial history or an outsider to the Whig tradition. With respect to George Macaulay Trevelyan, his biographer has made the point that by 1931, the year of Butterfield's attack on the Whig interpretation, "There was little in Butterfield's critique which could be applied to the eirenic, conservative, national historian which Trevelyan had become."[135] Not even the usual suspects fit the Whig profile.

Even Acton, the primary target of Butterfield in 1931, did not qualify. In a brilliant exegesis of Acton's work, Hugh Tulloch has demonstrated how the Regius professor was a far different historian than Butterfield portrayed. In the first place, Acton had little interest in or respect for the work of Stubbs (a Tory) and Freeman (a Liberal): "Its [the Whig interpretation's] stress on tangible institutions and edicts, what Acton called 'ethical materialism' and 'organic constitutionalism,' exerted a stultifying, deadening pull on historical writing."[136] In answer to Butterfield's accusation that Acton was an arch-Whig, Tulloch wrote: "Not only is this not so, it is possible to go further and assert categorically that Acton's entire historical canon is nothing less than a sustained assault of every variety of whig present-mindedness." Finally, Tulloch concluded: "The authority accorded to Butterfield's misunderstandings is curious, for even a cursory reading of Acton would help to dispel many persistent myths surrounding him." With the disqualification of Acton, we are left with a variety of definitions for Whig history but apparently no Whig historians.

Given the multiple meanings that have attached to Whig history, so that precise meaning and context have become impossible, has the phrase outlived its usefulness? Whig history has become a scholarly cadaver, a Frankenstein created by sewing together bits and pieces from defunct traditions of historical writing. The Whig monster still raises such fears that it has remained a favorite target for the historical mobs to pursue. In this case, the cliché holds true that if Whig historians had not existed, other historians would (and perhaps did) invent them. So sweeping has the term become, its initial incisiveness has long since disappeared. The assumed symmetry has deceived rather than explained English historiography. The adjective *Whig* has made its way into fields far removed from English history, notably American history, the history of science, and literary studies.[137] Such expansion has robbed the word *Whig* of any specific contemporary meaning.

The emphasis on constitutional history defined Whig history, and by extension national identity, as much as or more than any other single category. When restricted to this use, the concept of Whig history may still retain relevance for later historians. In the nineteenth century, constitutional history represented the most popular usable past, one that appealed to academic as well as public historians. The erosion of its hegemony as a research and as a taught tradition depended on numerous factors, but Round's role should not be discounted. His style of scholarship helped end the grand constitutional narrative, and it remains difficult to imagine that the general public cared about the narrow scholarly issues that obsessed Round. His pugnacity alienated academics who preferred a more genteel discourse about the past. In the end the national narrative found other forms of expression, and constitutional history suffered as a consequence. The widening chasm between academic and popular historians abetted the retreat from constitutional history. Whig history declined in tandem with the loss of prestige suffered by constitutional history, strengthening the equation of the two. It was perhaps not what the man from Brighton wished, but the field never truly recovered from his frequent contributions.

CHAPTER FIVE

"Our Law Is, in Fact, the Sum and Substance of What We Have to Teach in India; It Is the 'Gospel of the English'"

Constitutional History and the British Empire

This chapter does not deal with the constitutional history *of* the British Empire; rather, it attempts to explain the different ways that English constitutional history contributed to imperial purposes and, conversely, how imperial motives helped dramatize the significance of the constitutional past. After 1870, expansion in Africa and Asia resulted, famously, in British domination of roughly a fifth of the world's land area and a quarter of its people: 13 million square miles and 500 million inhabitants. The imperial mission was epic in scale, and how to govern this global edifice posed a fearsome challenge: "How was a civilized nation, one emphatically committed to the principle of the rule of law over men, to govern a burgeoning empire of dark-skinned and often violently recalcitrant subjects?"[1] The language of imperial goals stressed how nuanced this relationship was, for it was always the *British* Empire and *English* constitutional history in common parlance. Constitutional history traces one path among many to approach imperial history, because the topic addressed the changing fortunes of the empire itself. The majesty of this endeavor was summarized in 1929: "Thus we have traced constitutional development from the days when the only practical constitutional power rested in the folk-moots of parts of a remote little Island, to the time when that Island is the centre of the Constitution of a world-wide Empire."[2] The disappearance of the empire in the course of the twentieth century made the case for the study of English constitutional history less compelling. The constitutional model grounded in English history declined in direct proportion to the end of imperial rule.

The fate of English constitutional history in terms of its prestige as both a research and a taught tradition was linked also to the changes that have affected imperial historiography. The first among these conventions involved the tendency to describe the British Empire as a separate institution whose history had little to do with the mother country, acquired in a fit of absent-mindedness; in this interpretation, imperial events were almost mutually exclusive to those of domestic history.[3] The empire had expanded throughout the nineteenth century, and then suitable justifications had to explain this phenomenon, for power without moral purpose offended Victorian sensibilities. Imperial history meant one thing, and the internal history of the United Kingdom was another, and never the twain should meet. Next, there existed a focus on the empire whose influence worked reciprocally within Great Britain itself, when the imperial persona became a crucial element in how the British defined themselves. Even in this view, however, affairs in the metropole were intrinsically more important than those in the periphery. In yet another tradition, imperial history emphasized the areas of white settlement, where the replication of English constitutional development asserted its importance in new circumstances and under new conditions. More recently, historians have recognized the colonized as a crucial aspect of the imperial experience, for empire was never just about the British. Orientalism now serves as the symbol of the modern transformation in interpretations of the empire. The subtle shades of imperial relationships, including class, race, gender, and culture, have revived the study of imperial history in place of the empire as a "series of discrete components."[4] Integration of imperial history based on new tools of analysis has made the topic academically attractive once again.

The first category of historical interpretation stressed, in its constitutional manifestations, the formal elements of constitutional arrangements, with little or no room to examine the realities that hid behind these government structures. All too often imperial growth was justified as a series of constitutional changes, with special prominence accorded the crown as symbol of those alterations.[5] An excellent example of this consideration of the imperial past and present may be found in the extensive correspondence between A. V. Dicey and Arthur Berriedale Keith (1879–1944) from 1905 to 1919.[6] Dicey was in 1905 the aging Vinerian professor of English law at Oxford, while the much younger Keith served in the Colonial Office from 1901 to 1914. Their friendship emphasized the tendency to interpret the empire from an administrative and constitutional perspective.[7] The two scholars exchanged opinions about the variety of constitutional configurations that made up the empire, replete with the formalism of legal discussion, case and statute citations. Amid the sophisticated analyses of relationships within the empire, both settled and conquered, there lacked any hint that it impacted the lives of millions at home and abroad. The empire offered frequent opportunities for constitutional abstraction in a fashion that domestic realities did not allow. The constitutional superiority that flowed from its English past provided one part of the faith in empire that resembled the enthusiasm usually ascribed to religion. The empire offered ample occasions for rumination about the validity of Indian marriages at common law or the jurisdiction of the Supreme Court of Canada.[8] In the end, however, musings about technical elements of constitutional formalities rarely revealed the dynamics of daily life: "Its history was for the most part concerned with law, governance, and constitutional evolution."[9] In this school of imperial interpretation, constitutional precedents seemed most important, the tip of the imperial iceberg that hid many less attractive truths.

The "official mind" imperial analysis typified by making the Colonial Office or India Office the center of historical importance illustrated best the separation of empire from nation. As early as the work of John Robert Seeley in the 1880s, empire was regarded as an extension of the English nation state, but the habit of segregating imperial and domestic goals persisted. Only with the broader conception of British history a century later has the primacy of English history in isolation helped introduce new ways of looking at old subjects.[10] In imperial affairs the historian learned all that was essential among the domestic political elites. Empire represented a larger community united with, yet separate from, Great Britain; as James Anthony Froude wrote: "All of us are united at present by the invisible bonds of relationship and of affection for our common country, for our common sovereign, and for our joint spiritual inheritance."[11] If the historian moved away from the home islands, it was still the Briton on the spot who made the important decisions that affected millions. The overseas empire occupied a space removed from the homeland that might be remembered or forgotten as imperial circumstances dictated.[12] Even David Cannadine complained "that the history of the British Empire is still all too often written as if it were completely separate and distinct from the history of the British nation."[13] Ex parte histories of the empire have fallen from favor, but until the 1970s at least they formed the core of imperial historiography.

Over the past several decades scholarly trends have moved toward recognition of how integral the imperial experience became to the formation of modern national identity in Britain. The English nation was global in perspective and had created a much-admired brand of constitutional government. The imperial impulse had originated with the internal empire that encompassed Ireland, Scotland, and Wales; it then spread abroad over centuries to create the empire at its zenith in late Victorian Britain.[14] The evidence for this evolution has emerged from a wide variety of materials—literary, historical, and artistic—that continually represented how central empire was to self-image. To cite just one example from a vast body of excellent work, Kathleen Wilson has described how the English as a distinctive "island race" became important to national identity and legitimized the vision of a "particularly English genius and mission."[15] A self-belief in an altruistic moral capacity permitted the empire to appear as an important component in the progress of civilization. As Catherine Hall has argued: "The British nation was defined by its imperial task: it was this which raised the British above other nations. The empire was itself a sign of the conquering and colonizing genius of the Anglo-Saxon race."[16] Imperial expansion could not have occurred without the integrating symbols of English constitutional history and liberty.

Whether the United States could undertake such a task was debatable: "Their constitution and their traditions and their present political habits seem to unfit them for pursuing with success a great oceanic policy, perhaps from governing well distant territories inhabited by inferior subject races."[17] Sir Frederick Pollock added about the American conquest of the Philippines: "If anybody thinks these islands a particularly desirable possession for the United States, he must be pretty sanguine, but I don't see how you can safely or honorably get rid of them."[18] Few forecast how well the United States would succeed to global dominion in the latter half of the twentieth century. The reciprocity of imperial influences eclipsed the previous arguments that these effects only emanated outward from Britain. The acquisition of empire inaugurated the pride that Britain had produced a governing race capable of such dominion, as well as possessing the moral capacity to rule justly.

Where the early chroniclers of empire privileged the public sphere in which constitutional relationships loomed large, later scholars have emphasized the private sphere of women, missionaries, traders, and travelers. The rediscovery of imperial attachments on the part of many Victorians has shattered the argument of relative indifference to imperial concerns. James Fitzjames Stephen (1829–94), noted jurist and legal member of the Viceroy's Council in India from 1869 to 1872, "hailed the British empire as an outstanding moral and political feat."[19] Whether perceived as an abstract entity or an immediate reality, after 1870 the empire became an essential element of the manner in which Victorians fashioned themselves: "The very notion of a fixed English identity was doubtless a product of, and reaction to, the rapid change and transformation of both metropolitan and colonial societies which meant that, as with nationalism, such identities needed to be constructed to counter schisms, friction and dissent."[20] The recent trend of imperial scholarship has revolutionized conclusions about national identity and its connection to the empire: "What these critics (and countless others) have provoked is not a turn toward empire so much as *a critical return* to the connections between metropole and colony, race and nation, which imperial apologists and dissenters have appreciated at least since the nineteenth century, if not before."[21] Inclusion of previously marginalized groups has transformed the study of the British Empire away from its formal aspects to a dynamic analysis of its great variety, especially the violence and exploitation central to the colonial engagement.

Another facet to the identification of imperialism with national identity concerned the social nature of this attachment. However elite control of imperial policy may have been, after 1870 the allegiance of all segments of society to an imperial agenda became clear, symbolized by the creation of Queen Victoria (1819–1901) as empress of India in 1876. An educational system reformed in 1870 embraced the empire without hesitation, stressing "the grandeur of British dominions and the ideal of empire."[22] In the early twentieth century, the advent of Empire Day on May 24 celebrated British expansion amid pageantry and songs for schoolchildren and their parents at home and abroad.[23] One important element of popular culture that identified with the empire was the British civilizing mission. Few doubted that the British had become the greatest governing race in human history. Rudyard Kipling's (1865–1936) reference in *Recessional* (1897) to "lesser breeds without the law" may have originated in anxiety rather than triumphalism, but the allusion to Britain's constitutional exceptionalism struck a responsive chord.

The link between constitutional ideas and imperialism in popular culture perhaps was best expressed in Arthur Benson's (1862–1925) words to Edward Elgar's (1857–1934) *Pomp and Circumstance March #1* (1901), *Land of Hope and Glory*. Now the unofficial national anthem, at least for England, and favorite at the Proms, by 1914 the lyrics "had sufficiently permeated the national consciousness for crowds outside Buckingham Palace to join in spontaneously when a military band struck up."[24] The first stanza opened with these lines:

> Land of Hope and Glory
> Mother of the Free
> How shall we extol thee
> Who are born of thee?
> Wider still and wider
> Shall Thy bounds be set
> God who made Thee mighty
> Make Thee mightier yet

These words artfully combined the constitutional glory of the freeborn Englishman with the imperial concerns of British power and territory. We argue only that this constitutional dimension had a place in the imperial ideology that prevailed after 1870. Elgar certainly had his reservations about some of the vulgarity associated with popular imperialism, but some of his music both underpinned and drew from the general imperial mystique.[25] In the end, therefore, the self-fashioning of national identity in an imperial idiom invariably contained constitutional references.

The third general approach to imperial history focused on the areas of white settlement, because these colonies replicated the British experience, especially the model of English constitutional precedents. Imperial history in this vein stressed a Whiggish continuity of its own, whereby countries such as Canada followed a linear path of constitutional progress that ended with the attainment of responsible government and parliamentary democracy. Over time, the claims of national history diminished the importance of the imperial connection, and as generations passed, the United Kingdom ceased to represent home. The British diaspora fell victim to changing fashions of historiographical interest. Philip Buckner asked: "Whatever Happened to the British Empire?"[26] One response might be that the end of empire demanded new methods of inquiry and new questions elicited new answers.

Another explanation, supplied by Buckner, was that "as the Empire receded into history, so did the interest of imperial historians in the British colonies of settlement."[27] For historians the overseas British declined in importance as the issue of domestic British identity attracted greater attention. The ties of blood attenuated as memories of the mother country receded. Remaining British became the more difficult when colonial inhabitants increasingly took on a national identity of their own.[28] When dominion status gave way to national history, the typical unit of historical analysis, the nation-state dominated historical writing. The relationship between metropole and periphery lessened in importance when the settler colonies "matured" and new analytical frameworks were necessary.[29] With respect to constitutional matters specifically, the transition from English paradigms to indigenous jurisprudence also weakened the relevance of prior legal and constitutional precedents.

The most recent historiographical tradition, one that has revivified imperial history, might be termed, as some have done, The Empire Strikes Back.[30] Whether known as Orientalism, Subaltern Studies, or postcolonial discourse, the core of research has shifted to the colonized and the reciprocal cultural dynamics that characterized the colonial episode. In simplified form, imperial history happened in India and throughout the British possessions, not just within the confines of the Colonial Office. England and the empire did not exist as separate spheres but had profound reciprocal influences on each other. This trend has become the more remarkable in the face of dismay that "traditional" imperial history has lost much of its place in contemporary British education. Sophisticated multicultural analyses have altered the scope and purpose of imperial historiography forever. British and indigenous women, for example, once invisible among the administrative and constitutional preoccupations of imperial history, have gained inclusion in those groups whose voices have emerged, whether as memsahibs or objects of missionary proselytizing and sexual desire.

Similarity and difference, but especially the latter, defined the empire, no matter what hopes and intentions those in London harbored. Cannadine emphasized similarity in his argument that the empire attempted to recreate the hierarchical British social order in the colonies; Edward Said emphasized the cultural differences that defined imperial relationships. Empire always involved power connections, no matter what other ideals were invoked. Investigation into the inequality of force rather than constitutional forms has highlighted recent research: "Orientalism came to represent a construct, not a reality, an emblem of domination and a weapon of power. It lost its status as a sympathetic concept, a product of scholarly admiration for diverse and exotic cultures, and became the literary means of creating a stereotypical and mythic East through which European rule could be more readily asserted."[31] The British experience no longer predominated in the Orientalist vision of imperial history, making the older analyses even less relevant. If India was the jewel of the empire, then the interpretation of British ascendancy has taken on different contours in relation to the long centuries of Indian history: "We all live today in a 1026–1528–1992 present and not in the 1757–1885–1947 of the past."[32] Indian history in the global perspective has rested on Hindu-Muslim foundations in comparison to which the Raj now pales in significance. The irony that the British presence may well seem in the future an interlude has changed the view of Indian history as important only as long as the British occupied the country.

The nexus of English constitutional history to the preceding four traditions of imperial history varied considerably. It was fundamental to the interpretation of the empire as a formal set of legal bonds that tied together disparate global territories.[33] Constitutional history as a basic contribution to the imperial civilizing mission made the subject an excellent reference when the purity of British conduct needed restatement; as early as the 1780s, "government by law was already becoming the privileged basis for the conceptualization of the 'moral legitimacy' of British colonialism."The ideological justification for the British presence in India drew heavily on a much-vaunted tradition of ancient English liberty and lawfulness."[34] The topic also served as symbol for a governing race when the empire helped define a British national identity: the "Empire was benevolent, a gift to the natives, because in the end, the British genius for governance was taught to the imperial population."[35] To a somewhat lesser extent, constitutional history served as a model for the colonies of white settlement, although as a colonial national identity coalesced, these ties grew weaker. Finally, constitutional history has had no part in the Orientalist dissection of empire; in many ways the subject represented the shortcomings that distinguished the prior approaches. Constitutional history as a constituent part of the imperial story shared the fate of the empire itself: gone by the 1960s.

In official endorsements of imperial expansion after 1870, emphasis on the civilizing mission of Great Britain, whether railroads, religion, or the common law, played its part in the expression of British exceptionalism. Knowledge of English constitutional history imparted valuable lessons crucial to the spread of imperial blessings. In order to govern subject peoples, it was necessary to have a thorough familiarity with how the English people had governed themselves. As Prime Minister Arthur Balfour (1848–1930) noted in 1905: "Freedom and civilization have a common mission."[36] Britain was a chosen nation, and "empire, modern liberty, and benevolence were fully compatible."[37] The empire came to mean different things to distinct segments of the public and was never without critics, but as it expanded throughout the nineteenth century, it increasingly affected such issues as race and religion. In the aftermath of the Indian Mutiny of 1857, the divergence between the empire of conquest and the empire of settlement became more marked, especially in the dominion status granted to Canada in the British North America Act of 1867. The mutiny became an iconic event whereby "superior technology was read as the unmistakable sign of an essential racial superiority."[38] By 1870 the imperial enterprise had become so complex that responsible government throughout the empire remained a distant goal. The divorce between internal national history and overseas Britain no longer seemed tenable as the empire grew ever larger.[39] Duty, power, and mission required the construction of an imperial ideology that would give a moral foundation to the exercise of such vast authority. Needed for this task was an imperial history that recounted a romantic past as well as articulated a vision for the future.

Froude had made a start in this direction through his twelve volumes (1856–70) on the Tudor era, in which he located the spirit of English expansion. Not until the 1880s, however, did imperial history supplant Greater Britain. Seeley's *Expansion of England* (1883) filled this niche admirably. Three years later, Froude weighed in with his *Oceana*, a clarion call for imperial aggrandizement based on racial affinity. Seeley in a subtle fashion identified Britain with its overseas possessions to provide an interpretive framework that united nation and empire, for he paid less attention to contemporary racial theories than Froude had done in the justification of imperial purpose.[40] In the end, "the empire to which Seeley was committed provided England with a providential mission. ... he had tried to place Christ, social morality, and national destiny within a historical dynamic that propelled the present into a more spiritually satisfying future."[41] Most assertions of the imperial civilizing mission included some reference to the blessings of constitutional government that Britain would bestow through some form of political osmosis. In this manner the empire validated the national identity of a governing race with a special genius for ruling other people.

Each of the four topics (national identity, race, academic professionalization, and public policy debates) that contributed to the prominence of constitutional history also played a role in the ties that bound the subject to the empire, although not in equal measure. The acquisition of a global empire not only reinforced the image of a governing race; it also led inevitably to assertions of cultural superiority. Nowhere was this process better illustrated than in the fate of constitutional institutions abroad. In the process of the "mental miscegenation" that would make subject peoples "culturally English," the place of the common law and its constitutional accessories was central.[42] In addition to its imperial luster, the reputation of the English constitution attracted the admiration of European scholars as well: "There was an active debate as to the precise nature of British institutions and the extent to which they could be exported to other lands. Such men as Adolphe Thiers (1797–1877), François Guizot (1787–1874), Rudolf von Gneist, and Josef Redlich (1869–1936) became devoted scholars of English constitutional development because they wished to apply the lessons of English history in their own homeland."[43] In the imperial context, the common law and the Victorian constitution represented what was most characteristic of British integrity and morality; James Fitzjames Stephen wrote: "Our law is, in fact, the sum and substance of what we have to teach in India; it is the 'gospel of the English.'"[44] By the 1880s, justification for empire took a more prominent place in public discussions, and the provision of good government based on constitutional experience became more important to this argument.

Perhaps no better illustration of the links between religious faith and imperial ambition was the life and work of Lionel Curtis (1872–1955). Starting in South Africa at the time of the Boer War and for the remainder of his life, Curtis attempted to shape the development of the empire as an "internationalist who continued to idealize an older Anglo-Saxon world leadership."[45] In the face of imperial crises, Curtis was part of the Round Table movement that tried to reconstruct imperial organization in order to ensure its permanence. He never wavered in his belief that "he saw the hand of God in the British empire."[46] Such supercharged rhetoric amounted to self-deception on a grand scale. The conflict between spiritual commitment and the ordinary workings of the imperial order was never resolved; for example, Curtis's racial attitudes in 1907 represented a "conventional amalgam of prejudice, bad history, half-baked Darwinism, and spurious geography."[47] Internal imperial contradictions betrayed the highest ideals.

Imperial policy alternated between the claims of political realism and the demands of conscience symbolized by the reasoning that world power depended in the last resort on the moral rectitude of those who wielded such authority. Only a remarkably self-confident culture might construe imperial expansion as a civilizing mission.[48] Loyalty to the empire, as Lord Rosebery (1847–1929) remarked, entailed a higher form of patriotism that elite and popular culture strengthened at every social level. The unique imperial mission, including encouragement in constitutional progress for imperial peoples, satisfied the demand for moral purpose: "Empire had the power to regenerate not only the 'backward' world, but also the British themselves, to raise them from the gloom and apprehension of the later nineteenth century, and by creating a national purpose with a high moral content lead to class conciliation."[49] In writing of the British presence in India, Lord Cromer (1841–1917) specified that self-government "must manifestly constitute the corner-stone" upon which the principles of empire must depend.[50] The genius for self-government had produced in the English constitution a model of global significance. The putative capacity to govern others in their own best interest helped to give a noble tone to the fulfillment of imperial duty and simultaneously validated the nation's historical record: "In constitutional essentials England was qualified to be the tutor, not the pupil, of a more distracted world."[51] Constitutional history satisfied the realities of power and the needs of morality in supplying a primary rationale for imperial ascendancy. The result was a curious amalgam of arrogance and altruism that possessed a complexity still difficult to analyze.

The desire to justify and to flatter Britain in its imperial enterprises accounted for that curious historical effort, the comparison between the Roman Empire and the British Empire. Scholars and imperial officials considered in what ways was the earlier empire similar and how was it different from its later counterpart. Rome proved a useful foil because "the despotic example of Imperial Rome and the not more enlightening examples of subsequent imperial endeavors were bound to provoke concerned consideration among men who believed the chief virtue of the Anglo-Saxon race to be liberty."[52] Comparisons to Rome sought to answer an imperial conundrum: how to reconcile the English belief in liberty with the clear conclusion that the British Empire denied that same liberty to millions of others? The allusion to Rome served in a double fashion for imperial purposes; the Roman Empire might demonstrate the similar ruling capacity of the British Empire, yet also act as an example to show how the British succeeded where the Romans had failed. Foremost in this regard was the British retention of its moral purpose, whereas the Romans had faltered by drifting into moral decadence: "We may . . . learn . . . on the one hand to emulate the virtues that adorned [Rome's] prosperity, and on the other to shun the vices that were punished by her downfall. The sceptre which Rome relinquished, we have taken up. Great is our Honour—great our Responsibility."[53]

Perhaps the best illustration of this genre was delivered by James Bryce, who had the advantage of being both historian and jurist. In long essays he assessed the accomplishments of the two great empires. Bryce resolved the dilemma of blending power with morality by emphasizing the ideal of trusteeship in British imperial stewardship: "That the government of subject-races is to be regarded as a trust to be discharged with a sense of responsibility to God and to humanity at large has become generally accepted."[54] Both Rome and Britain aimed to bring justice in governance wherever the empires had expanded, but only Britain had refused to share that power with the conquered prematurely. Trusteeship permitted the British to reserve the realities of power while retaining the moral high ground of preparing their charges for eventual independence. This theme lasted well into the twentieth century, particularly in the work of historian Vincent Harlow (1898–1961), holder of the Beit chair in colonial history at Oxford from 1948 to 1961, who embarrassed probationers of the Colonial Service "in the final lecture of their course by bursting into tears as he spoke of their noble mission of trusteeship for the people of backward races."[55] This doctrine allowed the British, unlike the Romans, to maintain the upper echelons of governance in their own hands.

The dream of trusteeship never overcame the racial prejudices that festered within the British Empire. Racial difference made the retention of power necessary because color mattered to the British and created an atmosphere of superiority/inferiority. Bryce conceded the irrationality of such bias, but he argued that it was too ingrained to disappear: "Now to the Teutonic peoples, and especially to the English and Anglo-Americans, the difference of colour means a great deal. It creates a feeling of separation, perhaps even of a slight repulsion. Such a feeling may be deemed unreasonable or unchristian, but it seems too deeply rooted to be effaceable in any time we can foresee."[56] In the meantime, because the races within the empire existed at different levels of civilization, the laws of the conquerors must take precedence. This circumstance made Bryce acutely aware of the decline of Rome because it raised the question of whether such a fate awaited the British Empire and how might it be averted.[57] The global spread of the common law showed the vitality of the British Empire, whose sheer size made the Roman Empire puny by comparison, and the British governed a dependent population far greater than the Romans could have imagined. In moral terms, therefore, trusteeship legitimized conquest and racial discrimination, and it remained "among the permanent conventions of the British Empire."[58] The British had resolved, at least to their own satisfaction, the issue of racial difference within their own empire.

Comparison generated pride in British power because it contrasted favorably to that of Rome. Great Britain did not, and should not have, imitated its Roman predecessors in important respects such as moral standards and the severity of its dominion. Sir Charles Lucas (1853–1931), first head of the Dominions department within the Colonial Office in 1907, wrote that the Roman Empire meant the loss of freedom for its subjects whereas the British Empire, because of it "being born of freedom" and because "self-government is inherent in the British race," created liberty for all regardless of status.[59] For the British it remained the aspiration, if not the reality, that the empire ensured peace and harmony among all the subject races. His work with the self-governing dominions made Lucas careful to separate the empire into the settler countries and the dependent states, a racial distinction common to imperial discourse. The progress of the dominions toward self-government before World War I demonstrated the strength of English constitutional antecedents because these countries had shaped their own futures through imitation of common-law institutions. The success of the dominions fortified British identity as the nation blessed with the skills and experience of self-governance.

The kinship with Rome fostered optimism about the future of the empire. While the Roman Empire had ultimately disappeared, from the 1870s to the beginning of World War II it was axiomatic that a similar decline and fall could never happen. The British Empire would endure for as long as administrators purged those elements inconsistent with the common law from public life: "If the Roman example taught few lessons to the English as they tried to consolidate their empire, it did hold out the promise of historical prominence to the men and to the age responsible for that newer empire's final definition and destiny."[60] In a world replete with imperial rivals, the allusion to Rome portrayed the British as the successors to Justinian, the great codifier of Roman law. In the British instance over a much wider area the spread of the common law eclipsed the Roman achievement.

Finally, the allusion to Rome became a theme in Victorian art that in a few instances reflected the interest in the Roman Empire and the challenges of English imperial rule. Several artists focused on the Roman sense of duty to offset the sybaritic reputation that offended Victorian moral sensibilities, while others used the Roman legions in distant Britain to depict the difficulties of governing in remote lands. William Bell Scott's *Building a Roman Wall* (1856), where the construction of Hadrian's Wall continues in spite of barbarian attacks, called attention to the dangers of a beneficial role in an imperial setting. The more popular *Faithful Unto Death* (1865) by Edward John Poynter depicted a Roman soldier remaining at his post during the destruction of Pompeii, an act of obedience to duty that underlined the similar commitment necessary in the British Empire. Ford Madox Brown, in the fresco *Building the Roman Fort at Mansenion* (1879–80), emphasized the establishment of an empire that brought law and peace to the outer imperial boundaries: "the soldier striving in an unhospitable climate, far from home, to bring the protection of a great empire to the benighted barbarian."[61] Empire provided one element to national identity that gloried in the superior constitutional wisdom of the United Kingdom.

In the next instance of the imperial connection to English constitutional history, the advent of imperial history played a small part in the movement toward academic professionalization. Serious scholarship to chronicle the expansion of British power became imperative, the major academic recognition of which was the establishment of the Beit professorship of colonial history at Oxford in 1905, with Hugh Egerton (1855–1927) the first incumbent.[62] The research ideal encouraged the study of imperial history, particularly its constitutional ramifications. In the case of Canada, for example, the Whiggish theme of constitutional evolution went from settlement to the Durham Report of 1839 and responsible government, then to the British North America Act of 1867, and finally to dominion status with internal self-government. This process was characterized "by a teleology of constitutional progress—of British countries moving ever closer to the British ideal of good governance."[63] The history of the empire replicated the experience of England itself.

Historians married the imperial quest to the pageant of British history; imperial enthusiast J. A. Cramb (1862–1913) wrote in 1900 that "the Empire was Britain's destiny and her gift to the world; Britain had conquered, not for herself, but for humanity. The imperialism of the modern world, unlike the tyrannies or benevolent despotisms of earlier ages, had 'for its end the larger freedom,' a 'higher justice whose root is in the soul not of the ruler but of the race.'"[64] Less sophisticated imperial history for schoolchildren stressed the inferiority of subject peoples based on racial classifications. The 1911 *History of England* by C. R. L. Fletcher (1857–1934) and Rudyard Kipling accentuated the brilliant accomplishments of imperial administrators who had brought justice and mercy to areas of the world that had never known such blessings.[65] By 1922, questions about the empire had entered the examinations on constitutional law and legal history in the honor school of jurisprudence.[66] Whether frankly racist or sympathetically paternalist, the study of imperial history as an extension in part of the English constitutional legacy rested on assumptions of permanence and indigenous gratitude that soon ended. No sooner had scholarly research into imperial history made its debut than the institution it sought to serve began the decline that so few had anticipated. Only with the later advent of Orientalism in the 1980s did a more critical evaluation of empire place imperial history at the center of scholarly scrutiny.

In the area of public policy debates about empire there was no dearth of issues that prompted heated controversy. Two of these in particular involved constitutional issues in which historical evidence held an important place. The first was home rule for Ireland, certainly more recognizable as a continuing issue in British politics from 1874 to 1920. Many historians have cast the Anglo-Irish political relationship in a colonial (or perhaps decolonization) context, part of the process of English control of the Celtic fringe. In such an imperial environment, discussions of how home rule might affect (read jeopardize) that sovereignty were frequent. In the aftermath of the defeat of William Gladstone's first home rule bill in 1886, jurist Sir Frederick Pollock argued that home rule would blur the understanding of sovereignty vested in parliament, create substantial administrative confusion, but would not resolve the political issues at the heart of the problem. Pollock did not favor home rule, but he was prepared to accept it "as a fatal symptom that English political supremacy had outlived the English genius for politics."[67] The assumed English capacity for self-governance and for the altruistic rule of others made yet another appearance.

From the other perspective on this discussion, Irish patriot and historian Alice Stopford Green (1847–1929), the widow of John Richard Green, indicted British rule in Ireland on the eve of the Campbell-Bannerman government in 1905: "This is the kind of Nemesis that comes of the *temper* of outraging principles of law in Ireland & S. Africa."[68] The Conservative governments of Lord Salisbury and Balfour from 1895 to 1905 received their just reward in having to relinquish office because of their flawed policies that flouted English constitutional traditions. Although the home rule debate had dimensions that went well beyond the purely constitutional issues, nonetheless the debate returned again and again to the possibility of fundamental constitutional change and its potential dangers and opportunities.[69] Constitutional history contributed a small but significant foundation to this long-term source of political divisiveness. The battle between contemporary partisans of Orientalism and its critics has also raised the specter of a usable past, for Antoinette Burton has written: "History writing is one terrain upon which political battles are fought out."[70] Even today, questioning the validity and success of the imperial mission, especially with respect to the constitutional legacy, still has the power to arouse strong passions.

Another constitutional issue that had multiple consequences for political debates came in the form of federalism: for the empire and for the United Kingdom. In the first half of the nineteenth century, federalism, especially in its American incarnation, gained scant esteem; British observers in general regarded the American experiment as flawed because a federal system guaranteed weak central government. The doctrine of states' rights ensured that strong governance on the model of parliamentary sovereignty could not happen. The triumph of the Union cause in the American Civil War in preserving the federal government led to a reappraisal of the conventional wisdom about American federalism.[71] As the British Empire grew more diverse after 1870 with increased differences between the areas of white settlement on the fast track to self-government and the conquered colonies that were assumed to require centuries of political maturation before self-rule was possible, federalism as a potential principle to organize the imperial edifice entered public discussion.[72] In the years before World War I, opponents of federalism complained bitterly about the prospects for disaster. The primary constitutional critic was Dicey, who feared that an imperial parliament might result from the flirtation with federalism; and he dreaded the possibility that such a scheme might join the campaign for Irish home rule.[73] Dicey also thought that "the attempt to create a new Constitution which would federalize the British Empire, is as futile and as dangerous an experiment as any statesman has ever dreamed of. If it were carried out I believe myself it would break up the Empire."[74] Dicey hoped that any changes to the constitutional structure of the empire might occur through informal convention instead of statutory reform.

Proponents argued that a formal federal system would improve the imperial connection while permitting the dominions to evolve in a fashion that would strengthen commerce and defense. The empire in its many manifestations had no specific constitutional arrangements other than loyalty to the Crown, a situation that demanded remediation. An imperial parliament would resolve the problem; as Edward Freeman wrote: "The Great Witan *of the English Race* will not be elected by the residents in the two small islands from which English-speaking men have swarmed off to colonize the world. . . . The English world must either elect those who will direct its common policy, and decide all mat-

ters of general interest, or it will go to pieces."[75] Few questioned the existence of
the empire, because in the final analysis it served important ideals. Preservation
of the empire remained the shared goal, but how best to accomplish this task
led to continuous debate.

Politicians and jurists wrestled with these complex issues that ultimately
became identical in the minds of many and yet allowed various permutations
to generate public debate. Walter Long (1854–1924), for example, a Conservative party stalwart, wrote to Dicey: "I entirely agree with you that any form
of Federal Home Rule, such as has been adumbrated hitherto, would be even
more dangerous than Home Rule for Ireland alone."[76] The opponents of constitutional experimentation preferred what they thought a key lesson of constitutional history, the value of slow institutional development over decades or
even centuries. The proposal to mix imperial reform with home rule within the
United Kingdom struck critics as remarkably ill advised. In this context, Dicey
wrote: "I believe that sane imperialism would easily immensely increase the defensive power of the empire if fanatics would let the Empire grow by means of
understandings instead of trying to build a cumbrous Federal constitution wh.
is far more likely to break up than increase Imperial Unity of Action."[77] Dicey
admired the empire and the liberty that he supposed it imparted to subject
peoples, but he was adamant that to preserve its safety only active cooperation
with the self-governing dominions would work. He recognized that power relationships with the mother country had shifted in favor of the dominions and
coercion could no longer suffice. The United Kingdom would need to consult
with the dominions in the event of war, for example, for automatic participation could not be taken for granted.[78] Even with the advent of World War I and
the dominion willingness to share in the military burdens, Dicey still dreaded
the possibility of imperial federalism: "My utter distrust of a new Federation of
the Empire, makes me the more zealous, in favour of uniting the action & the
sentiment of the U.K. & the Dominions by making full use of Colonial Conferences."[79] Each side to this discussion appealed to precedent to support its case,
and this circumstance made invocations to constitutional history all the more
important.

The constitutional structure of the United Kingdom also caused controversy
because of proposals for devolution that would have established home rule all
around within the country. Proponents believed that only such a scheme could
settle the political complexities associated with home rule for Ireland. Opponents proclaimed that the political integrity of Great Britain related symbioti-
cally to the empire: "Integration and centralization of the United Kingdom was
central to the English constitution and fundamental to Britain's rise to a posi-

tion of global dominance."[80] Interpretations of European nationalism before 1914 usually argued that political movements on the model of Germany and Italy were exclusively centripetal. Federalism and the demand for Irish home rule ran counter to this historical path and implied decay and ruin. Dicey regarded federalism as "a delusion," one that destroyed the venerable traditions of English constitutionalism.[81] The place of England as the strongest component of the United Kingdom would suffer, and worse, it would send the wrong signal of decline if the internal British framework was dissolved: "This interlacing of concepts of England, Britain, and the British Empire, while a result of a process of obfuscation, was potentially rich in meanings and interpretations, by no means all of which worked to the advantage of English interests."[82] Dicey, who carefully monitored all discussions of this constitutional issue, wrote in criticism:

Federalism is opposed to the whole course of English history. No one who talks about it ever seems to have answered the plain question, what sort of Parliament do you intend to have for England? If you are to have a Federal Parliament or Congress, then you must have a separate English Parliament or legislature for by the most powerful State in the Confederacy. If on the other hand England is to be governed by the Federal or Imperial Parliament, then you let States such as Ireland or Wales, interfere in the local government of England. Then too it is certain that the English Parliament will by the force of historical tradition consider itself a sovereign Parliament. Federalism is folly and because people have never thought out what federalism is, they call it a solution of the Irish problem.[83]

Politics ultimately determined the outcome of these issues, but constitutional history offered a strong array of arguments that all sides utilized. Attempts to construct an imperial ideology based on English constitutional beneficence eventually foundered on the shoals of racial discrimination. No amount of paternalist rhetoric could disguise the fact that the empire depended upon conquest, not consent, and that the rule of law did not apply to all individuals equally. James Fitzjames Stephen, for example, stated that British rule in India rested on military power and the provision of good government: "By which I mean a firm and constant determination on the part of the English to promote impartially and by all lawful means, what they regard as the lasting good of the natives of India."[84] In contrast to this argument, Pollock provided this justification: "It signifies that our rule is better in the estimation of the majority of the dwellers in India than any other rule which they could probably look for in our absence. . . . It signifies that our empire is not of brute force, but of judgment and righteousness."[85] The tension between the self-image of constitutional magnanimity and the realities of power relations never found resolution, because race remained an intractable obstacle to the goals that the empire professed concerning self-realization of governance by colonial populations. In 1892 historian W. E. H. Lecky wrote of the optimism that had prevailed about the redemptive value of English constitutionalism: "Some thirty or forty years ago especially it was the custom of English statesmen to write and speak as if the salvation of every nation depended mainly upon its adoption of a miniature copy of the British constitution."[86] This faith, however admirable in its expression, never guided policy in its pragmatic applications because of assumed racial hierarchies: "If a rule of law was the settled theoretical standard of colonial politics, the institutional practices of the colonial state constantly fell short of such a standard."[87] The tension between ideal and practice ultimately came down to the race problem.

The conjunction of race and empire proved the cancer that destroyed the aspirations of the constitutional mission. Countries of white settlement were privileged because of race and resemblance to British constitutional practice. Race meant that English law could not be imposed wholesale on indigenous peoples, for the common law had to compromise with the customary law already in place. This racial division of the empire, particularly "the tendency to regard Anglo-Dominion relations as the key to imperial problems was not without its consequences for other areas of the empire, particularly India," signified that race legitimized the empire and demonstrated that government hinged on racial superiority.[88] If India was truly the jewel of the empire, it constituted the most important test of the constitutional mission. Racial attitudes that grew more abusive after 1870 made this all but impossible. Lecky wrote: "May we not say that the laws, the Constitutions, the habits of thought and character that have so largely made them what they are, are mainly of English origin?"[89] On their own, therefore, Indians lacked the capacity to govern themselves. Even progressives such as J. L. Hammond made the distinction that segregated the two imperial entities based on race: "The British Empire has survived certain other Empires because, so far as its relations to white men are concerned, it rests on consent and not on force."[90] Given this racial divide, the attitudes that had generated such a chasm proved too dramatic to overcome.

Several of the most famous episodes in imperial history connected racial feelings to constitutional issues. The Jamaican riots in 1865 and much later the massacre in India at Amritsar in 1919 raised issues of the powers that government might exercise when martial law existed.[91] Although the callous reaction of British public opinion and absence of legal sanctions to the death of large numbers of nonwhites has dominated the legacy of these incidents, whether the courts might scrutinize government conduct taken in a martial law situation also had a role. In the Ilbert Bill crisis of 1883, however, the arrogance of the British and the contempt of racial feelings for their Indian subjects became evident. This famous affair has received frequent mention but rarely with the full fury of racial hatred emphasized. The Mutiny of 1857 had destroyed the simplistic hopes of those reformers who thought that the transition to British constitutional standards would pose an easy task. Only the British could provide fair and impartial government, because the Muslims had imposed tyranny when they had ruled and thus were disqualified from exercising any further authority; the Hindus were a conquered population and thus unfamiliar with constitutional liberty. The British contrasted their vision of the rule of law to the oriental despotism that had characterized Indian history. British rule was necessary to raise both religious groups to the enjoyment of the freedoms that were a natural endowment of English constitutional history.[92] After the mutiny, however, racial attitudes "became less humanitarian and hardened into an imperialist ideology infused with assumptions about the rights and duties of superior master races over inferior subject races."[93] Racial solidarity proved too strong for these goals and for the policy of incorporating Indians into increasing signification in governing the country.

In January 1883, Courtenay Peregrine Ilbert (1841–1924), graduate of Balliol College, barrister who trained at Lincoln's Inn, draftsman for parliamentary bills and a law member on the council of the governor-general of India, produced a bill that made modest changes to the hierarchy of jurisdiction in India. The bill in select circumstances extended the "authority of a few Indian officials—experienced judges and magistrates—by giving them criminal jurisdiction over resident Europeans."[94] This proposal embodied the policy of incremental reform by the Gladstone government that would lead at some distant point to Indian self-government, which after all was a major rationale of British power. The Ilbert Bill provoked a firestorm of opposition in India and in Great Britain, and the controversy accentuated the racial hostility that divided the governors from the governed. Racial vitriol, liberally sprinkled with the gendered implications of effeminacy on the part of the Indians and the masculine call to duty on the side of the British, revealed the gulf that separated racial reality from the niceties of constitutional discussion.

In the Town Hall of Calcutta on 28 February 1883, a meeting to oppose the Ilbert Bill offered the opportunity to vent the anxieties of the British residents. J. J. J. Keswick offered these thoughts to the assembly:

Do you think that native judges will, by three or four years residence in England, become so Europeanised in nature and character, that they will be able to judge as well in false charges against Europeans as if they were Europeans bred and born? Can the Ethopian change his skin, or the leopard his spots? . . . The education which the Government has given them, and which they use chiefly to taunt it in a discontented spirit, would not put courage enough into their hearts to defend their hearths and homes, and these men . . . now cry out for power to sit in judgment on, and condemn the lion-hearted race whose bravery and whose blood have made their country what it is, and raised them to what they are. . . . A native judge, by reason of the conditions of his early nurture and early surroundings inculcated during his infancy from an educated mother, and by the fact that, to thoroughly understand European nature, it is necessary to have that nature innate, is unfitted when trying an European to put himself in his place, and to judge from an European stand-point of the likelihood of his having committed the crime of which he is charged. . . . But it will be a far future before they can achieve a position of confidence in the hearts of the non-official Europeans as judges of a race whose nature and whose characteristics they are yet unable to understand.

To these sentiments J. H. P. Branson added:

Now, a freeborn nation loves its freedom, and it would not be judged by a nation steeped in the tradition of the conquered, but by a nation glorious in the tradition of conquerors. Is it, then, to be wondered at that Englishmen protest that they are not to be tried, that they will not hand over the custody of their liberties to such a nation as the Hindus of India? . . . If then the Hindu has no patriotism . . . if he does *not* hate us, then it follows that he has not a single quality which we can understand or appreciate. I speak not of the Mahomedans. . . . You are not so ignorant of the nature of that people as to suppose that the Mahomedans do not hate us, as coveting the possession of the rich prize that they hoped to enjoy themselves. . . . Under these circumstances, is it any wonder that we should protest—if we should say that these men are not fit to rule over us, that we will not be judged by them? . . . We should call upon our brethren in England to appeal to the House of Commons to save our wives, and daughters, and sisters from being tried by those who cannot understand them, and in whose justice we cannot have, and have not any faith. . . . Many of you have brought from some far English home a girl for your wife who was entrusted to your hands and to your protection by a confiding father or a loving brother. You have brought her from a condition which ensured that she would never be brought up for trial except before one of her countrymen, and if you give in now you are betrayers of that sacred trust.[95]

The various racial attitudes revealed in these speeches illustrate the catch-22 of imperial racism. If a group such as the Muslims allegedly hated the British, then the potential for constitutional tutelage evaporated; if the Hindus lacked patriotism, then the path to constitutional self-realization stretched into an indefinite future. In both cases racial superiority meant cultural supremacy, and in the final analysis the actions of the government rarely lived up to the ideals promulgated by the British. Thus the British were faced with a dilemma of their own making, for modernization, a stated goal, could not occur until the limitations of racial prejudice disappeared.[96] In the aftermath of the Ilbert Bill explosion, Lord Ripon (1827–1909), governor-general of India, acknowledged this conundrum in stating that he had no idea of the "true feeling" of the British toward the Indian population and he despaired of the country's future on that account.[97]

The racial hatred and contempt expressed in the Ilbert Bill debate undermined the London conversations about constitutional forms and the frequent assertions of concern for the nonwhite imperial populace. As Linda Colley has written, insecurity was the imperial "flip side of arrogance and aggression."[98] Racial attitudes did not reflect some abstract intellectual construct, but rather they indicated a visceral emotion that belied imperial rhetoric. Racial hatred, even when acknowledged as irrational, was ascribed to an instinctual antipathy that would take generations to overcome if at all.[99] As racial feelings intensified, a crisis of imperial faith followed, because the goals of the center failed to bind those on the periphery. Well before the mutiny in 1857, East India Company official John Beames wrote about his destination: "All we knew was that it was 'beastly hot' and that there were 'niggers' there, and that it would be time enough to bother about it when you got there."[100] The end to the rhetoric of racial antagonism came slowly, tempered by the assumption in the first part of the twentieth century that the empire, especially in Africa, still had time on its side.[101] The legacy of the constitutional model for the empire in all its complexity remained; it ended much earlier than most had anticipated.

The reciprocal influence of constitutional history in the imperial context meant that not only did Great Britain bequeath a legacy of constitutional development, but the colonial world in return provided a mirror in which the British could find their behavior validated. The colonial Other reflected the purity of intentions that the British professed to see in their own conduct. The individuals who embraced this ideal were clearly a small minority, but they succeeded in linking constitutional history to the broader image of self-image and capacity for government. In addition to the opportunity to justify racial condescension, constitutional history offered the chance to praise the masculine elements of their own commitment to duty as opposed to the feminine qualities attributed to subject peoples; as Lecky wrote: "India is proving a school of inestimable value for maintaining some of the best and most masculine qualities of our race."[102] These presumed benefits included martial leadership as well as the protection for women so prominent in the Ilbert Bill speeches. The empire as proving ground for the constitutional self-image justified the importance of constitutional history in the mother country. Beyond the usual virtues of character, confidence, and loyalty, the imperial administrator professed allegiance to constitutional liberty in the mission to bring good government around the globe.[103] This "benevolent self-image" required a racial hierarchy in which subject races without the common law benefited from this constitutional device: "This entirely self-conforming ideological legitimization of the empire . . . justified the imperial enterprise (rationalizing the apparent contradiction between liberal democracy at home and benevolent despotism abroad)."[104] When Lord Cromer wished to illustrate the "uprightness, the benevolence, and the sincerity of the rulers of India," he quoted with approval various Indian luminaries to prove the case.[105] When the system did not work as intended or when resistance occurred, then local ingrates could always receive the blame, for the empire was never at fault.[106] Resistance to the imperial order was discounted or else ascribed to cranks and malcontents, for there was never any legitimacy to complaints: "It is, indeed, one of the inevitable incidents of the execution of an Imperial policy that, as a political force, the gratitude shown to the foreigner who relieves oppression is of a very ephemeral character."[107] The Victorian quest for moral purpose expressed in the dissemination of English constitutionalism never overcame the facts of racial discrimination. How persistent and how dramatic were racial attitudes was demonstrated in the 1950s in Kenya, where the attempts to defeat the Mau-Mau rebellion led to appalling brutality.[108] These events were all the more horrifying because of the hypocritical juxtaposition of lofty constitutional purpose and the murderous policy meted out to the Kenyan people: "British justice in 1950s Kenya was a blunt, brutal and unsophisticated instrument of oppression."[109]

The recalcitrance of subject populations to recognize the superiority of the British constitution made the performance of duty in the face of opposition all that much more morally praiseworthy. When demands for reform came from local groups, British authorities never conceded that this marked the true triumph of English constitutionalism, the ability to turn their principles against the British themselves. When Niall Ferguson listed the primary exports of British imperialism, four of the nine categories arguably belonged to the constitutional tradition: the common law, parliamentary government, English forms of land tenure, and the idea of liberty. It has become clear that this mission failed because no comprehensive plan of constitutional policy ever existed; despite a self-indulgent view of their endeavors, the British made up constitutional rules as they went along. Yet this legacy rested on a military supremacy that could not endure, and no amount of postconquest explanation could conceal the ambiguities of the situation. Some Victorians, such as James Fitzjames Stephen, faced this quandary directly:

Neither force nor justice will suffice by itself. . . . But so long as the masterful will, the stout heart, the active brain, the calm nerves and the strong body which make up military force are directed to the object which I have defined as constituting justice, I should have no fear, for even if we fail after doing our best, we fail with honour, and if we succeed, we shall have performed the greatest feat of strength, skill, and courage in the whole history of the world.[110]

Violence remained at the heart of the imperial enterprise, and no amount of constitutional rhetoric could disguise that fact. The commendable performance of duty without the expectation of thanks and the fatalism of eventual imperial decline was captured by Lecky:

> Whatever misfortunes, whatever humiliations the future may reserve to us, they cannot deprive England of the glory of having created this mighty Empire.
>
>> Not Heaven itself upon the Past has power
>> But what has been, has been—and we have had our hour.[111]

What many in 1900 thought impossible—the end of empire—was virtually complete by the 1960s; even the Roman Empire had lasted longer.

English constitutional history, of course, did bequeath an important legacy to imperial possessions, although not quite in the way governing authorities intended. Colonized peoples did internalize the ideas of liberty and equality before the law, but then demanded these constitutional guarantees for themselves without the impediment of racial subjectivities. The end of empire, not its perpetuation, in the long run indicated that the lessons of English constitutionalism had taken firm root. The process of decolonization liberated countries politically, and it also allowed them the freedom to settle their own constitutional institutions. Amid the lamentations still heard for the end of empire, the fact that former colonies found their own way still stands as the signal achievement of the constitutional legacy in which history played such an important part. We doubt that the admirers of empire in the twentieth century would have appreciated the irony.

As British power declined, the relevance of English constitutional history to the maintenance of empire disappeared with it down to the 1960s. The Statute of Westminster in 1931 held out the prospect of self-government for all parts of the empire on an equal basis and heralded a decolonization dictated by international events that took several decades to complete. About the 1930s, A. P. Thornton has written: "A legacy warrants the care of a trustee. Constitutional historians have regularly signed on for this duty. Following separate trails, they agree that law, not militance, second thoughts, nor first, ultimately shaped and justified England's expansion. Berriedale Keith's dry prose kindles when telling how jurisprudence and the common law nurtured not just England and her Empire, but the cause of civilization with it."[112] As a taught tradition, English constitutional history continued to regard the empire as a logical extension of

Britain; when movements for independence came to fruition, constitutional history was still crucial to the education of new commonwealth citizens. How fatuous this argument seems in retrospect, given the racial attitudes and unrealistic expectations that existed as late as the 1950s.[113] At the end of the decolonization process, constitutional history as a guide to the imperial present and future ebbed away. Its significance in 1900 still dominated as the putative model for global emulation, but by the 1960s the subject had no empire to influence: "constitutional foundations of imperial history had become irrelevant—Oxford graduates could no longer aspire to the administration of some far-flung outpost of greater Britain."[114] English constitutional history had played its own historical role, and the vicissitudes of British world power had helped its demise.

The relative decline of English constitutional history in academic status in the imperial environment has also resulted from the changing nature of scholarship. Emphasis by Orientalism scholars on the governed rather than the governors and the periphery rather than the metropole has made the topic symbolic of an era that no longer has answers to the questions historians now wish to ask. While the study of the empire has flourished in recent decades, interest in its constitutional history, real or theoretical, has diminished dramatically. The imperial context has added another dimension to the field's diminishment in scholarly prestige.

CHAPTER SIX

"Norman History Merges in That of England, the British Empire, and the United States"

Constitutional History and the Anglo-American Connection

In this chapter we argue that the particular turn toward institutional studies in constitutional history that was in ascendance by the end of the nineteenth century became an important vehicle for promoting Anglo-American rapprochement. However, it is important to realize that the older strain of racial analysis based on Anglo-Saxon descent remained a quite active force—indeed it was still the dominant strain in popular culture. Even within the historical profession, this interpretive line had by no means run its course. The frontiers of the profession were quite elastic, and as we have seen, "amateur" historians had taken an active part in the foundation and were still influential in the American Historical Association (AHA). Thus we must consider the historical profession within the United States at this juncture to still be in a formative state. Institutional studies of the kind undertaken by Charles McLean Andrews were certainly embraced by the professorial elite, but others left a place for racial interpretations, even as they selectively adopted an institutional approach. Sometimes this was no more than an added flourish of terminology, as when Woodrow Wilson, in his otherwise institutionally centered *History of the American People* (1902), could not resist naming the first volume "The Swarming of the English."[1] For literate members of the American public with an abiding interest in history, the racial paradigm offered a more stirring analysis, and one that gave a satisfying explanation of the great events of their day, especially their country's coming of age as a global power.

The 1890s were the heyday of imperialism in both the United States and Britain, which for some historians simply strengthened the appeal of Anglo-Saxonist ideology. It provided a clear justification for the English-speaking peoples to extend their civilizing sway around the globe, preferably in partnership. This was the tenor, for example, of *A Short History of Anglo-Saxon Free-*

dom (1890) by James K. Hosmer of Washington University in St. Louis. While most of Hosmer's book is straightforward English constitutional history, the final hundred pages are highly charged Anglo-Saxonist imperial propaganda.[2] Similarly, *The Discovery of America* (1892), by Boston Brahmin John Fiske, celebrated the superiority of the English-speaking peoples in the quest for empire. This was a theme that Fiske had developed before a London audience in 1880, when he lectured on "the Manifest Destiny of the English race" before the Royal Institution of Great Britain. In his popular book *The Critical Period of American History, 1783–1789,* Fiske claimed that the 1780s had been crucial because of the spread of Anglo-American political institutions throughout the world. Near the end of his life, he was invited to give a public lecture at Winchester in 1901 celebrating the one thousandth anniversary of Alfred the Great. He died several weeks before delivering this address, which was titled "The Beginnings of Federalism in New England, as related to the Expansion of Alfred's World." Had he survived to deliver it, the audience would have heard an impassioned plea for the federation of the English-speaking peoples.[3] Fiske, it should be added, had been president of the Immigration Restriction League, a powerful pressure group dedicated to keeping "undesirables" (e.g., non-Anglo-Saxons) out of the United States.[4] However, as we will see, it was the principle of federalism as a viable means of organizing the English-speaking world rather than the racist content of Fiske's thought that was to have a more enduring impact on Anglo-American relations.

Historians in Britain showed a growing interest in the history of the United States and an accompanying tendency to search for parallels to the main events of British history. Charles Firth, the leading expert on the constitutional struggles of seventeenth-century Britain, who was to be appointed Regius professor of history at Oxford in 1904, carried on a lengthy correspondence with James Ford Rhodes (1848–1927), the wealthy and well-connected amateur historian of the Civil War and Reconstruction. Writing in 1895 to express his admiration for Rhodes's *History of the Civil War,* Firth compared the work to that of Samuel Rawson Gardiner on the English Civil War, noting that the similarities between the two conflicts "are frequently very suggestive."[5] And in the midst of the Boer War, which Firth strongly supported, he told Rhodes that in the postwar reconstruction of South Africa, "your own history will throw some light on the problem, and I shall look to your next volume for political instruction as well as historical."[6] For his part, Rhodes wrote to Firth: "Mr. Gardiner, Bishop Stubbs and you are great object lessons to us. You have put us under weighty obligations. I am just reading the Letters of Johnny Green.[7] What a delightful book."[8]

In addition to the constitutional lessons offered by the two countries' civil wars, military history of a more expansionist kind provided a means of celebrating the superiority of the two peoples. The central event in this process was the publication in 1890 of *The Influence of Sea Power upon History* by Alfred Thayer Mahan (1840–1914), a captain in the U.S. Navy.[9] Besides giving valuable ammunition to ardent navalists like Theodore Roosevelt, himself no mean naval historian, Mahan's book was widely hailed in Britain. His celebration of Britain's dominance of the seas not only encouraged the building of modern capital ships, but endorsed the doctrine of Anglo-Saxon supremacy. When Mahan arrived in London in 1894 as captain of the *U.S.S. Chicago,* he was lionized at a sumptuous banquet at St. James's Hall attended by numerous British admirals and generals. The theme of the dinner, "Blood is thicker than water" (a phrase made famous during the second Opium War, when a "neutral" American vessel had assisted a British warship during an engagement), was emblazoned on a large streamer hanging in the hall. Moving on to receive honorary doctorates at Oxford and Cambridge, Mahan heard a highly unlikely rumor that he was being considered for an appointment as Regius professor of modern history at Cambridge.[10]

A similar interest in the history of empire was evinced by those professional historians undertaking an institutional analysis of the background of the American Revolution. Once again Andrews, along with Herbert Levi Osgood (1855–1918) and George Louis Beer (1872–1920), together constituting the so-called imperial school of American historians, took a leading role in reassessing the colonial period and British imperial policy. It should be noted that it was not at all unusual for historians of the era to work in widely disparate fields, such as American and medieval English history. For example, Charles Beard's first book, in 1904, was on the origins of justices of the peace in England,[11] while Charles Homer Haskins, who was to emerge as the most eminent of American medievalists, began his career as a historian of the United States. Andrews's interest in the colonial era became paramount after he was commissioned by the Pennsylvania Historical Society to undertake a study of the Board of Trade documents in the Public Record Office (PRO). What started as a peripheral activity to a continuing study of medieval institutions soon became his abiding interest. Before departing for England, Andrews's views on the American Revolution were already in flux, thanks in part to a conversation with Mellen Chamberlain (1821–1900), a judge noted for his lectures and writings on the constitutional questions involved in the revolution.[12] Chamberlain, who had taken an active part in the formation of the AHA, held that, constitutionally speaking, England had been in the right. He had already published his views in Justin Winsor's (1831–97) *Narrative and Critical History of America* (1888), to which he had contributed a chapter titled "The Revolution Impending." Andrews noted that Chamberlain's ideas were "rather radical in reference to the character of the revolution and other events of that period so that I saw many things from a quite different point of view."[13] Thus primed by Chamberlain, Andrews wrote to his mother from London in 1893 that studying the Board of Trade papers at the PRO had given him "a new and necessary point of view—which has not often enough been taken in America and shows the English side of the question. Of course in the difficulties during the colonial period our sympathies are largely with the Colonists but there is much to be said on the other side particularly as there was much conscientiousness and legal right in the position of the English officials."[14] Convinced of the necessity for cataloging and publishing all the relevant seventeenth- and eighteenth-century documents so that scholars could comprehend the basis of the colonial period (and by implication, the revolution), Andrews devoted nearly two decades of labor to the task. The result was two vitally important multivolume guides to British archival sources for American colonial history.[15]

Immersion in the day-to-day minutiae of British imperial officials was bound to produce a very different sense of eighteenth-century Anglo-American relations, one that had little room for heroes, villains, or patriotic effusions. Andrews and Osgood both delivered sharply revisionist papers to the 1898 meeting of the AHA, calling on their fellow scholars to place American colonial history within the framework of studying the larger difficulties of governing the British Empire. The cool, institutional approach of Andrews and the other "imperial" historians would become the new orthodoxy in the next couple of decades, at least within the historical profession. For the most part, these scholars avoided a head-on challenge to the older American chauvinist historiography on the revolution. Yet their drastic reframing of the colonial period, transatlantic perspective, and reliance on administrative documents necessarily did to the American Revolution what the anti-Whig historians were doing to the Norman Conquest: rendering it ideologically inert. As that eminent member of the imperial school of historians George Louis Beer concluded in his 1907 book, *British Colonial Policy, 1754–1765:* "It is easily conceivable, and not at all improbable that the political evolution of the next centuries may take such a course that the American Revolution will lose the great significance that is now attached to it, and will appear merely as the temporary separation of two kindred peoples whose inherent similarity was obscured by superficial differences."[16] In his scholarly publications, Andrews tended to avoid such rhetoric, but he showed no such restraint in a 1912 volume intended for a popular read-

m bent on destroying instead of amending it." He ended by depre-
en of lower stamp" in the government—a clear reference to David
.[29] It is impossible to identify the political affiliations of most of
onal historians of the era in the United States, but many of them
nilar to those of Adams, an ardent Republican and imperialist.
f Peter Novick's *That Noble Dream* will not be surprised at such
views. As Novick points out, the consensus among turn-of-the-
rican historians about the American Revolution, sectional recon-
imperialism was a function of their social and political values, in
own certainty of being objective.[30] What is being added to Novick's
s a transatlantic perspective as well as a linkage to the historiog-
Norman Conquest. The similar impulses at work in England were
ated with those in America, thanks in no small measure to the
s between scholars in the two countries. The Norman Conquest
ican Revolution, though separated by more than seven centuries,
ogether in a complex revisionist web. The sharply altered inter-
these topics offered by the new professional historians, besides
sting social and economic arrangements, also promoted closer
Anglo-American relations. While there were important strategic
k in shaping the so-called special relationship between Britain
d States, much of the ideological justification for it was produced
all of them of a "Normanizing" persuasion, whether they wrote
il England or colonial America.

al historians were determined that their writings should be based
archival research as well as embodying a transatlantic perspec-
d efforts like those of Andrews to catalog essential British materi-
an scholars soon began receiving major institutional support.
urn of the century, the Carnegie Institution and the American
ciation began a collaborative project for the systematic catalog-
archives and selective copying of key documents. The Carnegie
Vashington, founded in 1902, proved quite receptive to the fund-
leading historians like Jameson, head of the Historical Manu-
ission. The next year, the institution established a department
search, which quickly became a vital conduit of funding for the
h constitutional history. Even before its establishment, Jameson
dispensable in providing letters of introduction to leading Brit-
dams's letter to Jameson in 1900 prior to sailing to England is
American historians' requests: "I should like especially to meet
and York Powell."[31] From the outset there was a very close con-

ership. In *The Colonial Period,* part of the Home University Library published by Henry Holt and Co., the revolution is depicted as the product of "mobs" and "excitable and uncontrolled elements in America." As for the underlying principle which generations of Americans had revered as the essential basis of independence, Andrews concluded:

> The phrase "natural rights of Englishmen" is vague and meaningless in the history of constitutional development and political philosophy, and deserves to stand with that other equally abused phrase, much on the lips of the colonists at this time, "taxation without representation." Neither had any literal meaning in fact, but as historical influences each became a phenomenon of far-reaching significance. Men have died for a false creed; the colonists fought under a banner of a false philosophy.[17]

A parallel development to the "imperial" historians' transforming of eighteenth-century Anglo-American relations into a series of intricate administrative problems was framing the period through the lens of American social tensions. Carl Becker (1873–1945), after undergraduate study under Frederick Jackson Turner and C. H. Haskins at the University of Wisconsin, undertook graduate study at Columbia in 1896. Although he left Columbia after a year, he was greatly influenced by working under Herbert Levi Osgood, and he finally received his PhD from Wisconsin in 1907. His dissertation, published in 1909 as *The History of Political Parties in the Province of New York, 1760–1776,* focused on social tensions as the dominant factor in the rupture with Britain, an interpretation that became known as the Becker thesis. His former mentor, Turner, himself a decided revisionist, wrote to Becker to express his admiration of the book but also his concern about the boldness of Becker's rejection of the traditional interpretation: "With your belief that the Revolutionary history must be re-written with reference to its social aspects, I am in entire agreement, tho' I am not sure I should raise unnecessary issues by calling the movement for self-government (independence) secondary to this as the primary movement."[18] An additional affront to patriotic pieties was created by Charles Beard's *Economic Interpretation of the Constitution* (1913), with its insistence that the narrow class interests of the founders rather than high-minded principles provided the dynamic at the constitutional convention of 1787–89.

While the traditional interpretation continued to find favor with the general public as well as with historians outside the academy, it came in for increasingly severe criticism by professional historians. An example is provided by the professional reactions to George Otto Trevelyan's study of the American Revolution, the first volume of which appeared in 1899. Written by a British gentleman amateur historian (and nephew of the great Macaulay) and informed by an older Whig view of heroic American resistance to tyrannical officialdom, the book was sharply criticized by Osgood: "to the scientific historian, to the sober student of social and political forces, it will not be wholly convincing or satisfactory."[19] Even the author's son, George Macaulay Trevelyan, noted: "The style of thinking and writing had great merit, but it was subtly out of fashion."[20] However, a work by another British gentleman amateur historian, W. E. H. Lecky, proved less unfashionable in academic circles. His book on the American Revolution, published in 1898 (actually a separate reprinting of the chapters on America from his earlier *History of England in the Eighteenth Century*), was praised for giving a more balanced treatment than Trevelyan's. More importantly, Lecky postulated an "imperial feeling" as a central value of both branches of the Anglo-Saxon race: "It is a feeling which is rarely absent from any large section of the English race, and however much the Americans, during the War of Independence, may have reprobated it, it was never displayed more conspicuously or more passionately than by their own descendants when the great question of secession arose within their own border."[21] Andrew Dickson White wrote Lecky, commending the book for its fairness and reporting that Cornell students were being urged to read it "as the best antidote to the chauvinism of American historiography."[22] Lecky's insistence that the "imperial feeling" bound Americans and Englishmen together found considerable resonance in America. As late as 1924, when the book was reprinted, the editor, James A. Woodburn of Indiana University, declared in his introduction: "The intelligent reading of our Revolution should lead us to see that, while that unfortunate policy [of the British] may have disturbed, it has in no sense destroyed the essential unity of the Anglo-Saxon race."[23]

The essential unity of the Anglo-Saxon race was a doctrine often endorsed in the years before the Great War by American and British historians, especially those concerned with the American Revolution and the Norman Conquest. There was no more ardent advocate of closer Anglo-American ties than George Burton Adams of Yale. Adams (unrelated to the other historians with that surname who have already been discussed) had a PhD from Leipzig and was a specialist in English constitutional history. Following the lead of English medievalist John Horace Round, Adams rejected Whig "liberal descent" doctrine, asserting that English and American forms of limited government derived from feudalism, which, he insisted, had been introduced into England by William the Conqueror. As he explained to John Franklin Jameson, "it certainly makes an enormous difference with the interpretation of the XIII century in English history, whether one approaches it with a belief in the Saxon origin of everything good, or from the point of view of feudal institutional history."[24] For Adams, the key event in preventing the growth of absolutist government

in England had been Magna Carta.[25] Th[...] modern government with the sanctity c[...] of the medieval propertied elite in ensu[...] doctrine to conservatives on both side[...] such favor among British historians of[...] to write the volume on the later Midd[...] *of England* planned by Longmans and[...] wrote to express his satisfaction that *A*[...] izer."[26]

This term carried a good deal of co[...] tion to its historiographical meaning. [...] postulating postconquest institutional [...] glo-American government and law. It[...] of a conservative political and social c[...] hostility toward socialism, respect for [...] glo-American relations. Adams held a[...] leading constitutional historians on bo[...] to Hugh Egerton, a future professor of[...] his horror at the rise of populism and[...] America. Recalling the stridently anti-[...] istration and the American public dur[...] as the Anglophobic tone of William J[...] to the Democratic convention in 1896[...] a pure democracy like ours."[27] In Oc[...] Egerton at the recent electoral triumph[...] anticipated victory of the Republicans[...] would further the cause of empire and[...] of McKinley and the return of Lord Sa[...] certain, "secure the opportunity to c[...] prochement] forward . . . and the po[...] tance for the race and for the world."[...] recent biography of colonial admini[...] Thomas Stamford Raffles: "I hope we[...] do not see why we should not."[28] Willi[...] tor, proved an especially congenial co[...] worried about the pending assault on[...] Liberal government following the Bu[...] Parliament Act of 1911, Hunt exclaim[...] here as regards politics. Having a co[...]

nection with the AHA. The first director of the Department of Historical Research was University of Michigan professor Andrew Cunningham McLaughlin (1861–1947), a constitutional historian (as well as a trained lawyer) who simultaneously held the post of editor of the *American Historical Review*. In 1906, he became chair of the history department at the University of Chicago, a post he held for more than two decades. Under McLaughlin's leadership, the Department of Historical Research provided the funding for Andrews to resume his cataloging of English archives.[32] For the next few years, McLaughlin and his successor, Jameson, were inundated with requests from Andrews for yet more money as he discovered fresh troves of vital materials.[33] On one occasion, an exasperated Andrews argued successfully to Jameson the importance of West Indian materials (which he was to put to such effective use in his own scholarship): "No true understanding of British colonial policy can ever be obtained without a study of that policy applied to the West Indies, and England's attitude toward our colonies can be appreciated only by a thorough knowledge of the larger policy."[34] Andrews spent several more years in England before the first of his important guides was published by the Carnegie Institution in 1908.[35] His guide to the PRO appeared in 1912.[36] Even after the publication of his own masterly monograph, *The Colonial Background of the American Revolution* (1924), he pronounced the *Guides* "my chief contribution in the field."[37]

One important effect of the new emphasis on archival work was the necessity for American scholars to reside in England for long periods, during which they forged close relationships with their English counterparts. In the case of Andrews, Adams, and all the new professional historians who worked in either English or American colonial history, their research brought them to Britain frequently. Since the major repositories of documents upon which they based their work were there, extended visits of at least a few months, and sometimes a year or more at a time, became commonplace. This brought them into close contact with British scholars, and some enduring friendships developed. On his second trip to England in 1893, Andrews, who had started as an English constitutional historian, was invited to stay with Frederic Maitland and found his host "wonderfully genial and always ready to help and advise."[38] Invited to tea by F. York Powell (whom he had met the previous year), he ended up staying till midnight, declaring the English historian to be "cordial and hearty."[39] Andrews, however, was not uncritical of some aspects of English life and culture. In 1893, after witnessing the fawning adulation of the British press and public over the wedding of Princess May, Andrews wrote to his mother: "The instinct for servility and respectful subservience is deep in English society and for my part I don't like it."[40]

Hubert Hall, senior clerk of the PRO, proved very helpful to American historians who came there to study in increasing numbers, and in 1903 he wrote to Adams: "Your universities are full of good workers and your scholars are delightfully enthusiastic in their researches over here."[41] In 1909 a sumptuous banquet was given at the Holborn Restaurant by American historians resident in London in honor of Hall's thirtieth anniversary at the PRO.[42] Historians in the United States had already proved generous contributors to the Maitland Memorial Fund launched by Trinity College, Cambridge, in 1907.[43] Friendly relations between American and English scholars further enhanced the sense of transatlantic connectedness and a shared past. That sense eventually accelerated visits by British historians to lecture in the United States, a process pioneered in the 1880s by Edward Augustus Freeman and James Bryce, though Andrews complained to Thomas Frederick Tout in 1899 that English scholars came rarely to America, in spite of repeated invitations.[44] There was a marked increase in such visits after the turn of the century, with, for example, Paul Vinogradoff lecturing at Harvard and Yale in 1907[45] and George Prothero going on a lecture tour of the United States in 1910, including California.[46] Students also began to cross the Atlantic, at least eastward, for, thanks to the Rhodes scholarship program, the first systematic intake of American students into Britain had begun. The very point of the scholarships, to enhance international Anglophone solidarity, was entirely complementary to the bonds being forged by the historians, many of whom served enthusiastically on the Rhodes committees of their universities.

British and American historians alike also took advantage of the enhanced publishing opportunities afforded by their transatlantic contacts. Adams's volume in the Longmans series has already been discussed. A. P. Newton of the University of London, who had declared himself a "disciple" of Andrews, persuaded the latter to get Yale University Press to publish his master's thesis, *The Colonising Activities of the English Puritans*, in 1914.[47] As lecturer in American and colonial history at King's College, Newton drew American and Commonwealth students to study in London, a role that was magnified after his appointment as the first Rhodes professor of imperial history at the University of London in 1920.[48] American library purchases of limited-run scholarly publications by British scholars also enhanced publishing opportunities. Eminent medievalist John Horace Round found Adams sympathetic to his requests to get American libraries to order his works.[49] Publishing opportunities across the Atlantic worked in both directions and were becoming commonplace by the eve of the Great War.

In the first years of the new century, Anglophile historians began to note better public attitudes toward Britain, though Jameson told James Bryce that there was still much to do, especially in the Midwest.[50] Bryce, as the author of the notable *American Commonwealth* (1888), as well as the British ambassador in Washington from 1907 to 1913, was himself a major factor in improving relations. Popular with the American public as well as the academic community, Bryce was one of only three Britons to have been made honorary members of the American Historical Association (the other two, William Stubbs and Samuel Rawson Gardiner, had died in 1901 and 1902 respectively). He was also elected president of the American Political Science Association (APSA), whose membership in those days overlapped considerably with that of the AHA. The two organizations met jointly in 1908, the year of Bryce's APSA presidency. As a British scholar with a deep knowledge and love of America, as well as a Gladstonian little Englander, Bryce helped win over those American historians with misgivings about the imperialist raptures of people like Adams. Jameson and Bryce often worked closely on encouraging transatlantic exchanges and the convening of international conferences. In spite of this close partnership, however, Jameson became increasingly impatient with English scholars' unwillingness to take American history seriously as a field of study. In an otherwise positive report in the *American Historical Review* about the Third International Congress of Historical Studies held in London in 1913, he observed: "An American could not help thinking it to be a strange fact that, of more than a hundred papers presented by British subjects, only one was concerned wholly, and another partially, with the history of the United States, a country embracing nearly two-thirds of the English-speaking population of the globe."[51]

An opportunity to further the already rapidly improving state of Anglo-American relations came with the approaching centenary of the Treaty of Ghent, which had ended the War of 1812. The Carnegie Institution established the American Peace Centenary Committee, which sponsored various activities in American cities in 1913, some of them involving visiting British dignitaries.[52] To follow up these celebratory events, the committee commissioned a book by William Dunning of Columbia University. Since Dunning's own scholarship centered on the Reconstruction era in the United States, he was probably selected for the task because he was the president of the American Historical Association in 1913. For a book requiring no original research,[53] Dunning was paid fifteen hundred dollars.[54] It was, of course, popular with those already converted to the cause of transatlantic friendship. The rhetorical flourishes were many, and Dunning was not reluctant to invoke Divine Providence, concluding that "some special fiat of God and nature enjoins enduring peace among those whose blood or language or institutions or traditions . . . go back historically to the snug little island of Britain."[55] The president of the Ontario Historical Society wrote that he had bought numerous copies and was giving them to friends as Christmas presents.[56] However, the timing of the book's publication (August 1914) was unfortunate, at least in Britain, and James Bryce, who had written the foreword, informed Dunning in December that because of the war news there had been no reviews in the British press.[57] Since the total amount spent on this publication as well as the various visits and public events must have been considerable, it is instructive to consider the composition of the Peace Centenary Committee. It included such titans of industry, trade, and finance as Andrew Carnegie, Cornelius Vanderbilt II, and J. P. Morgan, all men with an important stake in fostering cordial Anglo-American relations.

Carnegie was also one who had long argued for the rejoining, or at least the federating of, America and Britain. Certain historians in the United States had made similar appeals in the years leading up to the war, and their efforts intensified after August 1914. Unsurprisingly, Adams was the foremost of these. In his 1896 book, *Why Americans Dislike England,* he lamented traditional American Anglophobia and pointed to the shared political values and systems of law of the United States and Britain, calling for a worldwide civilizing mission through the "common action of the Anglo-Saxon race."[58] An appreciative professor of history at the University of Minnesota, Frank Maloy Anderson (1871–1961), wrote to express his admiration for the book, telling Adams that in teaching his medieval English history class, "I always make a point to speak at least once briefly of the relations between England and the U.S.; next time I shall take the liberty to make your book the basis of my remarks."[59] In an 1897 article in the *Atlantic Monthly* titled "A Century of Anglo-Saxon Expansion," Adams celebrated improved relations but pointed to the challenge of "bringing the whole race into the lines of a common policy and the equal bearing of common burdens,—the problem of healing the breach made a century ago."[60] With the outbreak of war in 1914, Adams wrote numerous articles extolling the virtues of the British Empire, vilifying the Germans, and stressing the shared values of the American and English peoples. He also looked forward to a wider and closer Anglo-Saxon dominion over the postwar world.[61]

George Louis Beer, one of the "imperial" historians (as well as an independently wealthy New Yorker who had once taught at Columbia), is also of importance here. Beer, who along with Charles Gross (1857–1909) of Harvard, was one of the few prominent historians of the era whose background was Jewish, took up his pen to argue for a closer transatlantic union. We may wonder whether he would have been quite so ardent in the cause had the racially charged Teutonist version of history not been supplanted within the historical profession by the new institutional studies that he and others were writing. In fact, his devotion to the issue was such that he abandoned altogether his own scholarly work (part 2 of *The Old Colonial System*).[62] Articles that he wrote for *The Political Quarterly, The New Republic, The Forum,* and *The Annals of the American Academy* were published together in 1917, shortly after American entry into the war. The title of the book, *The English-Speaking Peoples: Their Future Relations and Joint International Obligations,*[63] suggests how closely aligned his views were with those of Adams.

Constitutional historians in the United States from the late nineteenth century on were concerned to bring their subject to a wider public and to change the public's generally unfavorable view of Britain. Herbert Baxter Adams quickly grasped the potential of using the numerous Chautauqua societies as a vehicle for a wider dissemination of pro-British views. When Kate F. Kimball of the Chautauqua Literary and Scientific Circle wrote to Adams in 1889 suggesting a three-year course in English history and literature, using John Richard Green's *Short History* as a foundation text, Adams responded enthusiastically. In the event, only seven students, all women, completed the first year's course, and Adams's hopes for turning the program into something more like a University Extension program were not realized.[64] Though he had told Daniel Coit Gilman of his hope that the program could be a force in "educating Democracy,"[65] he backed away from it in 1891 in favor of concentrating on the Johns Hopkins Extension.[66] Adams, however, continued to be intrigued by the potential for using popular institutions to spread what was, in his view, a more enlightened understanding of America's and England's shared past. The YMCA, with its seven hundred libraries, nine hundred reading rooms, and twenty-five thousand students in evening classes, was too tempting to ignore. After making a proposal for a series of courses, Adams received a favorable reply from the secretary of the International Committee of the YMCA, indicating that members of the committee

were rather pleased with the idea of your former letter in which a combination course of American and English history of one or two years' duration would especially fit into these times when the United States and England are becoming more closely allied in education, politics, and missionary efforts, was suggested. Such a course as you suggest might be called Anglo-American civilization or institutions or some such phrase.

A few months later, the YMCA added a course called "Anglo-American History."[67] The results could not have been more disappointing. Only six students signed up and just one finished the course, prompting the YMCA secretary to admit that, in selecting courses, young men "care very little for history."[68]

With such unpromising results, it was clear that the major effort needed to be concentrated on the schools. Many historians believed that better-informed teachers as well as a dramatically revised curriculum could help bring about improved relations with Britain. This had been a long-term concern on both sides of the Atlantic to those who wished to see improved relations. Considerable improvement had already taken place, according to Goldwin Smith, writing to a friend in 1897:

You speak of the American school histories as irritants of American feeling towards England. That was certainly the case when I first knew the United States. But the other day, seeing the remark made, I sent for the principal school histories, and on looking them over found that their tone was greatly improved. There was hardly anything to which exception could be taken. The feeling among the intelligent classes in the Eastern States is now not at all unkind towards us. The other day, at a great banquet at Princeton University, when I appealed to their gratitude towards the mother country, they all stood up and cheered. In the West there is more of the old bitterness, as plainly appeared when President Cleveland launched his Venezuelan message.[69]

Smith's own book on U.S. history, published in 1893,[70] though not strictly speaking a textbook, may have contributed to these warmer feelings, if the response of an academic admirer is accurate: "The book is destined to change materially the views of 'Young America.' We shall not love our country and its institutions less, but we shall love them more intelligently, and it is good to have the overwhelming conceit taken out of us, and to be made to feel that, next to America, England should be dear to us."[71] A similar improvement was taking place in textbooks in England, according to American journalist Julian Ralph. Writing in *Harper's New Monthly Magazine* in 1899, Ralph noted that when he had visited England ten years earlier, the history texts he looked at had ignored the American Revolution. On his recent trip he had examined the widely used *School History of England,* by Cunningham Geikie, and found a "full and sympathetic treatment, condemning English statesmen."[72]

However improved the tone of the texts, a considerable amount remained to be done, in the eyes of leaders of the American historical profession, especially to train young Americans to think more along "scientific" and institutional lines in regard to national history. They were doing their part with their own students, but it was the expanding realm of primary and especially secondary education that called out for attention. As George Burton Adams noted in 1896, "no class among us possesses a better opportunity . . . to create a right feeling towards England for the future as the public school teachers of this country."[73] A change in the kind of history that young Americans were subjected to in school was a high priority for the American Historical Association, which, encouraged by the National Education Association (NEA), in 1897 appointed the

Committee of Seven to investigate and issue a report. The NEA had requested a focus on college entrance requirements, but the committee expanded its brief to include a sweeping look at the history curriculum in high schools. This body, chaired by McLaughlin, included such Anglophiles as Herbert Baxter Adams of Johns Hopkins, Lucy Salmon of Vassar, Albert Bushnell Hart of Harvard, and H. Morse Stephens of Cornell. Between April 1897 and December 1898, the group held meetings at Cambridge, Massachusetts; Cleveland; Ann Arbor, Michigan; and New Haven, Connecticut, with each member engaged in considerable research in between. The committee studied secondary education in history in western Europe as well as the United States, noting that both Britain and America were far less systematic in their approach than France and Germany. McLaughlin, himself the author of a high school history textbook, took a dim view of the secondary education scene in his discipline: "Not only is the subject poorly taught, but there is no conception of what history is, and what it may be made to mean for high school students. At the best it is simply memorizing dry stuff in about ninety percent of the schools."[74]

The Committee of Seven agreed that English history, which was offered by only about half the American high schools surveyed, should be studied by all secondary students: "One cannot forget even in a high school course that England is the mother of modern constitutional government, that by the force of example she has become the lawgiver of nations." Moreover, the growth of the empire needed to be highlighted: "English history of the last three centuries without Drake, Raleigh, Pitt, Clive, and Gordon is not English history at all."[75] Not surprisingly, the committee's report recommended that high school juniors take a full year of English history, prior to American history in the senior year. English history in high schools, the committee suggested, should "be studied in its broader aspects" and should include "imperial development."[76] While that somewhat bland term was used in the printed official report, we can gain a better sense of the spirit of the committee's proceedings by considering this rhetorically rich justification for the study of the history of England and other countries from the committee's draft report: "The present war [the Spanish-American] has already shown that coal and steam, good ships, good guns, and Anglo-Saxon grit are destined to dominate the sea and all the earth."[77] The committee's published report called for the following sequence of study over the four years of high school: ancient history (to 800), medieval and modern European history, English history, and American history and government.[78]

The AHA revisited the issue in 1907, appointing the Committee of Five, of which McLaughlin was the only one from the previous body. Charles Homer Haskins of Harvard and James Harvey Robinson of Columbia were the most important of the new members. This time, English history was moved forward to the second year, and American colonial history was included in it, reflecting the ascendancy of the views of the "imperial historians": "English history, beginning with a brief statement of England's connection with the ancient world. The work should trace the main line of English development to about 1760, include as far as possible or convenient the chief facts of general European history, especially before the seventeenth century, and give something of the colonial history of America." Modern European history, in the third year, was to include "a suitable treatment of English history from 1760."[79]

An increased interest in the Normans was characteristic of these years and played an important part in fostering support for empire on both sides of the Atlantic. The most direct American promoter of a positive view of the Normans was Harvard professor (and later dean) Charles Homer Haskins, who published, during the First World War, two influential books detailing the accomplishments of the Normans in government, law, and culture.[80] Haskins, who had received his PhD at Johns Hopkins in 1890 after studying in France and Germany, asserted that the greatness of the Normans lay not only in their disciplined creativity but in their vigorous expansion, through which they carried the benefits of their civilization throughout Europe. The Normans, as a civilizing, imperial people, could be considered worthy forerunners of early-twentieth-century Americans. Pointing to a number of key constitutional and legal areas, Haskins declared that "the English-speaking countries are all heirs of the early Normans and of the Norman kings. . . . At such points, Norman history merges in that of England, the British Empire, and the United States."[81] Haskins's work further underscored the new orthodoxy in English constitutional history that the Normans were far more important than the Anglo-Saxons in forging the institutional foundations of Anglo-American law and government. Tout praised Haskins for his book *Norman Institutions,* noting the importance of stressing the Norman side of things.[82] It might be added that much of the research for Haskins's books on the Normans, like Andrews's research on eighteenth-century American materials in Britain, was funded by the Carnegie Institution, a markedly Anglophile body. The institution had provided repeated annual grants to Haskins for his "examination of the materials for Norman history in the eleventh and twelfth centuries with reference to the relations of Norman and English institutions."[83]

It is difficult to overestimate Haskins's influence within the profession on both sides of the Atlantic, as a writer, teacher, and molder of the next generation of medieval historians. As the great English medievalist F. M. Powicke put it in 1925: "As an American, he is free from our tradition of insularity; he knows his way around the manuscript collections . . . of Europe; yet his mind and outlook are English in the best sense of the word, and without a touch of pretentiousness."[84] One of the preeminent scholarly societies devoted to medieval studies is named in his honor. Founded in 1982, the Haskins Society is an "international scholarly organization dedicated to the study of Viking, Anglo-Saxon, Anglo-Norman, and early Angevin history and the history of neighboring areas and peoples."[85] Haskins had broken through the insular bonds of medieval institutional scholarship, taking a sweeping look at cultural as well as institutional developments in western Europe, albeit one that emphasized throughout the creative and shaping force of the Normans (as well as their Viking forebears). It was an approach that moved beyond the strictly institutional approach of earlier constitutional historians, yet one that underscored the importance of an adventurous, disciplined people who played a major role in shaping history and advancing civilization. It endorsed a cosmopolitan view of history yet stressed the leadership role of the most talented of northern peoples. It made the Normans worthy forerunners of early-twentieth-century America and England. As a people who were at once adventurous expansionists, cultural innovators, and wise, sober lawmakers, the Normans offered a compelling model for Haskins's contemporaries to carry on the mission of spreading civilization and the rule of law through the world. In addition to rendering imperialism a noble activity, his adulation of the Normans also bolstered a belief in the importance of strong central government. Just as Progressives (at least the Republican variety) in the United States and "New Liberals" in Britain were working toward a more activist state, the Anglo-Norman state's increasingly powerful and more intrusive central institutions were presented as a worthy constitutional model.

For George Burton Adams, Norman institutions were also laudable because they embodied a sober respect for authority and hierarchy. While Haskins was researching his books in France, Adams sent him an anxious letter, asking if he had discovered any pre-1066 Norman feudal charters, "for we need as many of them as we can get."[86] Adams held that feudalism had been introduced into England full-blown after 1066 and represented an exquisitely balanced polity, with many public duties in private hands, but subject, like the powers of the sovereign, to regulation by the precise contractual language of feudal charters. The evolution of postconquest law and government, shaped as it was by feudal contractualism, created not only a constitutional system but a constitutional culture, without which the carefully demarcated rights of subjects and limits on government, enforced by a growing body of law, could not have emerged. As he wrote in his *History of England from the Norman Conquest to the Death of John, 1066–1216* (1905), the introduction of the feudal system was as momentous as any which followed the Norman Conquest, as decisive in its influence as the enrichment of race or language; more decisive in one respect, since without the consequences in government and constitution, which were destined to follow from the feudalization of the English state, neither race nor language could have done the work in the world which they have already accomplished and are yet destined to perform in still larger measure.[87]

Such Norman descent of modern government was congenial to those throughout the English-speaking world who were determined to maintain the sanctity of contract and property rights against the menace of socialism, populism, and dangerous schemes of governmental "reform." It was a far cry from the views of the previous generation of constitutional historians, some of them still alive, for whom the "Norman Yoke" had been a central concept. One of the American historical counterparts to this inversion of the older view of Anglo-Saxons and Normans is the reversal, during the early years of the twentieth century, in the standing of Alexander Hamilton and Thomas Jefferson. The latter, whose near deification in the nineteenth century slipped substantially, was for a considerable time eclipsed by the suddenly ascendant Hamilton, whose vision of a strong capitalist America with vigorous central government was in tune with the times.[88]

Like the institutional approach of the "imperial" historians, pro-Norman views of the past were being methodically inserted into college and high school textbooks in the United States. The professional historians of this era were remarkably active in the writing of textbooks, certainly compared with later generations of scholars. While in part this activity may be attributed to low academic salaries, some of the best-paid leaders of the profession took the writing of texts for a mass (if captive) readership as seriously as they did the crafting of monographs for their scholarly peers. McLaughlin, in spite of his numerous other scholarly ventures, Carnegie Institution duties, and *American Historical Review* editing, found time to write a widely adopted high school text on U.S. history, the first edition of which appeared in 1899.[89] Claude H. Van Tyne (1869–1930), a rising star in the profession who at that time was at work on a book published a few years later as *The Loyalists in the American Revolution* (1902), wrote McLaughlin that as a schoolboy he had been subjected to the anti-British views of the standard text of the day, John C. Ridpath's *History of the United States:* "How I should have enjoyed being introduced to manly problems in a plain, straightforward way instead of being entertained with flowery jingoism."[90] The two men became close friends, and in 1903 McLaughlin offered Van Tyne a position at the University of Michigan, promising: "I'll look out for your interests and have no doubt all will come out well."[91] Indeed, all went well. Van Tyne had a long career at Michigan, publishing a number of influential books on the American Revolution and becoming department head in 1911. He also became McLaughlin's coauthor for subsequent editions of the U.S. history text.

Andrews, in his *Short History of England*, published in 1912 as part of the Allyn and Bacon School Histories series, was able to deal with the American Revolution as well as the Norman Conquest. After a nod toward the courage and "love of freedom" of the Anglo-Saxons, Andrews praised the conquest, "because in winning it the Normans displayed in military matters the same superiority which they were to show in government and law as well." He went on to observe that the Norman victory "prepared the way for a higher order of government, law, and industry, and for greater strength and stability in national affairs." Andrews's treatment of the American Revolution stressed the contingent nature of the event. Even after the battles of Lexington and Concord, he claimed, "a majority of the colonists, representing the best men in America, still hoped for reconciliation."[92]

There was a quite similar treatment of the causes, course, and results of the revolution in the relevant volumes of the most ambitious textbook undertaking of the era, the twenty-six-volume American Nation series, edited by Albert Bushnell Hart and published by Harpers. This series epitomized the professional approach by parceling out the work among numerous specialists in each time period, a method already being used in Britain in the *Cambridge Modern History*, edited by Lord Acton. Van Tyne, based on the success of his recent sympathetic book on the Loyalists, was selected to write volume 9, *The American Revolution*. In the same series, Andrews wrote volume 5, *Colonial Self-Government*, while McLaughlin wrote volume 10, *The Confederation and the Constitution*. The volumes dealing with the Civil War and Reconstruction also reflected the rapidly changing views of professional historians about that conflict—that the Civil War was not inevitable, that slavery had not been the overriding cause, and that radical reconstruction of the South had been overzealous and counterproductive. Volume 20, *Reconstruction, Political and Economic*, by Dunning, with its sympathetic portrayal of Southern resistance to the depredations of Northern carpetbaggers and near-savage freed slaves, was particularly effective in assuaging Southern resentments about the "Lost Cause." It also helped to bring the South, or rather the white South, more securely into the mainstream of national life and culture. Much of the ground for this nationalist-reconciliationist theme had been laid in doctoral dissertations at the end of the nineteenth century. At Johns Hopkins alone, eleven dissertations on the institutional aspects of slavery on a state-by-state basis had been undertaken in the

1880s and 1890s.[93] The welcoming back of the South to full honor was reflected in the extraordinary effusion of blue-grey comradeship by veterans' organizations, especially the fiftieth anniversary celebrations of the Battle of Gettysburg in 1913.[94] That same year also saw Dunning presiding over only the second annual meeting of the AHA to be held in the South (the first had been at New Orleans in 1903), at Charleston, South Carolina. In effect, what was done by historians to the Civil War was to bring it into the orbit of constitutional history, stripping it of its moral meanings. The struggle was transformed from a crusade against slavery into a constitutional question: states' rights versus national sovereignty. Both sides of the question could be deemed to have had solid justification for their views. As with the American Revolution, fanatical and obstreperous men on both sides could be blamed for having pushed the country unnecessarily over the precipice. North-South reconciliation became an analog to Anglo-American rapprochement.

It is hardly surprising that the Anglophile tone of the books by professional American historians of the era dealing with constitutional history and Anglo-American relations should also characterize the lectures they presented to their students. McLaughlin began his course on American colonial history at the University of Michigan by telling his students: "No one can study the history of England without seeing a steady progress towards freedom—and freedom in this sense—the consciousness of freedom," a process he claimed could also "be studied with minuteness, with satisfactory results in the history of our own country." To this unexceptionable Whig doctrine was added an expansionist and imperialist element, in which McLaughlin called on his students to recognize the "inherent audacity and boldness and capacity for government which has pushed the Anglo-Saxons all over the globe."[95] The lecture notes of Arthur Lyon Cross (1873–1940), who began teaching English constitutional history at the University of Michigan in 1899 after earning his PhD under Charles Gross at Harvard, are also preserved. It is not possible to date these notes precisely, but their dog-eared condition suggests repeated usage over many years. For the first day of the term, Cross's notes indicate the main points to be discussed, including such items as "co-op Eng. Sp. Peoples essential" and "Much anti-Br. feeling."[96] He also mentions the Round Table, a secretive, high-level political group founded in London in 1909 dedicated to imperial federation. There was growing interest in the movement among key American historians, who worked to expand the goals of the Round Table to include English-speaking federation. In 1914, there appeared Cross's college textbook, *A History of England and Greater Britain*[97] (note the Dilkean title), in which imperial federation and Anglo-American relations were prominent. Cross's lecture notes also contain a recommended reading list for various subtopics. Among the five titles suggested for Anglo-American relations are Dunning's *The British Empire and the United States,* the Carnegie-funded volume written for the Peace Centenary of 1913, and *The Pan-Angles* by Sinclair Kennedy (1875–1947). The latter, a Boston-born lawyer and enthusiast for English-speaking federation, was not an academic. His spirited book in favor of closely integrating the United States and the white settler dominions of the British Empire was published on the eve of the Great War and is filled with an air of anxiety about Britain's vulnerability to ruthless new powers like the German Empire, as well as the menace to all Pan-Angles represented by the "yellow races." In a tone not much different from the nationalist effusions of the Pan-German League, Kennedy concluded:

We have inherited not only lands but ideals from the men who fought for them, regardless of whether it was they or we, their children, who should inherit and enjoy them. To defend these lands, these ideals of personal freedom, and the language we speak, we once had unquestioned supremacy over the seas of the world. By a federation of the English-speaking white people of these seven nations [Britain, Canada, Newfoundland, Australia, New Zealand, South Africa, and the United States], the control of the world and the self-control of our own citizens will again be in the certain care of the Pan-Angle.[98]

When the Great War erupted in August 1914, English-speaking federationists, including a fair number of the constitutional historians in America, agitated for the United States to join Britain in her noble struggle. From Ann Arbor in January 1915, Van Tyne wrote to a friend at the Harvard Foundation in Paris: "I feel so strongly about the struggle that if I were an absolute despot I would be preparing this country to come to the aid of the allies. I should not need to do much urging either, for except for a few German and Irish the country is united in its hate of Prussian militarism and German arrogance."[99] Van Tyne's colleague Cross was quick to praise the stream of propagandistic publications written by British scholars as soon as the war broke out. From England, Ford Madox Ford thanked him for commending his book *When Blood Is Their Argument: An Analysis of Prussian Culture.*[100] One of Cross's former students, who was teaching at Knox College in Illinois, was determined to correct the apathy of his midwestern students: "I realize more than ever the great work that we, as teachers of history, can do in building up a state of opinion favorable to the cause of righteousness."[101] For his part, McLaughlin rejoiced to Cross that the dominions had rallied around the empire: "That is the structure which was to fall to pieces as soon as the war Lord [the Kaiser] pointed his finger at it."[102] Even the cosmopolitan Haskins wrote to assure Tout in Manchester that "the enormous preponderance of American opinion is on the English side, even among the large number of university men who have studied in Germany and feel a deep indebtedness to German scholarship. I am one of those who admire German scholarship when it is not shot from guns."[103] There was jubilation among the leading constitutional historians on both sides of the Atlantic when the United States joined the Allied cause in April 1917. From Oxford, Reginald Lane Poole, editor of the *English Historical Review,* wrote to Haskins: "We are all rejoicing at the turn which things have taken, and the stars and stripes are flying over the houses of parliament. I hope and believe that your intervention will materially shorten the war."[104]

Now that the United States was a combatant, a more massive and organized effort by U.S. historians on behalf of the war effort began. With America in the conflict, leaders of the profession considered it a patriotic and moral duty to instruct their compatriots about the righteousness of the Allied cause. The National Board for Historical Service (NBHS) was established under the leadership of Jameson and funded by the Carnegie Institution.[105] Cross, of Michigan, urged by NBHS vice chairman Carl Russell Fish (1876–1932) of the University of Wisconsin, became the very active chairman of the subcommittee on English history, organizing training camp lectures, writing articles for the *War Cyclopaedia,* and encouraging colleagues around the country to join the cause.[106] Fish, every bit as much an enthusiast for English-speaking federation as Cross, suggested some pointers for him in guiding the teachers who would carry out the public and training camp lectures: "In handling the American Revolution, the sympathy of the Whigs should be developed. The attempt then and later to organize the British Empire afford [*sic*] material on a possible World Federation, etc." We have, Fish continued, "a big job to fit the American people to be a world power."[107] Only a handful of American historians otherwise friendly to England refused to participate. One of them was Edward P. Cheyney of the University of Pennsylvania, author of two important college texts, *A Short History of England* and *Readings in English History.* Asked by the National Board to contribute something on the sixteenth century for a war-oriented series, "Timely Suggestions for Secondary School History," he replied:

when I think of putting before young people a plan of teaching English history in the 16th century, so as to show that the English and Dutch were right, the Spaniards and the Irish wrong, that the institutions then being developed were in themselves superior to those of other nations, with a constant suggestion of the righteousness of the present war and a deepening of the chasm between us and other nations—I simply cannot do it.[108]

Few others showed such scruples. In addition to public lectures, training camp lectures, and school essay contests, a steady stream of pamphlets issued from patriotic American historians, all extolling the virtues of England and demonizing the Germans.

Jameson, editor of the *American Historical Review,* also provided office space for the National Board in the Carnegie Institution building.[109] Moreover, as editor he refused to publish letters critical of National Board activities, such as one from John H. Latané of Johns Hopkins, who had challenged the historical accuracy of one of the board's pamphlets.[110] This issue was exacerbated by the lingering resentments over an earlier (1915) dispute about the running of the AHA, in which Latané and other insurgents had challenged the "oligarchic" character of the leadership long provided by Jameson, McLaughlin, and other grandees.[111] Among the grievances on that occasion was the "mysterious connection," as Latané put it, between the *American Historical Review* and the Carnegie Institution.[112] Jameson also took an active part in overseeing the kind of motivational training camp lectures that the National Board was providing. He explained to Bryce that it was necessary to show less-educated and thoughtful Americans

how great a change has come over Great Britain since the power passed from the hands of a ruling class into that of a democracy. I am just in these days engaged in preparing a syllabus for use by lecturers who go about in our various training camps and cantonments talking to thousands of boys, in simple fashion, on the origin and background of the war, and what it is all about, and I have been putting it very strongly to the lecturers that they must emphasize the particular results of British democracy, as well as to dwell on the British Empire as our ally more than on England alone.[113]

On another occasion, Jameson forwarded to the NBHS some articles sent by the head of British war publicity in the United States, including one from the *Round Table* called "The New German Empire," recommending it as the kind of approach the board should take in dealing with that topic.[114]

The tireless George Burton Adams gave his time unstintingly to the cause, writing numerous contributions for the National Board for Historical Service on such topics as the Triple Entente.[115] Such was his ardor that even Jameson had to express some reservations, though not to the point of impeding the steady flow of pro-British propaganda: "Personally, I do not think so highly of British unselfishness as I judge that you do. But that does not matter; if we are in alliance with them in any sense—and I am very glad that we are—it is right to 'play up' all their nobler and better qualities and all the evidences of willingness on their part to act in the interest of the whole world and its future."[116] Adams also went on numerous lectures around the country. Some of these were straight constitutional history rather than blatant war propaganda but served the same end quite effectively. At the start of a series of lectures at Pomona

College in California in 1917, he stressed to the students that the English constitution was the very bedrock of modern American society and gave them an institutional take on the civilizing role of the Anglo-Saxon "race":

The civilization of the United States is essentially Anglo-Saxon, for civilization and "race" are matters of institutions, not of mere blood. With the Anglo-Saxon race, progress in the main has been slow and steady, and its "constitution," the body of institutions by which it governs itself, has grown out of practical need, and not to serve any theoretical purpose. So far as general institutions are concerned, English constitutional history begins with the Norman Conquest.[117]

In regard to maintaining the close connections between American and British historians, Adams played a critical role in getting the AHA to continue renting a room for its members from the Royal Historical Society in London. The AHA had sought to discontinue the arrangement due to financial difficulties, but Adams, writing from London at the end of 1914, convinced Jameson of the value of maintaining such a vital point of contact during and after the war. In the end, the Morgan Bank (which had already done a good deal to promote close transatlantic scholarly relations), in the person of Dwight Morrow, paid the rent for the AHA London premises.[118]

While lecturing around the country and writing for the National Board, Adams was also heavily involved in promoting the work of the Round Table to bring about closer imperial federation that would ultimately include the United States. His labors in this arena were well under way even before the entry of the United States into the conflict in April 1917. There is a very large file of correspondence between Adams and Lionel Curtis, a leading force in the Round Table, as well as an active member of the Rhodes Trust. Curtis, who had served his apprenticeship as a member of Alfred Milner's "Kindergarten" in South Africa, told Adams that the fashioning of a closer Commonwealth was but a prelude to the movement's ultimate aim: "The immediate work we have to do is but a step towards the wider union which neither you nor I will see, by which the crowning catastrophy [sic] of modern history in the eighteenth century, will be undone. Then and then only the future of freedom will be secure and the world at length may rest in peace."[119] Eager to do his part, Adams wrote articles for the *Yale Review* and other magazines. These had been requested by Beer, who by this point had given up his own scholarly publications to devote himself to the Round Table. As Beer told Adams, the purpose of the articles was "to stimulate the interest of business men, lawyers, financiers, etc. in such questions and to form a bridge between the academic and the outer world."[120]

In early 1918, the National Board for Historical Service, whose activities to that point had been confined to the United States, sponsored a lecture tour of

Britain by McLaughlin. The initiative had come from the University of London, which had asked Jameson for an American historian to lecture to British teachers on the history of American institutions and Anglo-American relations. Writing to Firth, the Regius professor of modern history at Oxford, Jameson explained that the board not only agreed that McLaughlin was the best man, but expanded the project "into a scheme whereby he makes a tour of all the chief universities in Great Britain and Ireland, lecturing on such themes as were suggested."[121] The British, recognizing the value of such an extended and very public visit, pulled out all the stops. Shortly after his arrival, McLaughlin was feted at a gala dinner chaired by Lord Bryce and attended by a host of dignitaries, as well as the Duke of Connaught and the Archbishop of Canterbury.[122] The American professor was kept very busy. Newton had scheduled him for four lectures at University College alone. Moving on to Oxford, where he stayed with Firth, he lectured to seven or eight hundred "cadets, professors, and the women." In a set speech he gave throughout the United Kingdom titled "America's Entry into the War: An Historical Statement," he declared: "Nothing is to me, as I study American history and American institutions, is more impressive than the force of the essentials of Anglo-American civilization. The influence of language, of literature, of law have exerted and will continue to exert steady pressure, and the resulting civilization will be largely identical with your own."[123] A few weeks later, writing from Dublin, where he lunched with the Lord-Lieutenant, McLaughlin was able to report that he had "done most of the British—I mean English universities" and that "the audiences have been fairly numerous and always very responsive."[124] He hastened to assure Jameson that the theme of the necessity of long-term Anglo-American cooperation was front and center: "Hammered on that in all of my speeches." He also gave addresses before more professional audiences, such as the members of the Royal Historical Society, in which he highlighted the background of American Federalism.[125] Federalism had become the constitutional underpinning of all those groups seeking closer ties among the English-speaking nations and was to remain the central concept to stress during the interwar years. McLaughlin's satisfaction at the success of his lecture tour was soon eclipsed by a grievous loss, when his son Rowland was killed in battle in October 1918, a few weeks before the armistice. Yet, like the other historians involved in the war effort, he never doubted the rightness of the cause and celebrated not only the victory but the prospect of ever closer Anglo-American cooperation, both in diplomacy and scholarship.

McLaughlin was also the first American member of an important transatlantic organization established in 1918, the English-Speaking Union (E-SU).

Founded by an English journalist named Evelyn Wrench (1882–1966), the E-SU sought to build on earlier organizational efforts to foster closer Anglophone unity. We have already considered the Pan-Angle movement launched by Sinclair Kennedy before the war, but there were earlier enterprises and sentiments stretching back into the second half of the nineteenth century. Goldwin Smith had issued an early call for Anglo-American union on a visit to the United States during the last year of the Civil War. In 1882, he declared himself "a loyal and even ardent citizen of the Greater Britain" and longed "to see all children of England, including the people of the United States, linked to their parent by the bond of the heart."[126] While he never ceased to wish for closer bonds, as an unreconstructed Gladstonian "little Englander," Smith was put off by British and American jingoism and expansion at the end of the century.[127] Another staunch champion of the North in the Civil War who called for closer relations with America was Thomas Hughes, author of *Tom Brown's School Days*. In 1871, citing what he called the "lamentable ignorance of contemporary American history, which exists in England even amongst otherwise well instructed politicians,"[128] Hughes became chairman of the newly founded Anglo-American Association, which included such figures as Herbert Spencer and John Morley. A renewal of interest in forging a closer relationship came after the war scare associated with the Venezuelan boundary dispute of 1895. The Anglo-American League, containing both James Bryce and Sir Frederick Pollock, was established in 1898. After a promising start, including plans for an ambitious lecture series on American life, it lapsed into quiescence.[129]

A more enduring organization, and the immediate precursor to the English-Speaking Union, was the Atlantic Union, formed in 1901 by Sir Walter Besant (1836–1901). Besant was a speaker at the King Alfred Millenary celebrations in Winchester that year, and in his speech he managed to transform the king of Wessex into a modern symbol of imperial and Anglophone unity: "Alfred is, and will always remain, the typical man of our race—call him Anglo-Saxon, call him Englishman, call him Australian—the typical man of our race at his best and noblest."[130] In the aftermath of the Spanish-American and Boer Wars, the Atlantic Union called for the formation of a permanent military alliance of the English-speaking peoples to maintain the peace.[131] This was the organization that was amalgamated with the English-Speaking Union the year after the formal launch of the E-SU on 4 July 1918. Given the idealistic direction that the E-SU was to take in subsequent decades, with an emphasis on universal brotherhood, it is important to note its imperial and far-from-pacifistic roots. Evelyn Wrench had been a student in Germany in 1900 and during the next decade worked as a correspondent and editor for Lord Northcliffe's *Daily*

Mail. Inspired by the German Navy League, he sought to stimulate enthusiasm for the British Empire in Britain and the dominions. Resigning his journalistic post and giving himself over fully to the cause, Wrench established the Overseas Club in 1912, a group he described as a kind of "Grown-up Boy Scouts."[132] A four-thousand-mile train trip across the United States, including numerous visits to universities, confirmed his sense of the overriding importance of bringing all the English-speaking peoples together.

Wrench's wartime service in the Ministry of Information brought further American contacts, including the U.S. ambassador to Britain, Walter Hines Page, with whom he "agreed passionately . . . that the ending of the hundred and forty year estrangement between the English-speaking nations was 'the most momentous fact in the history of either people.'"[133] James Bryce and Winston Churchill became vice presidents of the English-Speaking Union, with Churchill assuming the chairmanship in 1921. Franklin Roosevelt, who was in England in 1917 and 1918, also became an early member. The E-SU's magazine, *The Landmark*, helped publicize the group's activities and prompted press baron Lord Rothermere (Alfred Harmsworth) to donate twenty thousand pounds to found a chair in U.S. history at Oxford in honor of his son Vyvyan Harmsworth, who had been killed in the war.[134] There was also a proposal that the E-SU itself found chairs of English history in American universities. It was decided that such a course would be "very unwise," a recognition that there was already growing alarm in America at the pro-British views emanating from the academic community.[135] In 1923, the E-SU did send a British teacher to the United States, the first of the Walter Hines Page Traveling Scholarships. The American branch of the E-SU flourished, with membership outstripping that in Britain by 1923, at which point there were 6,314 British members and 7,554 American ones.[136] The very success of the E-SU, however, as well as that of related organizations such as the Sulgrave Institution (named after the Washington ancestral home in Northamptonshire), was provoking strong opposition from traditionally minded American patriots, as well as ethnic organizations resentful at the slighting of their contributions to American history. During the 1920s this opposition was to erupt into a full-blown culture war.

CHAPTER SEVEN

"Designed to Disarm America by Destroying Patriotic Spirit and Inculcating National Pusillanimity in the Name of Peace"

Constitutional History and America's Culture Wars

Both the English-Speaking Union and the Round Table, including their historian members, continued to promote permanent Anglo-American cooperation in the world following the end of the Great War. But in the complex clash of ambitions and strategies at the peace conference, this would prove difficult, despite the presence of such Round Table luminaries as Lord Milner, the colonial secretary. In the American delegation, Round Table member George Louis Beer was colonial delegate to the Paris Peace Conference. An idealist as well as a believer in a wide U.S. role in the world (preferably in partnership with the British Empire), Beer pressed for America to become a mandate power in Africa, a scheme that fell victim to Anglo-French greed to acquire the former German colonies.[1] Even had the idea found favor, it would have come to nothing in the face of the U.S. Senate's refusal to ratify the Treaty of Versailles and enter the League of Nations. An even more extravagant role for America as a mandate power was envisaged by Reginald Lane Poole, the editor of the *English Historical Review*. Writing to George Burton Adams at the end of 1917, Poole ventured to suggest that, after the war, the United States

should be requested to accept the dominion of Constantinople and the immediately adjacent district, if not more. . . . I should like to see the whole Balkan territory from Bosnia to Greece placed under its hegemony. Those various (and largely mongrel) nationalities can only be kept in peace by being controlled by a great Power which has no prejudices in favour of Greeks, or Bulgarians, or Vlaks, or Serbs, or Turks, or Albanians.[2]

There were other historians in the American delegation in Paris besides Beer, about a dozen altogether, not counting President Wilson. Most of them had less grandiose ideas than Poole did about America's role in the postwar world, though they too wanted the United States to take a prominent part. Among the most important American scholars in Paris were Charles Homer Haskins, Charles Seymour (1885–1963), and James T. Shotwell (1874–1965). All three were brought into the secretive inner circle of presidential advisers known as "the Inquiry." Haskins, who had been in graduate school at Johns Hopkins with Wilson, became head of the western division and played a vital role in working out the territorial settlements in western Europe, as well as serving as Wilson's translator in key negotiations with President Clemenceau of France. The Yale-trained Seymour, whose first book, in 1915, had been on English constitutional history (*Electoral Reform in England and Wales*), was a confidant of Colonel House and was later editor of his papers. He played an important part in the territorial settlements in the Balkans. The Canadian-born Shotwell, who had earned his doctorate at Columbia in 1900 under James Harvey Robinson, was chairman of the National Board for Historical Service before becoming a close presidential adviser in Paris. He served as chief of the Division of History of the American delegation. Another American academic member of the delegation (like Shotwell, Canadian-born) was Isaiah Bowman (1878–1950). Though a geographer rather than a historian, he was vitally interested in both the history of the British Empire and the emergence of the United States as a global power, and the importance of close Anglo-American relations. In Paris, Bowman was the chief territorial adviser to President Wilson. Shortly after the peace conference, he published an important book called *The New World,* describing the process of boundary drawing at Paris and detailing the challenges faced by the British Empire as well as the emerging American one, accompanied by a call for a robust internationalism.[3]

All of these historical scholars were Anglophiles as well as internationalists. They were deeply disappointed by America's refusal to join the League of Nations and worked to foster international accord and Anglo-American partnership between the wars. Beer would have undoubtedly taken a leading part but for his untimely death in 1920. Haskins returned to Harvard, serving as dean of the graduate school until his death in 1937, having turned down numerous offers of government posts and university presidencies. Seymour also returned to academia, becoming president of Yale in 1930. Shotwell, both as a leading academic in the field of international relations (at Columbia) and as a major figure in the Carnegie Endowment for International Peace, continued to press for U.S. membership in the league. He was triumphantly present in San Francisco in 1945 (as a State Department consultant and one of the drafters of the UN charter) at the formation of the United Nations. Throughout his long career, Shotwell remained an admirer of the English constitution, but as befit a professional historian of the time, in the institutional sense rather than with any Anglo-Saxon racial associations.[4] And both Shotwell and Bowman were very active in the most influential of all the American foreign policy study groups formed after World War I, the Council on Foreign Relations.

The council, like its sister body in Britain, the Royal Institute of International Affairs, had its inception at the Paris Peace Conference. There the British and American advisers, some of them Round Table members, frustrated at their relatively modest influence on the final treaty, met to devise strategies to shape postwar foreign policy in a way that they believed would promote world peace and international cooperation under the guidance of the English-speaking nations. Beer and Shotwell took an important part in the early meetings. The leading figure on the British side was Lionel Curtis of the Round Table, now a professor at Oxford.[5] Once the Council on Foreign Relations was fully launched in 1921, the Morgan banking interest and the Carnegie Endowment proved generous benefactors, as they had done earlier with the Peace Centenary Committee of 1913 and various activities of the American Historical Association (AHA), but in the process they exacerbated the culture wars of the 1920s over the role of British influence on America.[6] Initially, the members of both the council and the Royal Institute of International Affairs looked on the proposed League of Nations as a device to foster closer cooperation within the Anglosphere, especially since the four white settler dominions (Canada, Australia, New Zealand, and the Union of South Africa) were to be represented. However, with the Senate's rejection of the Versailles Treaty, leaving the United States outside the league, and the dominions' evident determination to chart an independent course, the league's value was far more problematic. Still, the elite academics and business interests who steered the Council on Foreign Relations continued to press for American entry in the league, believing that the encouragement of any form of internationalism was a good thing and bound to foster Anglo-American cooperation. The relationship between the council and the Royal Institute of International Affairs (often referred to simply as Chatham House, its London headquarters), remained very close.[7]

The reaction against these developments was not long in coming. In the early postwar period, there was a growing outcry against the kind of history that had established itself at the universities, accompanied by an anxiety that it might spread through the high schools. The new historical orthodoxy had scant regard either for the traditional heroic national narrative or for the contributions of groups other than the British. The new constitutional history, by diminishing the importance of the American Revolutionary War, not only dimmed the luster of Washington and other leaders of the struggle for independence, but also took away heroes like Johann DeKalb and Tadeusz Kosciusko from the nation's history. Such figures had allowed generations of immigrants, not just Germans and Poles, to embrace the national past. The casting of the revolution as an unfortunate rupture of Anglo-Saxondom was especially galling to Irish Americans, their nationalism raised to a fever pitch by the Easter Rising of 1916 and the Anglo-Irish War of 1919–21. Nor did one need to be a "hyphenated American" (to borrow Theodore Roosevelt's derogatory term) to feel offended. The patriotic impulses of ordinary Americans, fashioned and renewed by annual Independence Day celebrations, were slighted by an institutionalized and internationalized recasting of the country's history. On top of these festering resentments against a professorial elite who were attempting to steal their history was the general disillusionment following the war and the growing sense that America had been gulled into entering the conflict by wily European powers, especially Britain. No Anglophile version of history, especially one that clearly carried an agenda of fostering ever closer cooperation with a victorious British Empire, could be allowed to undermine the sacred core of American life. For their part, the professors saw themselves fighting an uphill battle, with the majority of textbooks still conveying an anti-British bias. In 1917 there appeared a book by Charles Altschul detailing the dismal picture, with an introduction by Shotwell.[8] Reviewing the volume in the *American Historical Review,* Claude H. Van Tyne agreed that it gave "definite and concrete proof of an evil educational tendency of which many have been long but only vaguely aware."[9]

Many large American cities, controlled by the Irish and other ethnic communities, were sites of contentious wrangling in the 1920s over history textbooks in mayoral, council, and especially school board elections, in which the flames were fanned by the Hearst press and other media. Even rural and small-town America, though in thrall to nativist, anti-immigrant impulses, found some common ground with urban opponents of the new history. Patriotic organizations, led by the Daughters of the American Revolution, were also resistant to the new history, though, as Americans of largely British descent, they often found themselves at cross-purposes with the "ethnic" groups.[10] A culture war, centering on sharply divergent versions of the nation's history, erupted across a broad front. It mobilized people of all ethnicities and social classes, united by a determination to prevent the poisoning of American youth by what came to be called "treason texts."[11] Even many of those not as disposed to conspiracy theories were concerned that there was an evident agenda on the part of elite academics to transform not just the university curriculum but also the kind of history taught to children. Indeed, historians had often been quite frank about their intentions. In a 1918 pamphlet titled *America's Educational Problem,* that redoubtable Anglophile constitutional historian Claude H. Van Tyne of the University of Michigan had declared:

Except in our better colleges and universities the extent of our debt to England for most of the institutions which dominate in our republic has not been taught. Here and there in our grade and high schools a teacher of exceptional equipment has told his pupils of our indebtedness. But the leaven has not penetrated far. We have as a people taken unnoticed as the air we breathe the institutions of representative Government; trial by jury; no taxation without representation, habeas corpus, right of public assembly and of protest, free press, free speech and right of petition—rights that have all been created and developed by the English-speaking race. Many Americans seem to think that in some mysterious way Thomas Jefferson, George Washington, and Patrick Henry invented them before breakfast.[12]

Concern about the new constitutional history's impact upon schooling was evident even before the war, but with the dramatic expansion of secondary education after 1918, the issue assumed critical importance. All of the textbook writers discussed in Chapter 6 came in for heavy criticism, but one scholar above all became the symbol of the traitorous academic: David Saville Muzzey (1870–1965), the most prolific and successful author of high school and college history texts in the interwar years. Muzzey, who had received his doctorate from Columbia under James Harvey Robinson, taught at Columbia Teachers College, making him a double threat to traditionalists, both as a textbook writer and as a trainer of teachers. Muzzey's texts are lively and well written, so that there is little mystery about their widespread adoption by school districts throughout the country. His treatment of contentious issues like the American Revolution seems sound and evenhanded, but of course in the eyes of his critics, any attempt to see the situation through loyalist as well as patriot eyes undermined the stirring heroic epic they believed should be at the center of all accounts of the nation's past. Muzzey's slighting of the military side of the revolution also raised the ire of opponents. The scant ten pages (out of 540 pages of main text) given to the conflict in the 1923 edition of his text, *An American History* (first published 1911), is preceded by this comment: "A detailed description of battles and campaigns is profitable only to experts in military science, whereas the causes that lead a country into war, especially into a war for independence, are most important stages in the evolution of a people's political and moral life."[13] In spite of the many significant changes in the interpretive paradigms of constitutional history that had taken place by this point, such an assertion of the supremacy of constitutional issues over what John Richard Green had disparagingly called "drum and trumpet history" represents a profound continuity with the Whig historians of the nineteenth century. But in the 1920s, just as in the 1870s, traditionalists, who considered tales of martial glory an essential component of national identity, were incensed.

Among the gaggle of politicians, journalists, super-patriots, and cranks who took a prominent part in the opposition to the "treason texts" was Mayor William Hale ("Big Bill") Thompson of Chicago, who threatened to burn the texts of Muzzey, Andrew Cunningham McLaughlin, and Arthur Schlesinger Sr. on the lakefront. The AHA quickly sprang to the scholars' defense,[14] and Muzzey wrote Van Tyne that he was pleased that "all of the historical guild are solidly behind me in this rather disagreeable but necessary task of bringing the liars in Chicago to heel."[15] An outraged dean at the University of Chicago, C. S. Boucher, wrote Van Tyne: "Big Bill had given us many a laugh out here at the University, but has also caused us to hang our heads with shame for the city of Chicago. Personally, in my teaching I shall even make it more of a point than ever to bring out the English side in the American Revolution because that is what our citizens need."[16] On a more contemporary issue, other historians were working to reduce Britain's war debt to the United States. James T. Shotwell, now director of the Carnegie Endowment for International Peace, urged the University of Michigan to pass a resolution similar to that of Columbia, for the "statement . . . that Britain got so much out of the war that it can afford to pay the war debt many times over is so distinctly false that it is a shame to let it pass."[17]

In addition to Mayor Thompson, another key figure attacking the "traitorous" scholars was Hearst journalist Charles Grant Miller. Operating under the auspices of the Patriot League to Preserve American History, in 1922 Miller published *Treason to American Tradition: The Spirit of Benedict Arnold Reincarnated in United States History Revised in Textbooks: An Exposure of Ten Anglicized School Histories.* In this work he carefully documented the consistently pro-British views of prevalent American history texts, including that of Muzzey. In his 1928 work, *The Poisoned Loving-Cup: United States School Histories Falsified Through Pro-British Propaganda in Sweet Name of Amity,* Miller took his attack to new levels, setting forth what he considered an obvious network of academics, bankers, and business leaders with a mission to undermine national sovereignty and establish world government. The Carnegie Institution's close involvement with the historical profession from the start of the century was detailed, as was the interlocking directorate of a handful of academics and businessmen on the boards of elite universities and organizations like the English-Speaking Union and League of Nations Association. Nor did Miller overlook the Rhodes Scholarships, in which "hundreds of selected American young men are sent to Oxford University and returned to us Anglicized," all to bring about "the recovery of the United States as an integral part of the British Empire."[18] Typical of Miller's method of revealing the "interlocking directorate" of academics, business leaders, publishers, and internationalist organizations is the following: "George A. Plimpton, senior member of Ginn & Co. [Muzzey's publisher] is a trustee of the World Peace Foundation, the head of which is Nicholas Murray Butler, president of Columbia University. Ginn's and Carnegie's millions sustain the World Peace Foundation, which is designed to disarm America by destroying patriotic spirit and inculcating national pusillanimity in the name of peace."[19]

As far as constitutional matters proper, Miller zeroed in on the internationalists' slighting of the Declaration of Independence and emphasis on Magna Carta as the font of all things fine and noble in Anglo-American institutions. According to Miller, June 15, the date King John signed the charter in 1215, had been designated "Constitution Day" by the treasonous scholars and was to replace July 4 as the major national holiday. Moreover, it was to be the national holiday in all the seven Anglophone nations that had been the focus of Sinclair Kennedy's *The Pan-Angles*. This, Miller claimed, was the avowed aim of the Magna Carta Day Association, in a program that was "connected up with the alteration of our school histories directly and definitely." The proof of this assertion Miller found in the 1919 edition of McLaughlin and Van Tyne's *History of the United States for Schools*. While the 1911 edition of the text had made no mention whatever of Magna Carta, that of 1919 boasted a new fifteen-page chapter devoted to it, followed by a discussion of both the Declaration and the American constitution that stressed their derivation from English constitutional ideas.[20] A tone of breathless journalistic exposé pervades the whole of Miller's book, and the device of asserting the existence of a conspiracy on the basis of certain individuals being involved in the same organizations was a staple of the cranks and racists of the era who worked a credulous public. But after stripping away patriotic rant, hyperbole, and character assassination from the *Poisoned Loving-Cup*, there is more than a measure of truth at the core of Miller's diatribe.[21]

The constitutional historians were both bemused and provoked by the patriotic campaign. For the most part, the beleaguered historians simply carried on with their scholarship and continued to foster closer transatlantic ties. Immediately after the war, John Franklin Jameson hatched an ambitious, Carnegie-funded plan to publish all the correspondence between the British Ministers in Washington and the Foreign Office in London, with the clear intention of promoting closer transatlantic ties. As he explained to Charles Firth in March 1919: "It is of great importance to the future that history should do all it can to promote good relations, and mutual understanding as a means toward good relations, between Great Britain and the United States."[22] This project was still not completed when Jameson left the Carnegie Institution in 1928 to become chief of the Division of Manuscripts at the Library of Congress. It was turned over to others and not finally published till 1941, four years after his death.[23] Jameson also worked tirelessly to smooth the path of the international congress of historians, held at Brussels in 1923, overcoming the objections of Belgian scholars to inviting German, Austrian, and Hungarian historians.[24] Other American historians also worked to ensure the success of the gathering. From Wisconsin, Carl Fish wrote to T. F. Tout stressing the importance of the meeting in strengthening the Anglo-American connection: "We have most of us been working towards the cooperation of the United States and Great Britain in world affairs, and have felt that perhaps in scholarship we might look forward to accomplishing a little more than in matters of politics."[25]

In London in July 1921, the Institute of Historical Research, recently founded by A. F. Pollard, hosted an especially important event, the Anglo-American Conference of Professors of History, the forerunner of the later annual Anglo-American conferences. So successful was this gathering that Jameson organized a similar event to meet at the same time as the AHA convention at Richmond, Virginia, in December 1924. He secured sufficient funds from the Carnegie Endowment for International Peace to pay the expenses of ten British historians and also helped the visiting scholars to secure lecturing opportunities with honoraria. In promoting this program, Jameson wrote to Tout that preference would be given to those who had never before visited the United States "and who would feel that such a journey might be of some profit to their subsequent teaching, and through that teaching to the promotion of good relations between the two countries in the next generation."[26] In the event, a dozen British historians took up the offer, including such eminent figures as Pollard, J. H. Clapham, Hubert Hall, J. A. R. Marriott, F. M. Powicke, C. Grant Robertson, R. W. Seton-Watson, H. W. V. Temperley, and C. K. Webster. The centerpiece of the scholarly side of this meeting was a special session devoted to a consideration of how to further develop the study of the history of the British Empire.[27] Many of the visitors also took up the offer of lecturing at American colleges and universities.

British academic visitors to American campuses were becoming commonplace by the 1920s, and not only at elite east coast institutions. State universities, especially those with well-entrenched Anglophile faculty, were regular stops on the lecture tour—none more than the University of Michigan, where Arthur Lyon Cross still held sway. Among the eminent British visitors to Ann Arbor were Philip Kerr (later Lord Lothian), a former member of Milner's "Kindergarten" and secretary to Lloyd George, a major figure in the Round Table movement, and now secretary of the Rhodes Trustees (Cross was very active on the University of Michigan Rhodes committee). Among the British academics Cross brought to Michigan were C. K. Webster, J. H. Rose, C. Grant Robertson, R. B. Merriman, and Ramsay Muir (also a member of the Round Table), all of whom worked on the history of international relations and empire. Two other notable visitors were A. P. Higgins, professor of international law at Cambridge, and J. B. Brierly, Chichele professor of international law at Oxford.[28] Tout was an especially frequent visitor to North America, having lectured at twenty-six U.S. and Canadian colleges and universities, as well as having conducted research in medieval materials at the Huntington Library by the time of his death in 1929.[29] It seems likely, considering Tout's many visits and high level of contact with American academics, that real and enduring friendships resulted. Certainly this was the case with Haskins, who invited Tout not only to address the American Medieval Academy but also to have dinner with his family.[30] Tout was no doubt less cynical than his friend Poole, editor of the *English Historical Review*, who wrote to Tout after the death of George Burton Adams in 1925: "What a worthy wooly-headed man G. B. was, and how useful to us all through the war!"[31]

American academic visits to Britain were even more common than they had been before the war, facilitated by new programs like the Sir George Watson lectureships. The scheme had originally been hatched in 1913, at the time of the planning for the centenary of the Treaty of Ghent by the British-American Peace Centenary Committee, the British counterpart of the Carnegie-funded committee in the United States. The outbreak of war in 1914 delayed the implementation, but in 1919 the Anglo-American Society revived the project as the first element of the planned celebration of the tercentenary of the *Mayflower* and the Pilgrim Fathers, which, like the Treaty of Ghent, was to be observed on both sides of the Atlantic. Sir W. George Watson stepped forward with a grant of twenty thousand pounds, and Lord Bryce was selected as the inaugural chair in 1921. His lecture, delivered before a large and notable Anglo-American assemblage at the Mansion House and published in 1922 as *The Study of American History*, is informed by a rather old-hat Whig doctrine of liberal descent from the Angles, Saxons, and Jutes, the real starting point, Bryce claimed, of American history.[32] Alternately celebrating the advance of democracy and free institutions and fretting over the racial dilution of the original English stock by massive immigration, Bryce ended on a high note, calling for the United States and the British Empire to lead the world into a new age of prosperity and tranquility: "Will it not be in the days to come the glory of the free English-speaking peoples, to whom Providence has given the widest influence, and therewith the greatest responsibility, that any group of peoples has ever received, if they should join in using that influence to guide the feet of all mankind into the way of peace."[33]

Subsequent holders of the Watson chair were required to give a series of lectures at Oxford and other universities throughout the country. American holders of the chair were selected as much for their eminence in academic leadership circles as for their scholarly credentials. Two leading university presidents, Nicholas Murray Butler of Columbia and Arthur Twining Hadley of Yale, held the chair in the early 1920s. Among the leading constitutional historians, the most important American Watson lecturer was Van Tyne, who was praised by Evelyn Wrench, the English-Speaking Union founder, for "helping to dissipate prejudice against the British Empire throughout the United States."[34] Van Tyne's introductory lecture, entitled "The Struggle for the Truth about the American Revolution," was delivered at the Moses Chamber of the House of Lords on 13 May 1927. In a remarkably vituperative polemic, he devoted the whole of his speech to attacking and ridiculing the enemies of the new constitutional history.[35] His audience heard virtually nothing about the American Revolution but a great deal about the ignorance of traditional American patriots and the cynical manipulation of ethnic voters by rabble-rousing politicians and press magnates. Among his listeners at the House of Lords for that initial lecture was George Peabody Gooch (1873–1968), the diplomatic and intellectual historian, who told Van Tyne later that he was a "great admirer" of his work.[36] Also present that evening was George Haven Putnam (1844–1930), head of the publishing house and founder of the American branch of the English-Speaking Union. Writing to Van Tyne just before the event, Putnam informed him that the effort to get the University of London to establish a chair in American history was going well and that his friend American historian Robert McNutt McElroy (1872–1959), recently appointed to an American history position at Oxford, was doing "excellent service."[37] McElroy had indeed been Van Tyne's predecessor as Watson chair in 1926, lecturing on U.S. economic history,[38] but also dealing with Anglo-American relations. Putnam, who had attended his initial presentation as well (also in the House of Lords), noted that McElroy had been "quite frank with his damning, both ways on—various stupidities in Downing Street and various equal stupidities in Washington."[39]

Van Tyne's combativeness in attacking the American enemies of his kind of history in his opening lecture was bound to provoke those on the opposite side of the culture wars, especially "Big Bill" Thompson. When Van Tyne sent a prepublication copy of his lecture to Edith Scott, head of the Chicago branch of the English-Speaking Union, she took the greatest care when returning it to disguise its contents. Nevertheless, the parcel went missing in the post. Alarmed inquiries were made, but the postal authorities assured Scott that "Mayor Thompson was not allowed to roam through the post office and destroy anything that happened to displease him."[40] If Thompson and other patriots bothered to read Van Tyne's other five Watson lectures when they were published at the end of 1927, they would have found far less inflammatory material. The one titled "The Influence of English and American Lawyers in the American Revolution" was particularly well done, noting the strengths of the opposing constitutional interpretations and ending, not with a sense of regret over the breach but rather with a celebration of an alternate version of English liberty that had coalesced around the new republic.[41]

For Van Tyne, 1927 was an especially active year. In addition to the Watson lectures, he was also involved in the festivities for the bicentennial of George Washington's birth. Although Washington had been born in Virginia, a major part of the celebrations was held in Sulgrave Manor in Northamptonshire, the Washington ancestral home. The official name of the body organizing the event was the United States Commission for the Celebration of the Two Hundredth Anniversary of the Birth of George Washington, but much of the effort was undertaken by the Sulgrave Institution, one of the many Anglophile bodies in the United States working closely with the English-Speaking Union and other organizations to strengthen Anglo-American ties. Albert Bushnell Hart, Van Tyne, and other American historians planned to be on hand for the occasion.[42] On his return to Michigan, Van Tyne gave versions of his Watson lectures to large public audiences, like the one to a group of Iowa teachers titled "Truth, Propaganda, and the American Revolution," very likely similar in tone to his opening Watson lecture.[43] And he was pleased to hear that his successor in the Watson chair for 1928 would be Reginald Coupland, Beit professor of colonial history at Oxford, who would speak on the after-effects of the American Revolution on British policy as a kind of follow-up to Van Tyne's offerings.[44]

While Van Tyne was certainly more extreme in his pugnacity than most other constitutional historians of the time allowed themselves in public pronouncements, he does seem to have accurately reflected their feelings. Ever since the late nineteenth century, there had been within all segments of the academic community a strong undercurrent of iconoclasm in regard to traditional beliefs. The tone had been set by Andrew Dickson White's defiant books, *History of the Warfare of Science with Theology in Christendom* (1896) and *Seven Great Statesmen in the Warfare of Humanity with Unreason* (1910). In the post–

World War I era, there was a pronounced struggle over Darwin's theories of natural selection, centering on the famous Scopes trial of 1925. The protracted fight over "treason texts" and the wider contest over the American past was closely related, with historians, like their colleagues in the natural sciences, believing themselves to be voices of Reason and Progress contending with mass ignorance and prejudice. For the historians, there was the additional element of promoting internationalism (with a distinctly Anglophone cast, to be sure) and preparing America to take up its rightful place in the world. As with evolution, the fight over the new constitutional history concerned school curricula, with traditionalists rallying to protect youth from the corruption of dangerous new ideas.

This is not to suggest that historians in the United States during the interwar years were monolithic in their approaches and interpretations. There were numerous crosscurrents and some sharp debates. There was a fair amount of work by American scholars writing on English constitutional history, though it had a far lower public profile than the works on American constitutional history and tended to be largely uncontentious. Reginald Lane Poole lamented to Adams in 1918 that "medieval studies are languishing in England" and that the *English Historical Review* "depends largely upon Harvard and Cornell, Berkeley and Seattle for support in this department."[45] However, most of the work being done in the field was detailed administrative history, filling in the gaps of the earlier work initiated by John Horace Round, Frederic Maitland, Charles McLean Andrews, and others, but involving no new paradigm shift such as had taken place then. The doctoral students of major figures like Adams, Haskins, and Charles H. McIlwain (1871–1968), as they took up positions around the country, provided a good deal of the interwar scholarly output on English constitutional history, though Adams died in 1925 and Haskins had moved beyond the narrowly constitutional. He and his students were studying broader, more cosmopolitan trends in European history and culture, such as Haskins's own works on the twelfth-century renaissance and the rise of universities.[46]

McIlwain, who taught history and government at Harvard for many years, hewed most rigorously to the confines of constitutional history. He had published, in 1910, a work that arguably rivaled Haskins's volumes on the Normans as the most influential in the field by an American in the first half of the century. His book *The High Court of Parliament and Its Supremacy* wrenched the early history of parliament out of the realm of legislative history into that of judicial history, in the process undermining, inter alia, sanctified notions about Simon de Montfort and the Model Parliament.[47] McIlwain did not confine his studies to medieval England. His works on American constitutional history also made a considerable stir in the profession. His 1923 book, *The American Revolution: A Constitutional Interpretation,* was awarded the Pulitzer Prize for History. In this work McIlwain took issue with some of the more extreme views that had become fashionable in the field, like the claim that the constitutional position of patriot leaders like John Adams were "absurd." American opposition to parliamentary control before 1776 was consistent with well-established constitutional principles. However, McIlwain went on to point out that once Congress, through the Declaration of Independence, shifted its opposition to the king, whose prerogative in relation to colonial matters was unbounded, it was forced to abandon constitutionalism in favor of revolution, with a distinctly unconstitutional appeal to natural rights. McIlwain also gently chided those scholars who were pointing to economic motives and social tensions as the primary force driving events in the 1760s and 1770s.[48]

Ever since the work, referred to in Chapter 6, of Carl Becker on political parties in New York (1909) and that of Charles Beard on the economic interests of the constitution makers (1913), historians had accorded greater prominence to socioeconomic factors in precipitating the revolution. After the war, this trend increased, notably with the work of Arthur Meier Schlesinger (1888–1965) and J. F. Jameson. Schlesinger, who taught at Ohio State and then briefly at Iowa before finally settling in for a long tenure at Harvard, published in 1918 his important study of the role of merchants in the revolution.[49] Four years later these views, linked with those of similarly inclined scholars, were presented as a kind of new orthodoxy in Schlesinger's *New Viewpoints in American History.*[50] Even more influential in its long-term effects on the profession was Jameson's *The American Revolution Considered as a Social Movement* (1926). In this slender volume, based on lectures he presented at Princeton in 1925, Jameson painted a picture of an American population deeply divided over the revolution, with the propertied elite (except for certain groups like Virginia planters) tending toward accommodation, and the middling to lower sort, though not "the mob and rabble," pushing for independence.[51] The results of the upheaval were far-ranging, with economic equality foremost, producing an irresistible impulse toward political equality during the republic's first decades.

Thanks to the author's standing as the major organizer and leader of the historical profession, the "Jameson thesis" quickly acquired canonical status, though it is clearly hyperbole to claim, as Frederick B. Tolles did in 1954, that the book effected "a seismic disturbance in American society, a sudden quickening of the American mind."[52] It must be remembered that fewer than one thousand copies of the book were sold. Jack P. Greene was much closer to the mark in a 1962 article. Reviewing the historiography on the revolution, Greene drew a sharp distinction between the imperial school and what he called the "socio-economic or progressive school" that included Jameson together with Becker and Schlesinger.[53] Some form of this dichotomy has been evident in the scholarship on historical writing in America ever since, with John Higham's distinction between a progressive school and a "conservative evolutionist" school (read constitutional history of the institutional sort) as perhaps the dominant formulation.[54] In this reading, a slowly widening gap was opened up between the strictly institutional historians like Andrews and those looking at social change and economic tensions as important factors. The process of divergence is seen to start with Frederick Jackson Turner's frontier thesis in 1893 and began to quicken with the rise of progressivism. Robinson's "New History," with its emphasis on approaches borrowed from the social sciences and deploying historical scholarship in the service of contemporary social problems, is viewed as an especially important impulse to the progressive school of historians.

While this well-established interpretation has much to recommend it, there are some elements of the Jameson thesis, and some of the other works of the "progressive" school, that do not fit it particularly well. First of all, the lectures on which Jameson's book was based were not written in the 1920s but thirty years before. Before assuming that Jameson, in the twilight of his career, was suddenly converted to a "radical" interpretation of history, we should note the very long gestation period of his famous thesis. In their original form as lectures, in which he had specifically cast the American Revolution as a "social movement, they were prepared for delivery at Barnard College in 1895."[55] A dozen years earlier, James Bryce, when he first met Jameson in Baltimore in 1883, had encouraged this approach. When Bryce suggested to the young lecturer and newly minted PhD that determining the social aspects of politics would be a worthy undertaking, Jameson quietly resolved to undertake it.[56] Even before this, in a seminar paper titled "The Disturbances in Barbados in 1876" that Jameson had presented at Johns Hopkins in 1880, he had described how constitutional change, in this case proposed federation with other islands, had caused white planter resistance that in turn touched off a mass uprising by laborers.[57] His busy career of administering and editing deflected him from writing anything substantial from this perspective, apart from the Barnard lectures, for several decades. There was certainly no change of heart in his underlying social and political values, which had always been mildly progressive but fraught with suspicion of the masses. Interested as he was in social conflict, Jameson was no advocate of empowering the masses, whom he believed threatened American institutions. Populism he derided as a movement that threatened "to put the conduct of our public affairs into the hands of a vast horde of unintelligent farmers."[58] And as the exchange of correspondence with Bryce after World War I indicates, Jameson's patrician views had not abated on the eve of writing *The American Revolution Considered as a Social Movement*.[59]

As for figures like Becker and Schlesinger, their views of the revolution do seem to fit the "socio-economic or progressive" school model somewhat better, but here too caution is needed. First of all, many contemporaries, including professional historians as well as the general public, did not necessarily see this new history as a sharp break from the institutional kind of writing that the imperial school undertook. Patriotic traditionalists did not bother to distinguish between the "progressive" approach and the institutional. In their eyes, both denigrated the American Revolution and its heroes. Indeed, this is the central element shared by professional historians employing what seemed to a later generation sharply divergent approaches. Their approaches were complementary in that they both highlighted the failures of the old Bancroftian patriotic model. Both undermined the sense of righteousness and heroism of revolutionary era America, one by placing it in a wide institutional context, the other by demonstrating the far-from-edifying spectacle of selfishness and class interest. Both in effect internationalized the American Revolution, the one by considering it in the context of all the British colonies in the Americas and the difficulties experienced by imperial administrators in London, the other by showing that, when considering social structure and tension, America had much in common with Europe.

The class conflict model, borrowed partly from Marxism and evident in such works as Beard's *Economic Interpretation of the Constitution*, might seem to be fundamentally at odds with the institutional approach. The latter, as we have seen, carried a powerfully conservative political viewpoint, in favor of long-established structures and the sanctity of contract, and thus presumably in conflict with the "radical" nature of the progressive approach. But as we have seen with Jameson, it was quite possible to deploy this approach without personally endorsing a social or economic reform agenda of any kind. As historical scholarship started to become more ideologized from the 1930s, there was a tendency to look back and fit the two very different approaches into the left-wing/right-wing political model. There is, however, not much evidence in the interwar period, at either the personal or professional level, of conflict between historians following these different approaches. On the contrary, a spirit of genteel collegiality prevailed, friendships across this "divide" remained unaffected, and book reviews of the period do not reflect the sort of animosity we might expect from the left/right model. There were few institutional historians more conservative in their politics than Andrews, yet he was certainly not offended by Jameson's "radical" views. In 1931, he wrote Jameson to thank him for providing a graceful preface to a Festschrift to Andrews by his former students,[60] remarking that as a student of Jameson at Johns Hopkins, he "learned to admire your . . . wisdom and the majesty of your ideals of scholarship and I determined in those formative years to reach some of them no matter how hard was the climb to the top."[61]

The other point to bear in mind is that, despite the growth of socioeconomic interpretations of historical change, the institutional studies continued apace, not only in English constitutional history but in American as well. In 1924, the year that Andrews served as AHA president, he published his *Colonial Background of the American Revolution*.[62] And in 1934 there appeared the first volume of his four-volume magnum opus on which he had long toiled, *The Colonial Period in American History,* for which he was awarded the Pulitzer Prize for History in 1935. The other three volumes appeared over the next four years.[63] If Andrews's important books of the interwar period testify to the fact that institutional studies were not withering away, so did the publications of his many former students. The most eminent and productive of the Andrews-trained scholars was Lawrence Henry Gipson (1880–1971), who taught at Lehigh University for many years. He eventually produced, over a thirty-four-year period starting in 1936, a monumental (fifteen volumes) study of the British Empire before the American Revolution,[64] a fitting tribute to the institutional approach and to Andrews's imprint on the profession.

Another institutional historian who cast nearly as long a shadow as Andrews was McLaughlin. Partly this was a function of longevity. Both men lived into their eighties (Andrews died in 1943, McLaughlin in 1947), and both were active scholars in retirement. In 1935 McLaughlin published his *Constitutional History of the United States,* for which he was awarded the Pulitzer Prize for History in 1936. In this lengthy, wide-ranging survey, the author stressed the importance of federalism as the most significant component of constitutional development and examined its role as a possible solution to the tensions that culminated in the American Revolution. In McLaughlin's view, Benjamin Franklin's proposals in his unsuccessful Albany Plan of 1754, calling for enhanced colonial autonomy within a clearly defined federal imperial structure, might well have prevented a rupture. McLaughlin went on to point out that "the significance of these proposals lies not so much in their suggestions for a method of saving the old empire as in their indication of the route that was to be followed in later years."[65] This emphasis on federalism not only was consistent with McLaughlin's prewar and wartime views, but was also a staple of those who still argued for closer ties, even formal ones, between the United States and the British Empire. This included the members of the Round Table and many of those associated with the Council on Foreign Relations and the Carnegie Endowment for International Peace. The unfolding of events after 1918 held little cheer for them. The aloofness of the United States from the League of Nations, the largely independent course charted by Commonwealth nations, and even naval rivalries continued to dash the hopes of those who had anticipated the advent of an Anglophone imperium after the Great War.[66]

With growing international tensions and a confirmed internationalist (as well as English-Speaking Union member) in the White House, there were bound to be closer Anglo-American ties, especially after the outbreak of war on 1 September 1939. Remarkably, in 1940, in spite of the still prevailing isolationist sentiment in the country, both major party candidates were internationalists and in favor of increasing aid to Britain. Wendell Willkie had indeed been the only Republican internationalist in a crowded field of candidates, all the rest of whom held isolationist views.[67] Early in 1941, Clarence K. Streit's best-selling and widely discussed *Union Now With Britain* was published.[68] A clarion call for federal union of the United States, Britain, and the Commonwealth countries in order to preserve democracy and freedom, it grew out of Streit's experience as a *New York Times* correspondent covering the League of Nations. The author had attended Oxford, was a member of the Round Table, and had made a close study of American constitutional history.[69] Streit's detailed proposal was a virtual blueprint for the sort of federal Anglophone superstate that McLaughlin and many other constitutional historians had long hoped to see created. Of course, it had no chance of being implemented. The close wartime alliance that did take shape showed no signs of evolving into even the mildest form of union. And after the war, the United Nations, like the League of Nations before, was created around the sovereign nation state.

The heady international agenda of leading constitutional historians, never a realistic program, was finally laid aside. It was never completely extinguished, however, and periodically reappears, most recently in James C. Bennett's *The Anglosphere Challenge*.[70] After 1945, constitutional history lost its political sting, as earlier fears of America losing its national identity and even its independence by involving itself with the British Empire were overtaken by events. Britain, materially and financially shattered, would play a greatly reduced role in the postwar era. Unlike the situation in 1919, when the British Empire grew substantially with the addition of League of Nations mandates, Britain's dependent colonies were clearly on the road to gaining their independence. At any rate, with the rapid onset of the Cold War, the British Empire's role as a global menace was quickly taken by the Soviet Union in the minds of American patriots. In addition to shedding a global political agenda, constitutional history in the United States also began losing its savor within the profession. Even in the 1930s it was coming to be looked upon by younger scholars with little reverence. This tendency grew after 1945, as various new approaches and methodologies, most of them some form of social history, gained prominence. Moreover, at least in regard to general education, a wider sense of transatlantic connectivity than Anglo-American constitutionalism had been forged by historians in the form of the Western civilization course, which had become a standard feature of many universities' curricula by 1940. While the origins of this course can be traced to the nineteenth century and to the "New History" of Robinson, it had only begun to come into its own after World War I, partly the offspring of the War Issues course taught on campuses in 1918.[71] By offering a more broadly cultural affinity with Europe and yet one that was built on the Whiggish notion of the unfolding of freedom and rationality, the Western civ course offered many of the same benefits as constitutional history without its drawbacks—the impugning of traditional patriotic narratives and the perceived aridity of the subject matter. It is hardly surprising that with Britain's rapid decline as a power after 1945 Western civ would reign triumphantly on campuses for the next two decades. Its dominance would in turn fade in the closing decades of the century, undermined by the winding down of the Cold War and the rapid advance of multiculturalism.

Constitutional history, once the dominant discourse in the profession, had become, in the second half of the twentieth century, an increasingly marginalized subfield. The presidential address delivered by Robert Livingston Schuyler (1883–1966) at the annual meeting of the AHA in 1951 is instructive in this regard. Schuyler, who taught at Columbia, was the last constitutional historian of a traditional sort to hold the AHA presidency. His speech set no new research agenda, anticipated no new directions in the field. It was, rather, a graceful encomium of Frederic Maitland, in celebration of the hundredth anniversary (in 1950) of his birth.[72] It was also, perhaps unconsciously, a nostalgic tribute to the departed golden age of constitutional history. The decline of course was relative, and important work in the field continues.[73] Thus the trajectory of English constitutional history in the United States was remarkably similar to that in Great Britain. Originally the key element in the recording of American constitutional history, as it lost prestige it dragged its direct descendant with it. This record of leadership and then decline came full circle in 1963, when Paul Murphy published a plea to resuscitate the field from the malaise that had thinned the ranks of scholars, citing "the history profession's neglect of a vital area for which it is responsible, and about which it has done shamefully little in the last quarter century: American constitutional history and areas related to constitutional problems."[74] Murphy deplored the faddism in the historical profession that had lessened the status of constitutional history. He noted by the 1930s "both that its old practitioners were largely talking only to each other and that, with exceptions, the profession generally had rejected the discipline for other historical approaches and fields."[75] The increasing tendency of the Supreme Court to rely on historical evidence as part of constitutional interpretation demanded that historians contribute accurate information. The agenda that Murphy furnished helped to revive constitutional scholarship from the relative decline as a research field that had reduced its status.

Constitutional history also survived as a teaching field, albeit a considerably diminished one. American constitutional history might even be said to have a certain popularity, if we consider the public's seemingly insatiable appetite for biographies of the founders. A "rage for the founders," as Allan Kulikoff has termed it,[76] shows little sign of abating. This development does not necessarily gladden the hearts of academic specialists, however, for it shows the public's lack of taste for what most professional historians write about, an impatience with having to engage with broader social, economic, and cultural factors, and a straightforward delight in "great man" history. It also expresses a desire to have heroic individuals at the center of the nation's past, and to that extent it forms part of America's contemporary culture wars. While it is true that, compared to the 1920s, America's contemporary culture wars include numerous issues like multiculturalism and the atom-bombing of Japan,[77] one of the principal fault lines still runs through the era of the nation's founding. Although it no longer involves the question of whether the American Revolution was necessary, constitutional issues are still prominent. And if it is now the practitioners of social or cultural history rather than constitutional history who are apt to be pilloried by the champions of patriotic verities, the similarities to the earlier culture wars are nonetheless striking.

CHAPTER EIGHT

"The Endless Jar of Right and Wrong"

———◆◆◆———

Constitutional History and the History Women

We use the phrase "history women" with specific reference to John Kenyon's (1927–96) account in 1983 of historical writing in Britain, where only a single academic woman, Eileen Power (1889–1940), merited a brief citation in the consideration of five centuries of scholarship. Lucy Sutherland did earn a mention in the text but did not find her way into the index. A reader might have concluded that women never undertook the professional study of history, certainly never wrote anything memorable, or even mattered much in the processes of history. The relationship of women and their scholarly endeavors to constitutional history has two dimensions. The first was prominent in the golden age of constitutional history as a research tradition between 1870 and World War I, when the tradition accorded women little or no place in the articulation of the national narrative. The other category addressed the impact that women historians had in the field, including both the research and teaching traditions. Some women historians enthusiastically adopted the goals and methodologies of constitutional history as they embraced the prevailing norms of professional history. Several women historians even contributed to the field's decline in research status by pioneering the exploration of new fields of historical inquiry that eclipsed the academic status of constitutional history. Yet important women scholars also perpetuated the cachet of constitutional history as a taught tradition by virtue of their commitment to the topic as a crucial part of any history curriculum.

With respect to the omission of women as a subject of serious historical study, as early as 1803 even Jane Austen complained: "The quarrels of popes and kings, with wars and pestilences, in every age; the men are all so good for nothing, and hardly any women at all—it is very tiresome."[1] Interest in the other half of the human experience on either the local or national level was dismissed as mere antiquarianism. Constitutional history's emphasis on public law, the intersection of government and politics, reflected the absence of women from public power except in the case of the female monarchs. From the outset, therefore, after 1870 constitutional history had little or no room for attention to women. This commitment to public policy history rarely worried about the private sphere, where women had such a great impact. As a result, national identity up to and including John Bull was highly gendered in the scope and focus of constitutional history.

When queens did rule, both contemporaries and later historians treated these eras as aberrations or simply refused to recognize their legitimacy. Why, for example, was Matilda in the twelfth century never recognized as queen regnant? Why was the feckless Stephen credited with reigning for the entire period 1135–54, when this was clearly not the case for 1141–47? In the list of monarchs at the back of textbooks, Matilda might well never have existed. For the constitutional historians after 1870, this inattention to women expressed the belief that public authority, perhaps with the exception of Elizabeth I, rested more appropriately in male hands: "Most history written exemplified the centrality of white men and the marginalization of most others."[2] This approach showcased not only Elizabethan attitudes as in John Knox's phrase about the monstrous regiment of women, but also Victorian assumptions about the gendered nature of political hierarchy.

What about Lady Jane Grey, known forever after as the Nine Days' Queen, yet also never recognized in the roster of monarchs? One might argue that neither Matilda nor Lady Jane were ever crowned and so lacked the formal status that coronations entailed. Matilda styled herself "Lady of the English," but Jane Grey did claim the title of queen and acted as such, however briefly. By comparison, how has Edward V, that youthful victim of his villainous uncle Richard III, fared? Edward has always received his full three months as monarch, even though imprisoned for two of those three months and never crowned. When Mary Tudor and Elizabeth I governed England successively and then Mary Stuart came to the throne of Scotland, the situation presented special challenges, because Elizabeth succeeded in governing well whereas the other two had presumably failed in their royal duties. Victorian historians resorted to gendered language by stressing (as Elizabeth herself did) that she possessed the masculine virtues of judgment and courage whereas the two Marys foundered because they were consumed by the evils of feminine shortcomings in the public arena. Put another way, how could historians praise the success of Elizabeth while denouncing the decisions and actions of the other queens?[3] The definition of constitutional history as primarily public sphere activity made women invisible, with little place in the national past. Gerda Lerner has written that women "have appeared only as 'marginal' contributors to human development. What we see here is selective memory on the part of male historians which is grounded in the patriarchal values they hold."[4] Constitutional history and the practitioners thereof alike made a focus on women's history unlikely.

With the reminder that Clio, the muse of history, is female, the constitutional history so predominant after 1870 rejected this association. The more that constitutional history expressed the national narrative, the less inclusion for women was possible. Considerations of national identity have often emphasized the issue of marginalization: Who is included in the national story and who is excluded? Who belongs to the national community? Conveniently enough for this work, in 1869 the Royal Commission on the Laws of Naturalization and Allegiance took up this question.[5] The commission recommended, and parliament endorsed with a statute in 1870, that women born in Britain upon marriage took the nationality of their husbands. Common law had previously stipulated that the allegiance of the natural-born citizen lasted forever. The statute assumed that wives would embrace the nationality of their husbands as part of the overall new status that marriage conferred upon the wife.

While certainly there is no causal relationship, the conjunction of this statute with the growing importance of constitutional history made a useful symbol of the exclusion that women endured in the classic volumes of William Stubbs, Frederic Maitland, and others, in which the actions of men were inherently more serious than those of women. As Christina Crosby has argued: "In the nineteenth century 'history' is produced as men's truth, the truth of a necessarily historical Humanity, which in turn requires that 'woman' be outside history, above, below, or beyond properly historical and political life. . . . 'Women' are the unhistorical other of history."[6] The national narrative, premised on values such as continuity and progress, had no room for women: "Women were not seen as inhabiting history proper, but existing, like colonized peoples, in a permanently anterior time within the modern nation. White, middle-class men, by contrast, were seen to embody the forward thrusting agency of national progress."[7] This emphasis accounted for the argument "that continuity, as epitomized by the slow, orderly development of the English constitution, should have been thought of as a distinctive national virtue."[8] Constitutional history reinforced this outlook by defining historical significance at the expense of women. In the process, "history's representations of the past help construct gender for the present."[9] Little wonder then that Victorian values shaped the nature of constitutional history so dramatically.

Examination of historical gender issues is especially pertinent because the increasing utilization of gender as an analytical tool in order to "redefine the old questions in new terms" has permitted new insights into traditional documentary evidence.[10] If constitutional history removed women from the national narrative, what about the gendered assumptions of the historians? Robert C. K. Ensor (1877–1958) is now remembered for his volume on 1870–1914 in the Oxford History of England series. We do not want to place too much weight on a single piece of evidence, but the following surely reflected attitudes held on a much wider basis. Even more persuasive was that Ensor became a stalwart of the Fabian Society, an individual noted for his progressive views. In May 1902, while a young man at Oxford, Ensor wrote:

Oxford, always a pretty town in summer, is variegated at present with all manner of female flowers, who have come up partly to see the lights and chiefly to be seen: in dazzling raiment of white and colours, which only their selves could outshine. Eton match-wise they flood all colleges: with delicious artlessness calling quads "yards" and wondering why those silly men persist in rowing backwards—in a word revivifying all time-honoured foolishness. A strange piece of work is woman: there is no diviner thing on God's earth than a fine one: and none more uncommon. I suppose it is really their childishness that makes both their charm and their weakness. Their best side is their childish nearness to purity and the actualities of things; the shades of the prism-house close more gradually over the growing girl: unless indeed she be a bluestocking or a society woman. On whom may God have mercy, and hide from them the greatness of their loss.[11]

These sentiments on the part of Ensor, it might be argued, could be excused on the ground that they reflected broader currents of youthful opinion and that would be exactly the point. This passage symbolized why women intruded so little into the classic accounts of constitutional history.

Constitutional narratives privileged certain examples of historical significance such as the exercise of public authority at the expense of women and the private sphere that made women almost invisible.[12] Details of ordinary life, now a staple of the new social history, offered little attraction to those who chronicled the grave issues of (male) high politics and government. The use of gender analysis to reexamine the traditional foci of constitutional history has demonstrated how restrictive the older forms of constitutional inquiry were and how the asking of different questions has provided interesting new results. Judith Bennett provided an excellent example of this process in her reassessment of the medieval phenomenon known as leyrwite, an obscure offense mentioned briefly by the great medievalists Maitland and Paul Vinogradoff.[13] The latter scholars had argued that leyrwite "was a response to moral lapse and a manifestation of seigneurial power." They recognized but did not elaborate on the fact that this was a woman's offense. Bennett took the same evidence and by changing the boundaries of inquiry established that leyrwite "was a punitive fine that fell particularly on those ensnared by the hazards of marriage-making, rape and poverty." When examined as a gender issue, therefore, leyrwite represented an attempt to control women's sexuality, especially that of poor women. Bennett threw new light on what had previously seemed a minor subject in no need of revision. In this fashion, example by example, recent scholarship has redressed the imbalances of women's history inaugurated by constitutional history.[14] The ongoing process of revision has illustrated how much constitutional history had missed after 1870 by its relentless focus on public law.

Both before and after 1870, by asserting that only public affairs truly mattered, scholars allowed the Victorian private sphere of domesticity, matrimony, and maternity little role in constitutional history. Female historians before 1870, such as Agnes Strickland (1796–1874), took these latter topics as appropriate for their efforts. Many women historians specifically rejected the world of high politics in order to recount the private sphere, where their research showed that Victorian gendered values had always prevailed in the past:

Not direct, remarkable action but oblique, pervasive, beneficent sway over circumstances is the ideal for female behavior as well as an increasingly popular conception of historical significance. The women historians made the most of this congruence between ideology and historiography, legitimizing their scholarly projects by the parallels or overlap between women's history and social history while minimizing their challenge to the patriarchy by showing that their subjects contributed to history in acceptably ladylike ways.[15]

Even more, if women historians found it difficult to write history without gender restraints, "they certainly read it, thought about it, and discussed it, and their participation in the social circulation of historical knowledge of different sorts had effects that were long lasting."[16] In the face of these constraints, however, women scholars never lost sight of writing history according to their own lights.

In the decades prior to 1870, women historians attempted to carve out a niche for themselves, a process that "imitated, but did not mirror, that of her male counterpart."[17] Many factors affected the careers of women historians in this period: wealth, education, mentors, access to archives, and marriage. Even in the best of circumstances women faced obstacles that rarely confronted men. As a result, "British women's contributions to nineteenth-century historiography either went unremarked or were disrespected. British women were rarely seen as the most able historians."[18] It is arguable that, given the various hindrances that women writers faced, their level of attainment was all the more admirable: "Inevitably, the standard of women historians' scholarship varied and many women writers of history were essentially compilers and popularisers, but this is equally true of their male contemporaries."[19] The transformation of historical study by the elaboration of professional standards and the emphasis on constitutional history after 1870 added even more drawbacks, because while women might attend the ancient universities, neither students nor faculty were on the same footing as their male counterparts. They did, however, study a history curriculum on the same basis as their male colleagues. One example of this trend was the introduction of a graduate seminar by Vinogradoff at Oxford in which women gained valuable research instruction. Of the fifteen volumes that appeared in Vinogradoff's Oxford Studies in Social and Legal History between 1909 and 1927, five were written by women.[20]

To turn to our second purpose, the work of women historians within the field of constitutional history, given that the subject precluded consideration of all but elite women, it is the more ironic that the field provided an avenue for some women historians to establish their professional reputations. For others it served as a launching pad to strike out in new directions when constitutional history as a research tradition went into decline in the 1920s. The Great Tradition presented to several female historians the opportunity for scholarly greatness that might otherwise have eluded them. In order to pursue serious academic study, research women had to face the usual issues of financial independence, employment, marriage, and social attitudes. For these women an academic career offered many distinct problems. Kenyon's virtual exclusion of women historians has remained unfair because a number of women met and surpassed the standards of scholarship that measured their male colleagues. The biographer of Eileen Power, for example, wrote of Power's attempt, in a phrase redolent of E. P. Thompson (1924–93), "to redress the condescension of the History Men."[21]

With respect to employment prospects, the majority of women, regardless of background or training, faced formidable degrees of prejudice. A few women found solicitous patrons, as in the relationship between Mary Bateson (1865–1906) and Maitland, who provided encouragement, mentoring, and recommendations for various appointments. The potential for a position outside the women's college was even smaller: "For most women, historical research was of necessity a gentlemanly pursuit. Although many women were now trained in universities, few found employment there."[22] The men's colleges were an exclusive club where women in the first part of the twentieth century lacked any real opportunity to succeed, no matter what their qualifications.[23] For example, medieval historian V. H. Galbraith (1889–1976) wrote to Frank

Stenton in 1931: "By the way the M.S.S. Dept. at the B.M. are taking two new assistants—and would be very glad that one of them should be a man who knew or was prepared to learn Anglo-Saxon. *They are threatened with 2 women at the moment.*"[24] In the same year, King's College, Cambridge, had an opening for which "a mediaevalist, preferably a man, is required."[25] In the face of such attitudes, it was little wonder that women historians enjoyed few opportunities and chafed at the stereotypes that hindered recognition of their accomplishments.

Circumstances other than discrimination intervened as well. In the case of Rachel Reid (1876–1952), A. F. Pollard recorded: "Miss Reid gives up Girton because she prefers to come here [University of London]. I don't know that there is any particular 'goodness' about her doing so. Certainly it is not done to oblige me, though she is no doubt glad to be able to live with her mother and sister."[26] Domestic circumstances, whether marriage or caregiver duties, intruded far more often with women scholars than men. Whatever the vicissitude, in some cases the story turned out well. In 1938 Power wrote in reference to continental scholar Dorothea Oschinsky (1910–95) emigrating to England and her prospects of employment: "I don't know whether Dr. Oschinsky is preparing to take an English degree with a view to a job in England later; as to the chances of this I feel increasingly pessimistic. You will know the difficulties as well as I do & will certainly have warned her."[27] In this instance, matters worked out well. Oschinsky became a research student at the London School of Economics, was evacuated to Cambridge during World War II, and became reader in paleography at the University of Liverpool for many years. At her death, Oschinsky left a £450,000 bequest to the Cambridge University Library in order to support research in medieval history, a gift that commemorated the library's place in her own work as a student during the war. Success stories such as this one were all too infrequent.

The professionalization of history within the academy also served to limit opportunities for women. Access to training, job prospects, and the male domination of professional organizations worked against women's pursuit of history careers. As always, however, there were exceptions that proved the rule. The documents-based ideal that heralded the triumph of academic criteria provided the context for the labors of Mary Anne Everett Green (1818–95), who combined marriage and children with forty years of editorial work in preparing calendars of state papers in the domestic series, a total of forty-one in all.[28] In addition, Green wrote original scholarly works and contributed to the availability of records that made the research criterion possible. The abundance of documents drew women, as it did their male counterparts, to the study of

legal and constitutional history. The acquisition of ancient languages and paleography skills required for research in medieval records provided a standard
that male subjectivity could not diminish. It was only natural, therefore, that as
women sought to establish their scholarly credentials before World War I, they
would gravitate to the field in which male reputations had triumphed.

The final hurdle that women historians faced was the social baggage that accompanied the quest for an academic career. This category included the traditional stereotyping of female intellectuals as traitors to broader ideals of femi-
ninity, the difficult decision about political and feminist activism, and often
a career versus marriage choice. The Oxbridge colleges played an ambiguous
role in this process: "Although the women's colleges were remarkably successful in giving the necessary support to women seeking an independent intellectual life, they were often run by women of extremely conventional social
attitudes."[29] Tutorial commitments to students and contributions to college life
also posed difficulties for those who pursued an active research agenda. This
rarely included the history of women but rather the more prestigious field of
English constitutional history.[30] Yet even within the field, despite the enduring
quality of work by women historians, their scholarship rarely won the respect
and praise accorded male contemporaries of similar accomplishment.[31] These
women scholars have become remote in historiographical memory, receding in
consciousness along with the field they helped to illuminate.

The first historian in this category was Mary Bateson, the only student (although informally) that Maitland ever mentored. This scholarly support was
crucial for Bateson because technically she never earned a degree, not even a
bachelor's degree. Women's colleges such as Newnham at the time were not of-
ficially full members of the Cambridge University community, and so Bateson
received only a certificate stating that she had earned a first class in the history
tripos in 1887. In that year her essay titled "Monastic Civilisation in the Fens"
won the Historical Prize Essay.[32] Her first mentor was Mandell Creighton, who
guided her along the path of serious scholarship from 1887 to 1893 in pursuit
of monastic and ecclesiastical history. After Creighton became the bishop of
Peterborough in 1891, Bateson turned to the scholarly example provided by
Maitland, then at the height of his research and reputation.

Maitland directed her attention to the study and editing of medieval documents, especially for Leicester. The *Records of the Borough of Leicester,* extending
from 1103 to 1603, appeared in three volumes from 1899 to 1905. Although difficult to identify precisely, there appeared to be the assumption that editing work
was somehow more suited to the female temperament than original scholarship. Whether it was of her own choosing or not, this work required prodigious

learning and indefatigable purpose in equal measure. T. F. Tout noted "her zeal for historical investigation," which was the hallmark of her scholarship.[33] In her skill as an editor, Bateson emulated Maitland, much of whose own research appeared in volumes that he edited for the Selden Society. Bateson's work ethic soon breached gender barriers, for few contemporaries matched her commitment to the task of making medieval records accessible to scholars. As a result, when she did publish books of original scholarship, they were often so technical in nature that they did not produce an easy narrative.[34] Perhaps her greatest contribution came in the two edited volumes on borough customs that the Selden Society published in 1904 and 1906. Of this work Maitland wrote: "Such a work cannot make its mark in a couple of months, nor yet in a couple of years. It cannot attract 'the general reader'; it can be only a book for a few students of history. . . . Unless I am much mistaken, that book will 'sup late,' but in very good company. I see it many years hence on the same shelf with the *History of the Exchequer* and the *History of Tithes*. Neither Thomas Madox nor yet John Selden will resent the presence of Mary Bateson."[35] Bateson produced quality scholarship that matched the work of male historians in her editing skills, but an early death prevented her from writing the book that would have established her reputation fully. The topics of her edited work, however brilliant in editorial execution, proved too arcane even for academe.

Maitland recognized the barriers that Bateson had to surmount and rendered assistance whenever possible. When proposing Bateson to edit a volume for the Selden Society, Maitland thought it necessary to inquire of B. F. Lock (1849–1927), the society's secretary: "Are you opposed to female labour? I ask this because Miss Bateson occurred to me as a possible editor of Jew rolls. She has been editing the records of Leicester for the corporation, is careful and instructed. I have said no word to her."[36] In gratitude for this continuing support, Bateson, in the year before the death of both, wrote how much she appreciated his guidance.[37] Bateson adhered to the documents mania that made constitutional history so prominent; her reputation as an editor was reflected in the offer to become the editor of the *Cambridge Medieval History*, a position taken from her by her premature death.[38] At this loss Maitland wondered: "Where's our Medieval History now? We may find another editor, but not another Miss Bateson."[39] This testimony from Maitland alone should testify to her scholarly skills.

Although because of her independent means Bateson never was a full-time tutor at Newnham, her signature course on English constitutional history included her in the taught tradition as well. This brought to her students the topic that reigned supreme in Oxbridge men's colleges. Bateson fought for research fellowships for women, so that female students might choose a life of scholarship if they wished. She contributed a handsome sum to the endowment of the Newnham Research Fellowships, and she "firmly believed, 25 years before Virginia Woolf addressed the faculty and students of Newnham College about the necessity of 'A Room of One's Own,' that women could not pursue serious scholarship without the financial and professional support of an academic institution."[40] To the Great Tradition in both its research and teaching manifestations, Bateson made important and now generally forgotten contributions.

Blessed with financial independence, Bateson used this good fortune to live life on her own terms. In quaint fashion Tout underscored her personal agency in his memoir when he emphasized that the unmarried Bateson in Cambridge "lived in her own house in the Huntingdon Road."[41] In addition, despite advice to the contrary from her first patron, Creighton, Bateson remained active in the women suffragist movement throughout her life. In 1906 Bateson led a deputation on behalf of the cause to meet with Prime Minister Henry Campbell-Bannerman (1836–1908), when she gave the concluding speech in which she pointed out the absurdity that university women were disenfranchised.[42] When she died suddenly at the age of forty-one, Bateson had combined academic success and political activism in ways that few other women could envision.

Contemporaries remembered Bateson with obvious affection. Tout wrote of her as "high-spirited, good-humoured, and frank, she was innocent of academic stiffness, provincialism, or pedantry."[43] Her published work had already made its mark, but death claimed a scholar whose future promised even greater accomplishments. She had already earned her place in the Great Tradition, but her death took her before she had fulfilled her potential completely. The Selden Society Council acknowledged her scholarly status by its "desire to record their sense of the very valuable services of the late Mary Bateson in the masterly digest of Borough Customs edited by her for this Society."[44] This accolade has deserved a more prominent place in the legacy of constitutional history, for Bateson's work measured up to the quality of that of her male colleagues in the field.

Another historian whose life ended prematurely was Maude Violet Clarke, who died at forty-three after sixteen years as a tutor at Somerville College, Oxford. Clarke was born in Belfast and educated at Queen's University there and then at Lady Margaret Hall, Oxford; in each case she earned first-class honors. She devoted her scholarly research to the reign of Richard II and contributed an important reassessment of his reign and the advent of the Lancastrians: "I hope you didn't think that we were trying to whitewash Richard, a task which, at present, I think is beyond honesty. But I find Bolingbroke blacker the more

I work at him and cannot accept Stubbs's view of him as prince or king. I am afraid they were all ruffians, though Richard and his friends were ruffianly in a more interesting way."[45] As in the case of Mary Bateson, Clarke died with her best work still ahead of her and remained single: "In the early twentieth century the married woman could not be guaranteed the independence of mind, not to mention career, essential to scholarship."[46] Her most important book was finished just prior to her death and was published posthumously.[47] This work became a standard work in the understanding of fourteenth-century England, and Clarke was to write the volume in Oxford's History of England series for that time period until her illness and death prevented her contribution to the project. Eventually May McKisack (1902–81), Clarke's student and successor at Somerville, prepared the volume that covered the century.

As the Oxbridge college system sometimes permits, Clarke's influence was much greater than the corpus of her publications would have suggested. Her impact on Somerville and its educational standards lasted long after her death. No sooner did she take the vice principalship and its opportunity for change than her fatal illness intervened. In 1960, medievalist Margaret Hastings confessed to "a kind of diffidence perhaps about a scholar whose influence went very much further than her published work makes clear to me. Rosamund Sillen Tosh, the oldest of my English friends, speaks of her with both love and awe."[48] Clarke's impact on Somerville and on the larger Oxford community rested as much upon her teaching activities as upon her research. The historian of Somerville wrote about Clarke: "a great historian and a great tutor, one whose wisdom and judgement and taste Somerville had come to depend on in all sorts of ways. Fifty years later, those who knew her spoke still of her loss as irreparable."[49] The standards that Clarke fixed for her students set the academic tone for the entire college.

The primary course that Clarke offered was medieval English constitutional history. Tutorial notes made plain how Clarke transformed the subject into a proxy for all historical inquiry. Reason and imagination were the keys to historical understanding, and memory served them both. Trained in the Great Tradition herself, Clarke reinforced its position as a taught tradition in the 1920s and 1930s. Her own student days included papers on selected topics in Anglo-Saxon and Norman constitutional history; one of her essays noted that the abundance of early records were "at once the pride and bewilderment of the English historians."[50] When Clarke began teaching at Somerville in 1919, she set a demanding agenda for her students. "History is a most difficult subject, involving knowledge of and judgement on every aspect of human effort in the past," Clarke informed her pupils, whose purpose was "to encourage candidates to think for themselves instead of relying on memory for facts and for opinions."[51] Clarke proposed that "history is the science of ascertaining the facts of human affairs, but also the art of revealing the relations of the facts to each other."[52] In the study of history, Clarke insisted upon the integrity of research in original records and the absolute importance of seeking the truth.

Constitutional history, Clarke stressed to her students, meant that "how a country is governed and why it is so governed are the first questions to be asked and answered in attacking historical problems. It is therefore impossible to separate constitutional history from any other kinds of history."[53] The topic presented difficult challenges because it required understanding as well as memory. Clarke revered Stubbs and Maitland as the premier scholars in the shaping of constitutional history. Constitutional history, through Stubbs's demand for original documents and Maitland's emphasis on historical context, inculcated valuable lessons of caution and understanding. She wrote: "The student of C. history learnt that he must be suspicious, critical and above all things realistic in his use of words."[54] In what might stand as Clarke's apologia for her life's work, she wrote:

Two common factors lie behind all historical study: the desire to know all about the past and establish continuity with it and the desire to inform posterity about historical facts, which might otherwise be unrecorded . . . to break down the barriers of time and mortality and thus to extend the limits of human consciousness beyond the span of a single life. . . . The desire for continuity supplies what might be called *inner steel* towards historical studies.[55]

English constitutional history possessed a special value and interest because of its continuity, the variety of issues present, the independence from Roman law, and the common law's resistance to codification. In Clarke's custody, the subject endured beyond its loss of status as a research endeavor.

If fate had cut short the lives of Mary Bateson and Maude Clarke, no such tragedy curtailed the career of Helen Cam, who earned perhaps the strongest reputation of any woman historian working in the field of English constitutional history. Cam took a first in history in 1907 at Royal Holloway College, London, and she then spent a fellowship year at Bryn Mawr College in the United States. She received a master's degree from the University of London in 1909 and taught at Cheltenham Ladies College and Royal Holloway for the next twelve years. Cam spent most of her academic career at Girton College, Cambridge, where she served from 1921 to 1948. At Girton she faced the daunting task of replacing Eileen Power, who had left to join the London School of Economics. Like other female academics, Cam found that university life permitted an autonomy that other careers would not have allowed.

By the end of the 1920s, Cam had established herself as the leading authority on medieval English local government, especially that amorphous institution, the hundred.[56] As tutor, she insisted on the highest standards of academic work and was a role model for generations of Girton women. Cam published a number of important studies in constitutional history, and her reputation was secure. Her research and writing continued until the end of her long life, each contribution adding to her stature. Her standing in the profession remained as well, for she continued to offer information, encouragement, and advice to a wide variety of correspondents. For example, historian C. R. Cheney (1906–87) wrote to her in 1966: "One of my undergraduate students is keenly interested in 13th Century Hundreds. He asks—is anyone doing anything about hundreds besides Miss Cam & I answer: Miss Cam. There's no one else, is there?"[57] When Lord Denning (1899–1999), then Master of the Rolls, needed information about the dating of Magna Carta, he turned to Cam.[58] She remained at Cambridge long enough to witness the full recognition of Girton as a college within the university and the equality of male and female students in 1948.[59] In that year, Cam accepted the Zemarry Radcliffe professorship of history at Harvard, the first female professor in that university's College of Arts and Sciences. Another honor she received was her election in 1945 as a fellow of the British Academy, only the third woman so recognized; and in 1957, Cam and Doris Stenton became the first women elected to the Council of the Selden Society.

In both academics and politics, Cam took an active role. A committed supporter of the Labour Party, her one regret in life was "her inability to appreciate beer, the traditional drink of the English working man."[60] Throughout her life, Cam worked on behalf of adult education for women who had received scant schooling and needed extra help to seek education while still employed. She endorsed votes for women, although not with the same militancy that Bateson had shown. Within the Cambridge community, Cam fought in the same fashion, consistently but without public furor. Her specialty course in English constitutional history to 1485 retained great popularity with both those who aspired to the law as a profession and those who intended careers as schoolmistresses.[61] No matter what her other activities achieved, her reputation rested on her work as a historian.

In her course on constitutional history, Cam demonstrated strict allegiance to the standards set by her scholarly heroes, Stubbs and Maitland. Cam never joined the fashionable denigration of Stubbs, for she believed that in his stress on documentary evidence Stubbs had taught a lesson of enduring value; Cam taught her students that Stubbs's *Select Charters* "should be your stand by."[62] Cam emphasized that original documents were not merely illustrations, they were the fundamental evidence that students must weigh: "I know of no better means of acquiring the historian's technique for ascertaining & establishing truth than the careful study of const. documents."[63] Constitutional history concerned "real men with actual problems, how to live together in society."[64] The only fault Cam conceded in Stubbs's work was "his almost complete disregard of economic considerations, which now seem more relevant than 'political' or 'constitutional' ideas in treating primitive and decentralized communities."[65] Cam was therefore a true acolyte in the Great Tradition, even though she conceded in 1939 that the subject had lost some of its scholarly luster, "partly, I think, because we regarded it as being a closed chapter of history."[66] Although grieved by its diminishing status, Cam never abandoned the field either in its research or teaching expressions.

Cam defined constitutional history in a fashion that enlarged the narrow confines that other scholars regarded as its drawback: "The constitutional history is the study of the political institutions of the country: of the various ways in which the art and science of gov't has been practiced in England: often different answers that have been found."[67] The ultimate criterion of historical significance was an event's or a person's contribution to the constitution, for constitutional history subsumed all other avenues of inquiry. As Cam once remarked famously about the debate over the fate of the Princes in the Tower: "I just do not understand how people can become so upset over the fate of a couple of sniveling brats. After all, what impact did they have on the constitution?"[68] But she also believed that the study of legal institutions "provided the key to political and social growth."[69] To the usual justification of administrative, legal, and philosophical knowledge inherent in the study of constitutional history, Cam added the humanist perspectives that Maitland had given to the field.[70] These insights allowed the investigation of the constitution and common law to contain social dimensions and even permit the study of ordinary people: "As soon as you begin to say 'We do things this way—they do things that way—what is to be done about it?' men are beginning to feel towards justice, that resides between the endless jar of right and wrong."[71] In the standards to which Cam adhered: "The message was clear: in reading, as in writing, the first requirement for a historian was to be rigorous in regard to fact, evidence, and honesty of argument."[72] Cam earned her reputation not only by meeting the criteria for research into constitutional history, but also by making the subject more responsive to other forms of inquiry. She lived into the era of decline for constitutional history, so her own standing as a scholar has suffered an eclipse; but Cam surely helped pave the way by which constitutional history transformed itself into an ally of the new social history through such means as the study of wills and property transactions.

Still another profile for a woman historian's contribution to the Great Tradition came in the career of Doris Stenton. Her circumstances differed because she married, in this case distinguished medievalist Frank Stenton, and because she held an academic appointment outside the women's colleges at the University of Reading, where she served for decades on the faculty with her husband, although "in some sense she remained in Frank's shadow during his life."[73] Doris Stenton was dedicated to the editing and publication of original documents so much a part of constitutional history's scholarship. One great work that she performed was the resuscitation of the Pipe Roll Society from near extinction when she was appointed secretary in 1923. Stenton rescued the society from its moribund state in short order: "Under your energetic rule the Pipe Roll Society is getting on famously. To have increased the membership in so short a time by 58 per cent is a real triumph."[74] Even the difficult John Horace Round praised her: "Indeed it must make you proud to think that but for yourself, it [the Pipe Roll Society] must have come to an end long ago."[75] As an editor of primary records and as the author of original works, Stenton followed a well-trodden path. In other ways, however, she moved away from the core elements of constitutional history. The publication of *The English Woman in History* broke the dichotomy between the public/private spheres analysis that had dominated constitutional history once and for all.[76] Stenton anticipated but did not embody recent approaches to women's history:

Though in no way a feminist in the ordinary sense of that word, she herself had always consciously and gratefully enjoyed the complete freedom, so long denied to women, to develop to the utmost her intellectual faculties and to order her own life. The Anglo-Saxon attitude to women won her strongest commendation and her dislike of St. Paul's views on the proper place of females, accepted in feudal law and in the teaching of the church, was clearly expressed.[77]

Although Stenton conformed in a number of important ways to the legacy of constitutional history's impact on women, she also deviated from its basic principles through her personal agency and her attempt to extricate women from the silence of the subject.

Another female scholar who started in the conventions of English constitutional history but who departed even more dramatically than Stenton did was Lucy Sutherland. As an undergraduate tutored by Maude Clarke, Sutherland wrote essays on topics such as Magna Carta, the procedural changes in the law during the reign of Henry II, the representative principle in medieval parliaments, and the idea of lordship in Anglo-Saxon England.[78] The appearance of Lewis Namier's *Structure of Politics at the Accession of George III* in 1929 helped draw her into eighteenth-century history. Sutherland did focus much of her research on Parliament, as did Namier, but she was never a constitutional historian in the strict sense as defined by the Great Tradition. Sutherland relied upon the multivolume *History of English Law* by William Holdsworth rather than Stubbs and Maitland because the former had explained the "fundamental principles of constitutional law which had now become fixed."[79] Sutherland's scholarship often assisted Namier in the latter's History of Parliament project, and he relied heavily on her articles and on her advice: "I am most grateful to you for the two brilliant biographies of Beckford and Macpherson: they are both masterpieces each in its own style."[80] As the history of Parliament bogged down, Namier testified to the steadfastness of Sutherland's work; with 1,320 biographies done and 640 to go, he wrote: "I do trust I can still count on your co-operation. Almost everyone else outside my office has let me down. It is pretty hard."[81] Research on the East India Company, later on the history of Oxford University, and important administrative positions at Lady Margaret Hall and then the university pushed Sutherland's career far from the parameters delineated by Clarke.

In the long run, however, the affinity between constitutional history and women scholars ended most dramatically in the career of Eileen Power. Perhaps the most influential female historian of her generation, Power opened new intellectual venues for all scholars. Her biographer has written: "First she avoided the traditions of legal and constitutional history as a graduate and followed instead her inclination towards literary history and the history of religious life. This, together with the background she acquired at Girton in economic and social history, led her to develop her own route towards the social history of the Middle Ages."[82] Power left Girton to teach at the London School of Economics, preferring the excitement of the London institution to the cloistered atmosphere of the college. Power combined her gifts as a historian with study in France to pioneer in Britain what would eventually become known as the *Annales* school of historical analysis.[83] Her work placed her among the major historians of the interwar period.

Power's eminence did not last. She died in 1940 at the relatively early age of fifty-one, and while she had already published a corpus of significant scholarship, there was clearly more to come. The social history that Power had introduced went into eclipse, only to regain prestige in the latter part of the 1960s.[84] Her influence had created a niche for women historians, and her life served as a role model for women who aspired to an academic career.[85] The inclusion of women in the national narrative did not succeed in her lifetime, for social history had not yet taken its place at the apex of the professional status hierarchy. In the end, therefore, English constitutional history provided an arena where women scholars excelled on an equal basis with men; but the general decline of the field as a research tradition in the 1920s and afterward could not sustain this situation. Only Power, by striking out in new scholarly directions, pointed the way to the future.

Opportunities for women in higher education were no more promising in nineteenth-century America than they were in Britain, in spite of a handful of women's colleges like the Seven Sisters. Though the origins of at least two of these antedate the Civil War, their early histories, and in some cases their names, reflect the fact that they were, like Mount Holyoke (founded 1837), "female seminaries." Their transformation into institutions of higher learning comparable, in curriculum and methods of instruction, to the kind of experience enjoyed by male students at the best colleges and universities, was under way by the 1880s. The Ivy League colleges proved as resistant as Oxford and Cambridge to the admission of women, though Harvard and Columbia did affiliate with women's colleges and Yale was to prove relatively open to graduate students in history by the turn of the century. The private universities founded after the Civil War were marginally more accepting of women students, though only after considerable foot-dragging. At Cornell (founded 1869), there was supposedly no barrier to the admission of women, but it took a few years before they were grudgingly admitted, faculty like Goldwin Smith remaining adamantly opposed.[86] Only the University of Chicago (founded 1892) accepted women from the outset. State universities, founded in large numbers after the Civil War, were frequently coeducational, though usually with considerable resistance by faculty and male students. Even at "securely" coeducational institutions like the University of Michigan, women were in a distinct minority and marginalized both socially and in terms of the kind of professional preparation and mentoring men could take for granted. The first American woman to receive a PhD in history was Kate Everest Levi of the University of Wisconsin, who studied under Frederick Jackson Turner. The number of women historians holding a doctorate expanded modestly; there were still only forty-nine by 1915, with a disproportionate number of female PhD students clustered at Yale, Cornell, Chicago, and Wisconsin. Women were distinctly underrepresented in medieval history.[87]

An example of the kind of resistance faced by a determined woman scholar was provided by Lucy Maynard Salmon (1853–1927) at the University of Michigan. Even though she persisted, along with a handful of other women, in studying for a master's degree, the man under whom she studied, Charles Kendall Adams, was on record as saying that "of course the young women could not do seminary [i.e., seminar] work."[88] After teaching high school and teaching at the Indiana State Normal School (later Indiana State), she attempted to enter the doctoral program at Johns Hopkins, telling Herbert Baxter Adams that she hoped to "receive the same advantage of instruction in study in the department of history as are given to gentlemen."[89] In spite of his relative openness to women students and the help he proffered in getting her master's degree published,[90] Salmon did not end up pursuing a doctoral program at Johns Hopkins. Instead, she conducted additional graduate study at Bryn Mawr, where she was forced to study under Woodrow Wilson, who was even more negatively disposed toward women in advanced studies than Charles Kendall Adams had been.

In spite of such hostile mentoring, Salmon managed to get the master's thesis she had produced under Charles Kendall Adams, "History of the Appointing Power of the President," published in the first volume of the *Papers of the American Historical Association.* Herbert Baxter Adams was the editor of this series, and it was no doubt his friendly influence that made publication possible. Salmon stayed in close touch with Herbert Baxter Adams up to his death in 1901, and he was certainly closer to being her mentor than either of her actual graduate supervisors. Shortly before his death, she wrote him that some women (though obviously not her) pursued graduate study to escape the onerous charitable and civic duties that were expected of them, citing a friend who was "at the beck and call of everybody to do committee work and to serve the public in so many ways that she had not a moment's time from one year's end to another; she was looking for an occupation in self-protection."[91] Salmon's work on presidential appointive powers established itself as a classic study in American constitutional history over the next few years.[92] She was hired as Vassar's first history teacher in 1887, becoming a professor two years later and spending the remainder of her career there. Having achieved a measure of recognition through her scholarship and teaching, she was determined to carve out an active role for herself within that male bastion, the American Historical Association (AHA).

Salmon set out to achieve full participation in the AHA in publishing, presenting papers, and serving on committees. The first of these she had begun to achieve with the publication of her study of presidential appointive powers. When the *American Historical Review* was established in 1895, she wasted no time in putting herself forward, writing, with disarming diffidence to the editor, John Franklin Jameson: "I can not flatter myself that I have any special facility in the use of a pen, and so I hesitate to offer my services to the new review, but if at any time there is anything I am able to do, I should be glad to know of it."[93] Jameson did allow her to write a review for the second issue of the journal, but characteristically, it was of a biography of William the Silent by a popular woman historian, Ruth Putnam.[94] Considerable time elapsed before she would be entrusted with reviewing any serious constitutional history by male authors. To underscore her scholarly credentials to Jameson and others in this review, she criticized Putnam for lack of professional rigor in her treatment of the political and constitutional issues at stake in William the Silent's struggles.[95] Salmon also managed to get herself placed on the annual AHA program numerous times. In 1900, she wrote to Herbert Baxter Adams: "I have been waiting for someone to ask me to read a paper at the Detroit meeting. I wrote one on the steamer coming over!"[96] On this occasion, she was allowed to give a paper titled "The Advisability of Establishing a School for the Study of Roman History at Rome." But Andrew Cunningham McLaughlin, who thought it would be an interesting paper, assured Herbert Baxter Adams that, though a few women might find a restricted place on the program, they would continue to be excluded from any real social participation at the meeting:

We rather expect now to have a meeting Friday evening for the women only at some private house. This meeting will be of a social character, and I have thought it would be well if Miss Salmon and perhaps Miss Coman [Katharine Coman, a distinguished economic historian], would give short papers that evening. The men are to have a smoker at the Detroit Club from which, of course, the women would be excluded.[97]

This professional apartheid remained the norm until 1917. At the 1905 meeting in Baltimore, women historians were shunted off to separate festivities by Mrs. John Franklin Jameson, head of the Honorary Committee of Ladies, while their male colleagues gathered at the exclusive Arundel Club.[98]

Salmon became an active force on some of the AHA's leading committees, especially those dealing with secondary education. Partly this was because, as a teacher at a women's college, she played an important role in training secondary teachers. Moreover, as head of the History Teachers Association of the Middle States and Maryland, she was well placed to act as intermediary between secondary and postsecondary history educators. The AHA Committee of Seven (described in Chapter 6), on which Salmon was a most active member, recommended with her complete support a year of English history for high school juniors. She continued to monitor and to foster attempts to bring high school curricula into line with those of the universities, but found that progress was slow and patchy. Moreover, she found great resistance on the part of college faculty to adjust their methods and course structures to the work done in the high schools, complaining to Charles Homer Haskins in 1903: "recently some Harvard graduates who are now engaged in secondary school work spoke quite strongly in regard to the lack of adjustment in college courses in history to the work which is done in the secondary schools, saying that Harvard, Yale, and all the leading colleges were practically giving their college work without any reference to the work done in the schools."[99] This was probably not something most professional historians wanted to hear, and it is not surprising that, in spite of her expertise in pedagogy, Salmon was not appointed to the Committee of Five when the American Historical Association revisited the issue in 1907. Most male historians of the era were also put off by her insistence on opening up new channels of investigation into the history of everyday life. While not renouncing her earlier interest in constitutional history, she was opening new vistas on the history of society, including women's history, beginning with her book, *Domestic Service,* in 1897.[100] She quickly found, however, that the main professional journals, edited by men who continued to hold political and constitutional history as the essential core of the discipline, refused to publish her groundbreaking articles.[101]

The first generation of professional women historians faced a dilemma. When they tried to pursue scholarship on political and constitutional matters, they were considered by many of their male colleagues to lack any real ability to analyze the masculine world of public power. If, like Lucy Salmon, they turned to social history, this was considered trivial. Publication in leading journals like the *American Historical Review* was especially challenging for women, who accounted for only 3 percent of the articles between 1895 and 1940.[102] Women were also at a signal disadvantage in getting fellowships, travel grants, and other sources of funding. Typical of the expedients women scholars adopted in order to travel and research was a "Miss Kellogg," whom Haskins recommended to Jameson as a copyist for manuscript materials on American history in England. Haskins pointed out that she would be willing to work for a dollar a day plus passage for the fourteen weeks, "and would bring to it the advantage of extensive training in American history and considerable familiarity with the materials for American history in English archives."[103] The woman in question, Louise Phelps Kellogg (1862–1942), was in fact about to receive her doctorate under Frederick Jackson Turner from the University of Wisconsin. Her dissertation, "The American Colonial Charter," published in 1903 as part of the AHA annual report, won her the Justin Winsor Prize that year.[104] Unable to procure a teaching post commensurate with her abilities (probably due as much to age as to gender discrimination), she carved out an important career editing historical document collections at the Wisconsin Historical Society. She also found time to write a number of books and to mentor students sent from Vassar by Lucy Salmon to Wisconsin to pursue their doctorates.[105] In 1930 she became the first woman to be elected president of the Mississippi Valley Historical Association, the forerunner of the Organization of American Historians.

Clearly, in the absence of the kind of funding sources to which most male scholars had some access, it took uncommonly determined women like Lucy Salmon and Louise Kellogg to attain distinction within the profession. The next generation of women historians had somewhat greater opportunities but still had to undergo uncommon privations in order to carry out the necessary research for their publications. An important reason for the success of some of the leading women active in the first half of the twentieth century was the increased funding made available by women's colleges to their female faculty. That was certainly an important factor in the careers of both Bertha Haven Putnam (1872–1960) and Nellie Neilson (1873–1947). Putnam (unrelated to Ruth Putnam), as the daughter of George Haven Putnam, publisher and founder of the American branch of the English-Speaking Union, as well as a student of Charles McLean Andrews at Bryn Mawr, came by her interest in English constitutional history naturally. She went on to receive her PhD from Columbia. Her dissertation, on the enforcement of the Statute of Laborers of 1351, was published by Columbia University Press and established her as an authority on late medieval administration, economic regulation, and central/local relations.[106] Putnam epitomized the scholarly qualities that had characterized those who labored in English legal and constitutional history: "All of her work is meticulously and painstakingly supported by the original sources for medieval English legal history, which she knew as well or better than any other scholar who had worked with them before or has since."[107] Neilson was Putnam's classmate at Bryn Mawr and also a student of Andrews, staying on to take her master's degree (1894) and doctorate (1899) under his direction. Andrews proved an excellent mentor; both women testified to the importance of his encouragement and support.[108] Neilson's scholarly path followed that of many of her male colleagues: "Her commitment to English history is unsurprising given her apprenticeship at Bryn Mawr and the late-nineteenth-century fascination with English constitutional history."[109] Neilson's dissertation, "Economic Conditions on the Manors of Ramsey Abbey," was published in 1899,[110] though she had earlier published an article from it in the *American Historical Review*.[111] Like her subsequent works, both appeared under the gender-neutral name of N. Neilson.

If both Putnam and Neilson received a solid foundation at Bryn Mawr, their full professional development was nurtured at Mount Holyoke, where both spent the remainder of their teaching careers. The timing was important, as Mount Holyoke at the turn of the century was coming into its own as a bastion of the most rigorous sort of women's higher education. This was due in large measure to the strong leadership provided by Mary Emma Woolley (1863–1947), a historian who began her lengthy presidency of the college in 1901. The first woman to be admitted to Brown University, she had graduated in 1894 and finished her master's degree there, under the direction of John Franklin Jameson, the following year. She quickly moved to hire outstanding women scholars to staff the college, seeking advice beforehand from professional organizations like the AHA. One of her first acquisitions was Nellie Neilson, who had not landed a teaching position elsewhere for the previous four years, in spite of the great promise shown by her published dissertation. Without Woolley's offer, Neilson might well have languished in a seven-hundred-dollar-a-year job in Bryn Mawr's essay department. Hired as a lecturer in 1902, within three years she was made full professor and chair of the Department of History and Political Science.[112] Here she made her mark, not least through her teaching, by which she inspired a host of students, some of whom pursued graduate studies and became historians in turn. She was also able to provide opportunities for other women historians, and Putnam was one of her early (1908) hires.

With scholars like Neilson and Putnam on the faculty, the president and trustees of Mount Holyoke came to realize the importance of providing sources of funding for them to carry out the necessary research. Woolley convinced the trustees to offer half-pay sabbaticals to faculty.[113] This was a great help, though given the extremely low salaries of women faculty in this era, additional funding was usually necessary. Without this availability, such writers would have had to depend on the scant resources provided by the AHA and various male-dominated foundations, and as women they would have faced the likelihood of having their requests turned down. Putnam, for example, spent a year in England in 1912–13 researching her groundbreaking study of the justices of the peace in the fifteenth century, thanks to a grant from the Alice Freeman Palmer Memorial Fellowship given by the Association of Collegiate Alumnae. Out of the material gathered on this trip, she produced two articles in the *English Historical Review* and one in the *American Historical Review*. But when she applied to Jameson, as head of the department of historical research of the Carnegie Institution, for a grant to broaden the study and finish a book for which she already had a contract with Oxford University Press, his response was decidedly negative. He noted that, while she could submit an application for a research grant, as far as the Carnegie was concerned, "about all is now being done that is likely to be done" and that "my judgment is that it would not be successful."[114] Fortunately, Putnam eventually finished her important study with other sources of support. It was published in 1924 as part of the prestigious Oxford Studies in Social and Legal History edited by Paul Vinogradoff.[115]

For her part, Nellie Neilson continued to work on the details of medieval administrative and economic history, producing a number of important published editions of documentary material with learned commentaries. She was also increasingly active in the AHA and became a regular speaker and commentator at annual meetings, especially in the period after World War I. She had initially declined Haskins's offer to present a paper at the 1912 meeting, but as her confidence grew with the number of publications, she found her professional voice. Both she and Bertha Putnam were on the program of the 1920 meeting in Washington, D.C.[116] By this time the barriers were slowly coming down. More women were in the program, they were allowed to participate in smokers and other convivial gatherings, and they were being awarded more prizes for their books and articles, though certainly not in proportion to their numbers in the association.[117] Access to important AHA committees had started before the war but was, on the whole, granted reluctantly by most male scholars. There were, of course, important exceptions to this general pattern of resistance. Among the first generation of professional historians, Herbert Baxter Adams had been one of the most liberal in his openness to women scholars. Andrews, politically perhaps the most conservative of all the historians discussed and sometimes referred to behind his back as a "Tory," played a crucial role with his encouragement and active mentoring of women like Neilson and Putnam. This included badgering Jameson to publish Neilson's first article in the *American Historical Review*.[118] Jameson, the most powerful figure in the early profession, was not notably liberal on the issue of greater female participation in the profession, though he did occasionally prove helpful to individual women.[119]

With a number of the crucial choke points of the profession held by unsupportive men, it is not surprising that, in spite of greater social access to fellow historians at national meetings, women made only modest professional progress in the interwar period. Following Louise Phelps Kellogg's winning of the Winsor Prize in 1903, a handful of other women received prestigious awards, but it was still far from proportional to male prizewinners. The number of women historians certainly did increase after World War I. At the fiftieth anniversary meeting of the American Historical Association in 1935, George M. Dutcher (1874–1959) noted, somewhat optimistically: "There was a marked increase in the relative number of women . . . trained in university seminars, who made substantial contributions."[120] If the supply was increased, the prospects had become bleaker than ever, for a strong countervailing influence was at work. A number of women historians lost their positions during the Depression, as women's colleges were especially hard hit financially and showed an increasing tendency to hire male faculty. As a consequence, the share of full professorships in history held by women (16 percent in 1930) went into a steep decline and did not begin to climb again until the 1970s.[121]

In spite of these unfavorable developments, leading women scholars continued to work toward placing more women on AHA committees (including the program committee) and on the executive committee. By the 1910s, a few women began to gain access to committees. The first female executive committee member was Lucy Salmon, appointed in 1915.[122] Other women followed her onto the board over the next few years, including Nellie Neilson, whose scholarly output in the interwar era was especially impressive. She continued to do important work in medieval legal studies while further expanding into economic history, and she was invited by her friend Eileen Power to write a key section of *The Cambridge Economic History of Europe*.[123] While the more popularly written of her works showed a fascination with the details of social life not unlike that of Lucy Salmon and was hence apt to be considered "lightweight" by some of the profession's leaders, the solidity of her contributions in legal and economic history made her the leading candidate among women historians for a try at the AHA presidency. All but the most obdurate male historians were impressed by Neilson's scholarly rigor, her period of study in Britain with Paul Vinogradoff and Frederic Maitland, her presidency of the Medieval Academy of America, and her election as a Fellow of the Royal Historical Society.[124] And yet getting her elected president of the AHA required a decade of campaigning, with particularly effective work by the Berkshire Conference of Women Historians and male historians like Curtis P. Nettles and Howard K. Beale. Neilson was finally elected second vice president in 1940 and thus was in line to assume the presidency in 1943.[125] While certainly a triumph of sorts for gender equality within the profession, it was not to be repeated until 1987.

Neilson's presidential address, delivered at New York City on 29 December 1943, was a careful scholarly delineation of the many places within medieval England where the common law did not run, that welter of liberties and special franchises where a bewildering range of legal procedures and jurisdictions obtained.[126] She explained that contrary to usual practice in presidential addresses, she was not attempting to generalize from her lifelong immersion in her beloved specialty, but rather to present particular detailed findings that pointed up the slow, halting advance of a common legal system. Such a lengthy, gradual, and contested advance, she claimed, served to inculcate a powerful culture of limited government and a concomitant attachment to liberty characteristic of the English-speaking peoples. England's constitutional and legal history, Neilson insisted, was a fundamental component of America's culture of freedom:

Much of her history is our history. We think in large measure the same legal thoughts, in spite of many political and social differences. . . . The pattern of her common law she began to build very long ago, and throughout her history she has continued to elaborate it quietly without violent breaks or changes. It is a living organism and one the knowledge of which is especially essential to us Americans in war and in peace.[127]

More than a scholar's wartime patriotic effusion, Neilson's statement showed her abiding attachment to the central values of her nineteenth-century Whig predecessors and her insistence on the continuing relevance of the Great Tradition.

CHAPTER NINE

"I Never Met a Learned Man Who Less Oppressed One with His Learning"

Constitutional History as Lawyers' History and Historians' Law

The final issue in the rise and decline of English constitutional history was the uneasy relationship that developed between law and history, one that caused the subjects to separate increasingly into lawyers' history and historians' law. Originally, in the golden age of treatise writing by lawyers and constitutional narratives by historians of the 1870s and 1880s, both law and history had sought intellectual justification through appropriation of the language and goals of science. Initially the invocation of the prestige associated with science in relation to both law and history had not seemed problematic. The scientific bases for both topics were presumably destined to establish settled principles and objective truths in equal measure. As jurist Thomas Erskine Holland (1835–1926), Chichele professor of international law and diplomacy at Oxford from 1874 to 1909, wrote to Oliver Wendell Holmes about his seminal essay titled "The Path of the Law": "I was particularly interested in what you say as to the help of history in clearing away rubbish, so facilitating the approximation to accurately measured social sciences—as to all conduct being either lawful or unlawful, and as to the respective function of judge and jury."[1] The challenge of placing both disciplines securely within the changing environment of university life and validating their claims to scholarly respectability enlisted the energy of both jurists and historians. In tandem they helped spark the tremendous enthusiasm that made constitutional history so attractive in the decades after 1870. The strength of constitutional history as formulated by William Stubbs and his successors "came from concentrating on English history, above all on the institutions of Parliament and the common law,"[2] and had spread around the world. As A. L. Smith wrote: "To unravel a legal development, examine it historically. To illuminate a historical period, examine its legal ideas."[3] The increased separation between the two fields clouded the previous identification of constitutional history with national identity.

From the outset, however, law and history, despite frequent protestations to the contrary, went in different academic directions. The separation of law from history in 1872 in the undergraduate curriculum at Oxford produced varying results. Students flocked to the study of history, but few undertook reading the law. When James Bryce resigned the Regius professorship of civil law at Oxford in 1893, in his valedictory lecture he remarked on the disappointing results for legal studies that 1872 had produced. In 1897, A. V. Dicey wrote of his frustration that examination periods in history did not mesh well with constitutional law: "I don't feel convinced that it is possible to frame a scheme which is really satisfactory for both lawyers and historians."[4] In the end, therefore, what looked like an inevitable partnership expressed through constitutional history turned into a brief marriage of convenience.

The divorce between legal and historical scholarship was perhaps predestined. First united in 1852, the School of Law and Modern History combined Blackstone (or Justinian) with English history, either from 1066 to 1509 or from 1509 to 1837.[5] In retrospect, law was a junior partner whose student numbers remained small relative to those of history. Both historians and lawyers viewed the arrangement as something of a shotgun wedding. Montagu Burrows (1819–1905), Chichele professor of modern history at Oxford from 1862 to 1905, remarked that "history supplied interest and breadth to the somewhat repulsive science of law."[6] In 1866 Bryce wrote of the school: "As to the work of the men this time, it was, although in parts respectable, still as regards the law, certainly disappointing; so few men showed any originality or sparkle. If only we could have classical men—who have learned what the wide world was like from Herodotus, and what scientific politics are from Thucydides."[7] A half century later, Bryce had not changed his opinion: "But my professorial experience was disappointing, if not disheartening, for there was really no general interest among the best men in the subject [law], & the classes depended on the favour of the College Tutor who might, like a perfidious attorney send no briefs."[8] Given these difficulties from the outset, that law and history had an uneasy relationship was no surprise; as S. F. C. Milsom has written: "historians have long sought to expunge the lawyer."[9]

William Stubbs, for example, regarded lawyers with great suspicion for both theoretical and practical reasons. The more lawyers wished to systematize and to categorize, the more Stubbs regarded their endeavors as futile. Stubbs understood that the historical record rarely permitted exclusive judgments, for human affairs were contingent and complex.[10] As a result, lawyers too often misunderstood the context in which legal principles had originated: "It is quite ludicrous, to see the men, whose reading and training we know to be so merely empirical, as soon as they became wigged, secured from all risk of error—practice themselves, by hiring themselves out to confront right & wrong, to adjudicate on historical matters of which they know not the first elements & then lift up their hands in pious horror, because we do not see that what comes from their mouths is *law*."[11] The habit of jumping from precedent to precedent without regard for intervening events combined with a too reverential attitude toward the past precluded lawyers from a true understanding of the broader processes of history.

From a practical point of view, Stubbs thought that Norman lawyers had misunderstood Anglo-Saxon customary law, and the attempts to impose feudalism nearly had dire consequences for the evolution of the English constitution. The classificatory impulses of the legal profession, "its taste for what Stubbs stigmatized as 'theoretic principles'—constantly jeopardized the delicate growth of English institutions by attempting to impose the strait-jacket of legal formulae."[12] More specifically, Stubbs wrote that "I do not wonder that you are bothered about the military tenures; may the lawyers be hanged."[13] Feudalism had threatened to divert or even destroy the development of England's Germanic heritage but fortunately had not succeeded: "It was, Stubbs variously implied, the incomprehension of the Norman lawyers of anything not manifestly feudal, and of the policy of the Conqueror in retaining a direct link between himself and his subjects, which allowed the lower courts to survive."[14] Providentially, the strength of Anglo-Saxon institutional continuity had prevailed against the Norman assault and fortified English society in the process.

The serious study of history thus differed dramatically from the representation of a client or the musings of jurisprudence. Rather than synthesize the two disciplines, Stubbs wished to distance himself from the intellectual bases at the heart of legal study: a "general aversion to the approach of lawyers."[15] Given the academic rivalry that involved the different disciplines, interdisciplinary scholarship did not yet seem a reasonable strategy. For Stubbs, "the repudiation of lawyer-like habits of mind was a kind of declaration of intellectual independence."[16] This perspective created a culture that differentiated sharply between legal and historical research:

Just as in the reading rooms of the Public Record Office, historians and lawyers were participating in the same institutions and using the same documentary materials. How could the historians achieve and justify their independence? Stubbs's strategy is surely the exemplary one in these circumstances, since he places in the foreground the necessity of "judgment," yet withdraws from the term precisely those connotations which are appropriate to the legal sense of the term. Historians are not advocates, pleading for summary judgment. Their patient scrutiny of the documents of the case will never result in a condemnation or an acquittal, in the final sense, since that role belongs to God alone.[17]

From the outset, therefore, law and history had an uneasy alliance at best, one that foreshadowed future differences.

For his part, Edward Freeman, always more vociferous than his clerical friend Stubbs, extended the prejudice against lawyers. The pair delighted in exchanging lawyer jokes, for "both had a deep attachment for the English Constitution, as they understood it: it was not a theory or legalism to them, and they never wearied of jesting at philosophers' and lawyers' views of history."[18] Freeman's bias illustrated the preference for public law as the priority subject for historical inquiry and his reluctance to deal with the complexities of private law. Freeman admonished Bryce that he should turn away from the study of English law in order to concentrate on the more respectable subject of Roman law.[19] Freeman's suspicions of lawyers went even further than those of Stubbs because lawyers had damaged not only the study of history but history itself: "There can be no kind of doubt that lawyers' interpretations and lawyers' ways of looking at things have done no small mischief, not only to the true understanding of our history but to the actual course of our history itself."[20] The mistrust of lawyers' ability to arrive at an appropriate understanding of history provided a clandestine motif to constitutional history even at the time of its greatest prestige.

That the combative John Horace Round also harbored a deep mistrust of lawyers and their history came as no surprise either. This hostility emerged primarily when Round disapproved of decisions that concerned the details of peerage disputes. On one occasion T. F. Tout consoled Round with the advice that "the difficulty in arguing with the peerage lawyers is that they all see history as a flat plain, and could not, if they would, understand that conditions vary in different periods."[21] Round retained his general disdain for the lawyers' sense of history right up to his death in 1928. In 1916, for example, he wrote in disgust of an unspecified House of Lords decision about a peerage controversy that he thought "absolutely wrong": "It is interesting to note that this case illustrates afresh the great difference between law and history. For it is admitted, I believe, that historians would have, undoubtedly, decided it the other way."[22] In part, therefore, the reluctance of constitutional historians to explore the realms of private law depended on this general perception about the failings of lawyers to possess an appropriate historical vision; the fact that few historians had the technical training to deal with such subjects as torts or contracts, of course, also contributed to this prejudice.

For their part, lawyers came to have little sympathy for the endeavors of the new academic history. Dicey, for example, for all his renown as a jurist, evinced little interest in legal history. As he wrote at the beginning of his tenure as Vinerian professor of English law at Oxford:

> You will probably find out on nearer inspection better than you now appear to do, how very slender my own knowledge of history is. Partly for that reason & partly because I do not believe the historical aspect of law to be what the men here really need, I try as much as possible to learn myself what the law actually is rather than the process by which it has grown to be what it is. But I trust that I don't add to their historical confusions.[23]

This resulted primarily from Dicey's preoccupation with the analysis of legal institutions and relative lack of concern for how those institutions came into existence. His famous treatises identified legal principles whether in constitutional law or conflicts of law, but they did not narrate how those maxims came into existence except by reference to case law. In this methodology, Dicey carried the jurisprudence of John Austin (1790–1859) to an extreme: history had one purpose and legal analysis another, so cross-disciplinary scholarship had little appeal for him.[24] Dicey confessed: "I do not possess the gifts required for historical research, still less have I ever pursued it."[25] Dicey rejected the new standard of the discovery of new knowledge that academic history embraced, for he believed that the repetition of conventional truths without critical analysis sufficed for most purposes of historical explanation.

About the new emphasis on primary sources, Dicey once lamented the "fallacy of authorities and excesses in the way of industry" among historians.[26] He denounced the search for new facts and the desire to overturn established interpretations, because, as he once wrote: "History is no better than an old Almanack."[27] History could never supply scientific principles in the manner that legal axioms might become codified, and this legal history never attracted his attention. Dicey once wrote: "All I really maintain is that research is not everything. It is equally necessary for a good historian to be able to grasp results of other people's labours and to express these results with clearness and force."[28] This latter sentiment was surely correct, but Dicey preferred his history in literary form primarily, not in the language of extensive research. His attitude directly challenged the criteria on which constitutional history had built its reputation.

Law permitted impartial study, but history excited partisan passions, so scientific truths in the historical record escaped discovery.[29] Dicey held inflexible political beliefs, and he feared constantly that the advance of historical research might unsettle those truths he prized, especially with respect to the issue of

home rule for Ireland. As he wrote: "You ought not to use History for the purpose of adding bitterness to the controversies of the time in which you live."[30]
History did not supply precedents in the fashion that the common law did,
and so its conclusions were less reliable. History as a discipline was important
only for the perpetuation of moral reflections that might guide statesmen or
individuals. When applied to the home rule controversy, this meant that "I am
quite unable to persuade myself that the ill doings of 90 years ago can determine the rightness or wisdom of our [Unionist] policy today."[31] As a taught
tradition, Dicey did concede that constitutional history might "stimulate interest in Law," the only advantage that the subject possessed.[32] Beyond this sole
benefit, the teachings of history had little value for lawyers.

Even the work of Frederic Maitland made little favorable impression on
Dicey at first. He wrote, for example, in 1897 about the *History of English Law*
that Maitland's "results might easily be stated with greater clearness & his antiquarian researches have little more to do with law than with theology—perhaps not so much."[33] The great Maitland a mere antiquarian: to the modern
historian this seems not only heretical but downright sacrilegious in the bargain. Dicey's opinion, at least initially, ran counter to the enduring reputation
for excellence that Maitland has always enjoyed. In fairness, we should add
that Dicey changed his mind, writing to his widow after Maitland's death that
the posthumously published *Constitutional History* was "out and out the best
book written on the subject from the legal point of view which I have ever
read."[34] Dicey appreciated Maitland's regard for his own work, "such as Law
and Opinion which was in such a different line from his own labours & must
have seemed to him, rightly eno' so deficient in research."[35] Even here Dicey
recognized that the research standard to which historians adhered constituted
the primary demarcation between the scholarly work of lawyers and historians.

Jurist Sir Frederick Pollock, remembered today as the less famous half of
two partnerships, with Maitland as authors of the *History of English Law* and
with Oliver Wendell Holmes as his epistolary companion for nearly six decades,
had a more complex relationship with history. His undoubted learning never
extended to the new academic history. On the one hand, Pollock's section on
Anglo-Saxon law has long stood as the weakest part of the *History of English
Law,* and historians have long recognized Maitland's determination to negate
the partnership by completing the work so quickly before Pollock could inflict
more damage. Harold Laski (1893–1950) once wrote that he preferred his Holmes untainted by Pollock and quoted Harvard Law School professor Joseph H.
Beale: "Joey Beale used to say that the more he saw of Pollock the more he liked

Maitland, and I share that view. Pollock never lived after the Victorian age."[36] Pollock regarded the purpose of historical inquiry as the quest to rescue the common law from the chaos of its development: "Title by title, and chapter by chapter, the treasures of the Common Law must be consolidated into rational order before they can be newly grasped and recast as a whole."[37] History served as a handmaiden to the classificatory demands of treatise writers who sought to identify the principles that governed individual branches of the law. The analysis and codification of legal doctrine too often depended on "the tendency of the modern mind to impose modern concepts on the past" and resulted in a selective teleology to arrive at the contemporary rationality of the law.[38]

On the other hand, Pollock demonstrated a sympathetic attitude toward those historians who grappled with legal records from the distant past. This research had discovered many new dimensions of the common law that lawyers either had not known or simply neglected. Pollock did not presume to judge those historians such as Stubbs whom he called his masters: "As a lawyer I am free to admire the diligence and accuracy of their work on legal ground, and to express my thanks to them for the powerful aid they have given to dispel the fictions and perverse explanations of facts which have too long encumbered our law books."[39] Although Pollock, rightly, never claimed to be a historian, he did value the advances that academic professionalization had brought to the discipline. In his 1883 inaugural lecture as Corpus professor of jurisprudence at Oxford, Pollock argued: "For my own part I trust that Law and History may ever be too good allies and helpmates to wrangle over an imaginary boundary between their territories. Each of them has so much to do for the other and so much to learn from her that a dispute of this kind is a wasteful folly."[40] Despite these sincere sentiments, however, the alliance between jurists and historians never reached its full potential.

Both sides in the pursuit of legal history expressed good will, but priorities never reached a consensus. In his magisterial *Law and Custom of the Constitution,* for example, Sir William Anson (1843–1914) stipulated that "the lawyer primarily wants to know what an institution is, and then, the circumstances of its growth."[41] Holland confessed to retaining a decisive split between the two disciplines when he wrote to Anson: "You know my disbelief in the possibility of fairly comparing the merits of lawyers and historians."[42] The appearance in the 1880s of scholarly periodicals in both law and history further exacerbated the divisions between the perspectives dominant in each field. Law review history increasingly focused on private law to reconcile cases without significant attention to the context in which legal changes took place. History journals recounted developments in public law, but few historians entered the technical world of legal doctrine. As a result, in spite of the constant invocation of the necessity to bring law and history together, the uneasy relationship continued.

In the end, the "fundamental incompatibility of the two disciplines could be acknowledged only towards the end of the 19th century."[43] The gulf rested on the different approaches to the past utilized by each. For the lawyer, the common-law mind, deferential to precedent and immemorial custom, meant an emphasis on case law with little regard for the historical circumstances that accounted for the changing nature of the law: "The crossing of history with law is a mixture containing more snares than rewards, as it risks confusing rules of evidence basic to one profession with the canons of proof sacrosanct to another."[44] Legal scholars focused increasingly on case analysis, as Pollock had hoped for, in order to demonstrate that the existing law descended from reasonable judgments and was therefore the best law that could exist, a conservative conclusion that ignored the necessity of historical criticism: "Lawyers found academic history a time-consuming inconvenience. The only history they required was recorded in the statute book."[45] Conclusions of law alone merited appraisal, but findings of fact, so prized by historians, mattered little in the great chain of legal being. S. F. C. Milsom wrote: "Legal history means different things to different people. To historians it is usually a branch either of administrative or of social history; and legal thinking is not considered for its own sake. Lawyers are interested in legal thinking. But to them the subject usually appears as law read backwards, the inevitable unfolding of things as they came to be."[46] Legal evaluations of *stare decisis* or *ratio decidendi* had little attraction for historians, who dealt with the constitutional implications of high politics. The more technical legal doctrine became, the less likely it was that historians would acquire the training or the experience to deal with private law issues effectively. Maude Violet Clarke warned her students: legal and constitutional history "is so wide that the student must beware of floundering in the bogs of technical controversy. . . . Give a meaning to all technical expression."[47] For their part, lawyers needed an intellectual flexibility to deal with centuries of changing circumstances. The enlarging intellectual chasm was marked by the foundation in 1908 of the Society of Public Teachers of Law (which has been the Society of Legal Scholars since 2002), an organization that held its first meeting in July 1909: "This is not just turf war between two academic disciplines, not a simple question of who owns this sector of the past. There are large differences of approach."[48] Only one individual bridged both fields: the justly acclaimed Frederic Maitland.

The central position that Maitland still commands as the person who best combined the investigation of law and the writing of history has hinged in part on his brilliance in both areas. Maitland subsumed as did no other scholar the themes already discussed as constituent elements of the Great Tradition. For example, he never subscribed in any form to the racial interpretations that tried to explain English constitutional achievements in genetic terms. His *Constitutional History of England,* although published posthumously in 1908, was based on lectures delivered in 1887–88. At a time when the ideas of race promulgated by Freeman and Stubbs still reigned, Maitland had already formulated many of the conclusions that he would publish in later years. In the *Constitutional History,* Maitland had adopted a tone radically different from that of the Germanists: no racial nonsense, no grand narrative, topics divided along lines familiar to a lawyer, and a prose style so sober when contrasted to the fevered language of someone such as Freeman. The lectures, although less than a decade after the major works of Freeman and Stubbs, expressed a scholarly mentality so modern that the gap seems more like five decades. Against the preference for Anglo-Saxon institutions, Maitland argued: "The valuable thing that the Norman Conquest gives us is a strong kingship which makes for national unity."[49] In addition, in his Rede lecture published in 1901 as *English Law and the Renaissance,* Maitland "dismissed, in two sentences, the recurrent delusion that law in some occult fashion is a by-product of racial temperament."[50] Maitland's rejection of fashionable convention on race provided a prime example of his capacity for original thought and his determination never to accept historical arguments on faith.

With respect to the transformation of the history profession by virtue of the emphasis on research in original documents, Maitland personified this trend to perhaps an even greater degree than his contemporaries. His initial historical venture, after eight years of practice at the bar, led to the editing of an early Gloucestershire eyre roll, and his commitment to medieval documents remained unabated for the rest of his life. Part of this determination derived from admiration of his grandfather's labors in printing ecclesiastical records: "One still has to do for legal history something like the work that S[amuel] R[offey] M[aitland] did for ecclesiastical—to teach them, e.g., that some statement about the 13th century does not become truer because it has been constantly repeated, that a 'chain of testimony' is never stronger than its first link."[51] Like so many of his generation, Maitland corresponded with Maxwell Lyte and Hubert Hall at the Public Record Office in the ceaseless quest for manuscripts germane to medieval law in order to make available such sources to other scholars as well. Upon the publication of *Bracton's Note Book* in 1887, Pollock wrote to Maitland: "you must have had it in the blood to hunt medieval game of some kind."[52] Maitland read these documents in order to understand the society that had produced them, so when dealing with Parliament, for example, Maitland wished to know what business Parliament had actually accomplished. This functionalist approach to medieval law allowed Maitland to go beyond the rhetorical allusions to the grandeur of the common law in looking at its history.

A specific example of the commitment to the cult of original documents came in Maitland's work for the Selden Society from its foundation in 1887 to his death in 1906. Upon the inception of the society, in an unusually long letter, Maitland articulated his vision of the valuable work that might result: "It seems to me that at present the main object of the Society should be to print records and not to print essays."[53] Much archival material remained unexamined, so only publication could service the scholars who entered the field of English legal and constitutional history, especially its medieval period. England enjoyed remarkable collections of government records for the medieval era, but they would benefit no researcher if they remained hidden away in remote archives. Nearly two hundred of Maitland's extant letters dealt with the publications of the Selden Society.[54] While Maitland must share the credit for popularizing the emphasis on documentary evidence with German scholarly forebears and others in England such as Stubbs, his handling of archival materials set a high standard for the field.

In regard to culture wars, Maitland never took a role as public controversialist as Freeman and Round had done. He was not well known outside the academic community and for the most part expressed moderate liberal opinions. In some ways, however, as John Burrow has argued, Maitland's subtlety produced conclusions that had a much greater impact in the long run. For example, Maitland rejected the theory that Anglo-Saxon village life had depended upon community institutions at the expense of individual rights. Maitland was more concerned to discover how both categories had coexisted and the historical record of their development:

We are far from denying the existence of a communal sentiment, of a notion that somehow or another the men of the vill taken as a whole owned the lands of the vill, but this sentiment, this notion, if strong was vague. There were no institutions in which it could realize itself; there was no form of speech or thought in which it could find an apt expression. It evaded the grasp of law. At the touch of jurisprudence the township became a mere group of individuals, each with his separate rights.[55]

In the late Victorian context, this debate went to the issue of what was the more "natural" social condition: community (socialist) institutions or individualism (private property rights); Maitland took Sir Henry Maine's famous formula—from status to contract—and reversed it.[56] He also noted the paradox that so-called village communists such as Stubbs and Maine held conservative political views, while Frederic Seebohm, who stressed individual property rights in village life, was a strong liberal: "I am not speaking of votes at the polling booth but of radical and essential habits of mind."[57] Maitland's scholarship "transposed the veneration with which historians like Stubbs, Edward Freeman, and John Richard Green had regarded small self-governing social units, considered as the building blocks of English constitutional liberty, to the fluid conditions of a commercial and industrial society."[58] In shaping the contours of legal history in his image, Maitland left a political legacy greater than his more vocal contemporaries.

In imperial matters Maitland held moderate views, accepting the fact of empire while not permitting its existence to deflect him from his scholarly aims. He never expressed an imperial allegiance of the kind that enlisted the fervor of so many in Britain. For example, he opposed Irish home rule, remarking that no circumstance could make him sympathetic to this cause.[59] Yet he called the Boer War a "ghastly affair" and recorded how he "deeply mistrusted" Joseph Chamberlain, the war only making him more suspicious of Chamberlain's imperial machinations.[60] Maitland was certainly no political activist, and at his death his reputation did not extend beyond the boundaries of the academy, however famous he had become within that environment.

While Maitland did not anticipate the emphases of women's history so important since the 1970s, he supported women historians and university women to a greater degree than did most of his academic colleagues. His mentoring of Mary Bateson, including recommendations for various publishing projects, has already been discussed. The final break in his hitherto friendly relationship with Round came when Maitland could no longer abide one of Round's infamous scholarly assaults when the victim was Kate Norgate. Maitland's rebuke of Round for the unwarranted attack stemmed from Maitland's belief that Round would never have had the courage to express his venom in such a manner against a male colleague. For Maitland, this was bullying of an unacceptable nature and prompted him to act when so many other scholars feared Round's hostile pen. When the subject of degrees for women at Cambridge arose in 1897, Maitland was well ahead of his time in his support. He spoke eloquently on behalf of this cause, but in vain, for not until 1948 did women receive Cambridge degrees.[61] The generosity of character about which so many friends remarked was genuine, not merely the invention of pleasant obituaries.

Although Maitland never visited the United States, his reputation there was perhaps even greater than in Great Britain. The great devotion to English legal and constitutional history made Maitland the leading icon for those who professed to see a direct relationship between English medieval legal history and American law and jurisprudence. Maitland had many American scholars as friends, especially Harvard faculty such as James Barr Ames (1846–1910), Charles Gross, James Bradley Thayer (1831–1902), and Boston University law professor Melville Madison Bigelow (1846–1921).[62] In his inaugural lecture as Downing professor of English Law at Cambridge, Maitland stated simply: "Our law is their law."[63] Maitland acknowledged the strength of this connection when he noted: "I can't tell you why it is, but certainly you seem to care a deal more for legal history on your bank of the Atlantic than we do here. It is a malar-rangement of the universe which puts the records in one continent and those who would care to read them on another."[64] With his usual insight, Maitland also recognized that the emigration of English law to the United States could lead to exaggeration. For example, he cautioned Bigelow: "So the case of your American township seems to me rather a reproduction than a continuation of old English law—a reproduction all the more interesting because I dare say that the colonists knew little of legal antiquities."[65] Maitland received numerous in-vitations to lecture at American universities, but his health did not permit such trips, a source of constant regret: "You know how I regard the Harvard Law School: I feel as if I lived in the 12thy century and was rejecting a 'call' to Bolo-gna."[66] Maitland's enduring position as doyen of English legal history resulted in part, therefore, from the unique way in which he encapsulated the issues that had pushed the subject to the forefront of academic prestige.

Another sense in which Maitland dominated the world of legal history came from the experience he had acquired as a practicing lawyer who had taken up history. His views about his contemporaries in both camps made plain his abil-ity to synthesize successfully the norms of both disciplines. For some jurists who had attempted to write legal history, Maitland had significant reservations. About Maine and historical jurisprudence, for example, Maitland expressed substantial doubts on the ground that Maine undertook little serious research and thus his work was more theory than actual history. As a result, Maitland was reluctant to write about Maine, preferring silence to a thorough critique: "I am glad that you are to write of Maine; but glad also that this task is not mine."[67] In Maitland's judgment, Maine had not mastered the techniques of historical research: "You spoke of Maine. Well, I always talk of him with reluc-tance, for on the few occasions on which I sought to verify his statements of fact I came to the conclusion that he trusted much to a memory that played him tricks and rarely looked back at a book that he had once read."[68] Maitland resisted the seduction of Maine's methodology: "It is so pleasant to build theo-ries; so painful to discover facts."[69] The necessity for documentary research, so prized by Maitland, led him away from Maine's grand schemes.

The historical abilities of Pollock, Maitland's collaborator on the *History of*

English Law, likewise did not measure up to Maitland's standards for history. As noted earlier, Maitland hurried the completion of the great work lest Pollock submit other chapters. Maitland gave generous financial terms to Pollock in order to clear the way for him to be rid of his partner. Historians have conceded since its publication that the achievement was Maitland's alone. In the final analysis: "To Pollock history was the handmaid of the law. To Maitland law was but one aspect of history."[70] In the end, Maitland went his own way in the quest to unite law and history and in the process exemplified the conclusion of T. F. T. Plucknett (1897–1965): "Once the professor of law embarks upon history he has become a historian, for legal history is not law, but history."[71]

Maitland possessed ambivalent feelings about many of his history colleagues as well. He credited a reading of Stubbs's *Constitutional History* as one of the influences that helped steer him away from the bar and toward serious historical endeavors. He admired Stubbs's historical judgment and thought that Stubbs might have made a great judge.[72] In addition, he admired Stubbs's industry and the command of sources that allowed him to fashion a broad narrative. Finally, Maitland and Stubbs shared a passion for editing original documents, secure in the belief that this work contributed to scholarship as surely as any monograph.[73] At the same time, Maitland discredited many of Stubbs's own views, especially with respect to the history of Parliament. Maitland met Stubbs but once, and they never engaged in conversation, despite having so much in common.[74] Maitland respected Stubbs's contributions, but he also understood that scholarly fashion had increasingly consigned the greater part of his research to oblivion.

Maitland had less appreciation for Freeman, writing that "because the said Freeman believed that history was past politics, he never succeeded in adding anything to our knowledge of medieval politics but spoilt everything by inept comparisons."[75] Although the relationship with Round ended in 1899 because of the latter's bad scholarly manners, until that time the two had as cordial a friendship as Round's personality would allow. Maitland admired Round's research skills, his high standards, and his perseverance in seeking unpublished documents. Initially Round returned the approval, for upon the publication of the *History of English Law,* Round wrote: "You are a most wonderful man. How I have been marveling for years at your output, with which no one else's can compare. And now you top it off with this monumental work as if you had nothing else to do all these years but write it."[76] Yet in the end, the friendship foundered on the shoals of Round's rudeness. In fairness, Round did resolve his resentment against Maitland after the latter's death: "I make a point of introducing in my latest book a panegyric of Maitland because, although his work is as highly valued by scholars, his greatness is still too little known to the world at large."[77] With both jurists and historians, despite the many epistolary friendships, Maitland distanced himself from his peers as he proceeded with his work.

Only the Russian scholar Paul Vinogradoff merited Maitland's confidence. The Russian had also helped Maitland explore the road to legal history, and Maitland praised the manner in which this foreigner had mastered medieval records better than had English scholars themselves.[78] Maitland valued Vinogradoff's research skills highly and thought his scholarship on early medieval English history superior in every respect. When Pollock resigned the Corpus chair of jurisprudence at Oxford in 1903, Maitland supported Vinogradoff's candidacy for the position, and the Russian was duly elected. Maitland thought that his friend would make a much better professor than either Pollock or Maine because the Russian was a more gifted lecturer and his historical knowledge was so much greater.[79] Even in this case, however, Maitland tempered his enthusiasm by noting that Vinogradoff would fill the position well as long as he did not undertake to teach English law.[80] In the final analysis, therefore, Maitland's reputation rested on his ability to fuse profound historical knowledge and legal analysis in a fashion matched by no other scholar.

Not only did Maitland's editing skills and original writings over a period of just twenty-two years produce a prodigious outpouring of quality scholarship; his generous personality has attracted sympathetic attention since his death in 1906. Bryce wrote when Maitland died: "He was the first of our scholars in the field of legal history, taken away in his very prime."[81] Holmes admired Maitland's work—"accurate investigation of details in the interest of questions of philosophical importance"—and called his death "a great loss."[82] The passage of time did not diminish the great American jurist's opinion, for he wrote in 1928 to Felix Frankfurter (1882–1965) that "of course I agree with you about Maitland—everyone does."[83] From a much different historical tradition, George Macaulay Trevelyan noted Maitland's passing in this way: "He is one of those who has filled the world 'full of speed and glory and light.' His departure leaves English history, from the point of view of genius, in a poorer state than it has ever been since Macaulay began to write for the Edinburgh."[84] Even Dicey at the end had appreciated Maitland's gifts and personality: "I never met with a learned man who less oppressed one with his learning."[85] Such contemporary accolades might be multiplied endlessly, for if anyone begrudged Maitland his reputation, that person remained conspicuously silent.

In a most remarkable manner, Maitland's stature has remained fresh and enduring to the present. Frankfurter "termed Maitland 'the greatest voice of legal history.' "[86] The unanimity of praise for Maitland survived far longer than for any other historian of his generation. David Knowles (1896–1974) wrote of him: "Maitland, like Stubbs, is one of those historians whom every mediaevalist should read once a decade at least—it would save them from endless work and mistakes and give them ideas worth ten of any of their own."[87] Another distinguished medievalist, Richard Southern (1912–2001), echoed this judgment by referring to Maitland's "historical genius."[88] When Maitland stood as candidate for the Downing professorship of the laws of England, Lord Esher spelled out the qualities he expected: "I think that a good legal historian should have considerable staying power, never be in a hurry, and always ready to accept new light."[89] Maitland satisfied these criteria in a manner that has sustained his reputation ever after. The ceremony in January 2001, when Maitland became the first university historian honored with a memorial plaque in Westminster Abbey, reminded the historical profession of how strong his reputation was nearly a century after his death. We would argue that any historian who persuaded Geoffrey Elton to write a favorable biography had the qualities of "exceptional energy, diligence and excellence."[90] In Maitland's justly celebrated career, the field of English legal and constitutional history reached a pinnacle that it has never again attained. His death not only cut short his scholarly endeavors but heralded the end of the field's golden age as well.

How had Maitland achieved a level of success that would make any other historian green with envy? First of all, his eight years as a barrister had given to Maitland an insight into the position held by history within English legal culture. Maitland had discovered that contemporary rules of law depended on historical precedents that lay in the remote past and that nobody knew or cared what historical circumstances had called the rules into existence in the first place. To the utilitarian side of his training this situation was unacceptable: "He set himself to discover the system behind the wreckage which choked the legal machinery of the day."[91] In pondering why the history of English law had not been written, Maitland did not list legal training as a prerequisite. For both Stubbs and Vinogradoff, neither of whom were lawyers, Maitland had great respect. Yet he did discern some fundamental tensions between the two disciplines: "What the lawyer wants is authority and the newer the better; what the historian wants is evidence and the older the better."[92] Milsom has extended this perception: "The largest difficulty in legal history is precisely that we look at past evidence in the light of later assumptions, including our own assumptions about the nature and working of law itself."[93] The context so crucial for historical explanation rarely impinged on the lawyer's task.

Second, in agreement with most other academic lawyers of his generation,

Maitland believed that comparison was essential to historical understanding. Knowledge of Roman law could not help but improve the understanding of English law. The intellectual insularity of the English legal community had caused consternation among academic lawyers such as Pollock, who regularly campaigned for the benefits bestowed by acquaintance with Roman law. Familiarity with civil law provided the basis, it was asserted, for contrast and similarity that would sharpen the scientific basis for legal inquiry.[94] The ability to elicit general principles that buttressed the legal system served in Maitland's estimation the purposes of legal history well.

Third, Maitland brought a spirit of inquiry to legal history that enabled him to transcend the usual categories of historical explanation in his pursuit of truth. As he explained:

The only direct utility of legal history (I say nothing of its thrilling interest) lies in the lesson that each generation has an enormous power of shaping its own law. I don't think that the study of legal history would make men fatalists; I doubt it would make them conservatives: I am sure that it would free them from superstitions and teach them that they have free hands. I get more and more wrapped up in the middle ages but the only utilitarian justification that I ever urge *in foro conscientiae,* is that if history is to do its liberating work it must be as true to fact as it can possibly make itself, and true to fact it will not be if it begins to think what lessons it can teach.[95]

In this apologia, written at the height of his career, Maitland dismissed race as superstition, eschewed any attempt to provide political arguments, and proclaimed the factual basis of historical conclusions in accord with the prevailing definition that academic historians accepted. Interpretation of the facts was essential, but the subject should not be used as fodder for culture wars; private law was just as essential as the public face of the constitution. Maitland's work above all took constitutional history away from the germ theory of Teutonic origins by subjecting the racial argument to careful scrutiny. "Your mistrust of hasty generalisations and assumptions," Vinogradoff wrote to Maitland, "has given the death blow to many a theory cherished by antiquarians."[96] Given all these accomplishments, it was not surprising that "no English historian has been more lavishly praised from his own day to ours than Maitland."[97]

In the end, however, Maitland has remained somewhat elusive. His letters and his scholarship were straightforward with little revelation of the inner man. The celebration of his gifts has become almost routine. Early on Sir William Holdsworth wrote: "He has taught us to apply the methods of historical criticism to the sources of English law."[98] Decades later Elton summarized the staples of Maitland's reputation: "It is really astonishing to realize in how many ways Maitland stood at the beginning of a journey down the right road: teacher, research scholar, writer of history based on sound methods of work, founder of societies, inspirer of others. I think it no exaggeration to say that Maitland set the standards by which we—today's working historians—live."[99] Beyond these encomiums, there was a Maitland to whom the word *genius* was applied, but he defied this description as well. There were ineffable qualities about the man as historian and as lawyer that have been granted to few, or even to no other. Maitland and his reputation have stood firm beyond ordinary description—the deity who has continued to occupy a singular place in the pantheon of legal and constitutional historians.

Yet in the long run Maitland bequeathed an ambivalent legacy; he left no successors, and the prestige of legal and constitutional history as a research field declined in prestige among academic historians. In retrospect, at his death the subject began to divide into separate channels: historians who emphasized public law and lawyers who concentrated on the tracing of private law. Despite Maitland's star turn, the status of the field dwindled. He had set such a high standard of accomplishment that it was inevitable that the work of others would pale by comparison. Did other scholars seek elsewhere for research opportunities in the belief that Maitland's shadow would forever diminish their contributions? We will never know for sure. What we may conclude is that Maitland left no school to perpetuate his achievements and that his sole advisee, Mary Bateson, predeceased him by several weeks. Historians' law, defined by the Roundian crusade for the unpublished document, drifted away into narrower topics that defied easy synthesis. In brief, the lawyer regarded the past only as the path to the present without sufficient respect for historical context; Maitland fought vigorously against anachronism in his accounts of constitutional development, but historians too often succumbed to the task of learning more and more about less and less.[100]

Maitland's masterful analyses proved too triumphant. His research success "served, in fact, to create the general impression that Legal History is and must be essentially a study of medieval English legal institutions."[101] On both sides of the Atlantic, legal history withdrew from the spaciousness with which Maitland had infused the subject. In the United States, for example, American legal history found it difficult to emancipate itself from the prestige that attached to English legal history: "Hardly anything one could call American legal history was written in the 1880s and 90s, but one has to say something about the legal history that was written (English, mostly)."[102] The major American legal historians of this era (Ames, Bigelow, Holmes, and Thayer) made their reputations by their investigations into medieval English legal history. After Maitland, however, American scholars looked to their own case law increasingly to justify the logic of American judicial decisions. This formalist exercise narrowed the purview of legal history because it inevitably endorsed the present state of the law, precisely the legal teleology that Maitland had so wanted to destroy. Whether torts, contracts, or any other area of private law, the search for internal consistency widened the "gulf of incomprehension"[103] between historians and lawyers: "To the generation after Maitland the approach to history through law came to seem too formal a way at getting at the central problems of society in the past."[104] Although his own reputation remained high, the field that Maitland had personified gradually faded away from the center stage it had once occupied.

Another aspect of Maitland's ambiguous heritage has been his reputation as historian, where for the last several decades scholars have pointed out with distressing frequency errors of fact and interpretation in the Maitland canon. As early as 1968, in an introduction to a reprint of *History of English Law*, S. F. C. Milsom cast doubt upon major arguments that Maitland had made. In the first place, Milsom contended that Maitland had privileged the role of the king's courts at the expense of local courts. In addition, Maitland had worked backward from Bracton and therefore "supposes too great a degree of general sophistication and, in particular, despite all his care, that he sometimes places highly abstract notions of property too early."[105] This latter conclusion would doubtless have pained Maitland more than any other because his scholarship had tried to efface precisely this type of anachronism from legal and constitutional history.

Next, in looking at Maitland's work in totality, Milsom argued: "For me the question is how historical reconstruction can be so convincing, even so beautiful, and yet, as I have no doubt that it is, fundamentally wrong."[106] Finally, Milsom returned to the issue of Maitland's reputation in 1995, when he again tried to explain the conundrum of Maitland's diminishing stock of correct assertions and the reputation that he still enjoyed. On this occasion, Milsom emphasized Maitland's generally erroneous vision of how medieval law operated: "The extraordinary concentration of his mind produced a compelling picture. But the facts which lay outside the field of that concentrated vision remain; and there is no way of adjusting his account so as to accommodate them. Either you accept Maitland's authority and ignore that other evidence, or you work on a different picture."[107] Maitland had become an orthodoxy that discouraged fresh research, a result Maitland himself would have denounced. That a hundred years after its first publication the *History of English Law* still dominated the field amply proved Milsom's point.

Criticism of Maitland, when it came, was couched in the language of the utmost respect. Jurist Carleton K. Allen, for example, once wrote that the law student "is taught to venerate the name of Maitland, and rightly, but for once in his life Maitland was undoubtedly bewitched, through Gierke, by romanticism, and all that he wrote on 'Real Personality' is a snare to the student."[108] Historian Patrick Wormald (1947–2004) has also presented a thorough critique of Maitland's shortcomings with reference to the Anglo-Saxon period of legal development. First, Maitland erred in his belief that pre-1066 England had experienced a golden age of private justice supplanted by strong monarchs after the Norman Conquest. Next, Maitland gave little weight to Anglo-Saxon precedents for the jury of presentment. Finally, Maitland underestimated the extent to which the Anglo-Saxon criminal code had evolved from monetary compensation to punishment.[109] As scholarship in the 1890s increasingly focused attention on the postconquest importance of legal foundations, Maitland's reluctance to recognize the strength of the Anglo-Saxon state, so tainted by Stubbs's racial rationales, seemed intellectually justified. Wormald has demonstrated effectively that "Maitland underrated the part played by the earliest kings of England in shaping a distinctive English legal tradition."[110] Fearful of teleology as expressed in the Whig interpretation of history, Maitland devoted insufficient attention to continuity as he explained legal development from the Anglo-Saxons through Henry II to the reign of Edward I. Significant revision of any scholar's work occurs all the time—his or her conclusions reassessed and reputation adjusted, usually downward. Many iconic figures have suffered this fate and seen interpretations rejected by later research. In the face of this common academic cycle, how has Maitland attracted such trenchant criticism and yet remained such an admired scholar?

The answer, we believe, lies in the fact that, although his answers are now regarded as outdated, Maitland's questions remain relevant to modern scholars. Historians and lawyers have recognized that he addressed issues still relevant to both fields. His inquiries anticipated the concerns of social history for the lives and actions of ordinary individuals. Christopher Harvie wrote: "It can be argued that Maitland's respect for contemporary concerns made his work of seminal importance to the study of social history."[111] With due regard for the differences in approach, Maitland still practiced an early version of "history from below." Maitland's answers may no longer satisfy as they once did, but reading Maitland is still familiar because he wanted to know what contemporary legal historians wish to learn: "He never forgot the human beings who made and worked the institutions, or the human needs which shaped the laws, which he was describing."[112] However flawed Maitland's conclusions have become, a process that happens to all historians, to his everlasting credit Maitland synthesized law and history in a manner whose potential has reached fruition only in the past several decades: "For Maitland legal history became an inalienable part of history as a whole, necessary to discover the social reality of the past."[113] The abundant contributions to social history based on wills, trial statistics, and other legal phenomena have fashioned an understanding of crime, inheritance patterns, property distribution, and related social issues that would make Maitland proud.

Perhaps the scholar most victimized by the divorce between law and history was Sir William Holdsworth. His lifelong project to provide a comprehensive history of English law, the first volume of which appeared in 1903, attempted to follow in Maitland's wake. He believed that "law touches national life on all those many sides which the state finds it desirable to regulate, and so the historian of any of the important activities of mankind is sooner or later brought up against the law."[114] Holdsworth has often served as the whipping boy for the decline of legal history to the point where the question arose: "Did he truly handicap the development and advance of 'good' legal historical scholarship?"[115] Holdsworth had not completed the work at the time of his death, and it eventually finished at seventeen volumes when completed in 1972.[116] As a young man, Dicey had envisioned a similar project, but he had dismissed it for the reason Holdsworth had demonstrated: it was a lifelong task. Dicey wrote that "it might well have taken the whole of my remaining life first to realise what I meant and then carry out my conception, and no doubt the work would even now be a fragment."[117] In the end, Holdsworth did not match Maitland's achievement, because he did not live up to his goal: "In short, for Holdsworth, the common law and its practice were an overwhelming autonomous institution."[118] Holdsworth did not ground his work in attention to the common law as a living system, but rather he treated it in a formal way that did not introduce the reader to historical explanation on a broader scale.

Holdsworth's magnum opus is no longer read, if it ever was, at great length, although we suspect that scholars still consult individual volumes on specific points. Sampling Holdsworth piecemeal still works when the many volumes stagger the potential reader. As Pollock wrote to Holmes: "I have been nibbling through 3 vols. of Holdsworth's *History of English Law*, a great monument of industry & accuracy but I fear not very readable, though there are quite good bits."[119] Certainly no one mentions Holdsworth in the same breath with Maitland, although Arthur L. Goodhart (1891–1978), in an overabundance of enthusiasm for his good friend, once called Holdsworth "one of Oxford's greatest historians."[120] In the opposite vein, an equal exaggeration came from American jurist Roscoe Pound (1870–1964), who called Holdsworth "very mediocre" after a stay in Oxford in 1922.[121] The truth clearly lies somewhere between these hyperbolic assessments; yet in general Holdsworth's reputation has tended to languish ever since his death. His ambiguous legacy may be seen in the contrast between Laski's depiction of his conservatism in the desire "to fall flat on his face before a law lord."[122] Yet Holdsworth also fought Fascist attacks on academic freedom in an attempt to uphold faculty liberty: "We believe that the principle of academic freedom threatened as it is by dangerous developments, not in one place alone or from one cause alone, needs a specific defence."[123] The conclusions of both Maitland and Holdsworth have become dated, but only the latter's reputation has suffered as a result of this circumstance.

Holdsworth's reputation has received such disrespect in spite of the *History's* epic proportions, an enterprise never to be replicated. His habit of snagging the All Souls' port bottle in the evening and then writing until it ran out has become (in)famous, but this habit did point to a more underlying problem with Holdsworth's scholarship, because he perceived the trap of writing in Maitland's shadow. About Maitland and his achievement, Holdsworth wrote that his predecessor worked "in accordance with the exacting standards of modern historical scholarship."[124] These norms as initiated and promulgated by Stubbs emphasized the necessity for archival research. But as Holdsworth conceded in a letter to Maitland just a month before the latter's death: "I am afraid that the book does not go beyond the printed sources."[125] Holdsworth rarely engaged in original research and freely admitted that he worked from secondary authorities almost exclusively. As a result, Holdsworth lagged behind the march of scholarship, never quite catching up with modern interpretations: "I think he exaggerates the insularity of English institutions, and talks of a genius for self-government where I should talk of happy accident."[126] Without heavy reliance on the scholarship of others, Holdsworth would never have made any progress. His desire for topical coverage came at the expense of accuracy in too many cases, for he was "not on the whole good at explaining the history of particular strands of doctrine."[127] Holdsworth aimed to write an "intelligible history" that would encourage university study of legal history and arouse more general interest in the subject.[128] In every field of historical inquiry, those who have provided a broad, synthetic account of a large topic, even in seventeen volumes, deserve gratitude, not denunciation. In the end, however, Holdsworth's standing has slipped because he did not work according to the standards that became the measure for success among historians.

The breadth of the endeavor inevitably caused the earlier sections to become obsolete before the later volumes had appeared. When the seventh edition of volume 1 was published in 1956, for example, it took S. B. Chrimes seventy-seven pages to survey the arguments and conclusions that needed updating. In 1969 the work received this verdict from Frederick Bernays Weiner: "As far as I have gone it is obvious that his early portions are quite outdated, and that his treatment of Anglo-Saxon law in Vol. II is not saved by anything in Chrimes' supplementary essay in the 1956 version of Vol. I. E.g., H. is still under the shadow of Brunner; he has nothing to reflect your discoveries in the A-S origin of the jury."[129] The assignment that Holdsworth had set for himself proved too much, for keeping abreast of recent scholarship and new interpretations presented an impossible challenge. The poor man could not win, because no matter how rapidly he worked, the pace of new work rendered him outdated before his next volumes were finished. No wonder that Holdsworth's reputation, despite his immense learning, paled in comparison to that of Maitland.

By the 1930s the detachment of legal and constitutional history from wider historical contexts was complete. The admiration that had celebrated Maitland's career and the field remained only for the scholar. By 1937, in the judgment of David Sugarman, "modern legal history was, to put it kindly, dead."[130] Legal history fared no better in the United States, because the great academic work of the 1930s became the articulation of legal realism and legal history had not obtained a prominent place in the law school curriculum.[131] Counting cars in New Haven seemed a more reasonable scholarly project to Underhill Moore (1879–1949) than historical reconstruction. As noted earlier, English constitutional history continued into the 1960s as a taught tradition, but its research status had vanished. The gulf between legal and constitutional and the new frontiers of history widened; as Holdsworth explained: "The lawyer, immersed in technical rules, forgot the human beings for whom those rules were made and the human needs which gave them birth. The historian, because he was ignorant of the meaning of those technical rules, was apt to misapprehend the meaning of statutes and the reasoning of the courts."[132] Furthermore, the legal historian needed a "sense of how law works."[133] This line of argument became standard in lamenting the split between law and history.

No one complained more bitterly about this divide than Geoffrey Elton. Proudly embracing the title of constitutional historian, as one who dealt with politics and public law, he routinely denounced lawyers' history: "To a lawyer the doings of the past signify only inasmuch as they persist into and have life in the present. All very fine for them, but this teleological preoccupation, which ruins genuine history, they had imposed on the historians."[134] Elton charged lawyers' history with an "excessive preoccupation" with rules and technicalities, unwillingness to engage in appropriate source criticism, and indifference to historical background.[135] Such criticisms were not novel. As J. H. Baker has written of the excessively narrow vision of earlier legal historians: "The ten-dency of English legal historians to think of the common law solely as *juris-prudence*, by which I mean case-law produced by courts, is encouraged by the state of the evidence, in that the most accessible sources available to them for reconstructing the law of medieval and early-modern times have been the year books and later law reports."[136] We would argue, however, that by the time Elton made his protests, he was already flogging a dead horse.

The problems to which Elton objected were already in the process of re-mediation. Elton had the right issues but bad timing. The new social history that enabled historians to examine different indices of legal relevance made possible a new connection to Maitland's emphasis on broader social context. Legal history in the 1960s reunited the skills of the lawyer and the historian in order to produce a law and society approach to legal history: "A key platform in this approach has been exploration of the interface between the legal and the social."[137] As scholars in both disciplines realized that the domain of the law ex-tended beyond traditional boundaries, legal history made a strong comeback: "Important as case-law is, we have made an error if we have treated the history of the common law solely as a history of decided cases. There is a whole world of law which never sees a courtroom."[138] The return to Maitland came full cycle when Paul Brand wrote, "I have always believed that legal history should be a matter of interest not just to the narrow circle of my fellow specialists, but also to a much wider world of non-specialist lawyers and historians."[139] The recon-nection to Maitland since the 1960s symbolized the process by which English legal and constitutional history has rightly taken its place again among Clio's valued subdisciplines. If this renaissance has not exactly meant a return to the golden age of a century ago, it has undone the consequences of the rift between historians' law and lawyers' history.

Conclusion

Our argument concludes that the status of English constitutional history rose in the 1870s concurrently with new standards of historical research to a prominence that peaked before 1914. After World War I, its place as the premier area for historical investigation had already begun to erode. By 1930, its prestige as a research field had declined dramatically. As a taught tradition, however, constitutional history lasted into the early 1960s as a preferred teaching field. The belief in constitutional exceptionalism on both sides of the Atlantic, however, has never truly disappeared. As David Cannadine has written about Margaret Thatcher and John Major, the unique history of the constitution was a "commonplace of the Whig interpretation of English history which is now so much derided in professional circles, even if it retains its allure for Tory Prime Ministers."[1] This characterization has proved too narrow, for Tony Blair, in a speech about constitutional reform in the new century, sounded the tropes of the old century; constitutional change had to reflect "the core British values of fair play, creativity, tolerance and an outward-looking approach to the world."[2] Pride in the continuity of a constitution that has existed for a millennium, an essential feature of the Whig interpretation, has remained in public life. United States president George W. Bush, in a speech that many regarded as the finest of his first term, began his speech on "the calling of our time" in this fashion: "The roots of our democracy can be traced to England, and to its Parliament."[3] One may imagine Edward Freeman, William Stubbs, and James Bryce leading the applause for this sentiment.

We wish to stress, of course, that this chronology did not mean that important scholarly work in either tradition ceased; it signified only that the renown attached to the subject had dissipated in the face of changing academic fashion.

In his 1968 inaugural lecture as Regius professor at Cambridge, Geoffrey Elton noted: "The Chair is the chair of English Constitutional History. Now I chose that title myself, and I don't think I could have chosen worse, could I? I damned myself twice over."[4] A subdivision of history that a century ago enjoyed widespread admiration now ranks well down the hierarchy of fashionable historical specializations. Scholars who continue to work in medieval English constitutional history in particular, as well as legal and constitutional history in general, are likely to draw pity from colleagues. Exchanges on history Web sites sometimes allude to old-fashioned legal and constitutional history, reinforcing the lack of respect that the field now commands.

Changes in historiographical trends are sometimes symbolized by events that are not truly causative. For example, we suggest 1930 as a year when the prestige of constitutional history was finally acknowledged to have surrendered its primacy. This did not mean the calendar year specifically; the date serves as a useful symbol for the changes that clustered around it. As early as 1920, A. V. Dicey recorded his belief that the study of constitutions was as much underrated at that time as the subject had been overrated in the 1870s.[5] The death of John Horace Round in 1928, the publication of Lewis Namier's first major work in 1929, the appearance of that ultimate anti-Whig satire *1066 and All That* in 1930, and Herbert Butterfield's more serious attack on the Whig interpretation of history in 1931 in different ways affected the direction of historical research.

By 1930, English constitutional history, like so much else in British life, suffered from the consequences of World War I. To recount the complex diplomacy that led to war in 1914 became a patriotic duty in the respective combatant nations. In the 1920s and 1930s, historians such as Luigi Albertini (1871–1941), Sidney Bradshaw Fay (1876–1968), Pierre Renouvin (1893–1934), Bernadotte Schmitt (1886–1969), and many others made their reputations by writing on the origins of the war and the attendant debate on responsibility for starting the war. In England, George Peabody Gooch and Harold W. V. Temperley (1879–1939) enhanced their fame by editing the multivolume *British Documents on the Origins of the War*. Publication of national diplomatic archives in epic ventures such as *Die Grosse Politik* or the *Documents Diplomatiques Français* guaranteed visibility as historians disputed the war guilt question. Historians focused as routinely on foreign policy as they had previously done on national history.[6] After World War II, however, these questions suffered eclipse as new issues arose to attract the interest of academic historians.[7] With national honor in the balance in these discussions, constitutional history suffered by comparison.

Within the field of British history itself, the most influential event was the publication in 1929 and 1930 of the volumes on British politics in 1760 and shortly thereafter that established Namier's reputation: *The Structure of Politics at the Accession of George III* and *England in the Age of the American Revolution.* Through a remarkably meticulous analysis of politics combined with a passion for manuscript discovery, Namier not only attacked the Whig interpretation's version of this period but also removed the nation as the logical, natural vehicle for historical narrative. Even George Macaulay Trevelyan, the keeper of the Whig inheritance, recognized that the *Structure of Politics* had introduced a new form of historical inquiry, calling the book a "historical feat of a really novel character."[8] The undermining of portions of the national narrative was ironic, because Namier possessed such a deep admiration for the elites of the eighteenth century upon whom so much of the Whig interpretation depended. Namier believed that the House of Commons was "historically of the greatest interest in supplying a picture of the political community in Great Britain—a good part of the social and economic history of England could, in fact, be written in terms of membership of the House of Commons."[9] The Namier revolution proceeded slowly, but by the 1950s his reputation had reached its apex. The focus on what politicians did, not what they said, blazed a new path for research by means of structural analysis.

The claims of Namierite disciples for the biographical approach to history soon proved unsustainable. John Brooke predicted shortly after Namier's death in 1960 that "fifty years from now *all* history will be done as Sir Lewis does it."[10] That, of course, has not happened, and the Namierite approach to history has arguably suffered as dramatic a loss of professional respect as constitutional history once did. In the long run, therefore, the significance of Namier and his work lay not in issues of prosopography, dismissal of intellectual history, or the devaluation of art, literature, and music; rather it provided a sustained challenge to constitutional history's position as the most prestigious area of professional endeavor.

When Arnold Toynbee (1889–1975) published the first volumes of *The Study of History* in 1934, by which he meant the history of everything and everyone, he and Namier provided macroscopic and microscopic visions of historical writing that departed from established conventions: "We had, both of us, been unwilling to follow the broad highway that was being trodden by most contemporary Western historians."[11] The status of English constitutional history as a research field diminished as the result of rapidly diversifying methodologies. In the early 1960s, V. H. Galbraith acknowledged the decline: "It is *sad* how our generation has *funked* doing work on the basic sources."[12] This sentiment, while not exactly a requiem, did admit the demise of the subject's leadership within the academy. Those who worked in the field suffered from the benign neglect of the public as well as from the internecine battles of academe; as Margaret Hastings wrote of work in the 1930s: "I find I haven't said anything about Jolliffe's *Const. Hist.* or Wilkinson's except in the footnotes. J. seems to me unreadable (Someone said it was written in Anglo-Saxon.), and W. always makes me think of a knight in search of a dragon to kill."[13]

English constitutional history as a taught tradition, however, survived for another generation into the 1960s. Instead of weakening within the university curriculum and with the general public, the subject enjoyed an Indian summer of success after World War II in the extent and influence of its arguments: "Historians reaffirmed their prewar belief in the superiority of national English character and institutions."[14] Continuity and consensus dominated historical writing for the general public, witness the phenomenal sales enjoyed by Trevelyan's *English Social History* when it appeared in 1942. Victor Feske has written: "The acceptance of Whig history as the 'national interpretation' occurred between the wars."[15] World War I did not produce the same consequences for constitutional history as a taught tradition as it had done for the research emphasis: "Remarkably, the war, in which the victors lost so much, confirmed and even strengthened a nationalistic, Whiggish interpretation of both the past and the future."[16] On both sides of the Atlantic, English constitutional history still flourished as a central feature of undergraduate education; at Hartwick College in New York, for example, as late as the 1950s, the subject remained a graduation requirement for all students. In its teaching expression, English constitutional history still retained an honored place.

The prominence of constitutional history as a taught tradition ended in the early 1960s. Here again events symbolized the transition: the retirement of V. H. Galbraith in 1957,[17] the death of George Macaulay Trevelyan in 1962, and the publication of Edward P. Thompson's *The Making of the English Working Class* in 1963. On one level, political beliefs, few historians could have been more opposed; yet on another level, in an attachment to the ordinary people who passed through history, they were similar. J. H. Plumb wrote of Trevelyan: "His loyalty was boundless and he possessed reverence for the English past, the English countryside and for the English culture; but his deepest reverence was for the anonymous men and women of history, caught and lost in time."[18] Trevelyan thought of his social history "as the history of a people with the politics left out."[19] Thompson sought famously "to rescue the poor stockinger, the Luddite cropper, the 'obsolete' hand-loom weaver, the 'utopian' artisan, and even the deluded follower of Joanne Southcott, from the enormous condescension of posterity."[20] The anticipation of the new social history may be traced as far back as the foundation of the French journal *Annales* in 1929, an enterprise that eventually realized a breadth of investigation that eclipsed the limited range of a national constitutional history. Thompson's enormously influential work altered the focus of historical accomplishment, both research and teaching, to social history.

For those who had prospered in the belief that history relied primarily upon a narrative of literary distinction for the general public, the widening chasm between professional history and books written for a wider audience proved especially difficult. In the case of C. V. Wedgwood the result was particularly traumatic. Author of acclaimed works on a variety of topics in the 1940s and 1950s, Wedgwood regarded historical narrative as a fundamental prerequisite to issues of interpretation; as she wrote in 1959: "The careful, thorough and accurate answer to the question *How* should take the historian a long way towards answering the question *Why*."[21] The advent of computers, for Wedgwood, failed to realize the possibilities that others envisioned. In 1966, for example, Wedgwood wrote: "Maybe I use the word [*computer*] a little vaguely, to cover the idea of *statistical* research: in itself a very useful thing, but now advocated with altogether too much disregard of its applicability to certain quite non-statistical aspects of the subjects, and also without regard to the nature & quantity of the available evidence, which is often of a kind inadequate for such treatment."[22] By 1970, Wedgwood's best works were in the past and, after receiving a firestorm of academic criticism for her first two volumes on the English Civil War, she never completed the projected third volume. Changing historical culture had alienated her from Clio's tasks. In 1970 she confessed: "I would say, to explain my present difficulties in writing, that like some of the Great Victorians, I had 'lost my faith'—only in History, not as they did in God. One can't go on doing what one doesn't believe in." Wedgwood added that history was "all we have to teach us to understand the human part of the world we live in. I am doubtful if I believe this now—I can certainly never write or talk about it with confidence again."[23] In Wedgwood's opinion, history as a literary art had succumbed to a dangerously provincial academic model.

In addition, student ferment in the 1960s, with its accompanying demand for relevance, indicted constitutional history as precisely the type of history that had lost its utility. Three special issues of the *Times Literary Supplement* in 1966 mapped the new directions of historical inquiry. The dramatic change in historical fashion meant that English constitutional history could not retain its position as a taught tradition. For many within the academy, social history now reigned as the arbiter of professional cachet.[24] History from below served increasingly as a focal point for research, teaching, and political activism. The emphasis on individual agency for ordinary men and women opened many new fruitful avenues for historical research and offered a variety of directions that enriched the discipline. Thompson's attempt to depict the people's history for a broad audience paid handsome dividends.[25]

With respect to the empire, its loss created a malaise that engulfed constitutional history. As the national narrative seemingly lost its appeal, the field declined in prestige as well. The end of empire that culminated in the 1960s questioned the identity of a governing race. Faith in the imperial mission that had been sustained by constitutional history faded away in the face of changed circumstances; the dissolution of empire implied the relative unimportance of constitutional scholarship. Once again constitutional history appeared to have suffered an irreversible eclipse.

In the face of this great transformation, what became of English legal and constitutional history? In fact, without much notice from other historians, those legal and constitutional scholars who had kept the faith adapted well to the goals set by social history, and the field has flourished since the 1960s, although not with the prestige it had enjoyed earlier. In addition, social historians found that legal and constitutional materials provided excellent evidence in support of their research. The proliferation of journals,[26] conferences, monograph series,[27] and academic programs at both the graduate and undergraduate levels has testified to its continuing vitality. The innovative use of legal records such as wills, marriage documents, and criminal statistics, when placed in the appropriate legal context, has permitted historians to offer more sophisticated analyses of ordinary lives: "Backwoodsmen apart, there is a general sympathy with the idea that you cannot really understand law without attending both to its history, and to the way in which the operations of the various legal systems, and the professional culture of lawyers, interacts with what may, for the want of a better term, be called society generally."[28] The reunion of law and history has ceased to make legal history so intimidating, and both lawyers and historians now contribute to the field on a regular basis. Law permeates society so thoroughly that the recognition of their symbiotic relationship demonstrates, in retrospect, that indifference to this basic fact by previous scholars now seems a tragic mistake.

Legal and constitutional history has, in truth, never gone away; only its centrality for the academy has vanished. The extension of the subject beyond its traditional boundaries has led to research conclusions that "illustrate the varying paths legal history has taken since the days of Frederic W. Maitland and his friends."[29] The suspicion of constitutional history as too narrow in purview has lost its basis, for it has merged with social history to create a body of scholarship that transcends its earlier confines: "But the study of law has become much broader and more diverse than it used to be. One result has been to make much legal literature more accessible to ordinary readers. Law is far too important, too far-reaching and too interesting not to be part of general culture."[30] Legal and constitutional history has always produced excellent work,[31] as have all other fields, for no specialization has a monopoly on relevance or sophistication. Outreach to other scholars and merger with other methodologies has succeeded in attracting wider interest in what English legal and constitutional history has to offer; as Paul Brand has written: "Legal history written only for legal historians is a story which has lost its most important audience."[32] The field has, despite the stereotypes held by many other scholars, reinvented itself in a manner that has remained fully conversant with the broad advances of historical scholarship; in this respect Douglas Hay has written of "the extent to which the history of law is integral to understanding power, economy, gender, race, class, ideology, nation, and empire. The best of this writing integrates technically sophisticated accounts of legal doctrines and institutions with the most recent scholarship in cognate fields of history. All of it demonstrates the centrality of law to historical explanation."[33]

English legal and constitutional history has thus come full circle. More vibrant and productive than since before World War I, it lacks only academic recognition of its contributions. The publication of Ann Lyon's *Constitutional History* in 2003, the first endeavor of its kind in two generations, symbolized the resurrection of the discipline from its scholarly valley of death.[34] All that remains now is for other scholars to recognize that the subject is no longer a vestige of the historiographical past; its findings have reasserted the importance of the discipline itself. Over the last three decades the elegance of work in the field has returned to an extent that would please Stubbs, Maitland, and all the other scholars who created and have maintained the Great Tradition.

REFERENCE MATTER

Notes

------◆------

1. English Constitutional History as National Identity

1. See, for example, the April 2005 number of *Prospect*, in which, among others, politician Gordon Brown and historian Linda Colley discussed the national identity issue in advance of that year's general election.

2. Michael Wood, *In Search of England: Journeys into the English Past* (Berkeley: University of California Press, 1999).

3. Stefan Collini, *Public Moralists: Political Thought and Intellectual Life in Britain, 1850–1930* (Oxford: Clarendon Press, 1991), 287. See also: "Dicey set about making law the rallying-point of an English national identity, not least through the highly accessible style of his legal text books." Julia Stapleton, "Dicey and His Legacy," *History of Political Thought* 16 (Summer 1995), 235.

4. Benedict Anderson, *Imagined Communities: Reflections on the Origin and Spread of Nationalism*, 2nd ed. (London: Verso, 1991), 6.

5. Philip Schlesinger, "On National Identity: Some Conceptions and Misconceptions Criticised," *Social Science Information* 26 (June 1987), 241, 260.

6. Anthony D. Smith, *Theories of Nationalism* (London: Duckworth, 1983 [1971]), 22.

7. Anthony D. Smith, *The Ethnic Origins of Nations* (Oxford: Blackwell, 1986), 15.

8. James Loughlin, *Ulster Unionism and British National Identity since 1885* (London: Pinter, 1995), 8.

9. Theodore Marburg to Herbert Baxter Adams, 20 June 1893, Ms. 4, Box 8, Herbert Baxter Adams papers, Milton S. Eisenhower Library, Johns Hopkins University, Baltimore, MD.

10. Sir Edward Grey to Sir Edward Goschen, 9 December 1908, Sir Edward Grey papers, Foreign Office, 800/61, National Archives, Kew.

11. Judy Giles and Tim Middleton, eds., *Writing Englishness, 1900–1950: An Introductory Sourcebook on National Identity* (London: Routledge, 1995), 6.

12. Krishan Kumar, *The Making of English National Identity* (Cambridge: Cambridge

University Press, 2003); see also Richard Weight, *Patriots: National Identity in Britain, 1940–2000* (London: Macmillan, 2002).

13. Patrick Wormald, "The Eternal Angle," *Times Literary Supplement* (16 March 2001), 3; and "ENGLA LOND: The Making of an Allegiance," *Journal of Historical Sociology* 7 (March 1994), 2.

14. Patrick Wormald, "Sir Geoffrey Elton's *English*: A View from the Middle Ages," *Transactions of the Royal Historical Society,* Sixth Series 7 (1997), 319; Sarah Foot, "The Making of *Angelcynn:* English Identity before the Norman Conquest," *Transactions of the Royal Historical Society*, Sixth Series 6 (1996), 25–49; James Campbell, "The Late Anglo-Saxon State: A Maximum View," *Proceedings of the British Academy* 87 (1995), 47; Alfred P. Smyth, "The Emergence of English Identity, 700–1000," in Alfred P. Smyth, ed., *Medieval Europeans: Studies in Ethnic Identity and National Perspectives in Medieval Europe* (Basingstoke: Macmillan, 1998), 25; and Alan MacColl, "The Meaning of 'Britain' in Medieval and Early Modern England," *Journal of British Studies* 45 (April 2006), 249.

15. Susan Reynolds, *Kingdoms and Communities in Western Europe, 900–1300* (Oxford: Clarendon Press, 1984), 254.

16. David Crouch, "From Stenton to McFarlane: Models of Societies of the Twelfth and Thirteenth Centuries," *Transactions of the Royal Historical Society,* Sixth Series 5 (1995), 183; and John Gillingham, *The English in the Twelfth Century: Imperialism, National Identity and Political Values* (Woodbridge: Boydell, 2000), xxi.

17. Edward Jenks, *Edward Plantagenet (Edward I): The English Justinian or The Making of the Common Law* (Freeport, NY: Books for Libraries Press, 1969 [1901]), 346.

18. Edwin Jones, *The English Nation: The Great Myth* (Stroud: Sutton, 1998), 15.

19. Gerald Newman, "Nationalism Revisited," *Journal of British Studies* 35 (January 1996), 122.

20. Eric Evans, "Englishness and Britishness: National Identities, c. 1790–c. 1850," in Alexander Grant and Keith J. Stringer, eds., *Uniting the Kingdom: The Making of British History* (London: Routledge, 1995), 243.

21. Anthony Fletcher, "The First Century of English Protestantism and the Growth of National Identity," in Stewart Mews, ed., *Religion and National Identity* (Oxford: Blackwell, 1982), 316–17.

22. Linda Colley, "Britishness and Otherness: An Argument," *Journal of British Studies* 31 (July 1992), 316–17.

23. D. G. Paz, "Anti-Catholicism, Anti-Irish Stereotyping, and Anti-Celtic Racism in Mid-Victorian Working-Class Periodicals," *Albion* 18 (Winter 1986), 605.

24. William Stubbs to Edward Freeman, 3 November 1859, Bodl. Ms. Eng. Misc. e. 148, William Stubbs papers, Bodleian Library, Oxford.

25. Tony Claydon and Ian McBride, "The Trials of the Chosen Peoples: Recent Interpretations of Protestantism and National Identity in Britain and Ireland," in Tony Claydon and Ian McBride, eds., *Protestantism and National Identity: Britain and Ireland, c. 1650–c. 1850* (Cambridge: Cambridge University Press, 1999), 4–29.

26. J. C. D. Clark, "England's Ancien Regime as a Confessional State," *Albion* 21 (Fall 1989), 450–74.

27. Hugh McLoed, "Protestantism and British National Identity, 1815–1945," in Peter van der Veer and Hartmut Lehmann, eds., *Nation and Religion: Perspectives on Europe*

and Asia (Princeton, NJ: Princeton University Press, 1999), 53; see also John Wolffe, *God and Greater Britain: Religion and National Life in Britain and Ireland, 1843–1945* (London: Routledge, 1994), 18–19.

28. Keith Robbins, "Religion and Identity in Modern British History," in Stewart Mews, ed., *Religion and National Identity* (Oxford: Blackwell, 1982), 470.

29. D. Alan Orr, "From a *View* to a *Discovery*: Edmund Spenser, Sir John Davies, and the Defects of Law in the Realm of Ireland," *Canadian Journal of History* (December 2003), 399; and see more generally, Alan Cromartie, "The Constitutionalist Revolution: The Transformation of Political Culture in Early Stuart England," *Past and Present* 163 (May 1999), 77–120.

30. Margot C. Finn, *After Chartism: Class and Nation in English Radical Politics, 1848–1874* (Cambridge: Cambridge University Press, 1993), 141.

31. Timothy Lang, *The Victorians and the Stuart Heritage: Interpretations of a Discordant Past* (Cambridge: Cambridge University Press, 1995), 141.

32. Linda Colley, *Britons: Forging the Nation, 1707–1837* (New Haven, CT: Yale University Press, 1992).

33. Colley, "Britishness and Otherness," 327.

34. Gerald Newman, *The Rise of English Nationalism: A Cultural History, 1740–1830* (New York: St. Martin's Press, 1987), 129.

35. Norman Davies, "The Decomposing of Britain," *Times Literary Supplement* (6 October 2000), 15.

36. Murray G. H. Pittock, *Inventing and Resisting Britain: Cultural Identities in Britain and Ireland, 1685–1789* (Basingstoke: Macmillan, 1997), 1.

37. J. C. D. Clark, "Protestantism, Nationalism, and National Identity, 1660–1832," *Historical Journal* 43 (March 2000), 275.

38. R. J. Smith, *The Gothic Bequest: Medieval Institutions in British Thought, 1688–1863* (New York: Cambridge University Press, 1987), 94.

39. Susan Staves, "Chattel Property Rules and the Construction of Englishness, 1660–1800," *Law and History Review* 12 (Spring 1994), 124.

40. Richard Sheridan, Irish House of Commons, 10 January 1793.

41. Philippa Levine, *The Amateur and the Professional: Antiquarians, Historians and Archaeologists in Victorian England, 1838–1886* (Cambridge: Cambridge University Press, 1986).

42. Peter Mandler, "Against 'Englishness': English Culture and the Limits to Rural Nostalgia, 1850–1940," *Transactions of the Royal Historical Society*, Sixth Series 7 (1997), 158.

43. Charles Dellheim, *The Face of the Past: The Preservation of the Medieval Inheritance in Victorian England* (New York: Cambridge University Press, 1982), 71; see also Rosemary Mitchell, *Picturing the Past: English History in Text and Image, 1830–1870* (Oxford: Clarendon Press, 2000).

44. Valerie E. Chancellor, *History for Their Masters: Opinion in the English History Textbooks, 1800–1914* (London: Alden & Mowbray, 1970); Stephen Heathorn, *For Home, Country, and Race: Gender, Class, and Englishness in the Elementary School, 1880–1914* (Toronto: University of Toronto Press, 2000).

45. Philip Ayres, *Classical Culture and the Idea of Rome in Eighteenth-Century Eng-*

land (Cambridge: Cambridge University Press, 1997), xiii; see also Michael Liversidge and Catherine Edwards, eds., *Imagining Rome: British Artists and Rome in the Nineteenth Century* (London: Merrell Holberton, 1996); and Norman Vance, *The Victorians and Ancient Rome* (Oxford: Blackwell, 1997).

46. Frank M. Turner, *The Greek Heritage in Victorian Britain* (New Haven, CT: Yale University Press, 1981), 213; Richard Jenkyns, *Dignity and Decadence: Victorian Art and the Classical Inheritance* (London: Harper Collins, 1991); and Kyriacos Demetriou, "In Defence of the British Constitution: Theoretical Implications of the Debate over Athenian Democracy in Britain, 1770–1850," *History of Political Thought* 17 (Summer 1996), 289–91.

47. Andrew Wawn, *The Vikings and the Victorians: Inventing the Old North in Nineteenth-Century Britain* (Cambridge: D. S. Brewer, 2000), especially 98–99.

48. Janet L. Nelson, "England and the Continent in the Ninth Century: II, The Vikings and Others," *Transactions of the Royal Historical Society,* Sixth Series 13 (2003), 4.

49. Foot, "Making of *Angelcynn,*" 27.

50. Jenks, *Edward Plantagenet,* iii.

51. Peter Mandler, "'In the Olden Time': Romantic History and English National Identity, 1820–1850," in Lawrence Brockliss and David Eastwood, eds., *A Union of Multiple Identities: The British Isles, c. 1750–c. 1850* (Manchester: Manchester University Press, 1997), 83–89.

52. Lang, *Victorians and the Stuart Heritage,* 40.

53. The classic exposition of this evidence is Lewis P. Curtis, *Anglo-Saxons and Celts: A Study of Anti-Irish Prejudice in Victorian England* (Bridgeport, CT: Conference on British Studies, 1968); see also Michael de Nie, *The Eternal Paddy: Irish Identity and the British Press, 1798–1882* (Madison: University of Wisconsin Press, 2004); and Donald M. MacRaild, "'Principle, Party, and Protest': The Language of Victorian Orangism in the North of England," in Shearer West, ed., *The Victorians and Race* (Aldershot: Scolar Press, 1997), 131–37.

54. Sheridan Gilley, "English Attitudes to the Irish in England, 1780–1900," in Colin Holmes, ed., *Immigrants and Minorities in British Society* (London: Allen and Unwin, 1978), 85; for similar paradoxes of perception, see Jodie Kreider, "'Degraded and Benighted': Gendered Constructions of Wales in the Empire, ca. 1847," *North American Journal of Welsh Studies* 2 (Winter 2002), 1–12.

55. Lewis P. Curtis, "The Greening of Irish History," *Eire-Ireland* 29 (Summer 1994), 7–28; and Gabriel Doherty, "National Identity and the Study of Irish History," *English Historical Review* 111 (April 1996), 324–49.

56. Elizabeth K. Helsinger, *Rural Scenes and National Representation: Britain, 1815–1850* (Princeton, NJ: Princeton University Press, 1997), 13; see also John Taylor, *A Dream of England: Landscape, Photography and the Tourist's Imagination* (Manchester: Manchester University Press, 1994); and Stephen Daniels, *Fields of Vision: Landscape Imagery and National Identity in England and the United States* (Princeton, NJ: Princeton University Press, 1993).

57. David Lowenthal, "The Island Garden: English Landscape and British Identity," in Helen Brocklehurst and Robert Phillips, eds., *History, Nationhood and the Question of Britain* (New York: Palgrave Macmillan, 2004), 147; in the same collection see also Chris-

tine Berberich, "'I Was Meditating about England': The Importance of Rural England for the Construction of 'Englishness,'" 375–85.

58. Barbara English, "*Lark Rise* and Juniper Hill: A Victorian Community in Literature and in History," *Victorian Studies* 29 (Autumn 1985), 34.

59. John Stevenson, "The Countryside, Planning, and Civil Society in Britain, 1926–1947," in Jose Harris, ed., *Civil Society in British History: Ideas, Identities, Institutions* (New York: Oxford University Press, 2003), 195.

60. Standish Meacham, *Regaining Paradise: Englishness and the Early Garden City Movement* (New Haven, CT: Yale University Press, 1999), 1.

61. Anne Helmreich, *The English Garden and National Identity: The Competing Styles of Garden Design, 1870–1914* (Cambridge: Cambridge University Press, 2002), 22–23; and Alun Howkins, "Rurality and English Identity," in David Morley and Kevin Robins, eds., *British Cultural Studies: Geography, Nationality, and Identity* (New York: Oxford University Press, 2002), 146.

62. Catherine Brace, "Finding England Everywhere: Regional Identity and the Construction of National Identity, 1890–1940," *Ecumene* 6 (January 1999), 90; emphasis in the original.

63. Marjorie Morgan, *National Identities and Travel in Victorian Britain* (New York: Palgrave, 2001).

64. Adrian Gilgary, *The Silence of Memory* (Oxford: Berg, 1994).

65. Thomas W. Heyck, "Myths and Meanings of Intellectuals in Twentieth-Century British National Identity," *Journal of British Studies* 37 (April 1998), 192–221.

66. Stephen Brooke, "Identities in Twentieth-Century Britain," *Journal of British Studies* 40 (January 2001), 151–58; and James Vernon, "Englishness: The Narration of a Nation," *Journal of British Studies* 36 (April 1997), 243–49.

67. Andrew Higson, *Waving the Flag: Constructing a National Cinema in Britain* (Oxford: Clarendon Press, 1995), 275; see also Jeffrey Richards, *Films and British National Identity: From Dickens to Dad's Army* (Manchester: Manchester University Press, 1997).

68. Kathleen Wilson, *The Island Race: Englishness, Empire and Gender in the Eighteenth Century* (London: Routledge, 2003), 3.

69. John R. Gillis, "Introduction," in John R. Gillis, ed., *Commemorations: The Politics of National Identity* (Princeton, NJ: Princeton University Press, 1994), 7.

70. Paul Readman, "The Place of the Past in English Culture, c. 1890–1914," *Past and Present* 186 (February 2005), 149–50.

71. Newman, *Rise of English Nationalism*, xvii.

72. Anthony D. Smith, "The Origins of Nations," *Ethnic and Racial Studies* 12 (July 1989), 340.

73. A. Dwight Culler, *The Victorian Mirror of History* (New Haven, CT: Yale University Press, 1985), vii.

74. Mandler, "Against 'Englishness,'" 158.

75. David Miller, *On Nationality* (Oxford: Clarendon Press, 1995), 23.

76. James Bryce in 1882, quoted in Dellheim, *Face of the Past*, 90.

77. Reba N. Soffer, *Discipline and Power: The University, History, and the Making of an English Elite, 1870–1930* (Stanford, CA: Stanford University Press, 1994), 87.

78. James Epstein, "The Constitutional Idiom: Radical Reasoning, Rhetoric and Action in Early Nineteenth-Century England," *Journal of Social History* 23 (Spring 1990), 555.

79. Cited in Margot C. Finn, "A Vent Which Has Conveyed Our Principles: English Radical Patriotism in the Aftermath of 1848," *Journal of Modern History* 64 (December 1992), 641.

80. Reproduced in Roy C. Strong, *The Story of Britain* (New York: Fromm International, 1996), 440.

81. Winston Churchill, *A History of the English-Speaking Peoples*, 4 vols. (New York: Dodd, Mead, 1956–58), I: 158–65.

82. George Burton Adams, *The Origin of the English Constitution* (New Haven, CT: Yale University Press, 1912), 1.

83. James Bryce to Albert Venn Dicey, 20 August 1914, James Bryce papers, Bodleian Library, Oxford.

84. Eyre Crowe to Sir Francis Villiers, 14 January 1907, Sir Francis Villiers papers, Foreign Office 800/23, National Archives, Kew. We thank professor Lyle McGeoch of Ohio University for this reference.

85. Robert Colls, *Identity of England* (London: Oxford University Press, 2002), 73.

86. Herbert Butterfield, *The Whig Interpretation of History* (London: G. Bell & Sons, 1931).

87. H. A. L. Fisher, "The Whig Historians," *Proceedings of the British Academy* 14 (1928), 297–339.

88. Richard A. Cosgrove, "Reflections on the Whig Interpretation of History," *Journal of Early Modern History* 4 (2000), 147–67.

89. Fisher, "Whig Historians," 301.

90. Ian Ward, *The English Constitution: Myths and Realities* (Oxford and Portland, OR: Hart Publishing, 2004), viii.

91. Collini, *Public Moralists*, 287.

92. John W. Burrow, *A Liberal Descent: Victorian Historians and the English Past* (Cambridge: Cambridge University Press, 1981), 129.

93. Piet B. M. Blaas, *Continuity and Anachronism: Parliamentary and Constitutional Development in Whig Historiography and in the Anti-Whig Reaction between 1890 and 1930* (The Hague: Martinus Nijhoff, 1978), 34.

94. Stefan Collini, "Genealogies of Englishness: Literary History and Cultural Criticism," in Ciaran Brady, ed., *Ideology and the Historians* (Dublin: Lilliput Press, 1991), 135.

95. Helen Cam to Isao Higashide, n.d., October 1956, Helen Cam papers, Girton College, Cambridge; emphasis in the original.

96. "The Manor," n.d., Mss. Top. Oxon. d. 572, Henry W. C. Davis papers, Bodleian Library, Oxford.

97. Michael Powicke to J. Goronwy Edwards, 1 June 1962, Box 40, J. Goronwy Edwards papers, National Library of Wales, Aberystwyth.

98. Ian Ward, *A State of Mind? The English Constitution and the Popular Imagination* (Stroud: Sutton, 2000), 6.

99. Richard A. Cosgrove, *Our Lady the Common Law: An Anglo-American Legal Community, 1870–1930* (New York: New York University Press, 1987).

100. Oliver Wendell Holmes, *The Common Law* (Boston: Little, Brown, 1881).

101. Dicey to Bryce, 12 May 1898, Bryce papers.

102. Bench and Bar Banquet report, 14 April 1905, volume 37, Joseph Hodges Choate papers, Manuscript Division, Library of Congress, Washington, DC.

103. Sir William Holdsworth to Roscoe Pound, 29 February 1924, Box 67, File 5, Roscoe Pound papers, Harvard Law School Library, Cambridge, MA.

2. Constitutional History as Racial Hierarchy

1. Allen J. Frantzen and John D. Niles, "Anglo-Saxonism and Medievalism," in Allen J. Frantzen and John D. Niles, eds., *Anglo-Saxonism and the Construction of Social Identity* (Gainesville: University Press of Florida, 1997), 2.

2. Christopher Harvie, *The Lights of Liberalism: University Liberals and the Challenge of Democracy, 1860–1886* (London: Allen Lane, 1976), 136; see also Catherine Hall, "A Response to the Commentators," *Journal of British Studies* 42 (October 2003), 530–31.

3. Douglas Lorimer, *Colour, Class and the Victorians: English Attitudes to the Negro in the Mid-Nineteenth Century* (Leicester: Leicester University Press, 1978), 11.

4. Douglas Lorimer, "Theoretical Racism in Late-Victorian Anthropology, 1870–1900," *Victorian Studies* 31 (Spring 1988), 405.

5. Paul Crook, *Darwinism, War, and History: The Debate over the Biology of War from the 'Origin of Species' to the First World War* (Cambridge: Cambridge University Press, 1994), 80.

6. Ronald Rainger, "Race, Politics, and Science: The Anthropological Society of London in the 1860s," *Victorian Studies* 22 (Autumn 1978), 62; Jessica Harland-Jacobs, "All in the Family: Freemasonry and the British Empire in the Mid-Nineteenth Century," *Journal of British Studies* 42 (October 2003), 475.

7. G. K. Peatling, "The Whiteness of Ireland Under and After the Union," *Journal of British Studies* 44 (January 2005), 115–16.

8. Paul B. Rich, "Social Darwinism, Anthropology and English Perspectives of the Irish, 1867–1900," *History of European Ideas* 19 (July 1994), 779.

9. Lorimer, *Colour, Class and the Victorians*, 14.

10. Greta Jones, *Social Darwinism and English Thought: The Interaction between Biological and Social Theory* (Brighton: Harvester Press, 1980), 142.

11. K. Anthony Appiah, *In My Father's House: Africa in the Philosophy of Culture* (New York: Oxford University Press, 1992), 13.

12. Lorimer, "Theoretical Racism," 428.

13. Nancy Stepan, *The Idea of Race in Science: Great Britain, 1800–1960* (London: Macmillan, 1982), xx–xxi.

14. Hugh A. MacDougall, *Racial Myth in English History: Trojans, Teutons, and Anglo-Saxons* (Hanover, NH: University Press of New England, 1982), 95–97.

15. Billie Melman, "Claiming the Nation's Past: The Invention of an Anglo-Saxon Tradition," *Journal of Contemporary History* 26 (September 1991), 581.

16. Stephen Heathorn, *For Home, Country, and Race: Gender, Class, and Englishness in the Elementary School, 1880–1914* (Toronto: University of Toronto Press, 2000), 104.

17. Robert Miles, *Racism* (London: Routledge, 1989), 31; see also James Epstein, "The Constitutional Idiom: Radical Reasoning, Rhetoric and Action in Early Nineteenth-Century England," *Journal of Social History* 23 (Spring 1990), 555.

18. Lewis Curtis, *Anglo-Saxons and Celts: A Study of Anti-Irish Prejudice in Victorian England* (Bridgeport, CT: Conference on British Studies, 1968), 11.

19. Reginald Horsman, "Origins of Racial Anglo-Saxonism in Great Britain before 1850," *Journal of the History of Ideas* 37 (July 1976), 410.

20. Susan Reynolds, "What Do We Mean by 'Anglo-Saxon' and the 'Anglo-Saxons'?" *Journal of British Studies* 24 (October 1985), 414.

21. Cristian Capelli et al., "A Y Chromosome Census of the British Isles," *Current Biology* 13 (2003), 979–84; Michael E. Weale et al., "Y Chromosome Evidence for Anglo-Saxon Mass Migration," *Molecular Biology and Evolution* 19 (July 2002), 1008–21; and Bryan Ward-Perkins, "Why Did the Anglo-Saxons Not Become More British?" *English Historical Review* 115 (June 2000), 520.

22. Elisabeth Wallace, "Goldwin Smith on England and America," *American Historical Review* 59 (July 1954), 884; as well for Smith, see Paul T. Phillips, *The Controversialist: An Intellectual Life of Goldwin Smith* (Westport, CT: Praeger, 2002).

23. Goldwin Smith, *The Schism in the Anglo-Saxon Race* (New York: American News Company, 1887), 6.

24. Goldwin Smith, *Lectures on the Study of History* (New York: Harper & Bros., 1866), 66.

25. Charles Dilke, *Greater Britain: A Record of Travel in English-Speaking Countries*, 2 vols. (London: Macmillan, 1868), I: viii.

26. Hugh Tulloch, "Changing British Attitudes Towards the United States in the 1880s," *Historical Journal* 20 (December 1977), 825–40.

27. Charles Kingsley, *The Roman and the Teuton* (London: Macmillan, 1864), 1.

28. Thomas W. Thompson, *James Anthony Froude on Nation and Empire: A Study in Victorian Racialism* (New York: Garland, 1987), 210.

29. Frank Aydelotte, *The American Rhodes Scholarships: A Review of the First Forty Years* (Princeton, NJ: Princeton University Press, 1946), 18–19.

30. James Loughlin, "Joseph Chamberlain, English Nationalism and the Ulster Question," *History* 77 (June 1992), 203.

31. Marc Jason Gilbert, "Insurmountable Distinctions: Racism and the British Response to the Emergence of Indian Nationalism," in Roger D. Long, ed., *The Man on the Spot: Essays on British Empire History* (Westport, CT: Greenwood Press, 1995), 177.

32. Stuart Anderson, *Race and Rapprochement: Anglo-Saxonism and Anglo-American Relations, 1895–1904* (Rutherford, NJ: Associated University Presses, 1981), 26.

33. Ibid., 27–28.

34. John Lothrop Motley, *The Rise of the Dutch Republic*, 2 vols. (Philadelphia: Henry Altemus, 1898 [1855]), I: iv.

35. Leslie Stephen, ed., *Letters of John Richard Green* (London: Macmillan, 1901), 468.

36. Edward Augustus Freeman, *Lectures to American Audiences* (London: Trüburer, 1882), 55.

37. Stuart Anderson, "Racial Anglo-Saxonism and the American Response to the Boer War," *Diplomatic History* 2 (Summer 1978), 222.

38. Cushing Strout, *The American Image of the Old World* (New York: Harper & Row, 1963), 140–41; Bradford Perkins, *The Great Rapprochement: England and the United States, 1895–1914* (New York: Atheneum, 1968).

39. Anon., *Essays in Anglo-Saxon Law* (Boston: Little, Brown, 1876); Adams contributed an essay called "Courts of Law."

40. Goldwin Smith to George Waring, 25 April 1871, Goldwin Smith papers, Carl A. Kroch Library, Cornell University, Ithaca, NY.

41. James Bryce, undated handwritten draft titled "Goldwin Smith," bMS Am 1899 (48), folder 1, Joseph Halle Schaffner Autograph Collection, Houghton Library, Harvard University, Cambridge, MA.

42. Sybel was reviewing Erwin Nasse, *Über die Mittelalterliche Feldgemeinschaft und die Einhegungen des Sechszehnten Jahrhunderts in England* (Bonn: Carl Georgi, 1869) in *The Nation* 11 (22 September 1870), 192.

43. Herbert Baxter Adams to Daniel Coit Gilman, 11 October 1881, Ms. 4, Box 6, Herbert Baxter Adams papers, Milton S. Eisenhower Library, Johns Hopkins University, Baltimore, MD.

44. Charles McLean Andrews to his mother, 16 October 1886, Series I, Box 1, Charles McLean Andrews papers, Sterling Library, Yale University, New Haven, CT.

45. John Franklin Jameson to John Jameson, 13 February 1882, in Elizabeth Donnan and Leo F. Stock, eds., *A Historian's World: Selections from the Correspondence of John Franklin Jameson* (Philadelphia: American Philosophical Society, 1956), 21.

46. W. Stull Holt, ed., *Historical Scholarship in the United States, 1876–1901: As Revealed in the Correspondence of Herbert B. Adams* (Baltimore: Johns Hopkins Press, 1938), 90.

47. Herbert Baxter Adams, "The Germanic Origins of New England Towns," *Johns Hopkins University Studies in Historical and Political Science* 1 (1883), 8–9.

48. Herbert Baxter Adams, "Special Methods of Historical Study," in G. Stanley Hall, ed., *Methods of Teaching History*, 2nd ed. (Boston: Ginn, Heath, and Co., 1885), 122.

49. Herbert Baxter Adams to Daniel Coit Gilman, 3 July 1882, in Holt, *Historical Scholarship in the United States*, 55.

50. Thomas Gossett, *Race: The History of an Idea in America* (Dallas: Southern Methodist University Press, 1963), 110; and Peter Charles Hoffer, *Past Imperfect: Facts, Fictions, Fraud—American History from Bancroft and Parkman to Ambrose, Bellesiles, Ellis, and Goodwin* (New York: Public Affairs, 2004), 28.

51. Harvey Wish, *The American Historian: A Social-Intellectual History of the Writing of the American Past* (New York: Oxford University Press, 1960), 110–11.

52. Edward N. Saveth, *American Historians and European Immigrants, 1875–1925* (New York: Russell and Russell, 1965), 41.

53. Quoted in Saveth, *American Historians and European Immigrants*, 49.

54. Gregory A. VanHoosier-Carey, "Byhrnoth in Dixie: The Emergence of Anglo-Saxon Studies in the Postbellum South," in Allen J. Frantzen and John D. Niles, eds., *Anglo-Saxonism and the Construction of Social Identity* (Gainesville: University Press of Florida), 157–72.

55. Peter Novick, *That Noble Dream: The "Objectivity Question" and the American Historical Profession* (Cambridge: Cambridge University Press, 1988), 88.

56. Henry Adams to John Richard Green, 9 April 1882, John Richard Green papers, Jesus College, Oxford.

57. John W. Burrow, *A Liberal Descent: Victorian Historians and the English Past* (Cambridge: Cambridge University Press, 1981), 121.

58. Charles E. McClelland, *The German Historians and England: A Study in Nineteenth-Century Views* (Cambridge: Cambridge University Press, 1971), 102–3.

59. Steven W. Siak, "'The Blood That Is in Our Veins Comes from German Ancestors': British Historians and the Coming of the First World War," *Albion* 30 (Summer 1998), 233.

60. Keith Robbins, "Lord Bryce and the First World War," *Historical Journal* 10 (1967), 255.

61. Hugh Tulloch, *Acton* (London: Weidenfeld and Nicolson, 1988), 109.

62. Lord Acton to James Bryce, 8 May 1888, James Bryce papers, Bodleian Library, Oxford.

63. Hugh Tulloch, "Acton," in Benedikt Stuchtey and Peter Wende, eds., *British and German Historiography, 1750–1950: Traditions, Perceptions, and Transfers* (London: Oxford University Press, 2000), 167.

64. John W. Burrow, *Whigs and Liberals: Continuity and Change in English Political Thought* (Oxford: Clarendon Press, 1988), 133.

65. DeLloyd J. Guth, "How Legal History Survives Constitutional History's Demise," *Rechtsgeschichte und Quantitative Geschichte* 7 (1977), 126–27.

66. Remarks by Eliot, 6 March 1902, Charles William Eliot papers, Harvard University Archives, Cambridge, MA.

67. Howard L. Malchow, *Gothic Images of Race in Nineteenth-Century Britain* (Stanford, CA: Stanford University Press, 1996), 39.

68. Burrow, *Liberal Descent*, 125.

69. A. F. Pollard, *The Evolution of Parliament* (London: Longmans, Green, 1920), 3.

70. Edward Freeman to John Richard Green, 22 November 1881, Green papers.

71. Christopher J. W. Parker, "The Failure of Liberal Racialism: The Racial Ideas of E. A. Freeman," *Historical Journal* 24 (December 1981), 827.

72. Hugh Tulloch, *James Bryce's American Commonwealth: The Anglo-American Background* (Woodbridge: Royal Historical Society, 1988), 44; A. V. Dicey, Freeman's good friend, deplored this line of thought, complaining that "race was often mixed up with a quasi-permanent national character." A. V. Dicey to Bryce, 17 May 1912, Bryce papers.

73. Peter Dale, *The Victorian Critic and the Idea of History: Carlyle Arnold Pater* (Cambridge, MA: Harvard University Press, 1977), 5.

74. W. R. W. Stephens, ed., *The Life and Letters of Edward A. Freeman*, 2 vols. (London: Macmillan, 1895), I: 104.

75. Freeman to Edward B. Tylor, 20 July 1872, in Stephens, *Life and Letters*, II: 57.

76. Freeman to Bryce, 6 May 1867, Bryce papers.

77. Rosemary Jann, *The Art and Science of Victorian History* (Columbus: Ohio State University Press, 1985), 179.

78. The scholarly attempt to locate the origins of Parliament in the Anglo-Saxon period even enlisted the usually perspicacious Felix Liebermann, who in 1913 still wrote of the Anglo-Saxon witan as "one of the lineal ancestors of the British Parliament, to which the legislative assemblies of all the neighbours reverently look up to as their model and their teacher." Felix Liebermann, *The National Assembly in the Anglo-Saxon Period* (Halle, Germany: Max Niemeyer, 1913), 1. Yet as early as 1905, H. Munro Chadwick, *Studies on Anglo-Saxon Institutions* (Cambridge: Cambridge University Press, 1905), 355–66,

had provided a skeptical appraisal of the powers of the witan. "The witenagemot was little more than a court council" was the conclusion of T. J. Oleson, *The WITENAGEMOT in the Reign of Edward the Confessor: A Study in the Constitutional History of Eleventh-Century England* (London: Oxford University Press, 1955), 110.

79. John W. Burrow, "'The Village Community' and the Uses of History in Late Nineteenth-Century England," in Neil McKendrick, ed., *Historical Perspectives: Studies in English Thought in Honour of J. H. Plumb* (London: Europa, 1974), 268.

80. MacDougall, *Racial Myth in English History*, 102.

81. John Richard Green, *A Short History of the English People* (London: Macmillan, 1874), 45; in a letter to Green about the work, Freeman wrote: "Indeed I do use the name English before 449; it is something very important to use it." Freeman to Green, 26 March 1876, Edward A. Freeman papers, John Rylands Library, Manchester.

82. E. L. Godkin to James Bryce, 28 February 1882, in William Armstrong, ed., *The Gilded Age Letters of E. L. Godkin* (Albany: State University of New York Press, 1974), 282.

83. Edward Augustus Freeman, *Some Impressions of the United States* (New York: Henry Holt, 1883), 139; Freeman to F. H. Dickinson, 4 December 1881, in Stephens, *Life and Letters*, II: 242; Freeman to Green, 26 December 1881, Freeman papers.

84. Freeman to Boyd Dawkins, 15 October 1881, and Freeman to N. Pinder, 6 November 1881, in Stephens, *Life and Letters*, II: 234, 236.

85. Freeman to Green, 21 January 1875, Freeman papers; John Kenyon, *The History Men: The Historical Profession in England since the Renaissance* (London: Weidenfeld and Nicolson, 1983), 155.

86. Freeman to Green, 27 June 1875, Freeman papers.

87. Freeman to N. Pinder, 24 March 1882, in Stephens, *Life and Letters*, II: 254.

88. Freeman to Bryce, 24 July 1870, Bryce papers.

89. Freeman to Bryce, 28 March 1880, Bryce papers.

90. In 1892, the year of Freeman's death, Paul Vinogradoff published an excellent summary of this scholarly quarrel as part of his introduction to *Villainage in England: Essays in English Mediaeval History* (Oxford: Clarendon Press, 1892), 16–37.

91. Dicey to Bryce, 23 March 1892, Bryce papers.

92. Freeman to Bryce, 19 July 1880, Bryce papers.

93. Sir Frederick Pollock to Freeman, 26 August 1876, Freeman papers.

94. Parker, "Failure of Liberal Racialism," 837.

95. Peter Mandler, "'Race' and 'Nation' in Mid-Victorian Thought," in Stefan Collini, Richard Whatmore, and Brian Young, eds., *History, Religion, and Culture: British Intellectual History, 1750–1950* (Cambridge: Cambridge University Press, 2000), 240.

96. Edward Freeman, *The Growth of the English Constitution from the Earliest Times* (New York: Frederick A. Stokes Co., 1890 [1872]), 25–26.

97. Ibid., 33.

98. Ibid., 43.

99. Doris Goldstein, "Confronting Time: The Oxford School of History and the Non-Darwinian Revolution," *Storia Della Storiografia* 45 (2004), 15.

100. Freeman, *Growth of the English Constitution*, 80–81, 90–91. In private, Freeman referred to the "Great Witan of the English Race." Freeman to Bryce, 19 January 1887, Bryce papers.

101. Freeman, *Growth of the English Constitution,* 95.

102. Burrow, *Liberal Descent,* 126.

103. Tulloch, *James Bryce's American Commonwealth,* 43.

104. Freeman, *Growth of the English Constitution,* 8.

105. Ibid.

106. Edward Augustus Freeman, *The History of the Norman Conquest of England: Its Causes and Its Results,* 5 vols. (Oxford: Clarendon Press, 1867–1879), I: 1.

107. Ibid., I: 15.

108. Ibid., I: 50.

109. Ibid., III: 270.

110. Noel Annan, *Leslie Stephen: The Godless Victorian* (London: Weidenfeld and Nicolson, 1984), 85; and Kenyon, *History Men,* 155.

111. L. F. Salzman, "Senlac," *Times Literary Supplement* (1 May 1953), 285.

112. Burrow, *Liberal Descent,* 160.

113. Freeman to Bryce, 27 March 1881, Bryce papers.

114. H. A. Cronne, "Edward Augustus Freeman, 1823–1892," *History* 28 (March 1943), 83; and Kenyon, *History Men,* 155.

115. Freeman to Bryce, 6 March 1870, Bryce papers.

116. Freeman to Bryce, 20 April 1873, Bryce papers; emphasis in the original.

117. Freeman to Bryce, 10 April 1881, Bryce papers.

118. W. H. Dunn, *James Anthony Froude: A Biography,* 2 vols. (Oxford: Clarendon Press, 1961–63), II: 458.

119. Freeman to Bryce, 17 February and 7 March 1884, Bryce papers.

120. Freeman to Bryce, 22 July 1885, Bryce papers. Round's devastating critique of Freeman's work will be detailed later.

121. David C. Douglas, "The Norman Conquest and British Historians," [1946] reprinted in *Time and the Hour: Some Collected Papers of David C. Douglas* (London: Eyre Methuen, 1977), 63.

122. Kenyon, *History Men,* 155.

123. See Marjorie Chibnall, *The Debate on the Norman Conquest* (New York: St. Martin's Press, 1999). A collection of this kind, a sure sign of professional interest, indicates the continuing significance of this discussion.

124. Douglas, "Norman Conquest and British Historians," 63.

125. Clare A. Simmons, *Reversing the Conquest: History and Myth in Nineteenth-Century Literature* (New Brunswick, NJ: Rutgers University Press, 1990).

126. R. Allen Brown, "The Norman Conquest," *Transactions of the Royal Historical Society,* Fifth Series 17 (1967), 109.

127. Parker, "Failure of Liberal Racialism," 828.

128. M. Edwin Bratchel, *Edward Augustus Freeman and the Victorian Interpretation of the Norman Conquest* (Ilfracombe: Arthur H. Stockwell, 1969), 15.

129. Herbert Baxter Adams to Daniel Coit Gilman, 16 November 1882, Ms 1, Coll. 1, Daniel Coit Gilman papers, Milton S. Eisenhower Library, Johns Hopkins University, Baltimore, MD.

130. A. V. Dicey to Bryce, 22 June 1892, Bryce papers.

131. Frederic William Maitland, *Domesday Book and Beyond: Three Essays in the Early History of England* (Cambridge: Cambridge University Press, 1897), 150.

132. Anthony Brundage, *The People's Historian: John Richard Green and the Writing of History in Victorian England* (Westport, CT: Greenwood Press, 1994), 77–84.

133. Charles McLean Andrews, *The Old English Manor: A Study in Economic History* (Baltimore: Johns Hopkins Press, 1892), iii–xi.

134. Sir Frederick Pollock, *Oxford Lectures and Other Discussions* (London: Macmillan, 1890), 122.

135. Luke O. Pike, *A Constitutional History of the House of Lords: From Original Sources* (London: Macmillan, 1894), 18.

136. Sir Frederick Pollock, "The Continuity of the Common Law," *Harvard Law Review* 11 (February 1898), 427–28.

137. Charles H. McIlwain, *The High Court of Parliament and Its Supremacy: An Historical Essay on the Boundaries between Legislation and Adjudication in England* (New Haven, CT: Yale University Press, 1910), 12.

138. James F. Baldwin, *The King's Council in England during the Middle Ages* (Oxford: Clarendon Press, 1913), 2.

139. Geoffrey Elton, *The English* (Oxford: Blackwell, 1992), 4.

140. MacDougall, *Racial Myth in English History*, 127–30.

141. Pollard, *Evolution of Parliament*, 5.

142. Paul Freedman and Gabrielle Spiegel, "Medievalism Old and New: The Rediscovery of Alterity in North American Medieval Studies," *American Historical Review* 103 (June 1998), 685–86.

143. James Bryce, *The Study of American History* (New York: Macmillan, 1922); and Bryce to Goldwin Smith, 15 November 1900, Goldwin Smith papers.

144. Bryce to Hubert Hall, 29 June 1920, Public Record Office 44/1, Hubert Hall papers, National Archives, Kew.

145. See the Romanes lecture at Oxford: James Bryce, *The Relations of the Advanced and the Backward Races of Mankind* (Oxford: Clarendon Press, 1902); and the Creighton lecture at the University of London: James Bryce, *Race Sentiment as a Factor in History* (London: University of London Press, 1915). For other musings about race, see the exchange of letters with Charles Eliot in advance of the Romanes lecture: Bryce to Eliot, 7 February 1902, Eliot papers; and Eliot to Bryce, 14 March 1902, Bryce papers.

146. See especially James Bryce, "The Essential Unity of Britain and America," *Atlantic Monthly* 82 (July 1898), 22–29; and "The Influence of National Character and Historical Environment on the Development of the Common Law," *American Bar Association Reports* 31 (1907), 444–62.

147. Elazar Barkan, *The Retreat of Scientific Racialism: Changing Concepts of Race in Britain and the United States between the World Wars* (New York: Cambridge University Press, 1992), xi.

148. Dicey to J. St. Loe Strachey, 16 August 1899, J. St. Loe Strachey papers, House of Lords Record Office, London.

149. Carleton K. Allen to Sir John Linton Myres, 7 September 1935, Sir John Linton Myres papers, Bodleian Library, Oxford.

150. Theodore Roosevelt to Bryce, 31 March 1889, Bryce papers.

151. Bryce to William A. Dunning, 23 May 1918, Box 2, William A. Dunning papers, Butler Library, Columbia University, New York, NY.

3. Constitutional History as an Academic Profession

1. H. G. Richardson and G. O. Sayles, *The Governance of Medieval England from the Conquest to Magna Carta* (Edinburgh: Edinburgh University Press, 1963), vi, 20.

2. Edward Freeman to James Bryce, 24 October 1878, James Bryce papers, Bodleian Library, Oxford. The mutual admiration society formed by the two scholars led to humor at their expense: "See, ladling butter from alternate tubs, Stubbs butters Freeman, Freeman butters Stubbs." William Holden Hutton, ed., *Letters of William Stubbs: Bishop of Oxford, 1825–1901* (London: Constable, 1904), 149; or "Did you see in Saturday's *Times* an announcement on the front page? BETROTHAL. FREEMAN: STUBBS." Reginald Lane Poole to T. F. Tout, 19 June 1905, 1/953/5, T. F. Tout papers, Manchester University Library, Manchester.

3. John Horace Round, *"Barons" and "Knights" in the Great Charter* (Aberdeen: Aberdeen University Press, 1917), 7.

4. William Stubbs, *Select Charters and Other Illustrations of English Constitutional History: From the Earliest Times to the Reign of Edward the First* (Oxford: Clarendon Press, 1870). This remained "in successive editions a basis of English university courses for over a hundred years"; James Campbell, "Stubbs, Maitland, and Constitutional History," in Benedikt Stuchtey and Peter Wende, eds., *British and German Historiography, 1750–1950: Traditions, Perceptions, and Transfers* (Oxford: Oxford University Press, 2000), 102.

5. Charles Firth, *Modern History in Oxford, 1841–1918* (Oxford: Blackwell, 1920), 15.

6. Hugh A. MacDougall, *Racial Myth in English History: Trojans, Teutons, and Anglo-Saxons* (Hanover, NH: University Press of New England, 1982), 102.

7. Robert Brentano, "The Sound of Stubbs," *Journal of British Studies* 6 (May 1967), 1.

8. N. J. Williams, "Stubbs' Appointment as Regius Professor, 1866," *Bulletin of the Institute of Historical Research* 33 (1960), 123–24.

9. Llewellyn Woodward, "The Rise of the Professional Historian in England," in Kenneth C. Bourne and D. C. Watt, eds., *Studies in International History* (Hamden: Archon, 1967), 23.

10. William Gladstone to William Stubbs, 2 September 1883, in Hutton, *Letters of William Stubbs,* 231.

11. A. V. Dicey to Freeman, 18 March 1884, Edward A. Freeman papers, John Rylands Library, Manchester; as Oxford contemporary A. L. Smith put it, Stubbs had "given up to episcopacy what was meant for mankind." "Notes," Box 7, A. L. Smith papers, Balliol College Library, Oxford.

12. Norman F. Cantor, ed., *William Stubbs on the English Constitution* (New York: Thomas Y. Crowell, 1966), 4.

13. Campbell, "Stubbs, Maitland, and Constitutional History," 106.

14. Alon Kadish, "Scholarly Exclusiveness and the Founding of the *English Historical Review,*" *Historical Research* 61 (June 1988), 187.

15. C. H. S. Fifoot, *Law and History in the Nineteenth Century* (London: Bernard Quaritch, 1956), 5–6.

16. Arthur Marwick, "Two Approaches to Historical Study: The Metaphysical (Including 'Postmodernism') and the Historical," *Journal of Contemporary History* 30 (January 1995), 12. Emphasis in the original.

17. Hayden V. White, "Response to Arthur Marwick," *Journal of Contemporary History* 30 (April 1995), 243.

18. Stubbs to Freeman, 8 November 1857, Bodl. Ms. Eng. Misc. e. 148, William Stubbs papers, Bodleian Library, Oxford.

19. William Stubbs, *Seventeen Lectures on the Study of Medieval and Modern History and Kindred Subjects Delivered at Oxford, under Statutory Obligation in the Years 1867–1884* (Oxford: Clarendon Press, 1886), 76. About this lecture, "On the Purposes and Methods of Historical Study," James Bryce reported: "Stubbs's lecture is not on the study of history, but merely a sort of review of what has been doing lately in Oxford by himself and others; not likely to be of any use to you, though it is pleasant reading of course as a piece of composition." Bryce to Oscar Browning, 19 July 1876, Oscar Browning papers, King's College Library, Cambridge.

20. Stefan Collini, Donald Winch, and John W. Burrow, *That Noble Science of Politics: A Study in Nineteenth-Century Intellectual History* (Cambridge: Cambridge University Press, 1983), 200.

21. Stubbs to Freeman, 5 March 1867, Bodl. Ms. Eng. Misc. e. 148, Stubbs papers.

22. Stubbs, *Seventeen Lectures*, 83.

23. Doris Goldstein, "Confronting Time: The Oxford School of History and the Non-Darwinian Revolution," *Storia Della Storiografia* 45 (2004), 9.

24. Maurice Cowling, *Religion and Public Doctrine in Modern England*, 3 vols. (Cambridge: Cambridge University Press, 1980–2001), III: 234.

25. William Stubbs, *Lectures on Early English History. By William Stubbs* (New York: Longmans, Green, 1906), 3. The editing of these lectures by Arthur Hassall did not serve Stubbs well: "I am very sorry to hear such a bad account of the way in which Lord Acton's lectures have been edited. Much the same thing happened to Bishop Stubbs's lectures, and both were men fastidious in the highest degree about accuracy in detail." Reginald Lane Poole to Browning, 5 March 1907, Browning papers.

26. Peter Novick, *That Noble Dream: The "Objectivity Question" and the American Historical Profession* (Cambridge: Cambridge University Press, 1988), 37; on this point, see also Thomas Haskell, "Objectivity Is Not Neutrality: Rhetoric vs. Practice in Peter Novick's *That Noble Dream,*" *History and Theory* 29 (May 1990), 131, 143; and Gabrielle M. Spiegel, "History, Historicism and the Social Logic of the Text in the Middle Ages," *Speculum* 65 (January 1990), 74–75.

27. James Campbell, *Stubbs and the English State* (Reading: University of Reading Press, 1988), 5.

28. Reba N. Soffer, *Discipline and Power: The University, History, and the Making of an English Elite, 1870–1930* (Stanford, CA: Stanford University Press, 1994), 87.

29. Campbell, *Stubbs and the English State*, 3.

30. Henry Hallam, *Constitutional History of England: From Henry VII to George II*, 3 vols. (London: J. M. Dent, 1912 [1827]).

31. William Gladstone to Stubbs, 23 September 1875, in Hutton, *Letters of William Stubbs*, 147.

32. William Stubbs, *The Constitutional History of England in Its Origins and Development*, 3 vols. (Oxford: Clarendon Press, 1874–78).

33. Julia Crick, "*Pristina Libertas*: Liberty and the Anglo-Saxons Revisited," *Transactions of the Royal Historical Society*, Sixth Series 14 (2004), 47–48.

34. Charles E. McClelland, *The German Historians and England: A Study in Nineteenth-Century Views* (Cambridge: Cambridge University Press, 1971), 136.

35. Brentano, "Sound of Stubbs," 5. In 1883 Frederic Seebohm wrote, for example, that "more things went to the 'making of England' than were imported in the keels of the English invaders of Britain." *The English Village Community: Examined in Its Relations to the Manorial and Tribal Systems and to the Common or Open Field System of Husbandry* (London: Longmans, Green, 1905 [1883]), xv.

36. John W. Burrow, *A Liberal Descent: Victorian Historians and the English Past* (Cambridge: Cambridge University Press, 1981), 143.

37. Asa Briggs, "Saxons, Normans, and Victorians," *The Collected Essays of Asa Briggs,* 3 vols. (London: Harvester Press, 1985–91), II: 228.

38. John P. Kenyon, *The History Men: The Historical Profession in England since the Renaissance* (London: Weidenfeld and Nicolson, 1983), 153.

39. Campbell, "Stubbs, Maitland, and Constitutional History," 103.

40. Freeman to John Richard Green, 10 November 1878, Freeman papers.

41. Stubbs, *Constitutional History,* II: 17.

42. Ibid., II: 104.

43. Cantor, *Stubbs on the English Constitution,* 7.

44. Piet B. M. Blaas, *Continuity and Anachronism: Parliamentary and Constitutional Development in Whig Historiography and in the Anti-Whig Reaction between 1890 and 1930* (The Hague: Martinus Nijhoff, 1978), xiii.

45. Stubbs to Freeman, 23 November 1864, Bodl. Ms. Eng. Misc. e. 148, Stubbs papers.

46. T. F. Tout, *Chapters in the Administrative History of Mediaeval England: The Wardrobe, the Chamber, and the Small Seals,* 6 vols. Manchester: Manchester University Press, 1920–33, I: 3.

47. Goldstein, "Confronting Time," 27.

48. J. Goronwy Edwards, *William Stubbs* (London: George Philip & Son, 1952), 5.

49. Tout, *Administrative History of Mediaeval England,* I: 3.

50. Edward Powell, "After 'After McFarlane': The Poverty of Patronage and the Case for Constitutional History," in Dorothy J. Clayton, Richard G. Davies, and Peter McNiven, eds., *Trade, Devotion and Governance: Papers in Later Medieval History* (Stroud: Sutton, 1994), 1. Powell added that Stubbsian history, once thought extinct, was in the process of making a comeback, an indication of the cyclical nature of academic fashion.

51. Ludmilla Jordanova, *History in Practice* (London: Edward Arnold, 2000), 186–89.

52. Thomas W. Heyck, *The Transformation of Intellectual Life in Victorian England* (London: Croom Helm, 1982), 145.

53. Blaas, *Continuity and Anachronism,* xii.

54. Sir Frederick Pollock to Freeman, 17 January 1887, Freeman papers. Emphasis in the original.

55. Philippa Levine, "History in the Archives: The Public Record Office and Its Staff, 1838–1886," *English Historical Review* 101 (January 1986), 40.

56. John D. Cantwell, *The Public Record Office, 1838–1958* (London: Her Majesty's Stationary Office, 1991), 308.

57. C. T. Flower to Secretary of the Royal Literary Fund, 23 March 1945, PRO 44/1, Hubert Hall papers, National Archives, Kew.

58. Hubert Hall, *Studies in English Official Historical Documents* (Cambridge: Cambridge University Press, 1908).

59. Robert Bartlett, ed., *History and Historians: Selected Papers of R. W. Southern* (Oxford: Blackwell, 2004), 94.

60. Cowling, *Religion and Public Doctrine*, III: 227.

61. Soffer, *Discipline and Power*, 97.

62. Campbell, "Stubbs, Maitland, and Constitutional History," 103.

63. Raphael Samuel, "Continuous National History," in Raphael Samuel, ed., *Patriotism: The Making and Unmaking of British National Identity*, 3 vols. (New York: Routledge, 1989), I: 11.

64. Christopher J. W. Parker, *The English Historical Tradition since 1850* (Edinburgh: John Donald, 1990), 46.

65. Edwards, *William Stubbs*, 10.

66. H. A. L. Fisher to Gilbert Murray, 12 March 1893, Volume 54, H. A. L. Fisher papers, Bodleian Library, Oxford.

67. Gaillard Lapsley, "Some Recent Advance in English Constitutional History (Before 1485)," *Cambridge Historical Journal* 5 (1936), 119.

68. Kenyon, *History Men*, 152. Kenyon added that Stubbs's achievement was "the more astonishing when we remember that Stubbs was working virtually alone; he was so far above all his contemporaries as a medieval scholar that he could only assist them, not they him."

69. Stubbs, *Select Charters*, xv and xviii; the quotations in this and the next paragraph are from these two pages.

70. Bertie Wilkinson, *The Constitutional History of England, 1216–1399*, 3 vols. (London: Longmans, Green, 1948–58), I: vii.

71. Stubbs, *Seventeen Lectures*, 73.

72. Charles Oman, *On the Writing of History* (London: Methuen, 1939), 235.

73. Arthur J. Engel, *From Clergyman to Don: The Rise of the Academic Profession in Nineteenth-Century Oxford* (Oxford: Clarendon Press, 1983), 110.

74. Oman, *On the Writing of History*, 235.

75. George Otto Trevelyan to James Bryce, 24 March 1912, Bryce papers.

76. Charles Firth to John Linton Myres, 28 April 1912, Sir John Linton Myres papers, Bodleian Library, Oxford.

77. Hubert Hall to Browning, 21 November 1892, Browning papers; emphasis in the original.

78. Quoted in Charles Dellheim, *The Face of the Past: The Preservation of the Medieval Inheritance in Victorian England* (New York: Cambridge University Press, 1982), 90.

79. Reba N. Soffer, "Modern History," in M. G. Brock and M. C. Curthoys, eds., *The History of the University of Oxford*, VII, *Nineteenth Century Oxford*, Part 2 (Oxford: Clarendon Press, 2000), 361.

80. Soffer, *Discipline and Power*, 105.

81. Quoted in R. W. Lee, *Edward Jenks, 1861–1939* (London: Humphrey Milford, 1939), 23.

82. John W. Burrow, "'The Village Community' and the Uses of History in Late

Nineteenth-Century England," in Neil McKendrick, ed., *Historical Perspectives: Studies in English Thought in Honour of J. H. Plumb* (London: Europa, 1974), 267.

83. Campbell, "Stubbs, Maitland, and Constitutional History," 101.

84. Soffer, *Discipline and Power*, 63.

85. Reba N. Soffer, "Nation, Duty, Character and Confidence: History at Oxford, 1850–1914," *Historical Journal* 30 (March 1987), 91.

86. Oman, *On the Writing of History*, 252–53.

87. Firth, *Modern History in Oxford*, 29.

88. Burrow, *Liberal Descent*, 141.

89. John Clive, *Not by Fact Alone: Essays on the Writing and Reading of History* (New York: Knopf, 1989), 126.

90. Hall to Browning, 24 October 1887, Browning papers.

91. Soffer, "Modern History," 377.

92. Ibid., 368.

93. Dicey to Sir William Anson, 25 February 1898, Sir William Anson papers, Codrington Library, All Souls College, Oxford.

94. Soffer, "Modern History," 366; Smith's papers contain several examples of the care Smith devoted to making Stubbs's work accessible to the undergraduates. See Box 8, IA/2i, IA4/2iii, and IA4/3, A. L. Smith papers.

95. Soffer, *Discipline and Power*, 86.

96. Undergraduate Essays in Constitutional History, Box 2, J. Goronwy Edwards papers, National Library of Wales, Aberystwyth.

97. Tout to Edwards, 17 February 1922, Box 219, Edwards papers.

98. 1 March 1930, Box 50, Edwards papers.

99. N.d., Box 50, Edwards papers.

100. N.d., Box 268, Edwards papers.

101. 28 July 1949, Box 138, Edwards papers.

102. Christopher J. W. Parker, *The English Idea of History from Coleridge to Collingwood* (Aldershot: Ashgate, 2000), 214. See also W. J. Van Der Dussen, *History as a Science: The Philosophy of R. G. Collingwood* (The Hague: Martinus Nijhoff, 1981); David Boucher, *The Social and Political Thought of R. G. Collingwood* (Cambridge: Cambridge University Press, 1989); William H. Dray, *History as Re-Enactment: R. G. Collingwood's Idea of History* (Oxford: Clarendon Press, 1995); and Peter Johnson, *R. G. Collingwood: An Introduction* (Bristol: Thoemmes, 1998).

103. Christopher J. W. Parker, "English Historians and the Opposition to Positivism," *History and Theory* 22 (1983), 143.

104. Notes for a Philosophy of History, April 1928, Volume 12/4, Robin G. Collingwood papers, Bodleian Library, Oxford.

105. May 1928, Volume 12/4, Collingwood papers.

106. Soffer, *Discipline and Power*, 87.

107. Theodore Clarke Smith, "The Writing of American History in America, from 1884 to 1934," *American Historical Review* 40 (April 1935), 449; see also Novick, *That Noble Dream*, 259–60.

108. Can Historians Be Impartial? 27 January 1936, Volume 12/10, Collingwood papers.

109. Ibid.

110. Human Nature and Human History, March 1936, Volume 12/11, Collingwood papers.

111. The quotation and statistics are from Campbell, "Stubbs, Maitland, and Constitutional History," 101.

112. Marjorie McCallum Chibnall, "Memoir (1914–)," in Jane Chance, ed., *Women Medievalists in the Academy* (Madison: University of Wisconsin Press, 2005), 749.

113. Brian Harrison, "History at the Universities, 1968: A Commentary," *History* 53 (October 1968), 364.

114. Kenyon, *History Men*, 149.

115. Peter R. H. Slee, *Learning and Liberal Education: The Study of Modern History in the Universities of Oxford, Cambridge, and Manchester, 1800–1914* (Manchester: Manchester University Press, 1986), 86.

116. Paul T. Phillips, *Britain's Past in Canada: The Teaching and Writing of British History* (Vancouver: University of British Columbia Press, 1989), 50.

117. Undated syllabus, Maude Violet Clarke papers, Somerville College, Oxford.

118. Clarke papers. For a variation of this assessment, see J. R. Tanner, "The Teaching of Constitutional History," in William A. J. Archbold, ed., *The Teaching of History* (Cambridge: Cambridge University Press, 1901), 54.

119. Campbell, *Stubbs and the English State*, 4.

120. Richardson and Sayles, *Governance of Medieval England*, 1.

121. Edwards, *William Stubbs*, 11.

122. John Richard Green to Freeman, 28 January 1867, in Leslie Stephen, ed., *Letters of John Richard Green* (London: Macmillan, 1901), 172–73.

123. Freeman to Bryce, 15 March 1867, Bryce papers.

124. Browning, press clipping from the *Saturday Review*, 27 December 1906, in Volume 145, Fisher papers.

125. John W. Burrow, "Victorian Historians and the Royal Historical Society," *Transactions of the Royal Historical Society*, Fifth Series 39 (1989), 136.

126. Charles Oman to Browning, 9 March 1890, Browning papers. Just three days earlier, Oman had complained to Browning that "some of the present members' names inspire one with doubt, and most are perfectly unknown." Oman to Browning, 6 March 1890, Browning papers.

127. Edward Jenks to Browning, 13 February 1896, Browning papers.

128. Leslie Howsam, "Academic Discipline or Literary Genre? The Establishment of Boundaries in Historical Writing," *Victorian Literature and Culture* 32 (September 2004), 530–31.

129. Bryce to Freeman, 12 August 1883, Bryce papers.

130. Pollock to Freeman, 29 March 1884, Freeman papers.

131. Bryce to Browning, 28 June 1883, Browning papers.

132. Doris Goldstein, "The Origins and Early Years of the *English Historical Review*," *English Historical Review* 101 (January 1986), 13–14.

133. James Covert, *A Victorian Marriage: Mandell and Louise Creighton* (London: Hambledon, 2000), 204–8.

134. Bryce to Browning, 11 May 1899, Browning papers.

135. Poole to Tout, Easter Eve 1905, 1/953/3, Tout papers.

136. Doris Goldstein, "History at Oxford and Cambridge: Professionalization and

the Influence of Ranke," in Georg G. Iggers and James M. Powell, eds., *Leopold von Ranke and the Shaping of the Historical Discipline* (Syracuse, NY: Syracuse University Press, 1990), 141.

137. Harold Perkin, *The Rise of Professional Society: England since 1880* (London: Routledge, 1989), 369.

138. A. F. Pollard, *The Claims of Historical Research in London* (London: University of London Press, 1920), 6.

139. Edwards, *William Stubbs,* 20.

140. Helen Cam, "Stubbs Seventy Years After," *Cambridge Historical Journal* 9 (1948), 129.

141. Bartlett, *History and Historians,* 93.

142. Charles Kendall Adams to Herbert Baxter Adams, 9 February 1896, Ms. 4, Series 1, Box 1, Herbert Baxter Adams papers, Milton S. Eisenhower Library, Johns Hopkins University, Baltimore, MD.

143. *Dictionary of National Biography: The Concise Dictionary, Part II, 1901–1950* (Oxford: Oxford University Press, 1961), II: 399.

144. Charles Kendall Adams, *A Manual of Historical Literature, Comprising Brief Descriptions of the Most Important Histories in English, French and German, Together with Practical Suggestions as to Methods and Courses of Historical Study* (New York: Harper & Brothers, 1888).

145. Charles McLean Andrews to his mother, 9 November 1886, Series I, Box 1, Folder 20, Charles McLean Andrews papers, Sterling Library, Yale University, New Haven, CT.

146. Andrews to his mother, 22 April 1889, Series I, Box 2, Folder 28, Andrews papers.

147. "Graduate Studies in History at Brown University, 1887–1897," John Franklin Jameson to Herbert Baxter Adams, undated [1898] Ms. 4, Box 9, Herbert Baxter Adams papers.

148. Andrews published *The Old English Manor: A Study in English Economic History* (Baltimore: Johns Hopkins Press, 1892); Beard began his career with *The Office of Justice of the Peace in England in Its Origin and Development* (New York: Columbia University Press, 1904); and for Robinson, see Bryce to Browning, 20 April 1892, Browning papers.

149. Herbert Baxter Adams to Gilman 3 July 1882, in W. Stull Holt, ed., *Historical Scholarship in the United States, 1876–1901: As Revealed in the Correspondence of Herbert B. Adams* (Baltimore: Johns Hopkins University Press, 1938), 55.

150. Herbert Baxter Adams to Jameson, 15 July 1885, Box 46, File 19, John Franklin Jameson papers, Manuscripts Division, Library of Congress, Washington, DC.

151. Gilman to Herbert Baxter Adams, 15 July 1883, Ms. 4, Box 6, Herbert Baxter Adams papers; emphasis in the original.

152. Charles McLean Andrews, *The River Towns of Connecticut: A Study of Wethersfield, Hartford, and Windsor* (Baltimore: Johns Hopkins Press, 1889).

153. Andrews to Herbert Baxter Adams, 23 October 1891, Ms. 4, Box 1, Herbert Baxter Adams papers.

154. There is a file of reviews of his book in Series IV, Box 79, Folder 938, Andrews papers.

155. Charles McLean Andrews, *The Old English Manor: A Study in English Economic History* (Baltimore: Johns Hopkins Press, 1892), 286.

156. See, for example, Charles Oman's 1906 book, *The Great Revolt of 1381* (New York: Haskell House, 1968 [1906]).

157. John Franklin Jameson, "The American Historical Association, 1884–1909," *American Historical Review* 15 (October 1909), 1–20.

158. Herbert Baxter Adams to Jameson, 25 October 1889, Box 46, File 19, Jameson papers.

159. Arthur S. Link, "The American Historical Association, 1884–1984: Retrospect and Prospect," *American Historical Review* 90 (February 1985), 7.

160. John Higham, *History: Professional Scholarship in America* (Baltimore: Johns Hopkins University Press, 1983 [1965]), 16–17.

161. William M. Sloane, "History and Democracy," *American Historical Review* 1 (October 1895), 21, 22.

162. Moses Coit Tyler, "The Party of the Loyalists in the American Revolution," *American Historical Review* 1 (October 1895), 45.

4. Constitutional History as Culture Wars

1. Noel Annan, *The Dons: Mentors, Eccentrics, and Geniuses* (Chicago: University of Chicago Press, 1999), 91.

2. W. Raymond Powell, *John Horace Round: Historian and Gentleman of Essex* (Chelmsford: Essex Record Office, 2001).

3. John Horace Round, *Feudal England: Historical Studies in the Eleventh and Twelfth Centuries* (London: Allen & Unwin, 1895); and *Geoffrey de Mandeville: A Study of the Anarchy* (New York: B. Franklin, 1960 [1892]).

4. Among Round's targets were the famous, Edward Freeman, the quasi-famous, such as Kate Norgate and Hubert Hall, and the forgotten: H. Arthur Doubleday, W. H. B. Bird, and Walter Rye.

5. Frank M. Stenton, "Foreword," in the 1964 reprint of Round, *Feudal England,* 8.

6. John Horace Round to George Burton Adams, 16 July 1900, Box 6, Folder 30, George Burton Adams papers, Sterling Library, Yale University, New Haven, CT; emphasis in the original.

7. John Horace Round, *The King's Serjeants and Officers of State: With Their Coronation Services* (London: James Nisbet, 1911), 52.

8. David Stephenson, "The Early Career of J. H. Round: The Shaping of a Historian," *Essex Archaeology and History* 12 (1980), 3; Stephenson added one page later: "The master-pupil relationship with Stubbs, therefore, goes far to explain Round's failure to produce long works of connected history; his role, to a large extent quite consciously adopted, was to gloss Stubbs's work, and to develop the use of sources supplementary to those so successfully worked by the bishop."

9. John Horace Round, *"Barons" and "Knights" in the Great Charter* (Aberdeen: Aberdeen University Press, 1917), 7.

10. Frank M. Stenton, "Early English History, 1895–1920," *Transactions of the Royal Historical Society,* Fourth Series 28 (1946), 9.

11. Review of Round's *The Commune of London,* reprinted in Helen Cam, ed., *Selected Historical Essays of F. W. Maitland* (Cambridge: Cambridge University Press, 1957), 259–65.

12. Round to Oswald Barron, 26 May 1910, Add. Mss. 732, Oswald Barron papers, West Sussex Record Office, Chichester.

13. Round to Barron, 14 November 1912, Add. Mss. 732, Barron papers.

14. John Horace Round, "Introduction," in *Pipe Roll 29 Henry II 1182–83* (London: The Pipe Roll Society, 1911), xxviii.

15. Round to Barron, 9 January 1901, Add. Mss. 732, Barron papers.

16. Round to Barron, 23 October 1912, Add. Mss. 732, Barron papers.

17. Round to Maxwell Lyte, 5 July 1911, PRO 1/158, Maxwell Lyte papers, National Archives, Kew.

18. Round to Barron, 27 October 1908, Add. Mss. 732, Barron papers; emphasis in the original.

19. See, for example, the letter of Samuel Rawson Gardiner to Round, 4 April 1894, Volume 663, John Horace Round papers, University of London Library, London, in which Gardiner tried to explain to Round that a delay in proofs from the *English Historical Review* did not mean that a plot was afoot against him.

20. Round to Hubert Hall, 14 November 1886, U890, F5/1, Hubert Hall papers, Centre for Kentish Studies, Maidstone. See also Charles Johnson, "Hubert Hall, 1857–1944," *Transactions of the Royal Historical Society*, Fourth Series 28 (1946), 1–5.

21. Powell, *John Horace Round*, 137.

22. Frederic Maitland to Round, 7 September 1896, in C. H. S. Fifoot, ed., *The Letters of Frederic William Maitland* (Cambridge, MA: Harvard University Press, 1965), 150–51. Maitland believed that Round "should pick on someone his own size." Quoted in Edmund King, "John Horace Round and the 'Calendar of Documents Preserved in France,'" *Proceedings of the Battle Conference on Anglo-Norman Studies* 4 (1981), 100. In the same vein about Round, "a friend once remarked that if he would cease killing flies, what valuable work he would do." William Page, "Memoir," in John Horace Round, *Family Origins and Other Studies* (London: Constable, 1930), xxi.

23. Round to Lyte, 1 May 1897, PRO 1/158, Lyte papers. Lyte, Hall's superior at the PRO, continued to receive outraged missives from Round, especially the letters of 17 and 24 November 1897, PRO 1/158, Lyte papers.

24. Hubert Hall, *The Red Book of the Exchequer: A Reply to Mr. J. H. Round* (London: Spottiswoode, 1898), 3. Hall's judgment of Round's ethics might have gotten even more severe if he had known that Round occasionally used anonymous reviews to praise his own work. See Powell, *John Horace Round*, 74.

25. William Stevenson to Maitland, 27 March 1905, Add. Mss. 7007, Frederic Maitland papers, Cambridge University Library, Cambridge.

26. Lawrence Stone, "The Revival of Narrative: Some Reflections on a New Old History," *Past and Present* 85 (November 1979), 3.

27. Round to Lyte, 15 April 1896, PRO 1/158, Lyte papers.

28. King, "John Horace Round," 97–98.

29. John Horace Round, "Historical Research," *The Nineteenth Century* 44 (December 1898), 1007.

30. Round to Adams, 12 January 1909, Box 6, Folder 30, George Burton Adams papers. See also Lyte to Round, 5 February 1914, Volume 658, Round papers, where Lyte discusses the intricacies of such scholarly work with Round. Round produced fourteen of these volumes.

31. Round to Adams, 7 December 1914, Box 6, Folder 30, George Burton Adams papers.

32. A comparison, but without the personality issues, may be made to J. Conway Davies (1891–1971), whose publication record reflected the commitment to scholarly editing. See the J. Conway Davies papers, National Library of Wales, Aberystwyth, especially Boxes 34–50.

33. Round to Doris Stenton, 26 October 1926, Frank and Doris Stenton papers, University of Reading Library, Reading.

34. Tout to Frank Stenton, 17 January 1928, Stenton papers; see also Powell, *John Horace Round,* 120. In 1898 Round wrote that scholars had accepted his view of military tenure "except Mr. Charles Oman, who has not yet grasped it." Round, "Historical Research," 1006.

35. John P. Kenyon, *The History Men: The Historical Profession in England since the Renaissance.* (London: Weidenfeld and Nicolson, 1983), 283.

36. Round to Lord Acton, 23 January 1897, Add. Mss. 6443, Lord Acton papers, Cambridge University Library, Cambridge; and also the later letter of 7 February 1897.

37. Gardiner to Round, 5 February 1894, Volume 663, Round papers.

38. Reginald Lane Poole to Round, 17 October 1914, Volume 663, Round papers.

39. Round to Adams, 23 January 1897, Box 6, Folder 30, George Burton Adams papers. The work was presumably his *Feudal England.*

40. Round to Barron, 28 August 1911, Add. Mss. 732, Barron papers.

41. Poole to Round, 18 July 1920, Volume 638, Round papers.

42. Adams to Round, 16 December 1901, Box 6, Folder 30, George Burton Adams papers.

43. W. H. B. Bird to Round, 3 August 1903, Volume 663, Round papers.

44. Poole to Round, 18 October 1886, Volume 664, Round papers.

45. James Tait, "John Horace Round," *English Historical Review* 43 (October 1928), 576.

46. Frank Stenton, "Round, John Horace," in *Dictionary of National Biography, 1922–1930* (London: Oxford University Press, 1937), 728.

47. Stenton, "Foreword," 7.

48. Tait, "John Horace Round," 572.

49. William E. Kapelle, "Domesday Book: F. W. Maitland and His Successors," *Speculum* 64 (July 1989), 621.

50. Round called this the "fruit of long original research." Round to Lyte, 7 July 1891, PRO 1/158, Lyte papers. John Horace Round, "The Introduction of Knight Service into England," *English Historical Review* 6 (July 1891), 417–43; 6 (October 1891), 625–45; 7 (January 1892), 11–24. Soon after the appearance of Round's article, Paul Vinogradoff destroyed another conventional view with a brilliantly destructive opening sentence: "A word that occurs on three occasions, and, unless I am mistaken, on three occasions only, in our whole store of Anglo-Saxon documents, has become the parent of comprehensive theories of early English history." Paul Vinogradoff, "Folkland," *English Historical Review* 8 (January 1893), 1.

51. Round to Lyte, 31 May 1893, PRO 1/158, Lyte papers.

52. Poole to Round, 29 January 1891, Volume 663, Round papers.

53. John Gillingham, "The Introduction of Knight Service into England," *Proceedings of the Battle Conference on Anglo-Norman Studies* 4 (1981), 53–54.

54. Clare A. Simmons, *Reversing the Conquest: History and Myth in Nineteenth-Century Literature* (New Brunswick, NJ: Rutgers University Press, 1990), 5.

55. J. C. Holt, *Colonial England, 1066–1215* (Rio Grande, OH: Hambledon, 1997), 71.

56. N.d., Box 8, IA4/3, A. L. Smith papers, Balliol College Library, Oxford.

57. Poole to Maitland, 29 July 1901, Add. Mss. 7007, Maitland papers.

58. Frank M. Turner, *Contesting Cultural Authority: Essays in Victorian Intellectual Life* (Cambridge: Cambridge University Press, 1993), 35.

59. Olive Anderson, "The Political Uses of History in Mid-Nineteenth-Century England," *Past and Present* 36 (April 1967), 88.

60. Robert Bartlett, ed., *History and Historians: Selected Papers of R. W. Southern* (Oxford: Blackwell, 2004), 132.

61. Anthony Brundage, *The People's Historian: John Richard Green and the Writing of History in Victorian England* (Westport, CT: Greenwood Press, 1994), 74–75, 87.

62. Ludmilla Jordanova, *History in Practice* (London: Edward Arnold, 2000), 146.

63. Richard A. Cosgrove, "The Relevance of Irish History: The Gladstone-Dicey Debate about Home Rule, 1886–7," *Eire-Ireland* 13 (Winter 1978), 6–21.

64. William Gladstone to Dicey, 12 November 1886, Add. Mss. 44499, William Gladstone papers, British Library, London.

65. For full discussions see Piet B. M. Blaas, *Continuity and Anachronism: Parliamentary and Constitutional Development in Whig Historiography and in the Anti-Whig Reaction between 1890 and 1930* (The Hague: Martinus Nijhoff, 1978), 52–56; and Powell, *John Horace Round*, 94–102, 116–21.

66. Powell, *John Horace Round*, 98–99.

67. Poole to Round, 18 October 1886, Volume 664, Round papers.

68. John Horace Round, "Professor Freeman," *Quarterly Review* 175 (July 1892), 1–37.

69. Alon Kadish, "Scholarly Exclusiveness and the Founding of the *English Historical Review*," *Historical Research* 61 (June 1988), 198.

70. H. A. Cronne, "Edward Augustus Freeman, 1823–1892," *History* 28 (March 1943), 91–92.

71. Gardiner to Round, 25 May 1893, Volume 638, Round papers.

72. Blaas, *Continuity and Anachronism*, 54.

73. John Horace Round, *Feudal England: Historical Studies in the Eleventh and Twelfth Centuries* (London: Allen & Unwin, 1895), 303.

74. Ibid., 405.

75. Simmons, *Reversing the Conquest*, 195.

76. Round, *Feudal England*, 303.

77. Ibid., 302. Round's biographer suggests that the bitter battle with Hubert Hall may also in part have stemmed from Hall's connection to the new London School of Economics as a faculty member and his friendship with Beatrice and Sidney Webb. See Powell, *John Horace Round*, 137; and Beatrice Webb's thanks for Hall's contribution to the first decades of the London School of Economics: "What a splendid success the School is under Sir William Beveridge, and how much it owes to the pioneer work done by you and the first members of the staff." Beatrice Webb to Hall, 17 April 1926, U 890, F4/9, Hall papers, Centre for Kentish Studies.

78. Round to Barron, 17 May 1913, Add. Mss. 732, Barron papers; emphasis in the original.

79. Kate Norgate, "The Battle of Hastings," *English Historical Review* 9 (January

1894), 41–76; and Thomas Archer, "The Battle of Hastings," *English Historical Review* 9 (January 1894), 1–41.

80. John Horace Round, "Mr. Freeman and the Battle of Hastings," *English Historical Review* 9 (April 1894), 209–59.

81. Ibid., 256–59.

82. Round to Barron, 6 January 1910, Add. Mss. 732, Barron papers; emphasis in the original. This letter should be understood in the context of the first general election of 1910, then under way.

83. Peter Mandler, *History and National Life* (London: Profile Books, 2002), 50–51.

84. Alan O'Day, *Irish Home Rule, 1867–1921* (Manchester: Manchester University Press, 1998), 10–11.

85. Goldwin Smith to Bryce, 27 December 1888, James Bryce papers, Bodleian Library, Oxford.

86. Dicey to Lord Cromer, 12 April 1912, Lord Cromer papers, ING Bank NV, London.

87. A. F. Pollard to his parents, 7 April 1908, Box 3, A. F. Pollard papers, University of London Library, London.

88. Philip Kerr to H. A. L. Fisher, 11 February 1929, Lewis Namier papers, John Rylands Library (Deansgate), Manchester.

89. J. H. Plumb, *The Making of an Historian: The Collected Essays of J. H. Plumb*, 2 vols. (Athens: University of Georgia Press, 1988–89), I: 155.

90. Leslie Howsam, "Academic Discipline or Literary Genre? The Establishment of Boundaries in Historical Writing," *Victorian Literature and Culture* 32 (September 2004), 543.

91. W. E. H. Lecky, *The Political Value of History* (London: Edward Arnold, 1892), 24.

92. Ibid., 49.

93. See, for example, Dicey to W. E. H. Lecky, 17 July 1886, TCD Ms. 398, 10 November 1886, TCD Ms. 405, and 15 October 1890, TCD Ms. 614, W. E. H. Lecky papers, Trinity College, Dublin.

94. W. E. H. Lecky, *Historical and Political Essays* (London: Longmans, Green, 1908), 3–4.

95. Donal McCartney, *W. E. H. Lecky: Historian and Politician, 1838–1903* (Dublin: Lilliput Press, 1994), 54.

96. Richard H. Tawney, "J. L. Hammond, 1872–1949," *Proceedings of the British Academy* 46 (1949), 267.

97. Stewart A. Weaver, *The Hammonds: A Marriage in History* (Stanford, CA: Stanford University Press, 1998), 51. See also Julia Stapleton, *Englishness and the Study of Politics: The Social and Political Thought of Ernest Barker* (Cambridge: Cambridge University Press, 1994), 15.

98. This phrase is used in letters to John Hammond by Charles Trevelyan, 29 November 1911, and W. J. Ashley, 12 March 1913, Volume 18, John and Barbara Hammond papers, Bodleian Library, Oxford.

99. Mandler, *History and National Life*, 70.

100. David Cannadine, *G. M. Trevelyan: A Life in History* (London: Harper Collins, 1992), 183.

101. George Macaulay Trevelyan to H. A. L. Fisher, n.d. 1905, volume 59, Herbert. A. L. Fisher papers, Bodleian Library, Oxford.

102. Mandler, *History and National Life,* 74.

103. George Macaulay Trevelyan, *Clio, A Muse: and Other Essays Literary and Pedestrian* (London: Longmans, Green 1913), 4.

104. Quoted in Joseph M. Hernon, "The Last Whig Historian and Consensus History: George Macaulay Trevelyan, 1876–1962," *American Historical Review* 81 (February 1976), 72.

105. Rosemary Jann, *The Art and Science of Victorian History* (Columbus: Ohio State University Press, 1985), 209.

106. Quoted in Hernon, "Last Whig Historian," 79.

107. Herbert Butterfield to John Roselli, 12 November 1970, Add. Mss. 9314, Herbert Butterfield papers, Cambridge University Library, Cambridge.

108. Geoffrey Elton, "Herbert Butterfield and the Study of History," *Historical Journal* 27 (September 1984), 734.

109. Herbert Butterfield, *The Englishman and His History* (Cambridge: Cambridge University Press, 1944), 2. Among these similarities were a belief in a providential order, the prominence of historical narrative, and the importance of moral judgments.

110. W. O. Chadwick, *Freedom and the Historian* (Cambridge: Cambridge University Press, 1969), 37–38.

111. Butterfield to George N. Clark, 23 February 1965, George N. Clark papers, Bodleian Library, Oxford.

112. Keith C. Sewell, "The 'Herbert Butterfield Problem' and Its Resolution," *Journal of the History of Ideas* 64 (October 2003), 599–618.

113. Victor Feske, *From Belloc to Churchill: Private Scholars, Public Culture, and the Crisis of British Liberalism* (Chapel Hill: University of North Carolina Press, 1996), 4. Pages 1–14 of this work provide an excellent introduction to the Whig interpretation and its issues.

114. Herbert Butterfield, *The Whig Interpretation of History* (London: G. Bell & Sons, 1931), v.

115. C. T. McIntire, *Herbert Butterfield: Historian as Dissenter* (New Haven, CT: Yale University Press, 2004), 59.

116. Butterfield, *Whig Interpretation of History,* 30.

117. Keith C. Sewell, *Herbert Butterfield and the Interpretation of History* (New York: Palgrave Macmillan, 2005), 3.

118. Cannadine, *G. M. Trevelyan,* 197.

119. Butterfield, *Whig Interpretation of History,* 11.

120. Linda Colley, *Lewis Namier* (London: Weidenfeld and Nicolson, 1989), 46–47; see also Feske, *From Belloc to Churchill,* 2–3, for another excellent description of the Whig interpretation.

121. Jann, *Art and Science,* 78.

122. Blaas, *Continuity and Anachronism,* 75.

123. George Macaulay Trevelyan, *The English Revolution* (London: Oxford University Press, 1938), 20.

124. For an alternative argument about this consensus, see Theodore Koditschek, *Class Formation and Urban-Industrial Society: Bradford, 1750–1850* (Cambridge: Cambridge University Press, 1990), 26.

125. David Cannadine, "British History as a 'New Subject': Politics, Perspectives

and Prospects," in Alexander Grant and Keith J. Stringer, eds., *Uniting the Kingdom: The Making of British History* (London: Routledge, 1995), 16.

126. John W. Burrow, *A Liberal Descent: Victorian Historians and the English Past* (Cambridge: Cambridge University Press, 1981), 19.

127. Philippa Levine, *The Amateur and the Professional: Antiquarians, Historians and Archaeologists in Victorian England, 1838–1886* (Cambridge: Cambridge University Press, 1986), 78–79.

128. David Lowenthal, *The Past Is a Foreign Country* (Cambridge: Cambridge University Press, 1985), 102.

129. Burrow, *Liberal Descent*, 22.

130. Rosemary Jann, "From Amateur to Professional: The Case of the Oxbridge Historians," *Journal of British Studies* 22 (Spring 1983), 146.

131. David Cannadine, "British History: Past, Present—and Future?" *Past and Present* 116 (August 1987), 178.

132. T. G. Ashplant and Adrian Wilson, "Whig History and Present-centered History," *Historical Journal* 31 (March 1988), 2.

133. Henry Hallam, *Constitutional History of England: From Henry VII to George II*, 3 vols. (London: J. M. Dent, 1912 [1827]), I: 7.

134. Joseph Hamburger, *Macaulay and the Whig Tradition* (Chicago: University of Chicago Press, 1976), 49, 111.

135. Cannadine, *G. M. Trevelyan*, 209; pages 209–15 make a strong case for the appellation of Whig historian to be inaccurate in Trevelyan's case.

136. Hugh Tulloch, "Acton," in Benedikt Stuchtey and Peter Wende, eds., *British and German Historiography, 1750–1950: Traditions, Perceptions, and Transfers* (London: Oxford University Press, 2000), 80; the next two quotations in this paragraph are at 92 and 108–9 respectively.

137. See Peter Novick, *That Noble Dream: The "Objectivity Question" and the American Historical Profession* (Cambridge: Cambridge University Press, 1988), 85; David A. Hollinger, *Morris R. Cohen and the Scientific Ideal* (Cambridge, MA: MIT Press, 1975), 171–72; Stefan Collini, *Public Moralists: Political Thought and Intellectual Life in Britain, 1850–1930* (Oxford: Clarendon Press, 1991), 342–73; and Annabel Patterson, *Nobody's Perfect: A New Whig Interpretation of History* (New Haven, CT: Yale University Press, 2002).

5. Constitutional History and the British Empire

1. R. W. Kostal, *A Jurisprudence of Power: Victorian Empire and the Rule of Law* (New York: Oxford University Press, 2005), 461. Crucial to the imperial self-image, as characterized by Kipling's lesser breeds without the law, was the mission to bring the blessings of the common law to the governed: "The law was central to the British image of themselves in empire." Richard Price, "One Big Thing: Britain, Its Empire, and Their Imperial Culture," *Journal of British Studies* 45 (July 2006), 627.

2. Sidney Reed Brett, *The Story of the British Constitution* (Glasgow: Blackie and Son, 1929), 169.

3. Catherine Hall, "British Cultural Identities and the Legacy of the Empire," in David Morley and Kevin Robins, eds., *British Cultural Studies: Geography, Nationality, and Identity* (New York: Oxford University Press, 2001), 28; Bernard Porter, *The Absent-*

Minded Imperialists: Empire, Society, and Culture in Britain (London: Oxford University Press, 2004).

4. Tony Ballantyne, *Orientalism, Racial Theory and British Colonialism: An Aryan Empire* (Basingstoke: Palgrave, 2001), 3.

5. W. Ross Johnston, *Sovereignty and Protection: A Study of British Jurisdictional Imperialism in the Late Nineteenth Century* (Durham, NC: Duke University Press, 1973).

6. These letters may be found in the A. Berriedale Keith papers, Edinburgh University Library, Edinburgh. The entire correspondence has been published in Ridgway F. Shinn and Richard A. Cosgrove, eds., *Constitutional Reflections: The Correspondence of Albert Venn Dicey and A. Berriedale Keith* (Lanham, MD: University Press of America, 1996); see also Ridgway F. Shinn, *Arthur Berriedale Keith, 1879–1944: The Chief Ornament of Scottish Learning* (Aberdeen: Aberdeen University Press, 1990).

7. William Roger Louis, "Introduction," in Robin Winks, ed., *Historiography, The Oxford History of the British Empire*, 5 vols. (New York: Oxford University Press, 1998–99), V: 27–28.

8. Other topics included such issues as dominion neutrality in the event of war, transfers of Crown lands to dominion governments, or the semantics of colony, Crown colony, dominion, and independence; index to Dicey-Keith letters prepared by Ridgway F. Shinn, Gen 144/8/5, Keith papers.

9. David Cannadine, *Ornamentalism: How the British Saw Their Empire* (London: Oxford University Press, 2001), xiv.

10. David Armitage, "Greater Britain: A Useful Category of Historical Analysis?" *American Historical Review* 104 (April 1999), 441. In a recent article, Mark Proudman has castigated Armitage's approach, finding its treatment of Seeley patronizing, and calling for a wider constitutional analysis of the "Anglian world." Mark F. Proudman, "The Most Important History: The *American Historical Review* and Our English Past," *Journal of the Historical Society* 6 (June 2006), 177–211.

11. James Anthony Froude, *Oceana: or England and Her Colonies* (New York: Scribner's, 1886).

12. Ian Baucom, *Out of Place: Englishness, Empire, and the Locations of Identity* (Princeton, NJ: Princeton University Press, 1999), 6–7.

13. Cannadine, *Orientalism*, xvii.

14. Krishan Kumar, "'Englishness' and English National Identity," in David Morley and Kevin Robins, eds., *British Cultural Studies: Geography, Nationality, and Identity* (New York: Oxford University Press, 2002), 43.

15. Kathleen Wilson, *The Island Race: Englishness, Empire and Gender in the Eighteenth Century* (London: Routledge, 2003), 55.

16. Hall, "British Cultural Identities," 37.

17. James Bryce to Goldwin Smith, 6 July 1898, Goldwin Smith papers, Carl A. Kroch Library, Cornell University, Ithaca, NY.

18. Sir Frederick Pollock to A. Lawrence Lowell, 25 January 1899, A. Lawrence Lowell papers, Harvard University Archives, Cambridge, MA.

19. Julia Stapleton, "James Fitzjames Stephen: Liberalism, Patriotism, and English Liberty," *Victorian Studies* 41 (Winter 1998), 251.

20. Robert J. C. Young, *Colonial Desire: Hybridity in Theory, Culture and Race* (New York: Routledge, 1995), 3.

21. Antoinette Burton, "Introduction: On the Inadequacy and the Indispensability

of the Nation," in Antoinette Burton, ed., *After the Imperial Turn: Thinking with and through the Nation* (Durham, NC: Duke University Press, 2003), 2; emphasis in the original. See also Pamela Scully, "Imperial Crossings: British Identities and the 'Imperial Imaginary,'" *Journal of British Studies* 41 (October 2002), 520–25.

22. Valerie E. Chancellor, *History for Their Masters: Opinion in the English History Textbooks, 1800–1914* (London: Alden & Mowbray, 1970), 137.

23. Robert Roberts, *The Classic Slum: Salford Life in the First Quarter of the Century* (Manchester: Manchester University Press, 1971), 142–43.

24. Keith Robbins, *Nineteenth-Century Britain: Integration and Diversity* (Oxford: Clarendon Press, 1988), 62.

25. Jeffrey Richards, *Imperialism and Music: Britain, 1876–1953* (Manchester: Manchester University Press, 2001), 44–47.

26. Philip Buckner, "Whatever Happened to the British Empire," *Journal of the Canadian Historical Association*, New Series 4 (1993), 3–32.

27. Philip Buckner and Carl Bridge, "Reinventing the British World," *Round Table* 368 (January 2003), 78.

28. Angela Woollacott, "'All This Is the Empire, I Told Myself': Australian Women's Voyages 'Home' and the Articulation of Colonial Whiteness," *American Historical Review* 102 (October 1997), 1007.

29. Ballantyne, *Orientalism*, 14.

30. Andrew Thompson, *The Empire Strikes Back? The Impact of Imperialism on Britain from the Mid-Nineteenth Century* (Harlow: Longman, 2005).

31. John M. MacKenzie, *Orientalism: History, Theory and the Arts* (Manchester: Manchester University Press, 1995), xii.

32. Shahid Amin, quoted in Richard M. Eaton, ed., *India's Islamic Traditions, 711–1750* (New Delhi: Oxford University Press, 2003), 1.

33. The emphasis on governing legitimacy may be best seen in this great collection: Frederick Madden and David Fieldhouse, eds., *Select Documents on the Constitutional History of the British Empire and Commonwealth: The Foundations of a Colonial System of Government*, 8 vols. (Westport, CT: Greenwood Press, 1985–2000).

34. Nasser Hussain, *The Jurisprudence of Emergency: Colonialism and the Rule of Law* (Ann Arbor: University of Michigan Press, 2003), 3.

35. Paul Ward, *Britishness since 1870* (London: Routledge, 2004), 34.

36. Arthur Balfour to Joseph Hodges Choate, 1 June 1905, Volume 37, Joseph Hodges Choate papers, Manuscripts Division, Library of Congress, Washington, DC.

37. Linda Colley, *Captives: Britain, Empire and the World, 1600–1850* (London: Jonathan Cape, 2002), 367.

38. Gautam Chakravarty, *The Indian Mutiny and the British Imagination* (New York: Cambridge University Press, 2005), 4.

39. Armitage, "Greater Britain," 428.

40. Deborah Wormell, *Sir John Seeley and the Uses of History* (Cambridge: Cambridge University Press, 1980), 98.

41. Reba N. Soffer, "History and Religion: J. R. Seeley and the Burden of the Past," in R. W. Davis and R. J. Helmstadter, eds., *Religion and Irreligion in Victorian Society: Essays in Honor of R. K. Webb* (New York: Routledge, 1992), 145–46.

42. Benedict Anderson, *Imagined Communities: Reflections on the Origin and Spread of Nationalism*, 2nd ed. (London: Verso, 1991), 91.

43. H. J. Hanham, ed., *The Nineteenth-Century Constitution, 1815–1914* (Cambridge: Cambridge University Press, 1969), 1; for doubts about the power to transform other societies, see Porter, *Absent-Minded Imperialists,* 101.

44. Quoted in K. J. M. Smith, *James Fitzjames Stephen: Portrait of a Victorian Rationalist* (Cambridge: Cambridge University Press, 1988), 134.

45. Deborah Lavin, *From Empire to International Commonwealth: A Biography of Lionel Curtis* (Oxford: Clarendon Press, 1995), x.

46. Alex May, "Curtis, Lionel George (1872–1955)," in *Oxford Dictionary of National Biography,* Oxford University Press, 2004 [accessed 4 November 2004: http://www. oxforddnb.com/view/article/32678].

47. Lavin, *From Empire to International Commonwealth,* 60.

48. Philip Corrigan and Derek Sayer, *The Great Arch: English State Formation as Cultural Revolution* (Oxford: Blackwell, 1985), 194.

49. John M. MacKenzie, *Propaganda and Empire: The Manipulation of British Public Opinion, 1880–1960* (Manchester: Manchester University Press, 1984), 2.

50. Lord Cromer, *Ancient and Modern Imperialism* (London: John Murray, 1910), 121.

51. John W. Burrow, *A Liberal Descent: Victorian Historians and the English Past* (Cambridge: Cambridge University Press, 1981), 35. Imperial administrator Sir Charles Lucas noted the "mischievous characteristic of Englishmen at home to assume that the laws and institutions which are good for Englishmen in England must necessarily be good for all other races under all other conditions." Sir Charles P. Lucas, *Greater Rome and Greater Britain* (Oxford: Clarendon Press, 1912), 161.

52. Raymond F. Betts, "The Allusion to Rome in British Imperialist Thought of the Late Nineteenth and Early Twentieth Centuries," *Victorian Studies* 15 (December 1971), 153.

53. J. C. Bruce, *The Roman Wall* [1868], quoted in Christina Crosby, *The Ends of History: Victorians and "The Woman Question"* (New York: Routledge, 1991), 4.

54. James Bryce, *Studies in History and Jurisprudence,* 2 vols. (London: Oxford University Press, 1901), I: 25.

55. Richard Symonds, *Oxford and Empire: The Last Lost Cause?* (London: Macmillan, 1986), 55.

56. Bryce, *Studies in History and Jurisprudence,* I: 53.

57. J. G. Darwin, "The Fear of Failing: British Politics and Imperial Decline since 1900," *Transactions of the Royal Historical Society,* Fifth Series 36 (1986), 27.

58. H. A. L. Fisher, "The Whig Historians," *Proceedings of the British Academy* 14 (1928), 324.

59. Lucas, *Greater Rome and Greater Britain,* 141, 149.

60. Betts, "Allusion to Rome," 159.

61. Sam Smiles, *The Image of Antiquity: Ancient Britain and the Romantic Imagination* (New Haven, CT: Yale University Press, 1994), 143–44.

62. Symonds, *Oxford and Empire,* 51.

63. Stuart Ward, "Transcending the Nation: A Global Imperial History?" in Antoinette Burton, ed., *After the Imperial Turn: Thinking with and through the Nation* (Durham, NC: Duke University Press, 2003), 46.

64. Robert H. MacDonald, *The Language of Empire: Myths and Metaphors of Popular Imperialism, 1880–1918* (Manchester: Manchester University Press, 1994), 55.

65. Symonds, *Oxford and Empire,* 57–61.

66. F. H. Lawson, *The Oxford Law School, 1850–1965* (Oxford: Clarendon Press, 1968), 214.

67. Sir Frederick Pollock, *Oxford Lectures and Other Discussions* (London: Macmillan, 1890), 195.

68. Alice Stopford Green to Oliver Wendell Holmes, 3 December 1905, Volume 43, Folder 15, Oliver Wendell Holmes papers, Harvard Law School Library, Cambridge, MA; emphasis in the original.

69. John Kendle, *Ireland and the Federal Solution: The Debate over the United Kingdom Constitution, 1870–1921* (Kingston, ON: McGill-Queen's University Press, 1989); and *Federal Britain: A History* (London: Routledge, 1997).

70. Burton: "Introduction," 4.

71. Hugh Tulloch, "Changing British Attitudes Towards the United States in the 1880s," *Historical Journal* 20 (December 1977), 825–40.

72. John Kendle, *The Colonial and Imperial Conferences, 1887–1911: A Study in Imperial Organization* (London: Longmans, 1967); and *The Round Table Movement and Imperial Union* (Toronto: University of Toronto Press, 1975).

73. A. V. Dicey to J. St. Loe Strachey, 14 June 1911, J. St. Loe Strachey papers, House of Lords Record Office, London.

74. Dicey to A. Berriedale Keith, 10 May 1914, Gen 142/4/108, Keith papers.

75. Edward Freeman to Bryce, 19 January 1887, James Bryce papers, Bodleian Library, Oxford; emphasis in the original.

76. Walter Long to Dicey, 1 July 1911, General Manuscripts 508 (39), Glasgow University Library, Glasgow.

77. Dicey to M. Lupton, 26 July 1912, Working Men's College papers, London.

78. Dicey to Bryce, 31 July 1912, Bryce papers.

79. Dicey to Strachey, 28 March 1915, Strachey papers.

80. John S. Ellis, "'The Methods of Barbarism' and the 'Rights of Small Nations': War Propaganda and British Pluralism," *Albion* 30 (Spring 1998), 50.

81. Dicey to John Venn, 16 April 1914, C23/16B, John Venn papers, Gonville and Caius College, Cambridge.

82. G. K. Peatling, "Home Rule for England, English Nationalism, and Edwardian Debates About Constitutional Reform," *Albion* 35 (Spring 2003), 87.

83. Dicey to Venn, 30 April 1914, C25/17A, Venn papers.

84. Quoted in James A. Colaiaco, *James Fitzjames Stephen and the Crisis of Victorian Thought* (New York: St. Martin's Press, 1983), 114.

85. Pollock, *Oxford Lectures*, 53–54.

86. W. E. H. Lecky, *The Political Value of History* (London: Edward Arnold, 1892), 51.

87. Hussain, *Jurisprudence of Emergency*, 6.

88. Andrew S. Thompson, "The Language of Imperialism and the Meanings of Empire: Imperial Discourse in British Politics, 1895–1914," *Journal of British Studies* 36 (April 1997), 151.

89. W. E. H. Lecky, *Historical and Political Essays* (London: Longmans, Green, 1908), 62.

90. J. L. Hammond to Montague Bradley, 7 November 1903, Volume 18, John and Barbara Hammond papers, Bodleian Library, Oxford.

91. Hussain, *Jurisprudence of Emergency*, chap. 4.

92. Sudipta Sen, *Distant Sovereignty: National Imperialism and the Origins of British India* (New York: Routledge, 2002), 17.

93. Jessica Harland-Jacobs, "All in the Family: Freemasonry and the British Empire in the Mid-Nineteenth Century," *Journal of British Studies* 42 (October 2003), 475.

94. Edwin Hirschmann, *White Mutiny: The Ilbert Bill Crisis in India and the Genesis of the Indian National Congress* (New Delhi: Heritage, 1980), 2–3. See also Mrinalini Sinha, "'Chathams, Pitts, and Gladstones in Petticoats': The Politics of Gender and Race in the Ilbert Bill Controversy, 1883–1884," in Nupur Chaudhuri and Margaret Strobel, eds., *Western Women and Imperialism: Complicity and Resistance* (Bloomington: Indiana University Press, 1992), 98–116.

95. Both quotations are from Hirschmann, *White Mutiny,* 297–301. Emphasis in the original.

96. Partha Chatterjee, *The Nation and Its Fragments: Colonial and Postcolonial Histories* (Princeton, NJ: Princeton University Press, 1993), 21.

97. Niall Ferguson, *Empire: How Britain Made the Modern World* (London: Allen Lane, 2003), 198.

98. Colley, *Captives,* 371.

99. Cromer, *Ancient and Modern Imperialism,* 88.

100. Quoted in Sen, *Distant Sovereignty,* 17.

101. Paul B. Rich, *Race and Empire in British Politics* (Cambridge: Cambridge University Press, 1986), 26; and Suke Wolton, *Lord Hailey, the Colonial Office and the Politics of Race and Empire in the Second World War: The Loss of White Prestige* (New York: Palgrave, 2000), 154.

102. Lecky, *Historical and Political Essays,* 48.

103. Paul R. Deslandes, "'The Foreign Element': Newcomers and the Rhetoric of Race, Nation, and Empire in 'Oxbridge' Undergraduate College Culture, 1850–1920," *Journal of British Studies* 37 (January 1998), 57–58.

104. Stephen Heathorn, *For Home, Country, and Race: Gender, Class, and Englishness in the Elementary School, 1880–1914* (Toronto: University of Toronto Press, 2000), 201.

105. Cromer, *Ancient and Modern Imperialism,* 71.

106. Thompson, "Language of Empire," 169.

107. Cromer, *Ancient and Modern Imperialism,* 29.

108. Caroline Elkins, *Imperial Reckoning: The Untold Story of Britain's Gulag in Kenya* (New York: Henry Holt, 2005).

109. David Anderson, *Histories of the Hanged: Britain's Dirty War in Kenya at the End of Empire* (London: Weidenfeld and Nicolson, 2005), 7. See also Kostal, *Jurisprudence of Power,* 469; Kathryn Tidrick, *Empire and the English Character* (London: I. B. Tauris, 1990), 2; and Jennifer Pitts, *A Turn to Empire: The Rise of Imperial Liberalism in Britain and France* (Princeton, NJ: Princeton University Press, 2005), 123.

110. Quoted in Colaiaco, *James Fitzjames Stephen,* 114–15.

111. Lecky, *Historical and Political Essays,* 67. Dicey added in 1900 that "I am more and more convinced that to spread English ideas of law & justice is the one vocation of the English people as it will probably be our one permanent achievement." Dicey to Holmes, 3 April 1900, Volume 42, Folder 5, Holmes papers.

112. A. P. Thornton, "The Shaping of Imperial History," in Robin Winks, ed., *Historiography, The Oxford History of the British Empire,* 5 vols. (New York: Oxford University Press, 1998–99), V: 623.

113. Elkins, *Imperial Reckoning,* 5–7.

114. Ward, "Transcending the Nation," 47.

6. Constitutional History and the Anglo-American Connection

1. Actually, it is just chapter 2 of the first volume that is titled "The Swarming of the English," but there are only two chapters in the volume and this one comprises 90 percent of it. Woodrow Wilson, *History of the American People*, 2 vols. (New York: Harper and Brothers, 1902), I: 34–350.

2. James K. Hosmer, *A Short History of Anglo-Saxon Freedom: The Polity of the English-Speaking Race* (New York: Scribner's and Sons, 1890).

3. John Spencer Clark, *The Life and Letters of John Fiske*, 2 vols. (Boston: Houghton Mifflin, 1917), 2: 493–503.

4. Harvey Wish, *The American Historian: A Social-Intellectual History of the Writing of the American Past* (New York: Oxford University Press, 1960), 110–11.

5. Firth to Rhodes, 16 August 1895, Box 1, James Ford Rhodes Papers, Massachusetts Historical Society, Boston.

6. Firth to Rhodes, 28 January 1899, Box 2, Rhodes papers.

7. Leslie Stephen, ed., *Letters of John Richard Green* (London: Macmillan, 1901).

8. Rhodes to Firth, 17 November 1901, Box 2, Rhodes papers.

9. Robert Seager II, *Alfred Thayer Mahan: The Man and His Letters* (Annapolis, MD: Naval Institute Press, 1977), 68–69.

10. Ibid., 293, 297.

11. Charles A. Beard, *The Office of Justice of the Peace in England in Its Origin and Development* (New York: Burt Franklin, 1904).

12. Mellen Chamberlain, *The Constitutional Relations of the American Colonies to the English Government at the Commencement of the American Revolution*. Paper read to the American Historical Association, 23 May 1887 (New York: Knickerbocker Press, 1888).

13. Charles McLean Andrews to his mother, 9 June 1891, Series I, Box 3, Folder 42, Charles McLean Andrews papers, Sterling Library, Yale University, New Haven, CT.

14. Andrews to his mother, 20 June 1893, Series I, Box 4, Folder 53, Andrews papers.

15. Charles McLean Andrews, *Guide for the Manuscript Materials for the History of the United States to 1783, in the British Museum, in Minor London Archives, and in the Libraries of Oxford and Cambridge* (Washington, DC: Carnegie Institution, 1908); and *Guide to the Materials for American History, to 1783, in the Public Record Office of Great Britain*, 2 vols. (Washington, DC: Carnegie Institution, 1912–14).

16. George Louis Beer, *British Colonial Policy, 1754–1765* (London: Macmillan, 1907), 316.

17. Charles McLean Andrews, *The Colonial Period* (New York: Henry Holt and Co., 1912), 251–52.

18. Turner to Becker, 25 March 1909, Box 7, Carl Becker papers, Carl A. Kroch Library, Cornell University, Ithaca, NY.

19. Herbert Osgood, "Review of George Otto Trevelyan, *The American Revolution*," *Political Science Quarterly* 19 (September 1904), 505; George Otto Trevelyan, *The American Revolution*, 4 vols. (New York: Longmans, Green, 1899–1913).

20. George Macaulay Trevelyan, *Sir George Otto Trevelyan: A Memoir* (London: Longmans, Green, 1932), 140.

21. W. E. H. Lecky, *The American Revolution, 1763–1783: Being the Chapters and Passages Relating to America from the Author's History of England in the Eighteenth Century*, ed. James Albert Woodburn (New York: Appleton, 1924 [1898]), 348.

22. Donal McCartney, *W. E. H. Lecky: Historian and Politician, 1838–1903* (Dublin: Lilliput Press, 1994), 88–89.

23. Lecky, *American Revolution*.

24. George Burton Adams to John Franklin Jameson, 27 February 1900, Box 45, File 15, John Franklin Jameson papers, Manuscripts Division, Library of Congress, Washington, DC; George Burton Adams, "Anglo-Saxon Feudalism," *American Historical Review* 7 (October 1901), 11–35.

25. Reginald E. Rabb, "George Burton Adams," in Herman Ausubel, J. Bartlett Brebner, and Ealing M. Hunt, eds., *Some Modern Historians of Britain: Essays in Honor of R. L. Schuyler* (New York: Dryden Press, 1951), 177–91.

26. William Hunt to George Burton Adams, 24 November 1901, Box 5, Folder 25, George Burton Adams papers, Sterling Library, Yale University, New Haven, CT.

27. George Burton Adams to Hugh Egerton, 26 June 1898, Box 1, Folder 5, George Burton Adams papers.

28. George Burton Adams to Egerton, 15 October 1900, Box 1, Folder 5, George Burton Adams papers.

29. Hunt to George Burton Adams, 4 January 1911, Box 5, Folder 25, George Burton Adams papers.

30. Peter Novick, *That Noble Dream: The "Objectivity Question" and the American Historical Profession* (Cambridge: Cambridge University Press, 1988).

31. George Burton Adams to Jameson, 9 April 1900, Box 45, File 15, Jameson papers.

32. John Higham, *History: Professional Scholarship in America* (Baltimore: Johns Hopkins University Press, 1983 [1965]), 23.

33. Box 54, Files 103, 104, 105, Jameson papers.

34. Andrews to Jameson, 14 June 1906, Box 54, File 103, Jameson papers.

35. Andrews, *Manuscript Materials*.

36. Andrews, *Materials for American History*.

37. Andrews to Hastings Ells, 5 March 1926, quoted in A. S. Eisenstadt, *Charles McLean Andrews* (New York: Columbia University Press, 1956), 73.

38. Andrews to his mother, 29 August 1893, Box 5, Folder 55, Andrews papers.

39. Andrews to his mother, 5 September 1893, Box 5, Folder 56, Andrews papers.

40. Andrews to his mother, 11 July 1893, Box 4, Folder 54, Andrews papers.

41. Hubert Hall to George Burton Adams, 21 April 1903, Box 4, Folder 20, George Burton Adams papers.

42. Andrews to Jameson, 20 August 1909, Box 54, File 104, Jameson papers.

43. "Memorial to the Late Professor Frederic William Maitland," Box 111, File 1095, Jameson papers.

44. Andrews to T. F. Tout, 21 January 1899, 1/26/1, T. F. Tout papers, Manchester University of Manchester Library, Manchester.

45. Paul Vinogradoff to George Burton Adams, 23 March 1907, Box 4, Folder 20, George Burton Adams papers.

46. George Prothero to Jameson, 17 August 1910, Box 120, File 1368, Jameson papers.

47. Andrews to Jameson, 16 November 1913, Box 54, File 105, Jameson papers.

48. Margaret Marion Spector, "A. P. Newton," in Herman Ausubel, J. Bartlett Brebner, and Ealing M. Hunt, eds., *Some Historians of Modern Britain: Essays in Honor of R. L. Schuyler* (New York: Dryden Press, 1951), 286–305.

49. Round to George Burton Adams, 12 January 1909, Box 6, Folder 30, George Burton Adams papers.

50. Jameson to James Bryce, 17 April 1907, in Elizabeth Donnan and Leo F. Stock, eds., *A Historian's World: Selections from the Correspondence of John Franklin Jameson* (Philadelphia: American Philosophical Society), 105–6. As late as 1917 Bryce wrote that a primary cause of Anglo-American tension was "the misrepresentations in the school books." Bryce to Eliot, 19 September 1917, Eliot papers.

51. John Franklin Jameson, "The International Congress of Historical Studies, Held at London," *American Historical Review* 18 (July 1913), 687.

52. See *British-American Peace Centenary Secretary's Report of the Visit to the United States of the British Delegation May 1913* (privately printed, 1913), Misc., Box 3, File on the American Peace Centenary Committee, William A. Dunning papers, Butler Library, Columbia University, New York, NY.

53. William A. Dunning, *The British Empire and the United States: A Review of Their Relations during the Century of Peace Following the Treaty of Ghent* (New York: Scribner's, 1914).

54. James A. Stevens to Dunning, 26 February and 3 June 1914, Box 2, Dunning papers.

55. Dunning, *British Empire and the United States,* 362.

56. Clarence M. Warner to Dunning, 22 December 1914, Box 2, Dunning papers.

57. Bryce to Dunning, 23 December 1914, Box 2, Dunning papers.

58. George Burton Adams, *Why Americans Dislike England* (Philadelphia: Henry Altemus, 1896), 31.

59. Frank Maloy Anderson to George Burton Adams, 10 January 1898, Box 1, Folder 5, George Burton Adams papers.

60. George Burton Adams, "A Century of Anglo-Saxon Expansion," *Atlantic Monthly* 79 (April 1897), 538.

61. See, for example, George Burton Adams, "British Imperial Federation after the War," *Yale Review* 5 (April 1916), 687–701.

62. Grace A. Cockcroft, "George Louis Beer," in Herman Ausubel, J. Bartlett Brebner, and Ealing M. Hunt, eds., *Some Historians of Modern Britain: Essays in Honor of R. L. Schuyler* (New York: Dryden Press, 1951), 269–85.

63. New York: Macmillan, 1917.

64. Kate F. Kimball to Herbert Baxter Adams, 28 February 1889 and 14 December 1891, Ms. 4, Box 10, Herbert Baxter Adams papers, Milton S. Eisenhower Library, Johns Hopkins University, Baltimore, MD.

65. Herbert Baxter Adams to Daniel Coit Gilman, n.d. (partial letter), Ms. 1, Daniel Coit Gilman papers, Milton S. Eisenhower Library, Johns Hopkins University, Baltimore, MD.

66. George E. Vincent to H. B. Adams, 21 December 1891, MS. 4, Box 16, Herbert Baxter Adams papers.

67. George B. Hodges to Herbert Baxter Adams, 18 April and 20 June 1899, Ms. 4, Box 8, Herbert Baxter Adams papers.

68. George B. Hodges to C. W. Somerville, 1 May 1900, and C. W. Somerville to George B. Hodges, 4 May 1900, Ms. 4, Box 8, Herbert Baxter Adams papers.

69. Arnold Haultain, *A Selection from Goldwin Smith's Correspondence: Comprising*

Letters Chiefly to and from His English Friends, Written between the Years 1846 and 1910, collected by his literary executor, Arnold Haultain (London: T. W. Laurie, n.d. [1913?]), 300.

70. Goldwin Smith, *The United States: An Outline of Political History, 1492–1871* (New York: Macmillan, 1893).

71. Homer B. Sprague to Goldwin Smith, n.d. [1893], Goldwin Smith papers.

72. Julian Ralph, "Anglo-Saxon Affinities," *Harper's New Monthly Magazine* 98 (1899), 390–91.

73. Adams, *Why Americans Dislike England*, 13.

74. Andrew McLaughlin to Herbert Baxter Adams, 27 March 1897, Box 1, Andrew C. McLaughlin papers, Michigan Historical Collection, University of Michigan, Ann Arbor, MI.

75. Draft Report of the AHA Committee of Seven, 61–3, Ms. 4, Box 59, Herbert Baxter Adams papers.

76. Anon., "The Annual Meeting of the American Historical Association," *American Historical Review* 3 (April 1898), 412.

77. Draft Report of the AHA Committee of Seven, 61–3, Ms. 4, Box 59, Herbert Baxter Adams papers.

78. Anon., *The Study of History in Schools: Report to the American Historical Association by the Committee of Seven* (New York: Macmillan, 1904), 34–35.

79. Anon., *The Study of History in Secondary Schools: Report to the American Historical Association by the Committee of Five* (New York: Macmillan, 1911), 64.

80. Charles Homer Haskins, *The Normans in European History* (Boston: Houghton Mifflin, 1915); and *Norman Institutions* (Cambridge, MA: Harvard University Press, 1918).

81. Haskins, *Normans in European History*, 113.

82. T. F. Tout to Charles Homer Haskins, 30 March 1918, Box 12, Charles Homer Haskins papers, Firestone Library, Princeton University, Princeton, NJ.

83. Haskins to Pres. Woodward of the Carnegie Institution, 2 March 1908, Box 2, Haskins papers.

84. F. M. Powicke, "Review of Charles Homer Haskins, *Studies in the History of Mediaeval Science*," *English Historical Review* 40 (July 1925), 422.

85. The Haskins Society, http://www.haskins.cornell.edu. Accessed 22 October 2004.

86. George Burton Adams to Haskins, 29 October 1905, Box 1, Haskins papers.

87. George Burton Adams, *History of England from the Norman Conquest to the Death of John, 1066–1216* (London: Longmans, Green, 1905), 1067.

88. Joseph Ellis, "The Big Man: History vs. Alexander Hamilton," *New Yorker* (29 October 2001), 76–84.

89. Andrew C. McLaughlin, *A History of the United States for Schools* (New York: Appleton, 1899).

90. Claude H. Van Tyne to McLaughlin, 17 June 1899, Box 1, McLaughlin papers.

91. McLaughlin to Van Tyne, March 1903, Box 1, Claude H. Van Tyne papers, Michigan Historical Collections, University of Michigan, Ann Arbor, MI.

92. Charles McLean Andrews, *A Short History of England* (Boston: Allyn and Bacon, 1912), 62, 70, 344.

93. John David Smith, "James Ford Rhodes, Woodrow Wilson, and the Passing of the Amateur Historians of Slavery," *Mid-America* 64 (Oct. 1982), 24.

94. David W. Blight, *Race and Reunion: The Civil War in American History* (Cambridge, MA: Harvard University Press, 2001), 358, 387–93.

95. Notes for Lectures, Colonial, Vol. I, Box 1, McLaughlin papers.

96. Bentley 75/6/6, Box 12, Arthur Lyon Cross papers, Michigan Historical Collection, University of Michigan, Ann Arbor.

97. Arthur Lyon Cross, *A History of England and Greater Britain* (New York: Macmillan, 1914). English constitutional history textbooks by Americans included Albert B. White, *The Making of the English Constitution, 449–1485* (New York: G. P. Putnam's Sons, 1908); and George Burton Adams, *Constitutional History of England* (New York: Henry Holt, 1921); an American version of Stubbs's *Select Charters* was produced by George Burton Adams and H. M. Stephens, eds., *Select Documents of English Constitutional History* (New York: Macmillan, 1901); and a comprehensive guide was produced by Charles Gross, *The Sources and Literature of English History from the Earliest Times to about 1485* (New York: Longmans, Green, 1900).

98. Sinclair Kennedy, *The Pan-Angles: A Consideration of the Federation of the Seven English-Speaking Nations* (London: Longmans, Green, 1914), 235.

99. Van Tyne to James H. Hyde, 11 January 1915, Box 1, Van Tyne papers.

100. Ford Madox Ford to Cross, 75/5/2, Box 2, Cross papers.

101. Frederick A. Middlebush to Cross, 29 March 1917, 75/5/2, Box 2, Cross papers.

102. McLaughlin to Cross, 16 February 1915, 75/5/2, Box 2, Cross papers.

103. Charles Homer Haskins to T. F. Tout, 18 November 1914, 1/497/2, Tout papers.

104. Reginald Lane Poole to Haskins, 20 April 1917, Box 11, Haskins papers.

105. Jameson to Dana C. Munro, 5 January 1920, Box 115, File 1206, Jameson papers.

106. 75/5/6, Box 6, Cross papers.

107. Carl Fish to Cross, 22 May 1917, 75/6/1, Box 7, Cross papers.

108. Edward P. Cheyney to Cross, 2 August 1917, quoted in Novick, *That Noble Dream*, 120.

109. Novick, *That Noble Dream*, 121–28.

110. Harold Josephson, "History for Victory: The National Board for Historical Service," *Mid-America* 52 (1970), 214–16.

111. Ray Allen Billington, "Tempest in Clio's Teapot: The American Historical Association Rebellion of 1915," *American Historical Review* 78 (April 1973), 348–69.

112. John H. Latané to McLaughlin, 30 November 1915, 75/5/2, Box 2, Cross papers.

113. Jameson to Bryce, 6 February 1918, quoted in Leo Francis Stock, "Some Bryce-Jameson Correspondence," *American Historical Review* 50 (January 1945), 274–75.

114. Jameson to Waldo Gifford Leland, 17 July 1917, quoted in Morey Rothberg and Jacqueline Goggin, eds., *John Franklin Jameson and the Development of Humanistic Scholarship in America*, 3 vols. (Athens: University of Georgia Press, 1993–2001), III: 172–73.

115. Frank Maloy Anderson to George Burton Adams, 25 March 1918, Box 16, Folder 238, George Burton Adams papers.

116. Jameson to George Burton Adams, 3 May 1917, Box 45, File 15, Jameson papers.

117. Clipping from *Pomona College Quarterly Magazine* (1917), in Box 14, Folder 185, George Burton Adams papers.

118. George Burton Adams to Jameson, 15 December 1914, Box 45, File 15, Jameson papers; Jameson to W. H. Gardiner, 19 December 1917, Box 85, File 593, Jameson papers.

119. Lionel Curtis to George Burton Adams, 9 December 1915, Box 11, Folder 62, George Burton Adams papers.

120. Beer to George Burton Adams, 28 February and 13 March, 1916, Box 11, Folder 62, George Burton Adams papers.

121. Jameson to Charles Firth, 26 March 1918, Box 82, File 537, Jameson papers.

122. Printed program for dinner at University College, London, on Monday, 6 May 1918, Box 115, Jameson papers.

123. McLaughlin, *America and Britain* (New York: E. P. Dutton, 1918), 10.

124. McLaughlin to Jameson, 11 May and 31 May 1918, Box 115, Jameson papers.

125. McLaughlin to Jameson, 13 July 1918, Box 115, File 1206, Jameson Papers.

126. Goldwin Smith to John Tyndall, 6 October 1882, Goldwin Smith papers.

127. Paul T. Phillips, *The Controversialist: An Intellectual Life of Goldwin Smith* (Westport, CT: Praeger, 2002), 116–19.

128. Richard H. Heindel, *The American Impact on Great Britain, 1898–1914: A Study of the United States in World History* (Philadelphia: University of Pennsylvania Press, 1940), 38.

129. Ibid., 39.

130. Clare A. Simmons, *Reversing the Conquest: History and Myth in Nineteenth-Century Literature* (New Brunswick, NJ: Rutgers University Press, 1990), 189.

131. Bradford Perkins, *The Great Rapprochement: England and the United States, 1895–1914* (New York: Atheneum, 1968), 149–50.

132. Alex May, "Wrench, Sir (John) Evelyn Leslie (1882–1966)," in *Oxford Dictionary of National Biography* (Oxford: Oxford University Press, 2004). Accessed 11 November 2004: http://www.oxforddnb.com/view/article/37031.

133. Evelyn Wrench, "Recollections of Early Life and Foundation of the English-Speaking Union," *Concord* 1 (November 1962), 5.

134. Ibid.

135. Central Committee Meeting Minutes, 8 January 1920, English-Speaking Union papers, Dartmouth House, London.

136. Eighth Annual Report, 1925–26, English-Speaking Union papers.

7. Constitutional History and America's Culture Wars

1. William Roger Louis, "The United States and the African Peace Settlement of 1919: The Pilgrimage of George Louis Beer," *Journal of African History* 4 (1963), 413–33.

2. Reginald Lane Poole to George Burton Adams, 5 December 1917, Box 11, Folder 61, George Burton Adams papers, Sterling Library, Yale University, New Haven, CT.

3. Isaiah Bowman, *The New World* (Yonkers-on-Hudson, NY: World Book Co., 1922).

4. James T. Shotwell, *The Faith of an Historian* (New York: Walker and Company, 1964), 214.

5. Neil Smith, "Bowman's New World and the Council on Foreign Relations," *Geographical Review* 76 (October 1986), 438–60.

6. Laurence Shoup and William Minter, *Imperial Brain Trust: The Council on For-*

eign Relations and United States Foreign Policy (New York: Authors Choice Press, 2004 [1977]), 103–6.

7. Carroll Quigley, *The Anglo-American Establishment from Rhodes to Cliveden* (San Diego: GSL Associates, 1981), 248–63.

8. Charles Altschul, *The American Revolution in Our School Text-Books: An Attempt to Trace the Influence of Early School Education in the Feeling toward England in the United States* (New York: George H. Doran, 1917).

9. Claude H. Van Tyne, "Review of Altschul, *The American Revolution in Our School Text-Books,*" *American Historical Review* 23 (January 1918), 404.

10. Jonathan Zimmerman, *Whose America? Culture Wars in the Public Schools* (Cambridge, MA: Harvard University Press, 2002), 26.

11. Gary B. Nash, Charlotte Crabtree, and Ross E. Dunn, *History on Trial: Culture Wars and the Teaching of the Past* (New York: Knopf, 1997), 25–32.

12. Claude H. Van Tyne, *Democracy's Education Problem* (New York: National Security League, 1918), 4–5.

13. David Saville Muzzey, *An American History* (Boston: Ginn and Co., 1923), 116.

14. Nash, Crabtree, and Dunn, *History on Trial,* 30.

15. David Saville Muzzey to Claude H. Van Tyne, 26 October 1927, Box 2, Claude H. Van Tyne papers, Michigan Historical Collection, University of Michigan, Ann Arbor, MI.

16. Chauncey Samuel Boucher to Van Tyne, 28 November 1927, Box 2, Van Tyne papers.

17. James T. Shotwell to Van Tyne, 15 January 1927, Box 2, Van Tyne papers.

18. Charles Grant Miller, *The Poisoned Loving-Cup: United States School Histories Falsified Through Pro-British Propaganda in Sweet Name of Amity* (Chicago: National Historical Society, 1928), 111.

19. Ibid., 197.

20. Ibid., 119–20.

21. Conflicts over school history texts continued in ensuing decades, though rarely with the fireworks of the 1920s. As late as 1966, a joint committee of the AHA and the Historical Association deplored the national biases in both countries' textbook treatment of the other's history. Committee on National Bias in Anglo-American History Textbooks, *The Historian's Contribution to Anglo-American Misunderstanding* (London: Routledge and Kegan Paul, 1966).

22. John Franklin Jameson to Charles Firth, 19 March 1919, Box 82, File 537, John Franklin Jameson papers, Manuscripts Division, Library of Congress, Washington, DC.

23. Morey Rothberg, "John Franklin Jameson and the International Historical Community," *History Teacher* 26 (August 1993), 454–55.

24. Ibid., 454.

25. Carl Russell Fish to T. F. Tout, 13 January 1923, 1/369/1, T. F. Tout papers, University of Manchester Library, Manchester. Fish concluded his 1919 book, *The Path of Empire,* with a spirited call for the United States to take up a vigorous new international role. Carl Russell Fish, *The Path of Empire: A Chronicle of the United States as a World Power* (New Haven, CT: Yale University Press, 1919), 286–88.

26. Jameson to Tout, 13 December 1923, 1/582/3, Tout papers.

27. *American Historical Review* 30 (October 1924), 190.

28. "Random Recollections," Box 6, Bentley 75/5/6, Arthur Lyon Cross papers, Michigan Historical Collection, University of Michigan, Ann Arbor, MI.

29. Anon, "Obituary," *Manchester Guardian,* 24 October 1929.

30. Charles Homer Haskins to Tout, 31 March 1928, Box 12, Charles Homer Haskins papers, Firestone Library, Princeton University, Princeton, NJ.

31. R. L. Poole to Tout, 8 December 1925, 1/953/106, Tout papers.

32. James Bryce, *The Study of American History* (New York: Macmillan, 1922), 21–22.

33. Ibid., 90–91.

34. Evelyn Wrench to Robert Wilberforce, 15 March 1927, Box 2, Van Tyne papers.

35. Claude H. Van Tyne, *England and America: Rivals in the American Revolution* (New York: Macmillan, 1927), 1–28.

36. George Peabody Gooch to Van Tyne, 11 August 1927, Box 2, Van Tyne papers.

37. George Haven Putnam to Van Tyne, 11 May 1927, Box 2, Van Tyne papers.

38. Robert M. McElroy, *Economic History of the United States, Presented in Outline* (New York: Putnam, 1927).

39. Putnam to Van Tyne, 12 January 1927, Box 2, Van Tyne papers.

40. Edith Scott to Van Tyne, 4 November 1927; Marie A. Morris to Van Tyne, 7 November 1927, Box 2, Van Tyne papers.

41. Van Tyne, *England and America,* 90–118.

42. Albert Bushnell Hart to Van Tyne, 12 September 1927, Box 2, Van Tyne papers.

43. W. T. Root to Van Tyne, 25 November 1927, Box 2, Van Tyne papers.

44. Viscount Lee of Fareham to Van Tyne, 15 November 1927, Box 2, Van Tyne papers.

45. Poole to George Burton Adams, 14 June 1918, Box 4, Folder 20, George Burton Adams papers.

46. Charles Homer Haskins, *The Rise of Universities* (New York: Holt, 1923); and *The Renaissance of the Twelfth Century* (Cambridge, MA: Harvard University Press, 1927).

47. Charles Howard McIlwain, *The High Court of Parliament and Its Supremacy: An Historical Essay on the Boundaries between Legislation and Adjudication in England* (New Haven, CT: Yale University Press, 1910), *passim.*

48. Charles Howard McIlwain, *The American Revolution: A Constitutional Interpretation* (New York: Macmillan, 1923), 1.

49. Arthur Meier Schlesinger, *The Colonial Merchants and the American Revolution, 1763–1776* (New York: Columbia University Press, 1918).

50. Arthur Meier Schlesinger, *New Viewpoints in American History* (New York: Macmillan, 1922).

51. John Franklin Jameson, *The American Revolution Considered as a Social Movement* (Princeton, NJ: Princeton University Press, 1926), 18.

52. Frederick B. Tolles, "The American Revolution Considered as a Social Movement: A Re-Evaluation," *American Historical Review* 60 (October 1954), 1.

53. Jack P. Greene, "The Flight from Determinism: A Review of Recent Literature on the Coming of the American Revolution," *South Atlantic Quarterly* 61 (Spring 1962), 235.

54. John Higham, *History: Professional Scholarship in America* (Baltimore: Johns Hopkins University Press, 1983 [1965]).

55. Morey Rothberg, "John Franklin Jameson and the Creation of *The American Revolution Considered as a Social Movement*," in Ronald Hoffman and Peter J. Albert, eds., *The Transforming Hand of Revolution: Reconsidering the American Revolution as a Social Movement* (Charlottesville: University Press of Virginia Press, 1996), 16.

56. Ibid., 7.

57. Quoted in Ellen Fitzpatrick, *History's Memory: Writing America's Past, 1880–1980* (Cambridge, MA: Harvard University Press, 2002), 19.

58. Ibid., 27.

59. Leo Francis Stock, "Some Bryce-Jameson Correspondence," *American Historical Review* 50 (January 1945), 261–98.

60. Anon., *Essays in Colonial History Presented to Charles McLean Andrews by His Students* (New Haven, CT: Yale University Press, 1931).

61. Charles McLean Andrews to Jameson, 24 May 1931, quoted in Rothberg, *John Franklin Jameson*, vol. 3, 401.

62. Charles McLean Andrews, *The Colonial Background of the American Revolution* (New Haven, CT: Yale University Press, 1924).

63. Charles McLean Andrews, *The Colonial Period in American History*, 4 vols. (New Haven, CT: Yale University Press, 1934–38).

64. Lawrence H. Gipson, *The British Empire before the American Revolution*, 15 vols. (Caldwell: Caxton Printers, 1936–70).

65. Andrew C. McLaughlin, *A Constitutional History of the United States* (New York: Appleton-Century-Crofts, 1935), 21. This was the general tenor of studies of Franklin during the period. See Verner W. Crane, "Certain Writings of Benjamin Franklin on the British Empire," *The Papers of the Bibliographical Society of America* 28 (1934), 1–27. Also see the same author's *Benjamin Franklin, Englishman and American* (Baltimore: Williams and Wilkins, 1936).

66. For the struggles over naval policies, see Phillips Payson O'Brien, *British and American Naval Power, 1900–1936* (Westport, CT: Praeger, 1998).

67. Charles Peters, *Five Days in Philadelphia: The Amazing "We Want Willkie!" Convention of 1940 and How It Freed FDR to Save the Western World* (New York: Public Affairs, 2005).

68. Clarence K. Streit, *Union Now With Britain* (New York: Harper and Brothers, 1941). In his 1939 book, *Union Now*, Streit had called for federal union with other European democracies as well.

69. "The Case for Union," *Time*, 17 March 1941.

70. James C. Bennett, *The Anglosphere Challenge: Why the English-Speaking Nations Will Lead the Way in the Twenty-first Century* (Lanham, MD: Rowman and Littlefield, 2004).

71. Gilbert Allardyce, "The Rise and Fall of the Western Civilization Course," *American Historical Review* 87 (June 1982), 695–725. Allardyce's emphasis on the patriotic origins of the course have been challenged by Daniel A. Segal in "'Western Civ' and the Staging of History in American Higher Education," *American Historical Review* 105 (June 2000), 770–805.

72. Robert Livingston Schuyler, "The Historical Spirit Incarnate: Frederic William Maitland," *American Historical Review* 57 (January 1952), 303–22.

73. For an example of a recent lively constitutional history discussion in an *Ameri-*

can Historical Review forum, see Alan Brinkley, Laura Kalman, William E. Leuchtenburg, and G. Edward White, "The Debate over the Constitutional Revolution of 1937," *American Historical Review* 110 (October 2005), 1046–115.

74. Paul L. Murphy, "Time to Reclaim: The Current Challenge of American Constitutional History," *American Historical Review* 69 (October 1963), 64.

75. Ibid., 69.

76. Allan Kulikoff, "The Founding Fathers: Best Sellers! TV Stars! Punctual Plumbers!" *Journal of the Historical Society* 5 (Spring 2005), 155–87.

77. For a discussion of the wide range of historical issues in contemporary culture wars, see Nash, Crabtree, and Dunn, *History on Trial.*

8. Constitutional History and the History Women

1. Jane Austen, *Northanger Abbey* (1803).

2. Joan W. Scott, *Gender and the Politics of History* (New York: Columbia University Press, 1999 [1988]), 179.

3. Anne McLaren, "Gender, Religion, and Early Modern Nationalism: Elizabeth I, Mary Queen of Scots, and the Genesis of English Anti-Catholicism," *American Historical Review* 107 (June 2002), 745.

4. Gerda Lerner, *Why History Matters: Life and Thought* (New York: Oxford University Press, 1997), 52–53.

5. Pat Thane, "The British National State and the Construction of National Identities," in Billie Melman, ed., *Borderlines: Genders and Identities in War and Peace, 1870–1930* (London: Routledge, 1998), 35–36.

6. Christina Crosby, *The Ends of History: Victorians and "The Woman Question"* (New York: Routledge, 1991), 1.

7. Anne McClintock, "'No Longer in a Future Heaven': Women and Nationalism in South Africa," *Transition* 51 (1991), 105.

8. Raphael Samuel, "Continuous National History," in Raphael Samuel, ed., *Patriotism: The Making and Unmaking of British National Identity,* 3 vols. (New York: Routledge, 1989), I: 11.

9. Scott, *Gender and the Politics of History,* 2.

10. Joan W. Scott, "Gender: A Useful Category of Historical Analysis," *American Historical Review* 91 (December 1986), 1075.

11. Robert C. K. Ensor to Alfred E. Zimmern, 30 May 1902, Alfred E. Zimmern papers, Bodleian Library, Oxford.

12. Rohan Amanda Maitzen, *Gender, Genre, and Victorian Historical Writing* (New York: Garland, 1998), 34, 37.

13. Judith M. Bennett, "Writing Fornication: Medieval Leyrwite and Its Historians," *Transactions of the Royal Historical Society,* Sixth Series 13 (2003), 131–62. Quotations in this paragraph are from this article at 139, 153.

14. Joel T. Rosenthal, "Time to Share the Narrative: Late Medieval Women in Recent and Diverse Scholarship," *Journal of British Studies* 43 (October 2004), 506–13.

15. Maitzen, *Gender, Genre, and Victorian Historical Writing,* 41.

16. D. R. Woolf, "A Feminist Past? Gender, Genre, and Historical Knowledge in England, 1500–1800," *American Historical Review* 102 (June 1997), 678.

17. Rosemary Mitchell, "'The Busy Daughters of Clio': Women Writers of History from 1820 to 1880," *Women's History Review* 7 (1998), 108.

18. Devoney Looser, *British Women Writers and the Writing of History, 1670–1820* (Baltimore: Johns Hopkins University Press, 2000), 5.

19. Mitchell. "'Busy Daughters of Clio,'" 123.

20. The women scholars were Eleanor Lodge, Nellie Neilson, Ada Levett, Helen Cam, and Bertha Haven Putnam.

21. Maxine Berg, *A Woman in History: Eileen Power, 1889–1940* (Cambridge: Cambridge University Press, 1996), 1.

22. Bonnie G. Smith, "The Contribution of Women to Modern Historiography in Great Britain, France and the United States, 1750–1940," *American Historical Review* 89 (June 1984), 723.

23. Carol Dyhouse, *No Distinction of Sex? Women in British Universities, 1870–1939* (London: University College London Press, 1995), 134–35.

24. V. H. Galbraith to Frank Stenton, n.d. 1931, Frank and Doris Stenton papers, University of Reading Library, Reading; emphasis in the original.

25. F. J. C. Hearnshaw to Frank Stenton, 9 May 1931, Stenton papers.

26. A. F. Pollard to his parents, 9 March 1909, Box 3, A. F. Pollard papers, University of London Library, London.

27. Eileen Power to Veit Valentin, 6 July 1938, Add. Mss. 9355, Eileen Power papers, Cambridge University Library, Cambridge.

28. Christine L. Krueger, "Why She Lived at the PRO: Mary Anne Everett Green and the Profession of History," *Journal of British Studies* 42 (January 2003), 67.

29. Martha Vicinus, *Independent Women: Work and Community for Single Women, 1850–1920* (London: Virago, 1985), 133.

30. Barbara Hanawalt, "Golden Ages for the History of Medieval English Women," in Susan Stuard, ed., *Women in Medieval History and Historiography* (Philadelphia: University of Pennsylvania Press, 1987), 12.

31. Joan Thirsk, "The History Women," in Mary O'Dowd and Sabine Wishart, eds., *Chattel, Servant or Citizen: Women's Status in Church and State* (Belfast: Institute of Irish Studies, 1995), 10–11.

32. Mary Dockray-Miller, "Mary Bateson (1865–1906): Scholar and Suffragette," in Jane Chance, ed., *Women Medievalists in the Academy* (Madison: University of Wisconsin Press, 2005), 70.

33. T. F. Tout, "Mary Bateson (1865–1906)," in *Twentieth Century DNB 1901–1911* (Oxford: Clarendon Press, 1912), 110.

34. The best example is Mary Bateson, *Medieval England, 1066–1350* (London: Fisher Unwin, 1903). It should be added that this book was reprinted as recently as 1971 and that it attempted to explain topics that now would be included in the area of social history.

35. Frederic William Maitland, "Mary Bateson," in H. A. L. Fisher, ed., *The Collected Papers of Frederic William Maitland,* 3 vols. (Cambridge: Cambridge University Press, 1911), III: 542–43.

36. Frederic Maitland to B. F. Lock, n.d., 1898, Selden Society Archives, Cambridge University Library, Cambridge.

37. Mary Bateson to Maitland, 26 October 1905, Add. Mss. 7007, Frederic Maitland papers, Cambridge University Library, Cambridge.

38. Maitland obituary, *Solicitors' Journal,* 5 January 1907, Volume 144, copy in the H. A. L. Fisher papers, Bodleian Library, Oxford.

39. Peter Linehan, "The Making of the Cambridge Medieval History," *Speculum* 57 (July 1982), 467.

40. Dockray-Miller, "Mary Bateson," 71.

41. Tout, "Mary Bateson," 110.

42. Dockray-Miller, "Mary Bateson," 77.

43. Tout, "Mary Bateson," 112.

44. Selden Society Minute Book, 29 January 1907, Selden Society Archives.

45. Clarke to J. Goronwy Edwards, 29 March 1930, J. Goronwy Edwards papers, National Library of Wales, Aberystwyth.

46. Jennifer FitzGerald, " 'Persephone Come Back from the Dead': Maude Violet Clarke (1892–1935)," in Jane Chance, ed., *Women Medievalists and the Academy* (Madison: University of Wisconsin Press, 2005), 385.

47. Maude Violet Clarke, *Medieval Representation and Consent: A Study of Early Parliaments in England and Ireland, with Special Reference to the Modus Tenendi Parliamentum* (London: Longmans, Green, 1936).

48. Margaret Hastings to Helen Cam, 14 March 1960, Helen Cam papers, Girton College, Cambridge.

49. Pauline Adams, *Somerville for Women: An Oxford College, 1879–1993* (New York: Oxford University Press, 1996), 189.

50. Student essay, n.d., 1913–15, Maude Violet Clarke papers, Somerville College, Oxford.

51. Tutorial notes, n.d., Clarke papers.

52. Ibid.

53. Ibid.

54. Ibid.

55. Ibid. Emphasis in the original.

56. Helen Cam, *Studies in the Hundred Rolls: Some Aspects of Thirteenth Century Administration* (Oxford: Clarendon Press, 1921); and *The Hundred and the Hundred Rolls: An Outline of Local Government in Medieval England* (London: Methuen, 1930).

57. C. R. Cheney to Cam, 25 January 1966, Cam papers.

58. Lord Denning to Cam, 27 January 1965, Cam papers.

59. C. R. Cheney, "Helen Maud Cam, 1885–1968," *Proceedings of the British Academy* 55 (1969), 307–8.

60. Janet Sondheimer, "In Memoriam Helen Cam, 1885–1968," *Girton Review* (1969), 35.

61. Janet Sondheimer, "Helen Cam," in Edward Shils and Carmen Blacker, eds., *Cambridge Women: Twelve Portraits* (Cambridge: Cambridge University Press, 1996), 100.

62. Lecture Notes, 1931–1947, Cam papers.

63. Ibid.

64. Ibid.

65. Helen Cam, *Law-Finders and Law-Makers in Medieval England: Collected Studies in Legal and Constitutional History* (London: Merlin Press, 1962), 193.

66. Lecture Notes, 1931–1947, Cam papers.

67. Ibid.

68. Quoted in Charles T. Wood, "The Deposition of Edward V," *Traditio* 31 (1975), 286.

69. Cheney, "Helen Maud Cam," 303.

70. Lecture Notes 1931–1947, Cam papers.

71. Helen Cam, "Law as It Looks to a Historian," Founders Lecture, Girton College, 18 February 1956.

72. Sondheimer, "Helen Cam," 103.

73. Patricia R. Orr, "Doris Mary Stenton (1894–1971): The Legal Records and the Historian," in Jane Chance, ed., *Women Medievalists and the Academy* (Madison: University of Wisconsin Press, 2005), 452.

74. Reginald Lane Poole to Doris Stenton, 13 October 1924, Stenton papers.

75. John Horace Round to Doris Stenton, 23 January 1927, Stenton papers.

76. Doris Stenton, *The English Woman in History* (London: Allen & Unwin, 1957).

77. Kathleen Major, "Doris Mary Stenton, 1894–1971," *Proceedings of the British Academy* 58 (1972), 534.

78. Undergraduate Essays 1925–27, Lucy Sutherland papers, Bodleian Library, Oxford.

79. Lecture Notes, 14 November 1934, Sutherland papers.

80. Lewis Namier to Lucy Sutherland, 15 April 1958, Sutherland papers.

81. Namier to Sutherland, 30 June 1958, Sutherland papers.

82. Berg, *Woman in History,* 113.

83. Natalie Zemon Davis, "History's Two Bodies," *American Historical Review* 93 (February 1988), 21–22.

84. Eileen Power, "On Mediaeval History as a Social Study," in N. B. Harte, ed., *The Study of Economic History: Collected Inaugural Lectures, 1893–1970* (London: Frank Cass, 1971), 109–26.

85. Dyhouse, *No Distinction of Sex?,* 146–47.

86. Goldwin Smith to E. L. Godkin, 22 October 1871, Goldwin Smith papers, Carl A. Kroch Library, Cornell University, Ithaca, NY.

87. Julie Des Jardins, *Women and the Historical Enterprise in America: Gender, Race, and the Politics of Memory, 1880–1945* (Chapel Hill: University of North Carolina Press, 2003), 34.

88. Quoted in Bonnie G. Smith, *The Gender of History: Men, Women, and Historical Practice* (Cambridge, MA: Harvard University Press, 1998), 113.

89. Lucy M. Salmon to Herbert Baxter Adams, 30 March 1885, Ms. 4, Box 14, Herbert Baxter Adams papers, Milton S. Eisenhower Library, Johns Hopkins University, Baltimore, MD.

90. Ibid.

91. Salmon to Herbert Baxter Adams, 3 March 1901, Ms. 4, Box 14, Herbert Baxter Adams papers.

92. Des Jardins, *Women and the Historical Enterprise,* 38.

93. Salmon to John Franklin Jameson, 20 July 1895, Box 126, File 1479, John Franklin Jameson papers, Manuscripts Division, Library of Congress, Washington, DC.

94. Lucy Maynard Salmon, review of *William the Silent,* by Ruth Putnam, *American Historical Review* 1 (January 1896), 329–31.

95. Des Jardins, *Women and the Historical Enterprise,* 41.

96. Salmon to Herbert Baxter Adams, 24 October 1900, Ms. 4 Box 14, Herbert Baxter Adams papers.

97. Andrew C. McLaughlin to Herbert Baxter Adams, 7 November 1900, Ms. 4, Box 11, Herbert Baxter Adams papers.

98. Des Jardins, *Women and the Historical Enterprise,* 40.

99. Salmon to Charles Homer Haskins, 29 April 1903, Box 11, Charles Homer Haskins papers, Firestone Library, Princeton University, Princeton, NJ.

100. Des Jardins, *Women and the Historical Enterprise,* 74–75.

101. Smith, *Gender of History,* 206–9.

102. Jacqueline Goggin, "Challenging Sexual Discrimination in the Historical Profession: Women Historians and the American Historical Association, 1890–1940," *American Historical Review* 97 (June 1992), 781.

103. Haskins to Jameson, 26 February 1901, Box 88, File 669, Jameson papers.

104. Des Jardins, *Women and the Historical Enterprise,* 39.

105. Goggin, "Challenging Sexual Discrimination," 780.

106. Bertha Haven Putnam, *The Enforcement of the Statute of Labourers during the First Decade after the Black Death* (New York: Columbia University Press, 1908).

107. David Day, "The Justices' Chronicler: Bertha Haven Putnam (1872–1960)," in Jane Chance, ed., *Women Medievalists in the Academy* (Madison: University of Wisconsin Press, 2005), 157.

108. Margaret Hastings and Elisabeth G. Kimball, "Two Distinguished Medievalists: Nellie Neilson and Bertha Putnam," *Journal of British Studies* 18 (Spring 1979), 144.

109. Anne Reiber DeWindt, "Nellie Neilson (1873–1947): A Historian of 'Wit, Whimsy, and Sheer Poetry,' " in Jane Chance, ed., *Women Medievalists and the Academy* (Madison: University of Wisconsin Press, 2005), 167–68.

110. Nellie Neilson, *Economic Conditions on the Manors of Ramsey Abbey* (Philadelphia: Sherman and Co., 1899).

111. Nellie Neilson, "Boon-Services on the Estates of Ramsey Abbey," *American Historical Review* 2 (January 1897), 213–24.

112. DeWindt, "Nellie Neilson," 174.

113. Hastings and Kimball, "Two Distinguished Medievalists," 146.

114. Bertha Haven Putnam to Jameson, 26 March 1916, and Jameson to Putnam, 27 March 1916, Box 121, File 1377, Jameson papers.

115. Bertha Haven Putnam, *Early Treatises on the Practice of the Justices of the Peace in the Fifteenth and Sixteenth Century* (Oxford: Clarendon Press, 1924).

116. DeWindt, "Nellie Neilson," 174.

117. Des Jardins, *Women and the Historical Enterprise,* 39.

118. Charles McLean Andrews to Jameson, 3 June, 8 July, 31 July, and 23 November 1895, Box 54, File 103, Jameson papers.

119. Consider, for example, his strong recommendation of Louisa R. Loomis to McLaughlin: "I've come across but one or two men who can be compared with her in

insight, scholarship, and industry." Jameson to McLaughlin, 17 April 1903, Box 125, File 1444, Jameson papers.

120. Henry E. Bourne, "The Fiftieth Anniversary Meeting," *American Historical Review* 40 (April 1935), 425.

121. Goggin, "Challenging Sexual Discrimination," 776, 802.

122. Des Jardins, *Women and the Historical Enterprise*, 39.

123. Hastings and Kimball, "Two Distinguished Medievalists," 150.

124. Goggin, "Challenging Sexual Discrimination," 796.

125. Ibid., 799–802.

126. Nellie Neilson, "The Early Pattern of the Common Law," *American Historical Review* 49 (January 1944), 199–211.

127. Ibid., 200.

9. Constitutional History as Lawyers' History and Historians' Law

1. Thomas Erskine Holland to Oliver Wendell Holmes, 1 April 1899, Box 44, File 6, Oliver Wendell Holmes papers, Harvard Law School Library, Cambridge, MA.

2. Robert Bartlett, ed., *History and Historians: Selected Papers of R. W. Southern* (Oxford: Blackwell, 2004), 124.

3. A. L. Smith, "Notes on Maitland," Box 8, 1A, 4/3, A. L. Smith papers, Balliol College Library, Oxford.

4. A. V. Dicey to Sir William Anson, 29 November 1897, Sir William Anson papers, Codrington Library, All Souls College, Oxford.

5. F. H. Lawson, *The Oxford Law School, 1850–1965* (Oxford: Clarendon Press, 1968), 20–21.

6. Quoted in Charles Oman, *On the Writing of History* (London: Methuen, 1939), 228.

7. James Bryce to Edward Freeman, 24 June 1866, James Bryce papers, Bodleian Library, Oxford.

8. Bryce to Dicey, 29 May 1918, Bryce papers.

9. S. F. C. Milsom, "Maitland," *Cambridge Law Journal* 60 (July 2001), 267.

10. Stefan Collini, Donald Winch, and John W. Burrow, *That Noble Science of Politics: A Study in Nineteenth-Century Intellectual History* (Cambridge: Cambridge University Press, 1983), 202.

11. William Stubbs to Freeman, 14 November 1882, Bodl. Ms. Eng. Misc. e. 148, William Stubbs papers, Bodleian Library, Oxford; emphasis in the original.

12. Stefan Collini, *Public Moralists: Political Thought and Intellectual Life in Britain, 1850–1930* (Oxford: Clarendon Press, 1991), 296.

13. Stubbs to Freeman, 27 December 1871, Bodl. Ms. Eng. Misc. e. 148, Stubbs papers.

14. John W. Burrow, *A Liberal Descent: Victorian Historians and the English Past* (Cambridge: Cambridge University Press, 1981), 140.

15. James Campbell, "Stubbs, Maitland, and Constitutional History," in Benedikt Stuchtey and Peter Wende, eds., *British and German Historiography, 1750-1950: Traditions, Perceptions, and Transfers* (London: Oxford University Press, 2000), 111.

16. Burrow, *Liberal Descent*, 133.

17. Stephen Bann, *The Inventions of History: Essays on the Representation of the Past* (Manchester: Manchester University Press, 1990), 25.

18. William Holden Hutton, ed., *Letters of William Stubbs: Bishop of Oxford, 1825–1901* (London: Constable, 1904), 67.

19. Freeman to Bryce, 24 August 1873, Bryce papers.

20. Edward Augustus Freeman, *The Growth of the English Constitution from the Earliest Times* (New York: Frederick A. Stokes Co., 1890 [1872]), 168.

21. T. F. Tout to John Horace Round, 21 March 1912, Volume 683, John Horace Round papers, University of London Library, London.

22. Round to George Burton Adams, 26 February 1916, Box 30, Folder 6, George Burton Adams papers, Sterling Library, Yale University, New Haven, CT.

23. Dicey to Freeman, 18 March 1884, Edward A. Freeman papers, John Rylands Library, Manchester.

24. Albert Venn Dicey, "Digby on the History of English Law," *The Nation* (9 December 1875), 581.

25. Dicey to Bryce, 14 June 1916, Bryce papers. In the United States, similar attitudes were present. James Barr Ames, dean of the Harvard Law School from 1895 to 1910 and a scholar who made his reputation as a legal historian, wrote in 1887: "My new course in Legal History will be very crude this year. If I get anything into shape I sh'ld be glad to give you the benefit of it. I doubt however if I shall have time to do more than talk from scattered notes upon a few topics of early law & equity." James Barr Ames to Holmes, 30 January 1887, Box 37, Holmes papers.

26. Dicey to James Bradley Thayer, 28 March 1899, Box 17, File 3, James Bradley Thayer papers, Harvard Law School Library, Cambridge, MA.

27. A. V. Dicey, "History and Politics," General Manuscripts 192, Glasgow University Library, Glasgow; Richard A. Cosgrove, *The Rule of Law: Albert Venn Dicey, Victorian Jurist* (Chapel Hill: University of North Carolina Press, 1980), 170–94.

28. Dicey to Bryce, 11 January 1900, in R. S. Rait, ed., *Memorials of Albert Venn Dicey: Being Chiefly Letters and Diaries* (London: Macmillan, 1925), 181.

29. Dicey to W. E. H. Lecky, 5 March 1887, TCD MS 421, W. E. H. Lecky papers, Trinity College, Dublin.

30. Albert Venn Dicey, "History," *Working Men's College Journal* 6 (March 1900), 194.

31. Dicey to Lecky, 15 October 1890, TCD MS 614, Lecky papers.

32. Dicey to Anson, 16 November 1892, Anson papers.

33. Dicey to Bryce, 24 November 1897, Bryce papers.

34. Dicey to Mrs. Maitland, 25 September 1908, Add. Mss. 7006, Frederic Maitland papers, Cambridge University Library, Cambridge.

35. Dicey to Bryce, 23 December 1906, Bryce papers.

36. Harold Laski to Max Lerner, 29 October 1941, Max Lerner papers, Sterling Library, Yale University, New Haven, CT.

37. Sir Frederick Pollock, *Principles of Contract*, 4th ed. (London: Stevens & Sons, 1885), 6.

38. Jonathan Rose, "Doctrinal Development: Legal History, Law, and Legal Theory," *Oxford Journal of Legal Studies* 22 (Summer 2002), 338.

39. Sir Frederick Pollock, *Essays in Jurisprudence and Ethics* (London: Macmillan, 1882), 201.

40. Sir Frederick Pollock, *Oxford Lectures and Other Discussions* (London: Macmillan, 1890), 45.

41. Sir William R. Anson, *The Law and Custom of the Constitution,* 3 vols. (Oxford: Clarendon Press, 1886), I: ix.

42. Holland to Anson, 24 May 1898, Anson papers.

43. Piet B. M. Blaas, *Continuity and Anachronism: Parliamentary and Constitutional Development in Whig Historiography and in the Anti-Whig Reaction between 1890 and 1930* (The Hague: Martinus Nijhoff, 1978), 253.

44. John Phillip Reid, *The Ancient Constitution and the Origins of Anglo-American Liberty* (DeKalb: Northern Illinois University Press, 2005), 4.

45. Peter R. H. Slee, *Learning and Liberal Education: The Study of Modern History in the Universities of Oxford, Cambridge, and Manchester, 1800–1914* (Manchester: Manchester University Press, 1986), 58.

46. S. F. C. Milsom, *Historical Foundations of the Common Law* (London: Butterworth's, 1969), ix.

47. "Constitutional History," n.d., Maude Violet Clarke papers, Somerville College, Oxford.

48. S. F. C. Milsom, *A Natural History of the Common Law* (New York: Columbia University Press, 2003), xx.

49. Frederic William Maitland, *The Constitutional History of England* (Cambridge: Cambridge University Press, 1908), 9.

50. C. H. S. Fifoot, *Pollock and Maitland* (Glasgow: George Outram, 1971), 23; Frederic William Maitland, *English Law and the Renaissance* (Cambridge: Cambridge University Press, 1901).

51. Maitland to Selina Maitland Reynell, 22 November 1891, in C. H. S. Fifoot, ed., *The Letters of Frederic William Maitland* (Cambridge, MA: Harvard University Press, 1965), 95.

52. Sir Frederick Pollock to Frederic Maitland, 9 November 1887, Add. Mss. 7006, Maitland papers.

53. Maitland to P. E. Dove, 27 April 1887, in Fifoot, *Letters of Frederic William Maitland,* 29.

54. P. N. R. Zutshi, ed., *The Letters of Frederic William Maitland,* volume 2 (London: Selden Society, 1995), 13.

55. Frederic William Maitland, *Domesday Book and Beyond: Three Essays in the Early History of England* (Cambridge: Cambridge University Press, 1897), 150.

56. John W. Burrow, "'The Village Community' and the Uses of History in Late Nineteenth-Century England," in Neil McKendrick, ed., *Historical Perspectives: Studies in English Thought in Honour of J. H. Plumb* (London: Europa, 1974), 283.

57. Maitland to Paul Vinogradoff, 20 February 1889, in Fifoot, *Letters of Frederic William Maitland,* 57–58.

58. John W. Burrow, *Whigs and Liberals: Continuity and Change in English Political Thought* (Oxford: Clarendon Press, 1988), 150.

59. Maitland to Pollock, 10 October 1891, in Fifoot, *Letters of Frederic William Maitland,* 92.

60. Maitland to Leslie Stephen, 22 January 1900, in Fifoot, *Letters of Frederic William Maitland,* 208.

61. S. F. C. Milsom, "Maitland, Frederic William (1850–1906)," in *Oxford Diction-*

ary of National Biography, Oxford University Press, 2004 [accessed 29 November 2004: http://www.oxforddnb.com/view/article/34837].

62. About *Bracton's Note Book,* for example, Thayer wrote to Maitland that he had "conferred a very great benefit upon all students of *our* ancient law." Thayer to Maitland, 30 December 1887, Add. Mss. 7007, Maitland papers; emphasis added. For Ames, see H. D. Hazeltine, "Gossip About Legal History: Unpublished Letters of Maitland and Ames," *Cambridge Law Journal* 2 (1924), 1–18.

63. Frederic William Maitland, "Why the History of English Law Is Not Written," in H. A. L. Fisher, ed., *The Collected Papers of Frederic William Maitland,* 3 vols. (Cambridge: Cambridge University Press, 1911), I: 485.

64. Maitland to Melville Madison Bigelow, 31 July 1888, in Fifoot, *Letters of Frederic William Maitland,* 45.

65. Maitland to Bigelow, 19 April 1891, in Fifoot, *Letters of Frederic William Maitland,* 90.

66. Maitland to Charles Gross, 2 September 1898, in Fifoot, *Letters of Frederic William Maitland,* 179.

67. Maitland to Pollock, 15 December 1892, Ms. Eng. c. 2887, Arthur Lehman Goodhart papers, Bodleian Library, Oxford.

68. Maitland to Pollock, 21 January 1901, in Fifoot, *Letters of Frederic William Maitland,* 222.

69. H. A. L. Fisher, *Frederic William Maitland: A Biographical Sketch* (Cambridge: Cambridge University Press, 1910), 27.

70. Fifoot, *Pollock and Maitland,* 17.

71. Theodore F. T. Plucknett, "Maitland's View of Law and History," *Law Quarterly Review* 67 (April 1951), 190.

72. C. H. S. Fifoot, *Frederic William Maitland: A Life* (Cambridge, MA: Harvard University Press, 1971), 95.

73. Robert Livingston Schuyler, "The Historical Spirit Incarnate: Frederic William Maitland," *American Historical Review* 57 (January 1952), 312.

74. Fifoot, *Pollock and Maitland,* 7.

75. Maitland to Henry Sidgwick, 28 February 1896, in Fifoot, *Letters of Frederic William Maitland,* 148.

76. Round to Maitland, 28 March 1895, Add. Mss. 7006, Maitland papers.

77. Round to H. A. L. Fisher, 18 October 1910, Volume 59, H. A. L. Fisher papers, Bodleian Library, Oxford.

78. Maitland to Bigelow, 31 October 1885, in Fifoot, *Letters of Frederic William Maitland,* 15.

79. Maitland to Henry Jackson, 13 December 1903, in Fifoot, *Letters of Frederic William Maitland,* 288.

80. Maitland to Courtney Kenny, 14 January 1904, in Zutshi, *Letters of Frederic William Maitland,* 212.

81. Bryce to Holmes, 25 December 1906, Bryce papers.

82. Holmes to Pollock, 4 March 1888, in Mark DeWolfe Howe, ed., *Holmes-Pollock Letters: The Correspondence of Mr. Justice Holmes and Sir Frederick Pollock, 1874–1932,* 2 vols. (Cambridge, MA: Harvard University Press, 1941), I: 31; Holmes to John H. Wigmore, 2 January 1907, Box 51, Holmes papers.

83. Holmes to Frankfurter, 21 March 1928, Box 29, Holmes papers.

84. George Macaulay Trevelyan to Fisher, 14 January 1907, Volume 59, Fisher papers.

85. Dicey to Bryce, 23 December 1906, Bryce papers.

86. Quoted in Frederick Bernays Wiener, "Maitland the Incomparable," *American Journal of Legal History* 16 (April 1972), 178.

87. David Knowles to Cam, 10 August 1954, Helen Cam papers, Girton College, Cambridge.

88. Richard W. Southern, "The Letters of Frederic William Maitland," *History and Theory* 6 (1967), 106.

89. Lord Esher to Maitland, 7 June 1888, Add. Mss. 7006, Maitland papers.

90. Geoffrey Elton, *F. W. Maitland* (London: Weidenfeld and Nicolson, 1985), 97.

91. Southern, "Letters of Frederic William Maitland," 107.

92. Maitland, "Why the History of English Law," I: 491.

93. Milsom, *Natural History of the Common Law,* xvi.

94. Richard A. Cosgrove, *Our Lady the Common Law: An Anglo-American Legal Community, 1870–1930* (New York: New York University Press, 1987), 62.

95. Maitland to Dicey, ? July 1896, General Manuscripts 508 (14), Glasgow University Library.

96. Vinogradoff to Maitland, 6 April 1895, Add. Mss. 7006, Maitland papers.

97. John Watt, "Frederic Maitland," in John Cannon, ed., *The Historian at Work* (London: Allen & Unwin, 1980), 117.

98. William S. Holdsworth, *Some Makers of English Law* (Cambridge: Cambridge University Press, 1938), 278.

99. Elton, *Maitland,* 102.

100. Fifoot, *Maitland,* 93.

101. Calvin Woodard, "History, Legal History and Legal Education," *Virginia Law Review* 53 (January 1967), 107.

102. Robert W. Gordon, "Introduction: J. Willard Hurst and the Common Law Tradition in American Legal Historiography," *Law and Society Review* 10 (1975), 12.

103. Milsom, *Natural History of the Common Law,* xxiv.

104. Southern, "Letters of Frederic William Maitland," 110.

105. S. F. C. Milsom, "Introduction," in Sir Frederick Pollock and Frederic William Maitland, *The History of English Law before the Time of Edward I* (Cambridge: Cambridge University Press, 1968 [1895]), xxvii, lxxiii.

106. S. F. C. Milsom, "F. W. Maitland," *Proceedings of the British Academy* 66 (1980), 274.

107. S. F. C. Milsom, " 'Pollock and Maitland': A Lawyer's Retrospect," in John Hudson, ed., *The History of English Law: Centenary Essays on 'Pollock and Maitland'* (New York: Oxford University Press, 1996), 257.

108. Carleton K. Allen to Martin Wolff, 29 December 1938, Ms. Eng. c. 2889, Goodhart papers.

109. Patrick Wormald, "Frederic William Maitland and the Earliest English Law," *Law and History Review* 16 (Spring 1998), 6–17.

110. Ibid., 3.

111. Christopher Harvie, *The Lights of Liberalism: University Liberals and the Challenge of Democracy, 1860–1886* (London: Allen Lane, 1976), 214.

112. Holdsworth, *Some Makers of English Law,* 279; W. W. Buckland, a law faculty colleague of Maitland's, wrote that he discerned "medieval law was not something in a book, but the life-blood of a living people. That was the attraction of the Year Books to him. There and there only, as he held, was the real life of the law and of the people to be studied at first hand. For him the law was a living system." W. W. Buckland, "F. W. Maitland," *Cambridge Law Journal* 1 (1923), 299.

113. Blaas, *Continuity and Anachronism,* 258.

114. Holdsworth, *The Historians of Anglo-American Law* (New York: Columbia University Press, 1928), 151–52.

115. K. J. M. Smith and J. P. S. McLaren, "History's Living Legacy: An Outline of 'Modern' Historiography of the Common Law," *Legal Studies* 21 (June 2001), 265.

116. Sir William Holdsworth, *A History of English Law,* 17 vols. (Boston: Little, Brown, 1903–72).

117. Dicey to Bryce, 3 May 1918, Bryce papers.

118. Smith and McLaren, "History's Living Legacy," 267.

119. Pollock to Holmes, 20 March 1925, in Howe, *Holmes-Pollock Letters,* II: 157.

120. A. L. Goodhart, *Sir William Searle Holdsworth, O.M. 1871–1944* (London: Bernard Quaritch, 1954), 3.

121. Roscoe Pound to Felix Frankfurter, 6 June 1922, Volume 90, Felix Frankfurter papers, Manuscripts Division, Library of Congress, Washington, DC. This opinion did not prevent Pound from providing a handsome subsidy, both personally and as dean of the Harvard Law School, to Holdsworth's project. Round to Holdsworth, 12 November 1923, Box 67, File 15, Roscoe Pound papers, Harvard Law School Library, Cambridge, MA.

122. Laski to Holmes, 23 July 1932, in Mark DeWolfe Howe, ed., *Holmes-Laski Letters: The Correspondence of Mr. Justice Holmes and Harold J. Laski, 1916–1935,* 2 vols. (Cambridge, MA: Harvard University Press, 1953), II: 1398.

123. Report by Holdsworth, n.d., 1933, Volume 22/2, Society for the Protection of Science and Learning papers, Bodleian Library, Oxford.

124. Holdsworth, *Historians of Anglo-American Law,* 136.

125. Sir William Holdsworth to Maitland, 5 November 1906, Add. Mss. 7006, Maitland papers.

126. Laski to Holmes, 3 February 1925, in Howe, *Holmes-Laski Letters,* II: 707.

127. Lawson, *Oxford Law School,* 101.

128. Holdsworth to Maitland, 5 November 1906, Add. Mss. 7006, Maitland papers.

129. Frederick Bernays Wiener to Doris Stenton, 6 February 1969, Frank and Doris Stenton papers, University of Reading Library, Reading.

130. David Sugarman, "Reassessing Hurst: A Transatlantic Perspective," *Law and History Review* 18 (Spring 2000), 215.

131. Cosgrove, *Our Lady the Common Law,* 282.

132. Holdsworth, *Historians of Anglo-American Law,* 147.

133. Milsom, "Maitland," 268.

134. Geoffrey Elton, "Herbert Butterfield and the Study of History," *Historical Journal* 27 (September 1984), 735.

135. Clive Holmes, "G. R. Elton as a Legal Historian," *Transactions of the Royal Historical Society,* Sixth Series 7 (1997), 268.

136. J. H. Baker, *The Law's Two Bodies: Some Evidential Problems in English Legal History* (New York: Oxford University Press, 2001), 9.

137. Anthony Musson, *Medieval Law in Context: The Growth of Legal Consciousness from Magna Carta to the Peasants' Revolt* (Manchester: Manchester University Press, 2001), 3.

138. J. H. Baker, "Why the History of English Law Has Not Been Finished," *Cambridge Law Journal* 59 (March 2000), 78.

139. Paul Brand, *The Making of the Common Law* (London: Hambledon Press, 1992), xvi.

Conclusion

1. David Cannadine, "British History as a 'New Subject': Politics, Perspectives and Prospects," in Alexander Grant and Keith J. Stringer, eds., *Uniting the Kingdom: The Making of British History* (London: Routledge, 1995), 16.

2. Tony Blair, "Britishness and the Government's Agenda of Constitutional Reform," speech to regional newspaper executives, 28 March 2000, press release, British Consulate General, Los Angeles.

3. George W. Bush, "Age of Liberty: 'The Calling of Our Time,'" 6 November 2003. *Arizona Republic*, 30 November 2003.

4. Geoffrey Elton, *A Return to Essentials: Some Reflections on the Present State of Historical Study* (Cambridge: Cambridge University Press, 1991), 78.

5. A. V. Dicey to James Bryce, 24 August 1920, James Bryce papers, Bodleian Library, Oxford.

6. Christopher J. W. Parker, *The English Historical Tradition since 1850* (Edinburgh: John Donald, 1990), 109.

7. David Fromkin, *Europe's Last Summer: Who Started the Great War in 1914?* (New York: Vintage, 2004).

8. Philip Kerr to H. A. L. Fisher, 11 February 1929, Lewis Namier papers, John Rylands Library, Manchester.

9. Lewis Namier to Kerr, 11 August 1926, Namier papers.

10. Ved Mehta, *Fly and the Fly Bottle: Encounters with British Intellectuals* (Boston: Little, Brown, 1962), 183; emphasis in the original.

11. Arnold J. Toynbee, *Acquaintances* (London: Oxford University Press, 1967), 76.

12. V. H. Galbraith to Helen Cam, 25 July 1960 or 1961, Helen Cam papers, Girton College, Cambridge; emphasis in the original. R. V. Lennard (1885–1967) referred to the "strange museum of constitutional archaeology" in reflecting on the field's loss of prestige. Undated paper, Ms.Top.Oxon.c.564, R. V. Lennard papers, Bodleian Library, Oxford.

13. Margaret Hastings to Cam, 16 February 1960, Cam papers.

14. Reba N. Soffer, "The Conservative Historical Imagination in the Twentieth Century," *Albion* 28 (Spring 1996), 2.

15. Victor Feske, *From Belloc to Churchill: Private Scholars, Public Culture, and the Crisis of British Liberalism* (Chapel Hill: University of North Carolina Press, 1996), 13.

16. Reba N. Soffer, *Discipline and Power: The University, History, and the Making of an English Elite, 1870–1930* (Stanford, CA: Stanford University Press, 1994), 46.

17. Richard Southern called Galbraith "the last important representative of the modern history school at Oxford in the period when it concentrated on the continuous institutional and constitutional development of England from the early middle ages." Richard W. Southern, "Galbraith, Vivian Hunter (1889–1976)," rev., *Oxford Dictionary of National Biography*, Oxford University Press, 2004 [http://www.oxforddnb.com/view/article/31132, accessed 6 May 2005]. Historian H. A. Cronne wrote of Galbraith that he "was therefore steeped, one might say marinated, in original sources, so that he positively exuded the genuine flavour of Medieval History." H. A. Cronne, "Memoir of Balliol College 1925–27," c. 1977, in V. H. Galbraith papers, Bodleian Library, Oxford.

18. J. H. Plumb, *The Making of an Historian: The Collected Essays of J. H. Plumb*, 2 vols. (Athens: University of Georgia Press, 1988–89), I: 183.

19. George Macaulay Trevelyan, *English Social History: A Survey of Six Centuries, Chaucer to Queen Victoria* (London: Longmans, Green, 1942), vii.

20. Edward P. Thompson, *The Making of the English Working Class* (New York: Pantheon, 1963), 12.

21. C. V. Wedgwood, *History and Hope: The Collected Essays of C. V. Wedgwood* (London: Collins, 1987), 10; emphasis in the original.

22. C. V. Wedgwood to Michael Polanyi, 2 October 1966, Box 6, Folder 8, Michael Polanyi papers, University of Chicago Library, Chicago; emphasis in the original.

23. Both quotations are from C. V. Wedgwood, "Some Thoughts on History," 1 August 1970, Ms. Eng. c. 6839, C. V. Wedgwood papers, Bodleian Library, Oxford.

24. Richard Evans, *In Defence of History* (London: Granta Books, 1997), 168–69.

25. Peter Mandler, *History and National Life* (London: Profile Books, 2002), 110–11.

26. Some examples among many include the *American Journal of Legal History*, the *Journal of Legal History*, the *Law and History Review*, and the *Oxford Journal of Legal Studies*.

27. Examples here include the series published by the Cambridge University Press and the University of North Carolina Press.

28. A. W. B. Simpson, "Legal Education and Legal History," *Oxford Journal of Legal Studies* 11 (Spring 1991), 111.

29. Janet Senderowitz Loengard, "Beyond Maitland: The Maturing of a Discipline," *Journal of British Studies* 34 (October 1995), 530.

30. William Twining, *Blackstone's Tower: The English Law School* (London: Stevens & Sons/Sweet & Maxwell, 1994), 13.

31. See the programmatic essay by D. Alan Orr, "A Prospectus for a 'New' Constitutional History of Early Modern England," *Albion* 36 (Fall 2004), 430–50.

32. Paul Brand, *The Making of the Common Law* (London: Hambledon Press, 1992), xvi.

33. Douglas Hay, "Women, Men, and Empires of Law," *Journal of British Studies* 44 (January 2005), 212.

34. Ann Lyon, *Constitutional History of the United Kingdom* (London: Cavendish, 2003); Lyon wrote: "Constitutional history has not, perhaps surprisingly, been the subject of any recent specialist text" (xxxvii). Given the vagaries of historical fashion traced in our argument, this conclusion did not surprise us at all.

Bibliography

Manuscript Sources

Lord Acton Papers, Cambridge University Library, Cambridge.

George Burton Adams Papers, Sterling Library, Yale University, New Haven, Connecticut.

Herbert Baxter Adams Papers, Milton S. Eisenhower Library, Johns Hopkins University, Baltimore, Maryland.

Charles McLean Andrews Papers, Sterling Library, Yale University, New Haven, Connecticut.

Sir William Anson Papers, Codrington Library, All Souls College, Oxford.

Oswald Barron Papers, West Sussex Record Office, Chichester.

Carl Becker Papers, Carl A. Kroch Library, Cornell University, Ithaca, New York.

Oscar Browning Papers, King's College Library, Cambridge.

James Bryce Papers, Bodleian Library, Oxford.

Herbert Butterfield Papers, Cambridge University Library, Cambridge.

Helen Cam Papers, Girton College, Cambridge.

Joseph Hodges Choate Papers, Manuscripts Division, Library of Congress, Washington, DC.

George N. Clark Papers, Bodleian Library, Oxford.

Maude Violet Clarke Papers, Somerville College, Oxford.

Robin G. Collingwood Papers, Bodleian Library, Oxford.

Lord Cromer Papers, ING Bank NV, London.

Arthur Lyon Cross Papers, Michigan Historical Collection, University of Michigan, Ann Arbor, Michigan.

J. Conway Davies Papers, National Library of Wales, Aberystwyth.

Henry W. C. Davis Papers, Bodleian Library, Oxford.

William A. Dunning Papers, Butler Library, Columbia University, New York, New York.

J. Goronwy Edwards Papers, National Library of Wales, Aberystwyth.

Charles William Eliot Papers, Harvard University Archives, Cambridge, Massachusetts.

English-Speaking Union Papers, Dartmouth House, London.

H. A. L. Fisher Papers, Bodleian Library, Oxford.

Felix Frankfurter Papers, Manuscripts Division, Library of Congress, Washington, DC.

Edward A. Freeman Papers, John Rylands Library, Manchester.

V. H. Galbraith Papers, Bodleian Library, Oxford.

General Manuscripts, Glasgow University Library, Glasgow.

Daniel Coit Gilman Papers, Milton S. Eisenhower Library, Johns Hopkins University, Baltimore, Maryland.

William Gladstone Papers, British Library, London.

Arthur Lehman Goodhart Papers, Bodleian Library, Oxford.

John Richard Green Papers, Jesus College, Oxford.

Sir Edward Grey Papers, National Archives, Kew.

Hubert Hall Papers, Centre for Kentish Studies, Maidstone.

Hubert Hall Papers, National Archives, Kew.

John and Barbara Hammond Papers, Bodleian Library, Oxford.

Charles Homer Haskins Papers, Firestone Library, Princeton University, Princeton, New Jersey.

Oliver Wendell Holmes Papers, Harvard Law School Library, Cambridge, Massachusetts.

John Franklin Jameson Papers, Manuscripts Division, Library of Congress, Washington, DC.

A. Berriedale Keith Papers, Edinburgh University Library, Edinburgh.

W. E. H. Lecky Papers, Trinity College, Dublin.

R. V. Lennard Papers, Bodleian Library, Oxford.

Max Lerner Papers, Sterling Library, Yale University, New Haven, Connecticut.

A. Lawrence Lowell Papers, Harvard University Archives, Cambridge, Massachusetts.

Maxwell Lyte Papers, National Archives, Kew.

Frederic Maitland Papers, Cambridge University Library, Cambridge.

Andrew C. McLaughlin Papers, Michigan Historical Collection, University of Michigan, Ann Arbor, Michigan.

Sir John Linton Myres Papers, Bodleian Library, Oxford.

Lewis Namier Papers, John Rylands Library, Manchester.

Michael Polanyi Papers, University of Chicago Library, Chicago.

A. F. Pollard Papers, University of London Library, London.

Roscoe Pound Papers, Harvard Law School Library, Cambridge, Massachusetts.

Eileen Power Papers, Cambridge University Library, Cambridge.

James Ford Rhodes Papers, Massachusetts Historical Society, Boston.

John Horace Round Papers, University of London Library, London.

Joseph Halle Schaffner Autograph Collection, Houghton Library, Harvard University, Cambridge, Massachusetts.

Selden Society Archives, Cambridge University Library, Cambridge.

A. L. Smith Papers, Balliol College Library, Oxford.

Goldwin Smith Papers, Carl A. Kroch Library, Cornell University, Ithaca, New York.

Society for the Protection of Science and Learning Papers, Bodleian Library, Oxford.

Frank and Doris Stenton Papers, University of Reading Library, Reading.

J. St. Loe Strachey Papers, House of Lords Record Office, London.

William Stubbs Papers, Bodleian Library, Oxford.

Lucy Sutherland Papers, Bodleian Library, Oxford.
James Bradley Thayer Papers, Harvard Law School Library, Cambridge, Massachusetts.
T. F. Tout Papers, Manchester University Library, Manchester.
Claude H. Van Tyne Papers, Michigan Historical Collection, University of Michigan, Ann Arbor, Michigan.
John Venn Papers, Gonville and Caius College, Cambridge.
Sir Francis Villiers Papers, National Archives, Kew.
C. V. Wedgwood Papers, Bodleian Library, Oxford.
Working Men's College Papers, London.
A. E. Zimmern Papers, Bodleian Library, Oxford.

Published Sources

Armstrong, William, ed. *The Gilded Age Letters of E. L. Godkin*. Albany: State University of New York Press, 1974.

Ault, Warren O. "The Maitland-Bigelow Letters." *Boston University Law Review* 37 (Summer 1957): 285–326.

Bicknell, John W. *The Selected Letters of Leslie Stephen*. 2 vols. Basingstoke: Macmillan, 1996.

Clark, John Spencer. *The Life and Letters of John Fiske*. 2 vols. Boston: Houghton Mifflin, 1917.

Donnan, Elizabeth, and Leo F. Stock, eds. *A Historian's World: Selections from the Correspondence of John Franklin Jameson*. Philadelphia: American Philosophical Society, 1956.

Fifoot, C. H. S., ed. *The Letters of Frederic William Maitland*. Cambridge, MA: Harvard University Press, 1965.

Fisher, H. A. L., ed. *The Collected Papers of Frederic William Maitland*. 3 vols. Cambridge: Cambridge University Press, 1911.

Harriss, Gerald, ed. *K. B. McFarlane: Letters to Friends, 1940–1966*. Oxford: Magdalen College, 1997.

Haultain, Arnold, ed. *A Selection from Goldwin Smith's Correspondence: Comprising Letters Chiefly to and from His English Friends, Written between the Years 1846 and 1910*. London: T. W. Laurie, n.d. [1913?].

Hazeltine, H. D. "Gossip About Legal History: Unpublished Letters of Maitland and Ames." *Cambridge Law Journal* 2 (1924): 1–18.

Holt, W. Stull, ed. *Historical Scholarship in the United States, 1876–1901: As Revealed in the Correspondence of Herbert B. Adams*. Baltimore: Johns Hopkins Press, 1938.

Howe, Mark DeWolfe, ed. *Holmes-Laski Letters: The Correspondence of Mr. Justice Holmes and Harold J. Laski, 1916–1935*. 2 vols. Cambridge, MA: Harvard University Press, 1953.

———, ed. *Holmes-Pollock Letters: The Correspondence of Mr. Justice Holmes and Sir Frederick Pollock, 1874–1932*. 2 vols. Cambridge, MA: Harvard University Press, 1941.

Hutton, William Holden, ed. *Letters of William Stubbs: Bishop of Oxford, 1825–1901*. London: Constable, 1904.

Hyde, H. Montgomery, ed. *A Victorian Historian: Private Letters of W. E. H. Lecky, 1859–1878*. London: Home & Van Thal, 1947.

Kammen, Michael, ed. *"What Is the Good of History?": Selected Letters of Carl L. Becker, 1900–1945*. Ithaca, NY: Cornell University Press, 1973.

Madden, Frederick, and David Fieldhouse, eds. *Select Documents on the Constitutional History of the British Empire and Commonwealth: The Foundations of a Colonial System of Government*. 8 vols. Westport, CT: Greenwood Press, 1985–2000.

Rait, R. S., ed. *Memorials of Albert Venn Dicey: Being Chiefly Letters and Diaries*. London: Macmillan, 1925.

Shinn, Ridgway F., and Richard A. Cosgrove, eds. *Constitutional Reflections: The Correspondence of Albert Venn Dicey and Arthur Berriedale Keith*. Lanham, MD: University Press of America, 1996.

Stephen, Leslie, ed. *Letters of John Richard Green*. London: Macmillan, 1901.

Stephens, W. R. W., ed. *The Life and Letters of Edward A. Freeman*. 2 vols. London: Macmillan, 1895.

Stones, E. L. G., ed. *F. W. Maitland: Letters to George Neilson*. Glasgow: Glasgow University Press, 1976.

Zutshi, P. N. R., ed. *The Letters of Frederic William Maitland*, volume 2. London: Selden Society, 1995.

Primary Books

Adams, Charles Kendall. *A Manual of Historical Literature, Comprising Brief Descriptions of the Most Important Histories in English, French and German, Together with Practical Suggestions as to Methods and Courses of Historical Study*. New York: Harper & Brothers, 1888.

Adams, George Burton. *Constitutional History of England*. New York: Henry Holt, 1921.

———. *History of England from the Norman Conquest to the Death of John, 1066–1216*. London: Longmans, Green, 1905.

———. *The Origin of the English Constitution*. New Haven, CT: Yale University Press, 1912.

———. *Why Americans Dislike England*. Philadelphia: Henry Altemus, 1896.

Adams, George Burton, and H. M. Stephens, eds. *Select Documents of English Constitutional History*. New York: Macmillan, 1901.

Altschul, Charles. *The American Revolution in Our School Text-books: An Attempt to Trace the Influence of Early School Education in the Feeling toward England in the United States*. New York: George H. Doran, 1917.

Andrews, Charles McLean. *The Colonial Background of the American Revolution*. New Haven, CT: Yale University Press, 1924.

———. *The Colonial Period*. New York: Henry Holt and Co., 1912.

———. *The Colonial Period in American History*. 4 vols. New Haven, CT: Yale University Press, 1934–38.

———. *Guide for the Manuscript Materials for the History of the United States to 1783, in the British Museum, in Minor London Archives, and in the Libraries of Oxford and Cambridge*. Washington, DC: Carnegie Institution, 1908.

———. *Guide to the Materials for American History, to 1783, in the Public Record Office of Great Britain*. 2 vols. Washington, DC: Carnegie Institution, 1912–14.

———. *The Old English Manor: A Study in English Economic History*. Baltimore: Johns Hopkins Press, 1892.

———. *The River Towns of Connecticut: A Study of Wethersfield, Hartford, and Windsor.* Baltimore: Johns Hopkins Press, 1889.

———. *A Short History of England.* Boston: Allyn and Bacon, 1912.

Anon. *Essays in Anglo-Saxon Law.* Boston: Little Brown, 1876.

———. *The Study of History in Schools: Report to the American Historical Association by the Committee of Seven.* New York: Macmillan, 1904.

———. *The Study of History in Secondary Schools: Report to the American Historical Association by the Committee of Five.* New York: Macmillan, 1911.

Anson, Sir William R. *The Law and Custom of the Constitution.* 3 vols. Oxford: Clarendon Press, 1886.

Baldwin, James F. *The King's Council in England during the Middle Ages.* Oxford: Clarendon Press, 1913.

Bateson, Mary. *Medieval England, 1066–1350.* London: T. Fisher Unwin, 1903.

———, ed. *Borough Customs.* 2 vols. London: Bernard Quaritch, 1904–6.

Beard, Charles A. *The Office of Justice of the Peace in England in Its Origin and Development.* New York: Burt Franklin, 1904.

Beer, George Louis. *British Colonial Policy, 1754–1765.* London: Macmillan, 1907.

———. *The English-Speaking Peoples: Their Future Relations and Joint International Obligations.* New York: Macmillan, 1917.

Bowman, Isaiah. *The New World.* Yonkers-on-Hudson, NY: World Book Co., 1922.

Browning, Oscar. *Memories of Later Years.* London: T. Fisher Unwin, 1923.

Bryce, James. *Race Sentiment as a Factor in History.* London: University of London Press, 1915.

———. *The Relations of the Advanced and the Backward Races of Mankind.* Oxford: Clarendon Press, 1902.

———. *Studies in History and Jurisprudence.* 2 vols. London: Oxford University Press, 1901.

———. *The Study of American History.* New York: Macmillan, 1922.

———. *University and Historical Addresses.* New York: Macmillan, 1913.

Cam, Helen. *England before Elizabeth.* London: Hutchinson, 1950.

———. *The Hundred and the Hundred Rolls: An Outline of Local Government in Medieval England.* London: Methuen, 1930.

———. *Law as It Looks to a Historian.* Cambridge: W. Heffer & Sons, 1956.

———. *Law-Finders and Law-Makers in Medieval England: Collected Studies in Legal and Constitutional History.* London: Merlin Press, 1962.

———. *The Legislators of Medieval England.* London: Geoffrey Cumberlege, 1945.

———. *Liberties & Communities in Medieval England: Collected Studies in Local Administration and Topography.* Cambridge: Cambridge University Press, 1944.

———. *Selected Historical Essays of F. W. Maitland.* Cambridge: Cambridge University Press, 1957.

———. *Studies in the Hundred Rolls: Some Aspects of Thirteenth-Century Administration.* Oxford: Clarendon Press, 1921.

———. *What of the Middle Ages Is Alive in England Today?* London: Athlone Press, 1961.

Chamberlain, Mellen. *The Constitutional Relations of the American Colonies to the English Government at the Commencement of the American Revolution.* Paper read to the American Historical Association, 23 May 1887. New York: Knickerbocker Press, 1888.

Churchill, Winston. *A History of the English-Speaking Peoples.* 4 vols. New York: Dodd, Mead, 1956–58.

Clarke, Maude Violet. *Medieval Representation and Consent: A Study of Early Parliaments in England and Ireland, with Special Reference to the Modus Tenendi Parliamentum.* London: Longmans, Green, 1936.

Collingwood, Robin G. *The Idea of History.* New York: Oxford University Press, 1956 [1946].

Committee on National Bias in Anglo-American History Textbooks. *The Historian's Contribution to Anglo-American Misunderstanding.* London: Routledge and Kegan Paul, 1966.

Cromer, Lord. *Ancient and Modern Imperialism.* London: John Murray, 1910.

Cross, Arthur Lyon. *A History of England and Greater Britain.* New York: Macmillan, 1914.

Dicey, Albert Venn. *Introduction to the Study of the Law of the Constitution.* London: Macmillan, 1885.

Dilke, Charles. *Greater Britain: A Record of Travel in English-Speaking Countries.* 2 vols. London: Macmillan, 1868.

Doubleday, H. A. *Dr. Round's "Barons and Peers": A Reply.* London: W. H. Smith & Son, 1920.

Dunning, William A. *The British Empire and the United States: A Review of Their Relations during the Century of Peace Following the Treaty of Ghent.* New York: Scribner's, 1914.

Edwards, J. Goronwy. *Historians and the Medieval English Parliament.* Glasgow: Jackson, 1960.

———. *The Principality of Wales, 1267–1967: A Study in Constitutional History.* Denbigh: Caernarvonshire Historical Society, 1969.

———. *William Stubbs.* London: George Philip & Son, 1952.

Firth, Charles. *Modern History in Oxford, 1841–1918.* Oxford: Blackwell, 1920.

———. *A Plea for the Historical Teaching of History.* Oxford: Clarendon Press, 1904.

Fish, Carl Russell. *The Path of Empire: A Chronicle of the United States as a World Power.* New Haven, CT: Yale University Press, 1919.

Fisher, H. A. L. *Frederic William Maitland: A Biographical Sketch.* Cambridge: Cambridge University Press, 1910.

———. *Paul Vinogradoff: A Memoir.* Oxford: Clarendon Press, 1927.

———, ed. *The Collected Papers of Paul Vinogradoff.* 2 vols. Oxford: Clarendon Press, 1928.

Freeman, Edward Augustus. *The Growth of the English Constitution from the Earliest Times.* New York: Frederick A. Stokes Co., 1890 [1872].

———. *The History of the Norman Conquest of England: Its Causes and Its Results.* 5 vols. Oxford: Clarendon Press, 1867–79.

———. *Lectures to American Audiences.* London: Trüburer, 1882.

———. *The Reign of William Rufus and the Accession of Henry the First.* 2 vols. New York: AMS Press, 1970 [1882].

———. *Some Impressions of the United States.* New York: Henry Holt, 1883.

Froude, James Anthony. *History of England from the Fall of Wolsey to the Defeat of the Spanish Armada*. 12 vols. London: Longmans, Green, 1856–70.

———. *Oceana: or England and Her Colonies*. New York: Scribner's, 1886.

Gipson, Lawrence H. *The British Empire before the American Revolution*. 15 vols. Caldwell: Caxton Printers, 1936–70.

Green, John Richard. *A Short History of the English People*. London: Macmillan, 1874.

Gross, Charles. *The Sources and Literature of English History from the Earliest Times to about 1485*. New York: Longmans, Green, 1900.

Hall, Hubert. *Court Life under the Plantagenets: (Reign of Henry II)*. London: Swan Sonnenschein, 1899.

———. *The Red Book of the Exchequer: A Reply to Mr. J. H. Round*. London: Spottiswoode, 1898.

———. *Studies in English Official Historical Documents*. Cambridge: Cambridge University Press, 1908.

Hallam, Henry. *Constitutional History of England: From Henry VII to George II*. 3 vols. London: J. M. Dent, 1912 [1827].

Haskins, Charles Homer. *The Normans in European History*. Boston: Houghton Mifflin, 1915.

———. *Norman Institutions*. Cambridge, MA: Harvard University Press, 1918.

———. *The Renaissance of the Twelfth Century*. Cambridge, MA: Harvard University Press, 1927.

———. *The Rise of Universities*. New York: Henry Holt, 1923.

Hassall, Arthur, ed. *William Stubbs, Historical Introductions to the Rolls Series*. New York: Haskell, 1968 [1902].

Holdsworth, Sir William. *The Historians of Anglo-American Law*. New York: Columbia University Press, 1928.

———. *A History of English Law*. 17 vols. Boston: Little, Brown, 1903–72.

———. *Professor Sir Thomas Erskine Holland, 1835–1926*. London: Humphrey Milford, 1927.

———. *Some Makers of English Law*. Cambridge: Cambridge University Press, 1938.

Holland, Sir Thomas Erskine. *A Valedictory Retrospect (1874–1910)*. Oxford: Clarendon Press, 1910.

Holmes, Oliver Wendell. *The Common Law*. Boston: Little, Brown, 1881.

Hosmer, James K. *A Short History of Anglo-Saxon Freedom: The Polity of the English-Speaking Race*. New York: Scribner's and Sons, 1890.

Jameson, John Franklin. *The American Revolution Considered as a Social Movement*. Princeton, NJ: Princeton University Press, 1926.

Jenks, Edward. *The Book of English Law*. London: John Murray, 1928.

———. *Edward Plantagenet (Edward I): The English Justinian or The Making of the Common Law*. Freeport, NY: Books for Libraries Press, 1969 [1901].

———. *A Short History of English Law*. London: Methuen, 1912.

Jolliffe, J. E. A. *The Constitutional History of Medieval England: From the English Settlement to 1485*. London: Adam and Charles Black, 1937.

Kennedy, Sinclair. *The Pan-Angles: A Consideration of the Federation of the Seven English-Speaking Nations*. London: Longmans, Green, 1914.

Kingsley, Charles. *Hereward the Wake: "Last of the English."* London: J. M. Dent, 1907 [1866].

———. *The Roman and the Teuton.* London: Macmillan, 1864.

Lecky, W. E. H. *The American Revolution, 1763–1783: Being the Chapters and Passages Relating to America from the Author's History of England in the Eighteenth Century.* Arranged and edited, with historical and bibliographical notes, by James Albert Woodburn. New York: Appleton, 1924.

———. *Historical and Political Essays.* London: Longmans, Green, 1908.

———. *The Political Value of History.* London: Edward Arnold, 1892.

Liebermann, Felix. *The National Assembly in the Anglo-Saxon Period.* Halle, Germany: Max Niemeyer, 1913.

Lucas, Sir Charles P. *Greater Rome and Greater Britain.* Oxford: Clarendon Press, 1912.

Maitland, Frederic William. *The Constitutional History of England.* Cambridge: Cambridge University Press, 1908.

———. *Domesday Book and Beyond: Three Essays in the Early History of England.* Cambridge: Cambridge University Press, 1897.

———. *English Law and the Renaissance.* Cambridge: Cambridge University Press, 1901.

McElroy, Robert M. *Economic History of the United States, Presented in Outline.* New York: Putnam, 1927.

McIlwain, Charles H. *The American Revolution: A Constitutional Interpretation.* New York: Macmillan, 1923.

———. *The High Court of Parliament and Its Supremacy: An Historical Essay on the Boundaries between Legislation and Adjudication in England.* New Haven, CT: Yale University Press, 1910.

McLaughlin, Andrew C. *America and Britain.* New York: E. P. Dutton, 1918.

———. *A Constitutional History of the United States.* New York: Appleton-Century-Crofts, 1935.

———. *A History of the United States for Schools.* New York: Appleton, 1899.

Miller, Charles Grant. *The Poisoned Loving-Cup: United States School Histories Falsified Through Pro-British Propaganda in Sweet Name of Amity.* Chicago: National Historical Society, 1928.

Motley, John Lothrop. *The Rise of the Dutch Republic.* 2 vols. Philadelphia: Henry Altemus, 1898 [1855].

Muzzey, David Saville. *An American History.* Boston: Ginn and Co., 1923.

Neilson, Nellie. *Customary Rents.* Oxford: Clarendon Press, 1910.

———. *Economic Conditions on the Manors of Ramsey Abbey.* Philadelphia: Sherman and Co., 1899.

———. *Medieval Agrarian Economy.* New York: Henry Holt, 1936.

Norgate, Kate. *England under the Angevin Kings.* 2 vols. New York: Haskell, 1969 [1887].

———. *John Lackland.* New York: AMS Press, 1970 [1902].

———. *Richard the Lion Heart.* London: Macmillan, 1924.

Oman, Charles. *The Great Revolt of 1381.* New York: Haskell, 1968 [1906].

———. *Inaugural Lecture on the Study of History, 7 February 1906.* Oxford: Clarendon Press, 1906.

————. *On the Writing of History.* London: Methuen, 1939.

Pike, Luke O. *A Constitutional History of the House of Lords: From Original Sources.* London: Macmillan, 1894.

Plucknett, Theodore F. T. *A Concise History of the Common Law.* Rochester, NY: The Lawyers Co-Operative Publishing Co., 1929.

Pollard, A. F. *The Claims of Historical Research in London.* London: University of London Press, 1920.

————. *The Evolution of Parliament.* London: Longmans, Green, 1920.

Pollock, Sir Frederick. *Essays in Jurisprudence and Ethics.* London: Macmillan, 1882.

————. *Oxford Lectures and Other Discussions.* London: Macmillan, 1890.

————. *Principles of Contract.* 4th edition. London: Stevens & Sons, 1885.

Pollock, Sir Frederick, and Frederic William Maitland. *The History of English Law Before the Time of Edward I.* 2 vols. Cambridge: Cambridge University Press, 1895.

Poole, Reginald Lane. *The Exchequer in the Twelfth Century.* Oxford: Clarendon Press, 1912.

Putnam, Bertha Haven. *Early Treatises on the Practice of the Justices of the Peace in the Fifteenth and Sixteenth Century.* Oxford: Clarendon Press, 1924.

————. *The Enforcement of the Statute of Labourers during the First Decade after the Black Death.* New York: Columbia University Press, 1908.

————. *The Place in Legal History of Sir William Shareshull Chief Justice of the King's Bench, 1350–1361: A Study of Judicial and Administrative Methods in the Reign of Edward III.* Cambridge: Cambridge University Press, 1950.

————, ed. *Proceedings before the Justices of the Peace in the Fourteenth and Fifteenth Centuries: Edward III to Richard III.* London: Spottiswoode, Ballantyne, 1938.

Round, John Horace. *"Barons" and "Knights" in the Great Charter.* Aberdeen: Aberdeen University Press, 1917.

————. *Family Origins and Other Studies.* London: Constable, 1930.

————. *Feudal England: Historical Studies in the Eleventh and Twelfth Centuries.* London: Allen & Unwin, 1895.

————. *Geoffrey de Mandeville: A Study of the Anarchy.* New York: B. Franklin, 1960 [1892].

————. *The King's Serjeants and Officers of State: With Their Coronation Services.* London: James Nisbet, 1911.

Rye, Walter. *Dr. J. Horace Round and His Recent Attack on Mr. Walter Rye as to the Colchester Chronicle.* London: Roberts, 1922.

Schlesinger, Arthur Meier. *The Colonial Merchants and the American Revolution, 1763–1776.* New York: Columbia University Press, 1918.

————. *New Viewpoints in American History.* New York: Macmillan, 1922.

Seebohm, Frederic. *The English Village Community: Examined in Its Relations to the Manorial and Tribal Systems and to the Common or Open Field System of Husbandry.* London: Longmans, Green, 1905 [1883].

Seeley, John Robert. *The Expansion of England.* London: Macmillan, 1883.

Shotwell, James T. *The Faith of an Historian.* New York: Walker and Company, 1964.

Smith, A. L. *Frederic William Maitland: Two Lectures and a Bibliography.* Oxford: Clarendon Press, 1908.

Smith, Goldwin. *Lectures on the Study of History*. New York: Harper & Bros., 1866.

———. *The Schism in the Anglo-Saxon Race*. New York: American News Company, 1887.

———. *The United States: An Outline of Political History, 1492–1871*. New York: Macmillan, 1893.

Stenton, Doris M. *English Justice between the Norman Conquest and the Great Charter, 1066–1215*. Philadelphia: American Philosophical Society, 1964.

———. *The English Woman in History*. London: Allen & Unwin, 1957.

———, ed. *Preparatory to Anglo-Saxon England: Being the Collected Papers of Frank Merry Stenton*. Oxford: Clarendon Press, 1970.

Stenton, Frank M. *The First Century of English Feudalism, 1066–1166*. Oxford: Clarendon Press, 1932.

———. *Types of Manorial Structure in the Northern Danelaw*. Oxford: Clarendon Press, 1910.

Streit, Clarence K. *Union Now With Britain*. New York: Harper, 1941.

Stubbs, William. *The Constitutional History of England in Its Origins and Development*. 3 vols. Oxford: Clarendon Press, 1874–78.

———. *Lectures on Early English History. By William Stubbs*. New York: Longmans, Green, 1906.

———. *Select Charters and Other Illustrations of English Constitutional History: From the Earliest Times to the Reign of Edward the First*. Oxford: Clarendon Press, 1870.

———. *Seventeen Lectures on the Study of Medieval and Modern History and Kindred Subjects Delivered at Oxford, under Statutory Obligation in the Years 1867–1884*. New York: Howard Fertig, 1967 [1886].

Tait, James. *The Medieval English Borough: Studies in Its Origins and Constitutional History*. Manchester: Manchester University Press, 1936.

Tout, T. F. *Chapters in the Administrative History of Mediaeval England: The Wardrobe, the Chamber, and the Small Seals*. 6 vols. Manchester: Manchester University Press, 1920–33.

Trevelyan, George Macaulay. *Clio, A Muse: and Other Essays Literary and Pedestrian*. London: Longmans, Green, 1913.

———. *The English Revolution, 1688–1689*. London: Oxford University Press, 1938.

———. *English Social History: A Survey of Six Centuries, Chaucer to Queen Victoria*. London: Longmans, Green, 1942.

———. *History of England*. London: Longmans, Green, 1926.

———. *Sir George Otto Trevelyan: A Memoir*. London: Longmans, Green, 1932.

Trevelyan, George Otto. *The American Revolution*. 4 vols. New York: Longmans, Green, 1899–1913.

Van Tyne, Claude H. *Democracy's Education Problem*. New York: National Security League, 1918.

———. *England and America: Rivals in the American Revolution*. New York: Macmillan, 1927.

Vinogradoff, Paul. *The Growth of the Manor*. London: Allen & Unwin, 1904.

———. *Villainage in England: Essays in English Mediaeval History*. Oxford: Clarendon Press, 1892.

Wakeman, H. O., and Arthur Hassall, eds. *Essays Introductory to the Study of Constitu-*

tional History by Resident Members of the University of Oxford. London: Longmans, Green, 1901 [1886].

White, Albert B. *The Making of the English Constitution, 449–1485*. New York: G. P. Putnam's Sons, 1908.

Wilkinson, Bertie. *The Constitutional History of England, 1216–1399*. 3 vols. London: Longmans, Green, 1948–58.

Wilson, Woodrow. *History of the American People*. 2 vols. New York: Harper and Brothers, 1902.

Secondary Books

Adams, Pauline. *Somerville for Women: An Oxford College, 1879–1993*. New York: Oxford University Press, 1996.

Alter, Peter. *Nationalism*. London: Edward Arnold, 1989.

Anderson, Benedict. *Imagined Communities: Reflections on the Origin and Spread of Nationalism*. 2nd edition. London: Verso, 1991.

Anderson, David. *Histories of the Hanged: Britain's Dirty War in Kenya at the End of Empire*. London: Weidenfeld and Nicolson, 2005.

Anderson, Stuart. *Race and Rapprochement: Anglo-Saxonism and Anglo-American Relations, 1895–1904*. Rutherford, NJ: Associated University Presses, 1981.

Annan, Noel. *The Dons: Mentors, Eccentrics, and Geniuses*. Chicago: University of Chicago Press, 1999.

———. *Leslie Stephen: The Godless Victorian*. London: Weidenfeld and Nicolson, 1984.

Anon. *Essays in Colonial History Presented to Charles McLean Andrews by His Students*. New Haven, CT: Yale University Press, 1931.

Anstruther, Ian. *Oscar Browning: A Biography*. London: John Murray, 1983.

Appiah, K. Anthony. *In My Father's House: Africa in the Philosophy of Culture*. New York: Oxford University Press, 1992.

Appleby, Joyce, Lynn Hunt, and Margaret Jacob. *Telling the Truth about History*. New York: W. W. Norton, 1994.

Armitage, David. *The Ideological Origins of the British Empire*. Cambridge: Cambridge University Press, 2000.

Aydelotte, Frank. *The American Rhodes Scholarships: A Review of the First Forty Years*. Princeton, NJ: Princeton University Press, 1946.

Ayres, Philip. *Classical Culture and the Idea of Rome in Eighteenth-Century England*. Cambridge: Cambridge University Press, 1997.

Bailkin, Jordanna. *The Culture of Property: The Crisis of Liberalism in Modern Britain*. Chicago: University of Chicago Press, 2004.

Baker, J. H. *The Law's Two Bodies: Some Evidential Problems in English Legal History*. New York: Oxford University Press, 2001.

Ballantyne, Tony. *Orientalism, Racial Theory and British Colonialism: An Aryan Empire*. Basingstoke: Palgrave, 2001.

Bann, Stephen. *The Inventions of History: Essays on the Representation of the Past*. Manchester: Manchester University Press, 1990.

Banton, Michael. *Racial Theories*. Cambridge: Cambridge University Press, 1987.

Barczewski, Stephanie. *Myth and National Identity in Nineteenth-Century Britain: The Legends of King Arthur and Robin Hood*. New York: Oxford University Press, 2000.

Barkan, Elazar. *The Retreat of Scientific Racism: Changing Concepts of Race in Britain and the United States between the World Wars.* New York: Cambridge University Press, 1992.

Bartlett, Robert, ed. *History and Historians: Selected Papers of R. W. Southern.* Oxford: Blackwell, 2004.

Baucom, Ian. *Out of Place: Englishness, Empire, and the Locations of Identity.* Princeton, NJ: Princeton University Press, 1999.

Bennett, James C. *The Anglosphere Challenge: Why the English-Speaking Nations Will Lead the Way in the Twenty-first Century.* Lanham, MD: Rowman and Littlefield, 2004.

Bentley, Michael. *Modernizing England's Past: English Historiography in the Age of Modernism, 1870–1970.* Cambridge: Cambridge University Press, 2005.

Berg, Maxine. *A Woman in History: Eileen Power, 1889–1940.* Cambridge: Cambridge University Press, 1996.

Birch, Anthony H. *Nationalism and National Integration.* Winchester: Unwin, Hyman, 1989.

Blaas, Piet B. M. *Continuity and Anachronism: Parliamentary and Constitutional Development in Whig Historiography and in the Anti-Whig Reaction between 1890 and 1930.* The Hague: Martinus Nijhoff, 1978.

Blight, David W. *Race and Reunion: The Civil War in American History.* Cambridge, MA: Harvard University Press, 2001.

Boucher, David. *The Social and Political Thought of R. G. Collingwood.* Cambridge: Cambridge University Press, 1989.

Bowler, Peter J. *The Invention of Progress: The Victorians and the Past.* Oxford: Blackwell, 1989.

Boyes, Georgina. *The Imagined Village: Culture, Ideology and the English Folk Revival.* Manchester: Manchester University Press, 1993.

Brand, Paul. *The Making of the Common Law.* London: Hambledon Press, 1992.

Bratchel, M. Edwin. *Edward Augustus Freeman and the Victorian Interpretation of the Norman Conquest.* Ilfracombe: Arthur H. Stockwell, 1969.

Brett, Sidney Reed. *The Story of the British Constitution.* Glasgow: Blackie and Son, 1929.

Breward, Christopher, Becky Conekin, and Caroline Cox, eds. *The Englishness of English Dress.* Oxford and New York: Berg, 2002.

Briggs, Asa. *The Collected Essays of Asa Briggs.* 3 vols. London: Harvester Press, 1985–91.

Bromley, J. S., P. G. M. Dickson, and Ann Whiteman, eds. *Statesmen, Scholars and Merchants: Essays in Eighteenth Century History Presented to Dame Lucy Sutherland.* Oxford: Clarendon Press, 1973.

Brundage, Anthony. *The People's Historian: John Richard Green and the Writing of History in Victorian England.* Westport, CT: Greenwood Press, 1994.

Buckner, Phillip. *The Transition to Responsible Government: British Policy in British North America, 1815–1850.* Westport, CT: Greenwood Press, 1985.

Burrow, John W. *A Liberal Descent: Victorian Historians and the English Past.* Cambridge: Cambridge University Press, 1981.

———. *Whigs and Liberals: Continuity and Change in English Political Thought.* Oxford: Clarendon Press, 1988.

Butterfield, Herbert. *The Englishman and His History*. Cambridge: Cambridge University Press, 1944.

———. *Man on His Past: The Study of the History of Historical Scholarship*. Cambridge: Cambridge University Press, 1955.

———. *The Whig Interpretation of History*. London: G. Bell & Sons, 1931.

Campbell, James. *The Anglo-Saxon State*. London: Hambledon, 2000.

———. *Stubbs and the English State*. Reading: University of Reading Press, 1988.

Cannadine, David. *G. M. Trevelyan: A Life in History*. London: Harper Collins, 1992.

———. *In Churchill's Shadow: Confronting the Past in Modern Britain*. New York: Oxford University Press, 2002.

———. *Ornamentalism: How the British Saw Their Empire*. London: Oxford University Press, 2001.

Cantor, Norman F. *Inventing the Middle Ages: The Lives, Works, and Ideas of the Great Medievalists of the Twentieth Century*. New York: Morrow, 1991.

———, ed. *William Stubbs on the English Constitution*. New York: Thomas Y. Crowell, 1966.

Cantwell, John D. *The Public Record Office, 1838–1958*. London: Her Majesty's Stationary Office, 1991.

Chadwick, H. Munro. *Studies on Anglo-Saxon Institutions*. Cambridge: Cambridge University Press, 1905.

Chadwick, W. O. *Freedom and the Historian*. Cambridge: Cambridge University Press, 1969.

Chakravarty, Gautam. *The Indian Mutiny and the British Imagination*. New York: Cambridge University Press, 2005.

Chancellor, Valerie E. *History for Their Masters: Opinion in the English History Textbooks, 1800–1914*. London: Alden & Mowbray, 1970.

Chapman, Raymond. *The Sense of the Past in Victorian Literature*. London: Croom Helm, 1986.

Chatterjee, Partha. *The Nation and Its Fragments: Colonial and Postcolonial Histories*. Princeton, NJ: Princeton University Press, 1993.

Chibnall, Marjorie. *The Debate on the Norman Conquest*. New York: St. Martin's Press, 1999.

Clive, John. *Not by Fact Alone: Essays on the Writing and Reading of History*. New York: Alfred A. Knopf, 1989.

Cocks, R. C. J. *Sir Henry Maine: A Study in Victorian Jurisprudence*. Cambridge: Cambridge University Press, 1988.

Colaiaco, James A. *James Fitzjames Stephen and the Crisis of Victorian Thought*. New York: St. Martin's Press, 1983.

Colley, Linda. *Britons: Forging the Nation, 1707–1837*. New Haven, CT: Yale University Press, 1992.

———. *Captives: Britain, Empire and the World, 1600–1850*. London: Jonathan Cape, 2002.

———. *Lewis Namier*. London: Weidenfeld and Nicolson, 1989.

Collini, Stefan. *English Pasts: Essays in History and Culture*. New York: Oxford University Press, 1999.

———. *Public Moralists: Political Thought and Intellectual Life in Britain, 1850–1930*. Oxford: Clarendon Press, 1991.

Collini, Stefan, Donald Winch, and John W. Burrow. *That Noble Science of Politics: A Study in Nineteenth-Century Intellectual History*. Cambridge: Cambridge University Press, 1983.

Colls, Robert. *Identity of England*. London: Oxford University Press, 2002.

Corrigan, Philip, and Derek Sayer. *The Great Arch: English State Formation as Cultural Revolution*. Oxford: Blackwell, 1985.

Cosgrove, Richard A. *Our Lady the Common Law: An Anglo-American Legal Community, 1870–1930*. New York: New York University Press, 1987.

———. *The Rule of Law: Albert Venn Dicey, Victorian Jurist*. Chapel Hill: University of North Carolina Press, 1980.

Cousins, D. C. *English History in Forms of Essays: Political and Constitutional 1066–1688*. London: Allen & Unwin, 1927.

Covert, James. *A Victorian Marriage: Mandell and Louise Creighton*. London: Hambledon, 2000.

Cowling, Maurice. *Religion and Public Doctrine in Modern England*. 3 vols. Cambridge: Cambridge University Press, 1980–2001.

Crane, Verner W. *Benjamin Franklin, Englishman and American*. Baltimore: Williams and Wilkins, 1936.

Crook, Paul. *Darwinism, War, and History: The Debate over the Biology of War from the 'Origin of Species' to the First World War*. Cambridge: Cambridge University Press, 1994.

Crosby, Christina. *The Ends of History: Victorians and "The Woman Question."* New York: Routledge, 1991.

Culler, A. Dwight. *The Victorian Mirror of History*. New Haven, CT: Yale University Press, 1985.

Curtis, Lewis P. *Anglo-Saxons and Celts: A Study of Anti-Irish Prejudice in Victorian England*. Bridgeport, CT: Conference on British Studies, 1968.

Dale, Peter. *The Victorian Critic and the Idea of History: Carlyle Arnold Pater*. Cambridge, MA: Harvard University Press, 1977.

Daniels, Stephen. *Fields of Vision: Landscape Imagery and National Identity in England and the United States*. Princeton, NJ: Princeton University Press, 1993.

Debbins, William, ed. *Robin G. Collingwood: Essays in the Philosophy of History*. New York: McGraw-Hill, 1966.

Dellheim, Charles. *The Face of the Past: The Preservation of the Medieval Inheritance in Victorian England*. New York: Cambridge University Press, 1982.

De Nie, Michael. *The Eternal Paddy: Irish Identity and the British Press, 1798–1882*. Madison: University of Wisconsin Press, 2004.

Des Jardins, Julie. *Women and the Historical Enterprise in America: Gender, Race, and the Politics of Memory, 1880–1945*. Chapel Hill: University of North Carolina Press, 2003.

Deslandes, Paul R. *Oxbridge Men: British Masculinity and the Undergraduate Experience, 1850–1920*. Bloomington: Indiana University Press, 2005.

Dray, William H. *History as Re-Enactment: R. G. Collingwood's Idea of History*. Oxford: Clarendon Press, 1995.

Dunn, W. H. *James Anthony Froude: A Biography*. 2 vols. Oxford: Clarendon Press, 1961–63.

Dyhouse, Carol. *No Distinction of Sex? Women in British Universities, 1870–1939*. London: University College London Press, 1995.

Eaton, Richard M., ed. *India's Islamic Traditions, 711–1750*. New Delhi: Oxford University Press, 2003.

Eisenstadt, A. S. *Charles McLean Andrews*. New York: Columbia University Press, 1956.

Elkins, Caroline. *Imperial Reckoning: The Untold Story of Britain's Gulag in Kenya*. New York: Henry Holt, 2005.

Elton, Geoffrey. *The English*. Oxford: Blackwell, 1992.

———. *F. W. Maitland*. London: Weidenfeld and Nicolson, 1985.

———. *A Return to Essentials: Some Reflections on the Present State of Historical Study*. Cambridge: Cambridge University Press, 1991.

Engel, Arthur J. *From Clergyman to Don: The Rise of the Academic Profession in Nine-teenth-Century Oxford*. Oxford: Clarendon Press, 1983.

Evans, Richard. *In Defence of History*. London: Granta Books, 1997.

Ferguson, Niall. *Colossus: The Price of America's Empire*. New York: Penguin, 2004.

———. *Empire: How Britain Made the Modern World*. London: Allen Lane, 2003.

Feske, Victor. *From Belloc to Churchill: Private Scholars, Public Culture, and the Crisis of British Liberalism*. Chapel Hill: University of North Carolina Press, 1996.

Field, H. John. *Toward a Programme of Imperial Life: The British Empire at the Turn of the Century*. Westport, CT: Greenwood Press, 1982.

Fifoot, C. H. S. *English Law and Its Background*. London: G. Bell and Sons, 1932.

———. *Frederic William Maitland: A Life*. Cambridge, MA: Harvard University Press, 1971.

———. *Law and History in the Nineteenth Century*. London: Bernard Quaritch, 1956.

———. *Pollock and Maitland*. Glasgow: George Outram, 1971.

Finn, Margot C. *After Chartism: Class and Nation in English Radical Politics, 1848–1874*. Cambridge: Cambridge University Press, 1993.

Fitzpatrick, Ellen. *History's Memory: Writing America's Past, 1880–1980*. Cambridge, MA: Harvard University Press, 2002.

Forbes, Duncan. *The Liberal Anglican Idea of History*. Cambridge: Cambridge University Press, 1952.

Fromkin, David. *Europe's Last Summer: Who Started the Great War in 1914?* New York: Vintage, 2004.

Geary, Patrick J. *The Myth of Nations: The Medieval Origins of Europe*. Princeton, NJ: Princeton University Press, 2002.

Gervais, David. *Literary Englands: Versions of 'Englishness' in Modern Writing*. Cambridge: Cambridge University Press, 1993.

Giles, Judy, and Tim Middleton, eds. *Writing Englishness, 1900–1950: An Introductory Sourcebook on National Identity*. London: Routledge, 1995.

Gilgary, Adrian. *The Silence of Memory*. Oxford: Berg, 1994.

Gillingham, John. *The English in the Twelfth Century: Imperialism, National Identity and Political Values*. Woodbridge: Boydell, 2000.

Goodhart, A. L. *Sir William Searle Holdsworth, O.M. 1871–1944*. London: Bernard Quaritch, 1954.

Gossett, Thomas. *Race: The History of an Idea in America*. Dallas: Southern Methodist University Press, 1963.

Grainger, J. H. *Patriotisms: Britain, 1900–1939*. London: Routledge, 1986.

Gregory, Adrian. *The Silence of Memory: Armistice Day, 1919–1946*. Oxford: Berg, 1994.

Hall, Catherine. *Civilising Subjects: Metropole and Colony in the English Imagination, 1830–1867.* Chicago: University of Chicago Press, 2002.

Hamburger, Joseph. *Macaulay and the Whig Tradition.* Chicago: University of Chicago Press, 1976.

Hanbury, Harold G. *The Vinerian Chair and Legal Education.* Oxford: Blackwell, 1958.

Hanham, H. J., ed. *The Nineteenth-Century Constitution, 1815–1914.* Cambridge: Cambridge University Press, 1969.

Harvie, Christopher. *The Lights of Liberalism: University Liberals and the Challenge of Democracy, 1860–1886.* London: Allen Lane, 1976.

Hastings, Adrian. *The Construction of Nationhood: Ethnicity, Religion and Nationalism.* Cambridge: Cambridge University Press, 1997.

Heathorn, Stephen. *For Home, Country, and Race: Gender, Class, and Englishness in the Elementary School, 1880–1914.* Toronto: University of Toronto Press, 2000.

Heindel, Richard H. *The American Impact on Great Britain, 1898–1914: A Study of the United States in World History.* Philadelphia: University of Pennsylvania Press, 1940.

Helmreich, Anne. *The English Garden and National Identity: The Competing Styles of Garden Design, 1870–1914.* Cambridge: Cambridge University Press, 2002.

Helsinger, Elizabeth K. *Rural Scenes and National Representation: Britain, 1815–1850.* Princeton, NJ: Princeton University Press, 1997.

Heyck, Thomas W. *The Transformation of Intellectual Life in Victorian England.* London: Croom Helm, 1982.

Higham, John. *History: Professional Scholarship in America.* Baltimore: Johns Hopkins University Press, 1983 [1965].

Higham, N. J. *The Norman Conquest.* Stroud: Sutton, 1998.

Higson, Andrew. *Waving the Flag: Constructing a National Cinema in Britain.* Oxford: Clarendon Press, 1995.

Hill, Roland. *Lord Acton.* New Haven, CT: Yale University Press, 2000.

Himmelfarb, Gertrude. *The New History and the Old.* Cambridge, MA: Harvard University Press, 1987.

Hirschmann, Edwin. *White Mutiny: The Ilbert Bill Crisis in India and the Genesis of the Indian National Congress.* New Delhi: Heritage, 1980.

Hoffer, Peter Charles. *Past Imperfect: Facts, Fictions, Fraud—American History from Bancroft and Parkman to Ambrose, Bellesiles, Ellis, and Goodwin.* New York: Public Affairs, 2004.

Hollinger, David A. *Morris R. Cohen and the Scientific Ideal.* Cambridge, MA: MIT Press, 1975.

Holt, J. C. *Colonial England, 1066–1215.* Rio Grande, OH: Hambledon, 1997.

Hulsebosch, Daniel J. *Constituting Empire: New York and the Transformation of Constitutionalism in the Atlantic World, 1664–1830.* Chapel Hill: University of North Carolina Press, 2005.

Hussain, Nasser. *The Jurisprudence of Emergency: Colonialism and the Rule of Law.* Ann Arbor: University of Michigan Press, 2003.

Jann, Rosemary. *The Art and Science of Victorian History.* Columbus: Ohio State University Press, 1985.

Jenkins, Keith. *On "What Is History?": From Carr and Elton to Rorty and White.* New York: Routledge, 1995.

Jenkyns, Richard. *Dignity and Decadence: Victorian Art and the Classical Inheritance.* London: Harper Collins, 1991.

Johnson, Peter. *R. G. Collingwood: An Introduction.* Bristol: Thoemmes, 1998.

Johnston, W. Ross. *Sovereignty and Protection: A Study of British Jurisdictional Imperialism in the Late Nineteenth Century.* Durham, NC: Duke University Press, 1973.

Johnston, William M. *The Formative Years of R. G. Collingwood.* The Hague: Martinus Nijhoff, 1967.

Jones, Edwin. *The English Nation: The Great Myth.* Stroud: Sutton, 1998.

Jones, Greta. *Social Darwinism and English Thought: The Interaction between Biological and Social Theory.* Brighton: Harvester Press, 1980.

Jordanova, Ludmilla. *History in Practice.* London: Edward Arnold, 2000.

Judd, Denis. *The Lion and the Tiger: The Rise and Fall of the British Raj.* London: Oxford University Press, 2004.

Kadish, Alon. *Historians, Economists and Economic History.* London: Routledge, 1989.

———. *The Oxford Economists in the Late Nineteenth Century.* Oxford: Clarendon Press, 1982.

Kendle, John. *The Colonial and Imperial Conferences, 1887–1911: A Study in Imperial Organization.* London: Longmans, Green, 1967.

———. *Federal Britain: A History.* London: Routledge, 1997.

———. *Ireland and the Federal Solution: The Debate over the United Kingdom Constitution, 1870–1921.* Kingston, ON: McGill-Queen's University Press, 1989.

———. *The Round Table Movement and Imperial Union.* Toronto: University of Toronto Press, 1975.

Kenyon, John P. *The History Men: The Historical Profession in England since the Renaissance.* London: Weidenfeld and Nicolson, 1983.

Kidd, Colin. *British Identities before Nationalism: Ethnicity and Nationhood in the Atlantic World, 1600–1800.* Cambridge: Cambridge University Press, 1999.

King, Edmund, ed. *The Anarchy of King Stephen's Reign.* London: Oxford University Press, 1994.

Koditschek, Theodore. *Class Formation and Urban-Industrial Society: Bradford, 1750–1850.* Cambridge: Cambridge University Press, 1990.

Kostal, R. W. *A Jurisprudence of Power: Victorian Empire and the Rule of Law.* New York: Oxford University Press, 2005.

Kumar, Krishan. *The Making of English National Identity.* Cambridge: Cambridge University Press, 2003.

Lang, Timothy. *The Victorians and the Stuart Heritage: Interpretations of a Discordant Past.* Cambridge: Cambridge University Press, 1995.

Langford, Paul. *Englishness Identified: Manners and Character, 1650–1850.* New York: Oxford University Press, 2000.

Lavin, Deborah. *From Empire to International Commonwealth: A Biography of Lionel Curtis.* Oxford: Clarendon Press, 1995.

Lawson, F. H. *The Oxford Law School, 1850–1965.* Oxford: Clarendon Press, 1968.

Lee, R. W. *Edward Jenks, 1861–1939.* London: Humphrey Milford, 1939.

Lerner, Gerda. *Why History Matters: Life and Thought.* New York: Oxford University Press, 1997.

Levine, Philippa. *The Amateur and the Professional: Antiquarians, Historians and Ar-

chaeologists in Victorian England, 1838–1886. Cambridge: Cambridge University Press, 1986.

Liversidge, Michael, and Catherine Edwards, eds. *Imagining Rome: British Artists and Rome in the Nineteenth Century*. London: Merrell Holberton, 1996.

Looser, Devoney. *British Women Writers and the Writing of History, 1670–1820*. Baltimore: Johns Hopkins University Press, 2000.

Lorimer, Douglas. *Colour, Class and the Victorians: English Attitudes to the Negro in the Mid-Nineteenth Century*. Leicester: Leicester University Press, 1978.

Loughlin, James. *Ulster Unionism and British National Identity since 1885*. London: Pinter, 1995.

Lowenthal, David. *The Past Is a Foreign Country*. Cambridge: Cambridge University Press, 1985.

Lyon, Ann. *Constitutional History of the United Kingdom*. London: Cavendish, 2003.

MacDonald, Robert H. *The Language of Empire: Myths and Metaphors of Popular Imperialism, 1880–1918*. Manchester: Manchester University Press, 1994.

MacDougall, Hugh A. *Racial Myth in English History: Trojans, Teutons, and Anglo-Saxons*. Hanover, NH: University Press of New England, 1982.

MacKenzie, John M. *Orientalism: History, Theory and the Arts*. Manchester: Manchester University Press, 1995.

———. *Propaganda and Empire: The Manipulation of British Public Opinion, 1880–1960*. Manchester: Manchester University Press, 1984.

Maitzen, Rohan Amanda. *Gender, Genre, and Victorian Historical Writing*. New York: Garland, 1998.

Malchow, Howard L. *Gothic Images of Race in Nineteenth-Century Britain*. Stanford, CA: Stanford University Press, 1996.

Mandler, Peter. *History and National Life*. London: Profile Books, 2002.

McCartney, Donal. *W. E. H. Lecky: Historian and Politician, 1838–1903*. Dublin: Lilliput Press, 1994.

McClelland, Charles E. *The German Historians and England: A Study in Nineteenth-Century Views*. Cambridge: Cambridge University Press, 1971.

McDevitt, Patrick. *May the Best Man Win: Sport, Masculinity and Nationalism in Great Britain and the Empire, 1880–1935*. New York: Palgrave Macmillan, 2004.

McIntire, C. T. *Herbert Butterfield: Historian as Dissenter*. New Haven, CT: Yale University Press, 2004.

McNeill, William H. *Arnold J. Toynbee: A Life*. New York: Oxford University Press, 1989.

Meacham, Standish. *Regaining Paradise: Englishness and the Early Garden City Movement*. New Haven, CT: Yale University Press, 1999.

Mehta, Ved. *Fly and the Fly-Bottle: Encounters with British Intellectuals*. Boston: Little, Brown, 1962.

Miles, Robert. *Racism*. London: Routledge, 1989.

Miller, David. *On Nationality*. Oxford: Clarendon Press, 1995.

Milsom, S. F. C. *Historical Foundations of the Common Law*. London: Butterworth's, 1969.

———. *A Natural History of the Common Law*. New York: Columbia University Press, 2003.

———. *Studies in the History of the Common Law*. London: Hambledon, 1985.

Mink, Louis O. *Mind, History, and Dialectic: The Philosophy of R. G. Collingwood*. Bloomington: Indiana University Press, 1969.

Mitchell, Rosemary. *Picturing the Past: English History in Text and Image, 1830–1870*. Oxford: Clarendon Press, 2000.

Morgan, Marjorie. *National Identities and Travel in Victorian Britain*. New York: Palgrave, 2001.

Morillo, Stephen. *Warfare under the Anglo-Norman Kings, 1066–1135*. Woodbridge: Boydell Press, 1994.

Musson, Anthony. *Medieval Law in Context: The Growth of Legal Consciousness from Magna Carta to the Peasants' Revolt*. Manchester: Manchester University Press, 2001.

Nairn, Tom. *The Enchanted Glass: Britain and Its Monarchy*. London: Radius, 1988.

———. *Pariah: Misfortunes of the British Kingdom*. London: Verso, 2002.

Namier, Julia. *Lewis Namier: A Biography*. London: Oxford University Press, 1971.

Nash, Gary B., Charlotte Crabtree, and Ross E. Dunn. *History on Trial: Culture Wars and the Teaching of the Past*. New York: Knopf, 1997.

Newman, Gerald. *The Rise of English Nationalism: A Cultural History, 1714–1830*. New York: St. Martin's Press, 1987.

Novick, Peter. *That Noble Dream: The "Objectivity Question" and the American Historical Profession*. Cambridge: Cambridge University Press, 1988.

O'Brien, Phillips Payson. *British and American Naval Power, 1900–1936*. Westport, CT: Praeger, 1998.

O'Day, Alan. *Irish Home Rule, 1867–1921*. Manchester: Manchester University Press, 1998.

Oleson, T. J. *The WITENAGEMOT in the Reign of Edward the Confessor: A Study in the Constitutional History of Eleventh-Century England*. London: Oxford University Press, 1955.

Parker, Christopher J. W. *The English Historical Tradition since 1850*. Edinburgh: John Donald, 1990.

———. *The English Idea of History from Coleridge to Collingwood*. Aldershot: Ashgate, 2000.

Patterson, Annabel. *Nobody's Perfect: A New Whig Interpretation of History*. New Haven, CT: Yale University Press, 2002.

Paul, Herbert. *The Life of Froude*. New York: Scribner's, 1906.

Peardon, Thomas. *The Transition in English Historical Writing, 1760–1830*. New York: AMS Press, 1966 [1933].

Perkin, Harold. *The Rise of Professional Society: England since 1880*. London: Routledge, 1989.

Perkins, Bradford. *The Great Rapprochement: England and the United States, 1895–1914*. New York: Atheneum, 1968.

Peters, Charles. *Five Days in Philadelphia: The Amazing "We Want Wilkie!" Convention of 1940 and How It Freed FDR to Save the Western World*. New York: Public Affairs, 2005.

Phillips, Mark Salber. *Society and Sentiment: Genres of Historical Writing in Britain, 1740–1820*. Princeton, NJ: Princeton University Press, 2000.

Phillips, Paul T. *Britain's Past in Canada: The Teaching and Writing of British History*. Vancouver: University of British Columbia Press, 1989.

————. *The Controversialist: An Intellectual Life of Goldwin Smith.* Westport, CT: Praeger, 2002.

Pittock, Murray G. H. *Inventing and Resisting Britain: Cultural Identities in Britain and Ireland, 1685–1789.* Basingstoke: Macmillan, 1997.

Pitts, Jennifer. *A Turn to Empire: The Rise of Imperial Liberalism in Britain and France.* Princeton, NJ: Princeton University Press, 2005.

Plumb, J. H. *The Death of the Past.* London: Macmillan, 1969.

————. *The Making of an Historian: The Collected Essays of J. H. Plumb.* 2 vols. Athens: University of Georgia Press, 1988–89.

Porter, Bernard. *The Absent-Minded Imperialists: Empire, Society, and Culture in Britain.* New York: Oxford University Press, 2004.

Powell, W. Raymond. *John Horace Round: Historian and Gentleman of Essex.* Chelmsford: Essex Record Office, 2001.

Quigley, Carroll. *The Anglo-American Establishment from Rhodes to Cliveden.* San Diego: GSL Associates, 1981.

Ragussis, Michael. *Figures of Conversion: "The Jewish Question" and English National Identity.* Durham, NC: Duke University Press, 1995.

Reed, John S. *Glorious Battle: The Cultural Politics of Victorian Anglo-Catholicism.* Nashville: Vanderbilt University Press, 1996.

Reid, John Phillip. *The Ancient Constitution and the Origins of Anglo-American Liberty.* DeKalb: Northern Illinois University Press, 2005.

Reynolds, Susan. *Kingdoms and Communities in Western Europe, 900–1300.* Oxford: Clarendon Press, 1984.

Rich, Paul B. *Race and Empire in British Politics.* Cambridge: Cambridge University Press, 1986.

Richards, Jeffrey. *Films and British National Identity: From Dickens to Dad's Army.* Manchester: Manchester University Press, 1997.

————. *Imperialism and Music: Britain, 1876–1953.* Manchester: Manchester University Press, 2001.

Richardson, H. G., and G. O. Sayles. *The Governance of Medieval England from the Conquest to Magna Carta.* Edinburgh: Edinburgh University Press, 1963.

————. *Law and Legislation from Aethelbert to Magna Carta.* Edinburgh: Edinburgh University Press, 1966.

Robbins, Keith. *Nineteenth-Century Britain: Integration and Diversity.* Oxford: Clarendon Press, 1988.

Roberts, Robert. *The Classic Slum: Salford Life in the First Quarter of the Century.* Manchester: Manchester University Press, 1971.

Rothberg, Morey, and Jacqueline Goggin, eds. *John Franklin Jameson and the Development of Humanistic Scholarship in America.* 3 vols. Athens: University of Georgia Press, 1993–2001.

Rothblatt, Sheldon. *The Revolution of the Dons: Cambridge and Society in Victorian England.* New York: Basic Books, 1968.

————. *Tradition and Change in English Liberal Education: An Essay in History and Culture.* London: Faber and Faber, 1976.

Rowse, A. L. *Froude the Historian: Victorian Man of Letters.* Gloucester: Sutton, 1987.

————. *Historians I Have Known.* London: Duckworth, 1995.

————. *Memories of Men and Women*. London: Eyre Methuen, 1980.

Saveth, Edward N. *American Historians and European Immigrants, 1875–1925*. New York: Russell and Russell, 1965.

Scott, Joan W. *Gender and the Politics of History*. New York: Columbia University Press, 1999 [1988].

Seager, Robert, II. *Alfred Thayer Mahan: The Man and His Letters*. Annapolis, MD: Naval Institute Press, 1977.

Sellar, W. C., and R. J. Yeatman. *1066—And All That*. London: Methuen, 1930.

Sen, Sudipta. *Distant Sovereignty: National Imperialism and the Origins of British India*. New York: Routledge, 2002.

Sewell, Keith C. *Herbert Butterfield and the Interpretation of History*. New York: Palgrave Macmillan, 2005.

Shaw, Christopher, and Malcolm Chase, eds. *The Imagined Past: History and Nostalgia*. Manchester: Manchester University Press, 1989.

Shinn, Ridgway F. *Arthur Berriedale Keith, 1879–1944: The Chief Ornament of Scottish Learning*. Aberdeen: Aberdeen University Press, 1990.

Shoup, Lawrence, and William Minter. *Imperial Brain Trust: The Council on Foreign Relations and United States Foreign Policy*. New York: Authors Choice Press, 2004 [1977].

Simmons, Clare A. *Reversing the Conquest: History and Myth in Nineteenth-Century Literature*. New Brunswick, NJ: Rutgers University Press, 1990.

Simpson, Renate. *How the PhD Came to Britain: A Century of Struggle for Postgraduate Education*. Guildford: Society for Research into Higher Education, 1983.

Slee, Peter R. H. *Learning and Liberal Education: The Study of Modern History in the Universities of Oxford, Cambridge, and Manchester, 1800–1914*. Manchester: Manchester University Press, 1986.

Smiles, Sam. *The Image of Antiquity: Ancient Britain and the Romantic Imagination*. New Haven, CT: Yale University Press, 1994.

Smith, Anthony D. *The Ethnic Origins of Nations*. Oxford: Blackwell, 1986.

————. *Theories of Nationalism*. London: Duckworth, 1983 [1971].

Smith, Bonnie G. *The Gender of History: Men, Women, and Historical Practice*. Cambridge, MA: Harvard University Press, 1998.

Smith, K. J. M. *James Fitzjames Stephen: Portrait of a Victorian Rationalist*. Cambridge: Cambridge University Press, 1988.

Smith, R. J. *The Gothic Bequest: Medieval Institutions in British Thought, 1688–1863*. New York: Cambridge University Press, 1987.

Soffer, Reba N. *Discipline and Power: The University, History, and the Making of an English Elite, 1870–1930*. Stanford, CA: Stanford University Press, 1994.

Stapleton, Julia. *Englishness and the Study of Politics: The Social and Political Thought of Ernest Barker*. Cambridge: Cambridge University Press, 1994.

————. *Political Intellectuals and Public Identities in Britain since 1850*. Manchester: Manchester University Press, 2001.

Stepan, Nancy. *The Idea of Race in Science: Great Britain, 1800–1960*. London: Macmillan, 1982.

Stieg, Margaret. *The Origin and Development of Scholarly Historical Periodicals*. Tuscaloosa: University of Alabama Press, 1986.

Strong, Roy C., *Recreating the Past: British History and the Victorian Painter*. New York: Thames and Hudson, 1978.

———. *The Story of Britain*. New York: Fromm International, 1996.

Strout, Cushing. *The American Image of the Old World*. New York: Harper & Row, 1963.

Symonds, Richard. *Oxford and Empire: The Last Lost Cause?* London: Macmillan 1986.

Taylor, John. *A Dream of England: Landscape, Photography and the Tourist's Imagination*. Manchester: Manchester University Press, 1994.

Thompson, Andrew. *The Empire Strikes Back? The Impact of Imperialism on Britain from the Mid-Nineteenth Century*. Harlow: Longman, 2005.

Thompson, Edward P. *The Making of the English Working Class*. New York: Pantheon, 1963.

Thompson, Thomas W. *James Anthony Froude on Nation and Empire: A Study in Victorian Racialism*. New York: Garland, 1987.

Tidrick, Kathryn. *Empire and the English Character*. London: I. B. Tauris, 1990.

Toynbee, Arnold J. *Acquaintances*. London: Oxford University Press, 1967.

———. *A Study of History*. 12 vols. London: Oxford University Press, 1934–61.

Tulloch, Hugh. *Acton*. London: Weidenfeld and Nicolson, 1988.

———. *James Bryce's American Commonwealth: The Anglo-American Background*. Woodbridge: Royal Historical Society, 1988.

Turner, Frank M. *Contesting Cultural Authority: Essays in Victorian Intellectual Life*. Cambridge: Cambridge University Press, 1993.

———. *The Greek Heritage in Victorian Britain*. New Haven, CT: Yale University Press, 1981.

Turner, Katherine. *British Travel Writers in Europe 1750–1800: Authorship, Gender and National Identity*. Burlington: Ashgate, 2001.

Twining, William. *Blackstone's Tower: The English Law School*. London: Stevens & Sons/ Sweet & Maxwell, 1994.

Vance, Norman. *The Victorians and Ancient Rome*. Oxford: Blackwell, 1997.

Van Der Dussen, W. J. *History as a Science: The Philosophy of R. G. Collingwood*. The Hague: Martinus Nijhoff, 1981.

Vicinus, Martha. *Independent Women: Work and Community for Single Women, 1850–1920*. London: Virago, 1985.

Von Arx, Jeffrey. *Progress and Pessimism: Religion, Politics, and History in Late Nineteenth Century Britain*. Cambridge, MA: Harvard University Press, 1985.

Wallace, Stuart. *War and the Image of Germany: British Academics, 1914–1918*. Edinburgh: John Donald, 1988.

Ward, Ian. *A State of Mind? The English Constitution and the Popular Imagination*. Stroud: Sutton, 2000.

———. *The English Constitution: Myths and Realities*. Oxford and Portland, OR: Hart Publishing, 2004.

Ward, Paul. *Britishness since 1870*. London: Routledge, 2004.

Wawn, Andrew. *The Vikings and the Victorians: Inventing the Old North in Nineteenth-Century Britain*. Cambridge: D. S. Brewer, 2000.

Weaver, Stewart A. *The Hammonds: A Marriage in History*. Stanford, CA: Stanford University Press, 1998.

Webster, Wendy. *Englishness and Empire, 1939–1965*. New York: Oxford University Press, 2005.

Wedgwood, C. V. *History and Hope: The Collected Essays of C. V. Wedgwood*. London: Collins, 1987.

Weight, Richard. *Patriots: National Identity in Britain, 1940–2000*. London: Macmillan, 2002.

Wilson, Kathleen. *The Island Race: Englishness, Empire and Gender in the Eighteenth Century*. London: Routledge, 2003.

Wish, Harvey. *The American Historian: A Social-Intellectual History of the Writing of the American Past*. New York: Oxford University Press, 1960.

Wolffe, John. *God and Greater Britain: Religion and National Life in Britain and Ireland, 1843–1945*. London: Routledge, 1994.

Wolton, Suke. *Lord Hailey, the Colonial Office and the Politics of Race and Empire in the Second World War: The Loss of White Prestige*. New York: Palgrave, 2000.

Wood, Michael. *In Search of England: Journeys into the English Past*. Berkeley: University of California Press, 1999.

Wormald, Patrick. *The Making of English Law: King Alfred to the Twelfth Century*. Volume I: *Legislation and Its Limits*. Oxford: Blackwell, 1999.

Wormell, Deborah. *Sir John Seeley and the Uses of History*. Cambridge: Cambridge University Press, 1980.

Wright, Patrick. *On Living in an Old Country: The National Past in Contemporary Britain*. London: Verso, 1985.

Young, Robert J. C. *Colonial Desire: Hybridity in Theory, Culture and Race*. New York: Routledge, 1995.

Zimmerman, Jonathan. *Whose America? Culture Wars in the Public Schools*. Cambridge, MA: Harvard University Press, 2002.

Primary Articles

Adams, George Burton. "Anglo-Saxon Feudalism." *American Historical Review* 7 (October 1901): 11–35.

———. "British Imperial Federation after the War." *Yale Review* 5 (April 1916): 687–701.

———. "A Century of Anglo-Saxon Expansion." *Atlantic Monthly* 79 (April 1897): 528–38.

———. "The Origin of the English Courts of Common Law." *Yale Law Journal* 30 (June 1921): 798–813.

Adams, Herbert Baxter. "The Germanic Origins of New England Towns." *Johns Hopkins University Studies in Historical and Political Science* 1 (1883): 1–21.

———. "Special Methods of Historical Study." In G. Stanley Hall, ed., *Methods of Teaching History*, 2nd ed., pp. 113–47. Boston: Ginn, Heath, and Co., 1885.

Anon. "The Annual Meeting of the American Historical Association." *American Historical Review* 3 (April 1898): 405–17.

Archer, T. A. "The Battle of Hastings." *English Historical Review* 9 (January 1894): 1–41.

Bryce, James. "The Essential Unity of Britain and America." *Atlantic Monthly* 82 (July 1898): 22–29.

———. "The Influence of National Character and Historical Environment on the Development of the Common Law." *American Bar Association Reports* 31 (1907): 444–62.

Cam, Helen. "Law as It Looks to a Historian." Founders Lecture, Girton College, 18 February 1956.

———. "Stubbs Seventy Years After." *Cambridge Historical Journal* 9 (1948): 129–47.

Dicey, Albert Venn. "Digby on the History of English Law." *The Nation* (9 December 1875): 581–82.

———. "History." *Working Men's College Journal* 6 (March 1900): 193–98.

Fisher, H. A. L. "The Whig Historians." *Proceedings of the British Academy* 14 (1928): 297–339.

Freeman, Edward. "Last Words on Mr. Froude." *Contemporary Review* 35 (May 1879): 214–36.

Jameson, John Franklin. "The American Historical Association, 1884–1909." *American Historical Review* 15 (October 1909): 1–20.

———. "The International Congress of Historical Studies, Held at London." *American Historical Review* 18 (July 1913): 679–91.

Neilson, Nellie. "Boon-Services on the Estates of Ramsey Abbey." *American Historical Review* 2 (January 1897): 213–24.

———. "The Early Pattern of the Common Law." *American Historical Review* 49 (January 1944): 199–211.

Norgate, Kate. "The Battle of Hastings." *English Historical Review* 9 (January 1894): 41–76.

Osgood, Herbert. "Review of George Otto Trevelyan, *The American Revolution*." *Political Science Quarterly* 19 (September 1904): 502–5.

Plucknett, Theodore F. T. "Maitland's View of Law and History." *Law Quarterly Review* 67 (April 1951): 179–94.

Pollock, Sir Frederick. "The Continuity of the Common Law." *Harvard Law Review* 11 (February 1898): 423–33.

Power, Eileen. "On Mediaeval History as a Social Study." In N. B. Harte, ed., *The Study of Economic History: Collected Inaugural Lectures, 1893–1970*, pp. 109–26. London: Frank Cass, 1971.

Powicke, F. M. "Review of Charles Homer Haskins, *Studies in the History of Mediaeval Science*." *English Historical Review* 40 (July 1925): 421–23.

Ralph, Julian. "Anglo-Saxon Affinities." *Harper's New Monthly Magazine* 98 (1899): 385–91.

Round, John Horace. "As Established by Law." *Contemporary Review* 75 (June 1899): 814–22.

———. "Historical Research." *The Nineteenth Century* 44 (December 1898): 1004–14.

———. "Introduction." In *Pipe Roll 29 Henry II 1182–83*, i–xxxi. London: The Pipe Roll Society, 1911.

———. "The Introduction of Knight Service into England." *English Historical Review* 6 (July 1891): 417–43; 6 (October 1891): 625–45; and 7 (January 1892): 11–24.

———. "Mr. Freeman and the Battle of Hastings." *English Historical Review* 9 (April 1894): 209–59.

———. "Professor Freeman." *Quarterly Review* 175 (July 1892): 1–37.

Sloane, William M. "History and Democracy." *American Historical Review* 1 (October 1895): 1–23.

Smith, Theodore Clarke. "The Writing of American History in America, from 1884 to 1934." *American Historical Review* 40 (April 1935): 439–49.

Stenton, Frank M. "Early English History, 1895–1920." *Transactions of the Royal Historical Society,* Fourth Series 28 (1946): 7–19.

———. "Foreword." In John Horace Round, *Feudal England: Historical Studies in the Eleventh and Twelfth Centuries,* pp. 1–8. London: G. Allen & Unwin, 1964 [1895].

———. "Round, John Horace." In *Dictionary of National Biography, 1922–1930,* pp. 727–31 (London: Oxford University Press, 1937).

Stock, Leo Francis. "Some Bryce-Jameson Correspondence." *American Historical Review* 50 (January 1945): 261–98.

Tait, James. "John Horace Round." *English Historical Review* 43 (October 1928): 572–77.

Tanner, J. R. "The Teaching of Constitutional History." In William A. J. Archbold, ed., *The Teaching of History,* pp. 51–68. Cambridge: Cambridge University Press, 1901.

Tout, T. F. "Mary Bateson (1865–1906)." In *Twentieth Century DNB 1901–1911.* pp. 110–12 (Oxford: Clarendon Press, 1912).

Tyler, Moses Coit. "The Party of the Loyalists in the American Revolution." *American Historical Review* 1 (October 1895): 24–45.

Van Tyne, Claude H. "Review of Altschul, *The American Revolution in Our School Text-Books.*" *American Historical Review* 23 (January 1918): 404.

Vinogradoff, Paul. "Folkland." *English Historical Review* 8 (January 1893): 1–17.

Wrench, Evelyn. "Recollections of Early Life and Foundation of the English-Speaking Union." *Concord* 1 (November 1962): 3–6.

Secondary Articles

Adamson, J. S. A. "Eminent Victorians: S. R. Gardiner and the Liberal as Hero." *Historical Journal* 33 (September 1990): 641–57.

Allardyce, Gilbert. "The Rise and Fall of the Western Civilization Course." *American Historical Review* 87 (June 1982): 695–725.

Anderson, Olive. "The Political Uses of History in Mid-Nineteenth-Century England." *Past and Present* 36 (April 1967): 87–105.

Anderson, Stuart. "Racial Anglo-Saxonism and the American Response to the Boer War." *Diplomatic History* 2 (Summer 1978): 219–36.

Anon. "Obituary." *Manchester Guardian* (24 October 1929).

Armitage, David. "Greater Britain: A Useful Category of Historical Analysis?" *American Historical Review* 104 (April 1999): 427–45.

Arnstein, Walter L. "George Macaulay Trevelyan and the Art of History: A Centenary Appraisal." *Midwest Quarterly* 18 (Autumn 1976): 78–97.

Ashplant, T. G., and Adrian Wilson. "Present-centred History and the Problem of Historical Knowledge." *Historical Journal* 31 (June 1988): 253–74.

———. "Whig History and Present-centred History." *Historical Journal* 31 (March 1988): 1–16.

Bailey, Charles E. "The British Protestant Theologians in the First World War: Germanophobia Unleashed." *Harvard Theological Review* 77 (April 1984): 195–221.

Baker, J. H. "Why the History of English Law Has Not Been Finished." *Cambridge Law Journal* 59 (March 2000): 62–84.

Bates, David. "Medieval Historiography: Stenton, Maitland, Round." *Journal of British Studies* 38 (January 1999): 93–97.

Bennett, Judith M. "Medievalism and Feminism." *Speculum* 68 (April 1993): 309–31.

——. "Writing Fornication: Medieval Leyrwite and Its Historians." *Transactions of the Royal Historical Society,* Sixth Series 13 (2003): 131–62.

Berberich, Christine. "'I Was Meditating about England': The Importance of Rural England for the Construction of 'Englishness.'" In Helen Brocklehurst and Robert Phillips, eds., *History, Nationhood and the Question of Britain*, pp. 375–85. New York: Palgrave Macmillan, 2004.

Berg, Maxine. "The First Women Economic Historians." *Economic History Review* 45 (May 1992): 308–29.

Betts, Raymond F. "The Allusion to Rome in British Imperialist Thought of the Late Nineteenth and Early Twentieth Centuries." *Victorian Studies* 15 (December 1971): 149–59.

Billington, Ray Allen. "Tempest in Clio's Teapot: The American Historical Association Rebellion of 1915." *American Historical Review* 78 (April 1973): 348–69.

Blair, Tony. "Britishness and the Government's Agenda of Constitutional Reform." 28 March 2000, Press Release, British Consulate-General, Los Angeles.

Bourne, Henry E. "The Fiftieth Anniversary Meeting." *American Historical Review* 40 (April 1935): 423–38.

Boyden, Peter B. "J. H. Round and the Beginnings of the Modern Study of Domesday Book: Essex and Beyond." *Essex Archaeology and History* 12 (1980): 11–24.

Brace, Catherine. "Finding England Everywhere: Regional Identity and the Construction of National Identity, 1890–1940." *Ecumene* 6 (January 1999): 90–109.

Brentano, Robert. "The Sound of Stubbs." *Journal of British Studies* 6 (May 1967): 1–14.

Brinkley, Alan, Laura Kalman, William E. Leuchtenburg, and G. Edward White. "The Debate over the Constitutional Revolution of 1937." *American Historical Review* 110 (October 2005): 1046–115.

"Britain Rediscovered." *Prospect* 109 (April 2005): 1–14.

Brooke, Stephen. "Identities in Twentieth-Century Britain." *Journal of British Studies* 40 (January 2001): 151–58.

Brown, Elizabeth A. R. "The Tyranny of a Construct: Feudalism and Historians of Medieval Europe." *American Historical Review* 79 (October 1974): 1063–88.

Brown, R. Allen. "The Norman Conquest." *Transactions of the Royal Historical Society,* Fifth Series 17 (1967): 109–30.

Buckland, W. W. "F. W. Maitland." *Cambridge Law Journal* 1 (1923): 279–301.

Buckner, Phillip. "Whatever Happened to the British Empire?" *Journal of the Canadian Historical Association,* New Series 4 (1993): 3–32.

Buckner, Phillip, and Carl Bridge. "Reinventing the British World." *Round Table* 368 (January 2003): 77–88.

Burrow, John W. "Victorian Historians and the Royal Historical Society." *Transactions of the Royal Historical Society,* Fifth Series 39 (1989): 125–40.

——. "'The Village Community' and the Uses of History in Late Nineteenth-Century England." In Neil McKendrick, ed., *Historical Perspectives: Studies in English Thought and Society in Honour of J. H. Plumb*, pp. 255–84. London: Europa, 1974.

Burton, Antoinette. "Introduction: On the Inadequacy and the Indispensability of the Nation." In Antoinette Burton, ed., *After the Imperial Turn: Thinking with and through the Nation*, pp. 1–23. Durham, NC: Duke University Press, 2003.

Bush, George W. "Age of Liberty: 'The Calling of Our Time.'" 6 November 2003; *Arizona Republic*, 30 November 2003.

Campbell, James. "The Late Anglo-Saxon State: A Maximum View." *Proceedings of the British Academy* 87 (1995): 39–65.

———. "Stenton's *Anglo-Saxon England* with Special Reference to the Earlier Period." In Donald Matthew, ed., *Stenton's Anglo-Saxon England Fifty Years On*, pp. 49–59. Reading: University of Reading Press, 1994.

———. "Stubbs, Maitland, and Constitutional History." In Benedikt Stuchtey and Peter Wende, eds., *British and German Historiography, 1750–1950: Traditions, Perceptions, and Transfers*, pp. 99–122. Oxford: Oxford University Press, 2000.

———. "William Stubbs (1825–1901)." In Helen Damico and Joseph B. Zavadil, eds., *Medieval Scholarship: Biographical Studies on the Formation of a Discipline*, pp. 77–87. New York: Garland, 1995.

Cannadine, David. "British History as a 'New Subject': Politics, Perspectives and Prospects." In Alexander Grant and Keith J. Stringer, eds., *Uniting the Kingdom: The Making of British History*, pp. 12–28. London: Routledge, 1995.

———. "British History: Past, Present—and Future?" *Past and Present* 116 (August 1987): 169–91.

Capelli, Cristian, Nicola Redhead, Julia K. Abernethy, et al. "A Y Chromosome Census of the British Isles." *Current Biology* 13 (2003): 979–84.

Carpenter, Christine. "Political and Constitutional History: Before and After McFarlane." In Richard H. Britnell and A. J. Pollard, eds., *The McFarlane Legacy: Studies in Late Medieval Politics and Society*, pp. 175–206. Stroud: Sutton, 1995.

Chadwick, Owen. "Acton and Butterfield." *Journal of Ecclesiastical History* 38 (July 1987): 386–405.

Chase, Malcolm. "This Is No Claptrap: This Is Our Heritage." In Malcolm Chase and Christopher Shaw, eds., *The Imagined Past: History and Nostalgia*, pp. 128–46. Manchester: Manchester University Press, 1989.

Cheney, C. R. "Helen Maud Cam, 1885–1968." *Proceedings of the British Academy* 55 (1969): 293–310.

Chibnall, Marjorie McCallum. "Eileen Edna Le Poer Power (1889–1940)." In Jane Chance, ed., *Women Medievalists in the Academy*, pp. 311–21. Madison: University of Wisconsin Press, 2005.

———. "Memoir (1914–)." In Jane Chance, ed., *Women Medievalists in the Academy*, pp. 747–58. Madison: University of Wisconsin Press, 2005.

Clark, J. C. D. "England's Ancien Regime as a Confessional State." *Albion* 21 (Fall 1989): 450–74.

———. "Protestantism, Nationalism, and National Identity, 1660–1832." *Historical Journal* 43 (March 2000): 249–76.

Claydon, Tony, and Ian McBride. "The Trials of the Chosen Peoples: Recent Interpretations of Protestantism and National Identity in Britain and Ireland." In Tony Claydon and Ian McBride, eds., *Protestantism and National Identity: Britain and Ireland, c. 1650–c. 1850*, pp. 3–29. Cambridge: Cambridge University Press, 1999.

Cockcroft, Grace A. "George Louis Beer." In Herman Ausubel, J. Bartlett Brebner, and Ealing M. Hunt, eds., *Some Historians of Modern Britain: Essays in Honor of R. L. Schuyler*, pp. 269–85. New York: Dryden Press, 1951.

Cohen, Deborah. "Who Was Who? Race and Jews in Turn-of-the-Century Britain." *Journal of British Studies* 41 (October 2002): 460–83.

Colley, Linda. "Britishness and Otherness: An Argument." *Journal of British Studies* 31 (July 1992): 309–29.

Collini, Stefan. "Genealogies of Englishness: Literary History and Cultural Criticism in Modern Britain." In Ciaran Brady, ed., *Ideology and the Historians*, pp. 128–45. Dublin: Lilliput Press, 1991.

Colls, Robert. "The Constitution of the English." *History Workshop Journal* 46 (Autumn 1998): 97–127.

———. "Englishness and the Political Culture." In Robert Colls and Philip Dodd, eds., *Englishness: Politics and Culture, 1880–1920*, pp. 29–61. London: Croom Helm, 1986.

Cosgrove, Richard A. "The Culture of Academic Legal History: Lawyers' History and Historians' Law 1870–1930." *Cambrian Law Review* 33 (2002): 23–34.

———. "Reflections on the Whig Interpretation of History." *Journal of Early Modern History* 4 (2000): 147–67.

———. "The Relevance of Irish History: The Gladstone-Dicey Debate about Home Rule, 1886–7." *Eire-Ireland* 13 (Winter 1978): 6–21.

Crane, Verner W. "Certain Writings of Benjamin Franklin on the British Empire." *The Papers of the Bibliographical Society of America* 28 (1934): 1–27.

Crick, Julia. "*Pristina Libertas*: Liberty and the Anglo-Saxons Revisited." *Transactions of the Royal Historical Society*, Sixth Series 14 (2004): 47–71.

Cromartie, Alan. "The Constitutionalist Revolution: The Transformation of Political Culture in Early Stuart England." *Past and Present* 163 (May 1999): 77–120.

Cronne, H. A. "Edward Augustus Freeman, 1823–1892." *History* 28 (March 1943): 78–92.

Crouch, David. "From Stenton to McFarlane: Models of Societies of the Twelfth and Thirteenth Centuries." *Transactions of the Royal Historical Society*, Sixth Series 5 (1995): 179–200.

Curtis, Lewis P. "The Greening of Irish History." *Eire-Ireland* 29 (Summer 1994): 7–28.

Darwin, J. G. "The Fear of Failing: British Politics and Imperial Decline since 1900." *Transaction of the Royal Historical Society*, Fifth Series 36 (1986): 27–43.

Davies, Norman. "The Decomposing of Britain." *Times Literary Supplement* (6 October 2000): 15–16.

Davis, Natalie Zemon. "History's Two Bodies." *American Historical Review* 93 (February 1988): 1–30.

Day, David. "The Justices' Chronicler: Bertha Haven Putnam (1872–1960)." In Jane Chance, ed., *Women Medievalists in the Academy*, pp. 157–66. Madison: University of Wisconsin Press, 2005.

Dellheim, Charles. "Interpreting Victorian Medievalism." In Florence S. Boos, ed., *History and Community: Essays in Victorian Medievalism*, pp. 39–58. New York: Garland, 1992.

De Nie, Michael. "'A Medley Mob of Irish-American Plotters and Irish Dupes': The British Press and Transatlantic Fenianism." *Journal of British Studies* 40 (April 2001): 213–40.

Demetriou, Kyriacos. "In Defence of the British Constitution: Theoretical Implications of the Debate over Athenian Democracy in Britain, 1770–1850." *History of Political Thought* 17 (Summer 1996): 280–97.

Deslandes, Paul R. "'The Foreign Element': Newcomers and the Rhetoric of Race, Nation, and Empire in 'Oxbridge' Undergraduate Culture, 1850–1920." *Journal of British Studies* 37 (January 1998): 54–90.

DeWindt, Anne Reiber. "Nellie Neilson (1873–1947): A Historian of 'Wit, Whimsy, and Sheer Poetry.'" In Jane Chance, ed., *Women Medievalists in the Academy*, pp. 167–81. Madison: University of Wisconsin Press, 2005.

Dockray-Miller, Mary. "Mary Bateson (1865–1906): Scholar and Suffragist." In Jane Chance, ed., *Women Medievalists in the Academy*, pp. 67–78. Madison: University of Wisconsin Press, 2005.

Doherty, Gabriel. "National Identity and the Study of Irish History." *English Historical Review* 111 (April 1996): 324–49.

Douglas, David C. "The Norman Conquest and British Historians." In *Time and the Hour: Some Collected Papers of David C. Douglas*, pp. 57–76. London: Eyre Methuen, 1977.

Ellis, John S. "'The Methods of Barbarism' and the 'Rights of Small Nations': War Propaganda and British Pluralism." *Albion* 30 (Spring 1998): 49–75.

Ellis, Joseph. "The Big Man: History vs. Alexander Hamilton." *New Yorker* (29 October 2001): 76–84.

Elton, Geoffrey. "Herbert Butterfield and the Study of History." *Historical Journal* 27 (September 1984): 729–43.

English, Barbara. "*Lark Rise* and Juniper Hill: A Victorian Community in Literature and in History." *Victorian Studies* 29 (Autumn 1985): 7–34.

Epstein, James. "The Constitutional Idiom: Radical Reasoning, Rhetoric and Action in Early Nineteenth-Century England." *Journal of Social History* 23 (Spring 1990): 553–74.

Evans, Eric. "Englishness and Britishness: National Identities, c. 1790–c. 1870." In Alexander Grant and Keith J. Stringer, eds., *Uniting the Kingdom: The Making of British History*, pp. 223–43. London: Routledge, 1995.

Finn, Margot C. "Law's Empire: English Legal Cultures at Home and Abroad." *Historical Journal* 48 (March 2005): 295–303.

———. "A Vent Which Has Conveyed Our Principles: English Radical Patriotism in the Aftermath of 1848." *Journal of Modern History* 64 (December 1992): 637–59.

FitzGerald, Jennifer. "'Persephone Come Back from the Dead': Maude Violet Clarke (1892–1935)." In Jane Chance, ed., *Women Medievalists and the Academy*, pp. 381–98. Madison: University of Wisconsin Press, 2005.

Fletcher, Anthony. "The First Century of English Protestantism and the Growth of National Identity." In Stewart Mews, ed., *Religion and National Identity*, pp. 309–17. Oxford: Blackwell, 1982.

Foot, Sarah. "The Making of *Angelcynn*: English Identity before the Norman Conquest." *Transactions of the Royal Historical Society*, Sixth Series 6 (1996): 25–49.

Frantzen, Allen J., and John D. Niles. "Anglo-Saxonism and Medievalism." In Allen J. Frantzen and John D. Niles, eds., *Anglo-Saxonism and the Construction of Social Identity*, pp. 1–14. Gainesville: University Press of Florida, 1997.

Freedman, Paul, and Gabrielle Spiegel. "Medievalism Old and New: The Rediscovery of Alterity in North American Medieval Studies." *American Historical Review* 103 (June 1998): 677–704.

Fyfe, Christopher. "Race, Empire and the Historians." *Race and Class* 33 (April–June 1992): 15–30.

Galbraith, V. H. "Sir Frank Stenton (1880–1967)." *American Historical Review* 76 (October 1971): 1116–23.

Gilbert, Marc Jason. "Insurmountable Distinctions: Racism and the British Response to the Emergence of Indian Nationalism." In Roger D. Long, ed., *The Man on the Spot: Essays on British Empire History*, pp. 161–81. Westport, CT: Greenwood Press, 1995.

Gilley, Sheridan. "English Attitudes to the Irish in England, 1780–1900." In Colin Holmes, ed., *Immigrants and Minorities in British Society*, pp. 81–110. London: Allen & Unwin, 1978.

Gillingham, John. "The Introduction of Knight Service into England." *Proceedings of the Battle Conference on Anglo-Norman Studies* 4 (1981): 53–64.

Gillis, John R. "Introduction." In John R. Gillis, ed., *Commemorations: The Politics of National Identity*, pp. 3–24. Princeton, NJ: Princeton University Press, 1994.

Goggin, Jacqueline. "Challenging Sexual Discrimination in the Historical Profession: Women Historians and the American Historical Association, 1890–1940." *American Historical Review* 97 (June 1992): 769–802.

Goldstein, Doris. "Confronting Time: The Oxford School of History and the Non-Darwinian Revolution." *Storia Della Storiografia* 45 (2004): 3–27.

———. "History at Oxford and Cambridge: Professionalization and the Influence of Ranke." In Georg G. Iggers and James M. Powell, eds., *Leopold von Ranke and the Shaping of the Historical Discipline*, pp. 141–53. Syracuse, NY: Syracuse University Press, 1990.

———. "The Organizational Development of the British Historical Profession, 1884–1921." *Bulletin of the Institute of Historical Research* 55 (November 1982): 180–93.

———. "The Origins and Early Years of the *English Historical Review*." *English Historical Review* 101 (January 1986): 6–19.

Gordon, Robert W. "Introduction: J. Willard Hurst and the Common Law Tradition in American Legal Historiography." *Law and Society Review* 10 (1975): 9–55.

Greene, Jack P. "The Flight From Determinism: A Review of Recent Literature on the Coming of the American Revolution." *South Atlantic Quarterly* 61 (Spring 1962): 235–59.

Guth, DeLloyd J. "How Legal History Survives Constitutional History's Demise." *Rechtsgeschichte und Quantitative Geschichte* 7 (1977): 117–53.

Hall, Catherine. "British Cultural Identities and the Legacy of the Empire." In David Morley and Kevin Robins, eds., *British Cultural Studies: Geography, Nationality, and Identity*, pp. 27–39. New York: Oxford University Press, 2001.

———. "A Response to the Commentators." *Journal of British Studies* 42 (October 2003): 530–38.

Hanawalt, Barbara. "Golden Ages for the History of Medieval English Women." In Susan Stuard, ed., *Women in Medieval History and Historiography*, pp. 1–24. Philadelphia: University of Pennsylvania Press, 1987.

Harland-Jacobs, Jessica. "All in the Family: Freemasonry and the British Empire in the Mid-Nineteenth Century." *Journal of British Studies* 42 (October 2003): 448–82.

Harrison, Brian. "History at the Universities, 1968: A Commentary." *History* 53 (October 1968): 357–80.

Haskell, Thomas. "Objectivity Is Not Neutrality: Rhetoric vs. Practice in Peter Novick's *That Noble Dream*." *History and Theory* 29 (May 1990): 129–57.

Hastings, Margaret, and Elisabeth G. Kimball. "Two Distinguished Medievalists—Nellie Neilson and Bertha Putnam." *Journal of British Studies* 18 (Spring 1979): 142–59.

Hay, Douglas. "Women, Men, and Empires of Law." *Journal of British Studies* 44 (January 2005): 204–12.

Heathorn, Stephen. "'Let Us Remember That We, Too, Are English': Constructions of Citizenship and National Identity in English Elementary School Reading Books, 1880–1914." *Victorian Studies* 38 (Spring 1995): 395–427.

Hernon, Joseph M. "The Last Whig Historian and Consensus History: George Macaulay Trevelyan, 1876–1962." *American Historical Review* 81 (February 1976): 66–97.

Heyck, Thomas W. "Freelance Writers and the Changing Terrain of Intellectual Life in Britain, 1880–1980." *Albion* 34 (Fall 2002): 233–67.

———. "Myths and Meanings of Intellectuals in Twentieth-Century British National Identity." *Journal of British Studies* 37 (April 1998): 192–221.

Hollister, C. Warren. "The Norman Conquest and the Genesis of English Feudalism." *American Historical Review* 66 (April 1961): 641–63.

Holmes, Clive. "G. R. Elton as a Legal Historian." *Transactions of the Royal Historical Society,* Sixth Series 7 (1997): 267–79.

Holton, Sandra. "Gender Difference, National Identity and Professing History: The Case of Alice Stopford Green." *History Workshop Journal* 53 (Spring 2002): 118–27.

Hopkins, A. G. "Back to the Future: From National History to Imperial History." *Past and Present* 164 (August 1999): 198–243.

Horsman, Reginald. "Origins of Racial Anglo-Saxonism in Great Britain before 1850." *Journal of the History of Ideas* 37 (July 1976): 387–410.

Howkins, Alun. "Rurality and English Identity." In David Morley and Kevin Robins, eds., *British Cultural Studies: Geography, Nationality, and Identity,* pp. 145–56. New York: Oxford University Press, 2002.

Howsam, Leslie. "Academic Discipline or Literary Genre? The Establishment of Boundaries in Historical Writing." *Victorian Literature and Culture* 32 (September 2004): 525–45.

Jann, Rosemary. "From Amateur to Professional: The Case of the Oxbridge Historians." *Journal of British Studies* 22 (Spring 1983): 122–47.

Johnson, Charles. "Hubert Hall, 1857–1944." *Transactions of the Royal Historical Society,* Fourth Series 28 (1946): 1–5.

Josephson, Harold. "History for Victory: The National Board for Historical Service." *Mid-America* 52 (July 1970): 205–24.

Kadish, Alon. "Scholarly Exclusiveness and the Founding of the *English Historical Review*." *Historical Research* 61 (June 1988): 183–98.

Kapelle, William E. "Domesday Book: F. W. Maitland and His Successors." *Speculum* 64 (July 1989): 620–40.

King, Edmund. "John Horace Round and the 'Calendar of Documents Preserved in France.'" *Proceedings of the Battle Conference on Anglo-Norman Studies* 4 (1981): 93–103.

Koditschek, Theodore. "The Making of British Nationality." *Victorian Studies* 44 (Spring 2002): 389–98.

Kostal, R. W. "A Jurisprudence of Power: Martial Law and the Ceylon Controversy of 1848–51." *Journal of Imperial and Commonwealth History* 28 (January 2000): 1–34.

Kramer, Paul A. "Empires, Exceptions, and Anglo-Saxons: Race and Rule between the British and the United States Empires, 1880–1910." *Journal of American History* 88 (March 2002): 1315–53.

Kreider, Jodie. "'Degraded and Benighted': Gendered Constructions of Wales in the Empire, ca. 1847." *North American Journal of Welsh Studies* 2 (Winter 2002): 1–12.

Krueger, Christine L. "Why She Lived at the PRO: Mary Anne Everett Green and the Profession of History." *Journal of British Studies* 42 (January 2003): 65–90.

Kulikoff, Allan. "The Founding Fathers: Best Sellers! TV Stars! Punctual Plumbers!" *Journal of the Historical Society* 5 (Spring 2005): 155–87.

Kumar, Krishan. "'Englishness' and English National Identity." In David Morley and Kevin Robins, eds., *British Cultural Studies: Geography, Nationality, and Identity*, pp. 41–55. New York: Oxford University Press, 2002.

Lapsley, Gaillard. "Some Recent Advance in English Constitutional History (Before 1485)." *Cambridge Historical Journal* 5 (1936): 119–61.

Levett, Elizabeth. "Sir Paul Vinogradoff." *Economic Journal* 36 (June 1926): 310–17.

Levine, Philippa. "History in the Archives: The Public Record Office and Its Staff, 1838–1886." *English Historical Review* 101 (January 1986): 20–41.

Linehan, Peter. "The Making of the Cambridge Medieval History." *Speculum* 57 (July 1982): 463–94.

Link, Arthur S. "The American Historical Association, 1884–1984: Retrospect and Prospect." *American Historical Review* 90 (February 1985): 1–17.

Loengard, Janet Senderowitz. "Beyond Maitland: The Making of a Discipline." *Journal of British Studies* 34 (October 1995): 529–36.

Lorimer, Douglas. "Race, Science and Culture: Historical Continuities and Discontinuities, 1850–1914." In Shearer West, ed., *The Victorians and Race*, pp. 12–33. Aldershot: Scolar Press, 1997.

———. "Theoretical Racism in Late-Victorian Anthropology, 1870–1900." *Victorian Studies* 31 (Spring 1988): 405–30.

Loughlin, James. "Joseph Chamberlain, English Nationalism and the Ulster Question." *History* 77 (June 1992): 202–19.

Louis, William Roger. "Introduction." In Robin Winks, ed., *Historiography*, vol. 5, pp. 1–42. *The Oxford History of the British Empire*. 5 vols. New York: Oxford University Press, 1998–99.

———. "The United States and the African Peace Settlement of 1919: The Pilgrimage of George Louis Beer." *Journal of African History* 4 (1963): 413–33.

Lowenthal, David. "The Island Garden: English Landscape and British Identity." In Helen Brocklehurst and Robert Phillips, eds. *History, Nationhood and the Question of Britain*, pp. 137–48. New York: Palgrave Macmillan, 2004.

MacColl, Alan. "The Meaning of 'Britain' in Medieval and Early Modern England." *Journal of British Studies* 45 (April 2006): 248–69.

MacKenzie, John M. "Empire and National Identities: The Case of Scotland." *Transactions of the Royal Historical Society*, Sixth Series 8 (1998): 215–31.

MacRaild, Donald M. "'Principle, Party and Protest': The Language of Victorian Orangeism in the North of England." In Shearer West, ed., *The Victorians and Race*, pp. 128–40. Aldershot: Scolar Press, 1997.

Major, Kathleen. "Doris Mary Stenton, 1894–1971." *Proceedings of the British Academy* 58 (1972): 525–35.

Mandler, Peter. "Against 'Englishness': English Culture and the Limits to Rural Nostalgia, 1850–1940." *Transactions of the Royal Historical Society,* Sixth Series 7 (1997): 155–75.

——. "'In the Olden Time': Romantic History and English National Identity, 1820–1850." In Lawrence Brockliss and David Eastwood, eds., *A Union of Multiple Identities: The British Isles, c. 1750–c. 1850,* pp. 78–92. Manchester: Manchester University Press, 1997.

——. "'Race' and 'Nation' in Mid-Victorian Thought." In Stefan Collini, Richard Whatmore, and Brian Young, eds., *History, Religion, and Culture: British Intellectual History, 1750–1950,* pp. 224–44. Cambridge: Cambridge University Press, 2000.

Mangan, J. A. "'The Gist of Our Forefathers': Invented Traditions, Propaganda and Imperialism." In John M. MacKenzie, ed., *Imperialism and Popular Culture,* pp. 113–39. Manchester: Manchester University Press, 1986.

Marwick, Arthur. "Two Approaches to Historical Study: The Metaphysical (Including 'Postmodernism') and the Historical." *Journal of Contemporary History* 30 (January 1995): 5–36.

May, Alex. "Curtis, Lionel George (1872–1955)." In *Oxford Dictionary of National Biography,* Oxford University Press, 2004 [accessed 4 November 2004: http://www.oxforddnb.com/view/article/32678].

——. "Wrench, Sir (John) Evelyn Leslie (1882–1966)." In *Oxford Dictionary of National Biography,* Oxford: Oxford University Press, 2004 [accessed 11 November 2004: http://www.oxforddnb.com/view/article/37031].

McClintock, Anne. "'No Longer in a Future Heaven': Women and Nationalism in South Africa." *Transition* 51 (1991): 104–23.

McIntyre, W. David. "Clio and Britain's Lost Dream: Historians and the British Commonwealth of Nations in the First Half of the 20th Century." *Round Table* 376 (September 2004): 517–32.

McLaren, Anne. "Gender, Religion, and Early Modern Nationalism: Elizabeth I, Mary Queen of Scots, and the Genesis of English Anti-Catholicism." *American Historical Review* 107 (June 2002): 739–67.

McLeod, Hugh. "Protestantism and British National Identity, 1815–1945." In Peter van der Veer and Hartmut Lehmann, eds., *Nation and Religion: Perspectives on Europe and Asia,* pp. 44–70. Princeton, NJ: Princeton University Press, 1999.

Melman, Billie. "Claiming the Nation's Past: The Invention of an Anglo-Saxon Tradition." *Journal of Contemporary History* 26 (September 1991): 575–95.

Milsom, S. F. C. "F. W. Maitland." *Proceedings of the British Academy* 66 (1980): 265–81.

——. "Introduction." In Sir Frederick Pollock and Frederic Maitland, *The History of English Law before the Time of Edward I,* pp. 25–91. Cambridge: Cambridge University Press, 1968 [1895].

——. "Maitland." *Cambridge Law Journal* 60 (July 2001): 265–70.

——. "Maitland, Frederic William (1850–1906)." In *Oxford Dictionary of National Biography,* Oxford University Press, 2004 [accessed 29 November 2004: http://www.oxforddnb.com/view/article/34837].

——. "'Pollock and Maitland': A Lawyer's Retrospect." In John Hudson, ed., *The History of English Law: Centenary Essays on 'Pollock and Maitland,'* pp. 243–59. New York: Oxford University Press, 1996.

Mitchell, Rosemary. "'The Busy Daughters of Clio': Women Writers of History from 1820 to 1880." *Women's History Review* 7 (1998): 107–34.

Murphy, Paul L. "Time to Reclaim: The Current Challenge of American Constitutional History." *American Historical Review* 69 (October 1963): 64–79.

Nelson, Janet L. "England and the Continent in the Ninth Century: II, The Vikings and Others." *Transactions of the Royal Historical Society*, Sixth Series 13 (2003): 1–28.

Newman, Gerald. "Nationalism Revisited." *Journal of British Studies* 35 (January 1996): 118–27.

Noonan, Kathleen M. "'The Cruell Pressure of an Enraged, Barbarous People': Irish and English Identity in Seventeenth Century Propaganda and Policy." *Historical Journal* 41 (March 1998): 151–77.

———. "'Martyrs in Flames': Sir John Temple and the Conception of the Irish in English Martyrologies." *Albion* 36 (Summer 2004): 223–55.

Obelkevich, Jim. "New Developments in History in the 1950s and 1960s." *Contemporary British History* 14 (Winter 2000): 125–42.

Oldfield, Adrian. "Metaphysics and History in Collingwood's Thought." In David Boucher, James Connelly, and Tariq Mahood, eds., *Philosophy, History and Civilization: Interdisciplinary Perspectives on R. G. Collingwood*, pp. 182–202. Cardiff: University of Wales Press, 1995.

Orr, D. Alan. "From a *View* to a *Discovery*: Edmund Spenser, Sir John Davies, and the Defects of Law in the Realm of Ireland." *Canadian Journal of History* 38 (December 2003): 395–408.

———. "A Prospectus for a 'New' Constitutional History of Early Modern England." *Albion* 36 (Fall 2004): 430–50.

Orr, Patricia R. "Doris Mary Stenton (1894–1971): The Legal Records and the Historian." In Jane Chance, ed., *Women Medievalists and the Academy*, pp. 441–58. Madison: University of Wisconsin Press, 2005.

Owen, Nicholas. "British Progressives and Civil Society in India, 1905–1914." In Jose Harris, ed., *Civil Society in British History: Ideas, Identities, Institutions*, pp. 149–75. New York: Oxford University Press, 2003.

Parker, Christopher J. W. "English Historians and the Opposition to Positivism." *History and Theory* 22 (May 1983): 120–45.

———. "The Failure of Liberal Racialism: The Racial Ideas of E. A. Freeman." *Historical Journal* 24 (December 1981): 825–46.

Paz, D. G. "Anti-Catholicism, Anti-Irish Stereotyping, and Anti-Celtic Racism in Mid-Victorian Working-Class Periodicals." *Albion* 18 (Winter 1986): 601–17.

Peatling, G. K. "Home Rule for England, English Nationalism, and Edwardian Debates About Constitutional Reform." *Albion* 35 (Spring 2003): 71–90.

———. "The Whiteness of Ireland Under and After the Union." *Journal of British Studies* 44 (January 2005): 115–33.

Pilling, Norman. "Lecky and Dicey: English and Irish Histories." *Eire-Ireland* 16 (Autumn 1981): 43–56.

Poole, Austin Lane. "J. H. Round and the Battle of Senlac." *Times Literary Supplement* (17 April 1953): 253.

Porter, Bernard. "Edward Elgar and Empire." *Journal of Imperial and Commonwealth History* 29 (January 2001): 1–34.

Powell, Edward. "After 'After McFarlane': The Poverty of Patronage and the Case for

Constitutional History." In Dorothy J. Clayton, Richard G. Davies, and Peter Mc-
Niven, eds., *Trade, Devotion and Governance: Papers in Later Medieval History*, pp.
1–16. Stroud: Sutton, 1994.

Powell, W. Raymond. "J. Horace Round, the County Historian: The Victorian County
Histories and the Essex Archaeological Society." *Essex Archaeology and History* 12
(1980): 25–38.

Price, Richard. "One Big Thing: Britain, Its Empire, and Their Imperial Culture." *Journal
of British Studies* 45 (July 2006): 602–27.

Proudman, Mark F. "The Most Important History: The *American Historical Review* and
Our English Past." *Journal of the Historical Society* 6 (June 2006): 177–211.

Rabb, Reginald E. "George Burton Adams." In Herman Ausubel, J. Bartlett Brebner, and
Ealing M. Hunt, eds., *Some Modern Historians of Britain: Essays in Honor of R. L.
Schuyler*, pp. 177–91. New York: Dryden Press, 1951.

Rainger, Ronald. "Race, Politics, and Science: The Anthropological Society of London in
the 1860s." *Victorian Studies* 22 (Autumn 1978): 51–70.

Readman, Paul. "The Place of the Past in English Culture c. 1890–1914." *Past and Present*
186 (February 2005): 147–99.

Reynolds, Susan. "What Do We Mean by 'Anglo-Saxon' and the 'Anglo-Saxons'?" *Journal
of British Studies* 24 (October 1985): 395–414.

Rich, Paul B. "British Imperial Decline and the Forging of English Patriotic Memory, c.
1918–1968." *History of European Ideas* 9 (1988): 659–80.

———. "Social Darwinism, Anthropology and English Perspectives of the Irish, 1867–
1900." *History of European Ideas* 19 (July 1994): 777–85.

Robbins, Keith. "History, the Historical Association and the 'National Past.'" *History* 66
(October 1981): 413–25.

———. "Lord Bryce and the First World War." *Historical Journal* 10 (1967): 255–78.

———. "Religion and Identity in Modern British History." In Stewart Mews, ed., *Religion and National Identity*, pp. 465–87. Oxford: Blackwell, 1982.

Rose, Jonathan. "Doctrinal Development: Legal History, Law, and Legal Theory." *Oxford
Journal of Legal Studies* 22 (Summer 2002): 323–40.

Rosenthal, Joel T. "Time to Share the Narrative: Late Medieval Women in Recent and
Diverse Scholarship." *Journal of British Studies* 43 (October 2004): 506–13.

Rothberg, Morey. "John Franklin Jameson and the Creation of *The American Revolution
Considered as a Social Movement*." In Ronald Hoffman and Peter J. Albert, eds., *The
Transforming Hand of Revolution: Reconsidering the American Revolution as a Social
Movement*, pp. 1–26. Charlottesville: University of Virginia Press, 1996.

———. "John Franklin Jameson and the International Historical Community." *History
Teacher* 26 (August 1993): 449–57.

Salzman, L. F. "Senlac." *Times Literary Supplement* (1 May 1953): 285.

Samuel, Raphael. "Continuous National History." In Raphael Samuel, ed., *Patriotism:
The Making and Unmaking of British National Identity*, 3 vols., I: 9–17. New York:
Routledge, 1989.

Schlesinger, Philip. "On National Identity: Some Conceptions and Misconceptions Criticised." *Social Science Information* 26 (June 1987): 219–64.

Schuyler, Robert Livingston. "The Historical Spirit Incarnate: Frederic William Maitland." *American Historical Review* 57 (January 1952): 303–22.

Schwarz, Bill. "The Expansion and Contraction of England." In Bill Schwarz, ed., *The*

Expansion of England: Race, Ethnicity and Cultural History, pp. 1–8. London: Routledge, 1996.

Scott, Joan W. "Gender: A Useful Category of Historical Analysis." *American Historical Review* 91 (December 1986): 1053–75.

Scribner, Robert. "Communalism." In Hans J. Hillerbrand, ed., *The Oxford Encyclopedia of the Reformation*, I: 385–88. New York: Oxford University Press, 1996.

Scully, Pamela. "Imperial Crossings: British Identities and the 'Imperial Imaginary.'" *Journal of British Studies* 41 (October 2002): 520–25.

Segal, Daniel A. "'Western Civ' and the Staging of History in American Higher Education." *American Historical Review* 105 (June 2000): 770–805.

Sewell, Keith C. "The 'Herbert Butterfield Problem' and Its Resolution." *Journal of the History of Ideas* 64 (October 2003): 599–618.

Siak, Steven W. "'The Blood That Is in Our Veins Comes from German Ancestors': British Historians and the Coming of the First World War." *Albion* 30 (Summer 1998): 221–52.

Simpson, A. W. B. "Legal Education and Legal History." *Oxford Journal of Legal Studies* 11 (Spring 1991): 106–13.

Sinha, Mrinalini. "'Chathams, Pitts, and Gladstones in Petticoats': The Politics of Gender and Race in the Ilbert Bill Controversy, 1883–1884." In Nupur Chaudhuri and Margaret Strobel, eds., *Western Women and Imperialism: Complicity and Resistance*, pp. 98–116. Bloomington: Indiana University Press, 1992.

Sklar, Kathryn Kish. "American Female Historians in Context, 1770–1930." *Feminist Studies* 3 (Fall 1975): 171–84.

Slee, Peter. "Professor Soffer's 'History at Oxford.'" *Historical Journal* 30 (December 1987): 933–42.

Smith, Anthony D. "The Origins of Nations." *Ethnic and Racial Studies* 12 (July 1989): 340–67.

Smith, Bonnie G. "The Contribution of Women to Modern Historiography in Great Britain, France and the United States, 1750–1940." *American Historical Review* 89 (June 1984): 709–32.

Smith, John David. "James Ford Rhodes, Woodrow Wilson, and the Passing of the Amateur Historians of Slavery." *Mid-America* 64 (October 1982): 17–24.

Smith, K. J. M., and J. P. S. McLaren. "History's Living Legacy: An Outline of 'Modern' Historiography of the Common Law." *Legal Studies* 21 (June 2001): 251–324.

Smith, Neil. "Bowman's New World and the Council on Foreign Relations." *Geographical Review* 76 (October 1986): 438–60.

Smyth, Alfred P. "The Emergence of English Identity, 700–1000." In Alfred P. Smyth, ed., *Medieval Europeans: Studies in Ethnic Identity and National Perspectives in Medieval Europe*, pp. 24–52. Basingstoke: Macmillan, 1998.

Soffer, Reba N. "The Conservative Historical Imagination in the Twentieth Century." *Albion* 28 (Spring 1996): 1–17.

———. "History and Religion: J. R. Seeley and the Burden of the Past." In R. W. Davis and R. J. Helmstadter, eds., *Religion and Irreligion in Victorian Society: Essays in Honor of R. K. Webb*, pp. 133–50. New York: Routledge, 1992.

———. "Modern History." In M. G. Brock and M. C. Curthoys, eds., *The History of the University of Oxford*, VII, *Nineteenth Century Oxford*, Part 2, pp. 361–84. Oxford: Clarendon Press, 2000.

———. "Nation, Duty, Character and Confidence: History at Oxford, 1850–1914." *Historical Journal* 30 (March 1987): 77–103.

Sondheimer, Janet. "Helen Cam." In Edward Shils and Carmen Blacker, eds., *Cambridge Women: Twelve Portraits*, pp. 93–112. Cambridge: Cambridge University Press, 1996.

———. "In Memoriam Helen Cam, 1885–1968." *Girton Review* (1969): 32–36.

Southern, Richard W. "Galbraith, Vivian Hunter (1889–1976)," rev., *Oxford Dictionary of National Biography*, Oxford University Press, 2004 [accessed 6 May 2005, http://www.oxforddnb.com/view/article/31132].

———. "The Letters of Frederic William Maitland." *History and Theory* 6 (1967): 105–11.

Spector, Margaret Marion. "A. P. Newton." In Herman Ausubel, J. Bartlett Brebner, and Ealing M. Hunt, eds., *Some Historians of Modern Britain: Essays in Honor of R. L. Schuyler*, pp. 286–305. New York: Dryden Press, 1951.

Spiegel, Gabrielle M. "History, Historicism and the Social Logic of the Text in the Middle Ages." *Speculum* 65 (January 1990): 59–86.

Stapleton, Julia. "Dicey and His Legacy." *History of Political Thought* 16 (Summer 1995): 234–56.

———. "James Fitzjames Stephen: Liberalism, Patriotism, and English Liberty." *Victorian Studies* 41 (Winter 1998): 243–63.

Staves, Susan. "Chattel Property Rules and the Construction of Englishness, 1660–1800." *Law and History Review* 12 (Spring 1994): 123–53.

Stephenson, David. "The Early Career of J. H. Round: The Shaping of a Historian." *Essex Archaeology and History* 12 (1980): 1–10.

Stevenson, John. "The Countryside, Planning, and Civil Society in Britain, 1926–1947." In Jose Harris, ed., *Civil Society in British History: Ideas, Identities, Institutions*, pp. 191–211. New York: Oxford University Press, 2003.

Stone, Lawrence. "The Revival of Narrative: Some Reflections on a New Old History." *Past and Present* 85 (November 1979): 3–24.

Sugarman, David. "Reassessing Hurst: A Transatlantic Perspective." *Law and History Review* 18 (Spring 2000): 215–21.

Tawney, Richard H. "J. L. Hammond, 1872–1949." *Proceedings of the British Academy* 46 (1949): 267–94.

Taylor, Euan, and Gina Weaver. "Helen Cam (1885–1968): Charting the Evolution of Medieval Institutions." In Jane Chance, ed., *Women Medievalists and the Academy*, pp. 255–72. Madison: University of Wisconsin Press, 2005.

Taylor, Miles. "Patriotism, History and the Left in Twentieth-Century Britain." *Historical Journal* 33 (December 1990): 971–87.

Taylor, Peter J. "The English and Their Englishness: 'A Curiously Mysterious, Elusive and Little Understood People.'" *Scottish Geographical Magazine* 107 (December 1991): 146–61.

Thane, Pat. "The British National State and the Construction of National Identities." In Billie Melman, ed., *Borderlines: Genders and Identities in War and Peace, 1870–1930*, pp. 29–45. London: Routledge, 1998.

Thirsk, Joan. "The History Women." In Mary O'Dowd and Sabine Wichart, eds., *Chattel, Servant or Citizen: Women's Status in Church and State*, pp. 1–11. Belfast: Institute of Irish Studies, 1995.

Thompson, Andrew S. "The Language of Imperialism and the Meanings of Empire: Imperial Discourse in British Politics, 1895–1914." *Journal of British Studies* 36 (April 1997): 147–77.

Thornton, A. P. "The Shaping of Imperial History." In Robin Winks, ed., *Historiography,* vol. 5, pp. 612–34. *The Oxford History of the British Empire,* 5 vols. New York: Oxford University Press, 1998–99.

Tolles, Frederick B. "The American Revolution Considered as a Social Movement: A Re-Evaluation." *American Historical Review* 60 (October 1954): 1–12.

Tulloch, Hugh. "Acton." In Benedikt Stuchtey and Peter Wende, eds., *British and German Historiography, 1750–1950: Traditions, Perceptions, and Transfers,* pp. 159–72. London: Oxford University Press, 2000.

———. "Changing British Attitudes Towards the United States in the 1880s." *Historical Journal* 20 (December 1977): 825–40.

VanHoosier-Carey, Gregory A. "Byhrnoth in Dixie: The Emergence of Anglo-Saxon Studies in the Postbellum South." In Allen J. Frantzen and John D. Niles, eds., *Anglo-Saxonism and the Construction of Social Identity,* pp. 157–72. Gainesville: University Press of Florida, 1997.

Vernon, James. "Englishness: The Narration of a Nation." *Journal of British Studies* 36 (April 1997): 243–49.

———. "Narrating the Constitution: The Discourse of the 'Real' and the Fantasies of Nineteenth-Century Constitutional History." In James Vernon, ed., *Re-reading the Constitution: New Narratives in the Political History of England's Long Nineteenth Century,* pp. 204–29. Cambridge: Cambridge University Press, 1996.

Wallace, Elisabeth. "Goldwin Smith on England and America." *American Historical Review* 59 (July 1954): 884–94.

Ward, Stuart. "Transcending the Nation: A Global Imperial History?" In Antoinette Burton, ed., *After the Imperial Turn: Thinking with and through the Nation,* pp. 44–56. Durham, NC: Duke University Press, 2003.

Ward-Perkins, Bryan. "Why Did the Anglo-Saxons Not Become More British?" *English Historical Review* 115 (June 2000): 513–33.

Watson, George. "The War Against the Whigs: Butterfield's Victory . . . and Defeat." *Encounter* 66 (January 1986): 19–25.

Watt, John. "Frederic Maitland." In John Cannon, ed., *The Historian at Work,* pp. 103–20. London: Allen & Unwin, 1980.

Weale, Michael, Deborah A. Weiss, Rolf F. Jager, Neil Bradman, and Mark G. Thomas. "Y Chromosome Evidence for Anglo-Saxon Mass Migration." *Molecular Biology and Evolution* 19 (July 2002): 1008–21.

White, Hayden V. "Response to Arthur Marwick." *Journal of Contemporary History* 30 (April 1995): 233–46.

Wiener, Frederick Bernays. "Maitland the Incomparable." *American Journal of Legal History* 16 (April 1972): 177–91.

Williams, N. J. "Stubbs' Appointment as Regius Professor, 1866." *Bulletin of the Institute of Historical Research* 33 (May 1960): 121–25.

Wolfe, Patrick. "History and Imperialism: A Century of Theory, from Marx to Postcolonialism." *American Historical Review* 102 (April 1997): 388–420.

Wood, Charles T. "The Deposition of Edward V." *Traditio* 31 (1975): 247–86.

Woodard, Calvin. "History, Legal History and Legal Education." *Virginia Law Review* 53 (January 1967): 89–121.

Woodward, Llewellyn. "The Rise of the Professional Historian in England." In Kenneth C. Bourne and D. C. Watt, eds., *Studies in International History,* pp. 16–34. Hamden: Archon, 1967.

Woolf, D. R. "A Feminine Past? Gender, Genre, and Historical Knowledge in England, 1500–1800." *American Historical Review* 102 (June 1997): 645–79.

Woollacott, Angela. " 'All This Is the Empire, I Told Myself': Australian Women's Voyages 'Home' and the Articulation of Colonial Whiteness." *American Historical Review* 102 (October 1997): 1003–29.

Wormald, Patrick. "ENGLA LOND: The Making of an Allegiance." *Journal of Historical Sociology* 7 (March 1994): 1–24.

———. "The Eternal Angle." *Times Literary Supplement* (16 March 2001): 3–4.

———. "Frederic William Maitland and the Earliest English Law." *Law and History Review* 16 (Spring 1998): 1–25.

———. "Maitland and Anglo-Saxon Law: Beyond Domesday Book." In John Hudson, ed., *The History of English Law: Centenary Essays on 'Pollock and Maitland,'* pp. 1–20. New York: Oxford University Press, 1996.

———. "Sir Geoffrey Elton's *English*: A View from the Early Middle Ages." *Transactions of the Royal Historical Society,* Sixth Series 7 (1997): 318–25.

Index